International Investment Terms

Jae K. Shim, Ph.D.
Professor of Finance and Accounting
California State University, Long Beach

Joel G. Siegel, Ph.D., CPA
Professor of Finance and Accounting
Queens College of the City University of New York

BARRON'S

Copyright © 2001 Barron's Educational Series, Inc.

All rights reserved. No part of this book may be reproduced in any form, by photostat, microfilm, xerography, or any other means, or incorporated into any information retrieval system, electronic or mechanical, without the written permission of the copyright owner.

All inquiries should be addressed to:
Barron's Educational Series, Inc.
250 Wireless Boulevard
Hauppauge, NY 11788
http://www.barronseduc.com

Library of Congress Catalog Card No. 2001035722

International Standard Book No. 0-7641-1864-1

Library of Congress Cataloging-in-Publication Data

Shim, Jae K.
    Dictionary of international investment terms / Jae K. Shim,
    Joel G. Siegel.
      p. cm.
    Includes bibliographical references.
    ISBN 0-7641-1864-1
    1. International finance—Dictionaries. 2. Investments,
Foreign—Dictionaries. 3. Investments—Dictionaries. I. Siegel,
Joel G. II. Title.
HG3880 .S548   2001
332.6′03—dc21   2001035722

PRINTED IN THE UNITED STATES OF AMERICA

9 8 7 6 5 4 3 2 1

CONTENTS

Preface		v
How to Use This Dictionary Effectively		vii
Terms A–Z		1
Appendices		
Appendix A	Present Value Tables	324
Appendix B	Web Sites for Global Investing	327
Appendix C	World Stock Markets	329
Appendix D	Foreign Ticker Symbols	333
Appendix E	World Currencies and Symbols	382

PREFACE

This dictionary is directed toward the public at large. The idea behind the *Dictionary of International Investment Terms* is for the layperson, consumer, and professional to be able to read and comprehend terms and concepts continuously appearing in magazines (such as *Money, Worth, Individual Investor, Smartmoney,* and *Euromoney*) and finance dailies (such as *The Wall Street Journal, Investor's Business Daily,* and *Financial Times*) dealing with foreign investing, money management, personal finance, international finance, and consumer economics.

Due to an advance in information technology and telecommunications, we live and do investing in a real-time environment. What occurs in one part of the financial world immediately impacts the rest of the world. International investing is exploding as a direct result of technological advancements, World Wide Web (WWW), and rapidly advancing economies. Global investing has become one of the fastest expanding and intriguing areas affecting individuals, as planning personal affairs is crucial to success in life. Foreign investing is analogous to foreign travel. It is expensive, time-consuming, and often frustrating, but in the end, it can be highly rewarding.

This dictionary will be a constant reference tool for investors who want to learn about the rewards and risks of global investing. It covers all areas and terms of investing and finance with heavy emphasis on international investment arenas. The topics include global investing, multinational finance, international mutual funds, foreign exchange markets, international economics, and other related fields. Definitions and descriptions cover a wide array of topics, including institutions such as International Monetary Fund, major currencies including the Euro, and much more. The dictionary includes the latest terminology and thinking. It is essential for the individual to go beyond domestic investments and to understand investing and finance in global markets in order to achieve personal financial goals.

Newest in Barron's series of business dictionaries, this book presents more than 1500 terms with definitions applicable to international markets. Readers interested in global investment opportunities can cut through unfamiliar international financial and investment jargon and gain understanding of both risks and the available protections that govern multinational business, investment, and trade organizations.

The *Dictionary of International Investment Terms* contains a host of practical applications, examples, illustrations, tables, graphs, Internet sources, and checklists to aid reader comprehension and use. In the Appendices are tables referred to in the text, such as present value tables, and other valuable information such as foreign ticker symbols, world stock markets, and Internet global investing web sites.

This dictionary can also be used as a supplement by students taking courses in finance and investing in adult education programs, extension centers, and colleges and universities. It is also valuable for people who wish to study for professional certifications, such as Certified Financial

PREFACE

Planner (CFP), Chartered Financial Consultant (ChFC), and Chartered Financial Analyst (CFA).

The authors would like to thank Ms. Max Reed, Senior Editor, and the entire editorial staff at Barron's Educational Series for their consistently professional and enthusiastic support and guidance.

HOW TO USE THIS DICTIONARY EFFECTIVELY

Alphabetization: All entries are alphabetized by word; for example, *capital stock* precedes *capitalization*. In some cases, abbreviations or acronyms appear as entries in the main text. This occurs when the short form, rather than the formal name, predominates in common business usage. For example, NASDAQ is more commonly used when speaking of the National Association of Securities Dealers Automated Quotations system than the name itself, so the entry is located at **NASDAQ**. Numbers in entry titles are alphabetized as if they were spelled out.

Cross references: In order to gain a fuller understanding of a term, it will sometimes help to refer to the definition of another term. In these cases the additional term is printed in SMALL CAPITALS. Such cross references appear in the body of the definition or at the end of the entry (or subentry). Cross references at the end of an entry (or subentry) may refer to related or contrasting concepts rather than give more information about the concept under discussion. As a rule, a term is printed in small capitals only the first time it appears in an entry. It is noted that some terms are so common and appear so frequently that they are generally not cross referenced. Examples include (but are not limited to) *stocks, bonds*, and *broker*. Where an entry is fully defined at another entry, a reference rather than a definition is provided. For example, **either-or order** *see* ALTERNATIVE ORDER.

Italics: *Italic* type is generally used to indicate that another term has a meaning identical or very closely related to that of the entry. Occasionally, *italic* type is also used to highlight the fact that a word used is a business term and not just a descriptive phrase. *Italics* are also used for the titles of publications.

Parentheses: Parentheses are used in entry titles for two reasons. The first is to indicate that an entry's opposite is such an integral part of the concept that only one discussion is necessary. For example, **realized profit (or loss)**. The second and more common reason is to indicate that an abbreviation is used with about the same frequency as the term itself. For example, **over-the-counter (OTC)**.

Examples, Illustrations, Figures, Internet Screens, and Tables: The numerous examples in this dictionary are designed to help readers gain understanding and to help them relate abstract concepts to the real world of international finance and investment. Line drawings are provided in addition to text to clarify concepts best understood visually, for example, technical chart patterns used by securities analysts and graphic concepts used in financial analysis. Tables supplement definitions where essential detail is more effectively condensed and expressed in tabular form. Examples include currency changes vs. foreign returns in U.S. dollars and the differences between open-end mutual funds and closed-end mutual funds. Some key web site screens are shown as captured.

A

absolute rate a quote made that is given as an absolute rate rather than in reference to a funding base such as LONDON INTERBANK OFFERED RATE (LIBOR), U.S. Treasury rates, and so on. For example, rather than LIBOR + 0.75%, the bid is expressed as 10.375%.

account executive a staff member of a BROKERAGE FIRM who provides financial recommendations and executes orders to buy and sell financial and/or real assets; also called *registered representative*. The account executive acts as the client's agent. The account executive must pass certain examinations in order to be properly registered before he or she can practice.

accrual bonds bonds that do not pay interest on a periodic basis, but accumulate interest for payment when the bond is redeemed.

accrued dividend DIVIDEND a company usually pays on its stock but that the board of directors has not formally declared. Until the board of directors does make a formal declaration, an accrued dividend is not a legal obligation of the company, and if, in the opinion of management, the dividend should be reduced or not paid, management is free to make this recommendation. The board would still have to declare a reduced dividend. As opposed to an accrued dividend, a dividend formally declared but not paid is a dividend in arrears. *See also* ACCUMULATED DIVIDEND.

accrued interest interest due for the period from the last interest date to the date the bond is sold. At the sale date, the investor must pay the seller not only the price of the bond but also the accumulated interest. Accrued interest equals the nominal (stated, coupon) interest rate multiplied by the face value of the bond multiplied by the elapsed months from the last payment date divided by 12 months in a year.

EXAMPLE:
A $100,000, 10% bond pays interest on 1/1 and 7/1. If the bond is issued on 3/1, the accrued interest equals $1667 (10% × $100,000 × 2/12).

accumulated dividend unpaid DIVIDEND due, typically to owners of cumulative preferred shares.

accumulation
1. buying large amounts of shares in anticipation of a major increase in stock price, often by people with a lot of knowledge about the company who believe the stock is undervalued. The accumulation phase is the beginning stage of a major upward trend

from informed investors who are purchasing securities. The stock is viewed as going from small investors to large investors. Perhaps bad news has already been discounted and incorporated in the stock price. Accumulation occurs when the demand for a security exceeds its supply. An INSTITUTIONAL INVESTOR may try to buy a significant number of corporate shares in a controlled manner so as to minimize driving up the stock price. The institutional investor's accumulation plan may involve weeks or months to finalize.

2. cumulative retained profit.
3. periodic addition of interest to the principal amount.
4. investment of a fixed dollar amount regularly and reinvestment of DIVIDENDS and CAPITAL GAINS.

acquisition cost sales charge assessed by a mutual fund for purchase of a share of the fund. This cost is also called FRONT-END LOAD.

active account any type of account in which recurring activities occur. Such accounts include bond accounts, checking accounts, stock accounts, and so on. An active account is a current account. It may have a high volume of activity. If a bank account has not been used for five years for a deposit or withdrawal, the money may have to be transferred to the state, for example, as required by New York State law; however, some banks require a withdrawal to be made rather than a deposit. The reason for this is that the depositor may be deceased. Some brokerage firms and banks may charge a fee if there have been no transactions in an account for a period of time.

active investment investment practice in which an investor makes investment choices and continuous monitoring, in contrast to PASSIVE INVESTMENT.

active market any market, whether stock, bond, commodity, option, or foreign exchange, may have a high volume of buying or selling in a particular day, week, month, quarter, or year. Investing in an active stock is advantageous from a LIQUIDITY point of view and there is less spread between bid and asked prices. Active stocks, which often reflect the activity of institutional investors, account for more than 30% of the total New York Stock Exchange volume. If the number of shares traded is very high, but market prices are fairly constant, securities are fairly stable. However, an increasing price on heavy volume is a BULLISH sign of a strong upward movement. On the other hand, decreasing price on heavy volume may signal a significant downward movement. Institutional investors like an active market because there is less of an effect on price when a large block of stock is traded. Questions to be answered include: Is the heavy trading due to an announcement of superior earnings, heavy buying by institutions, or a takeover attempt? Can the volume and price movement be sustained?

actively managed funds
1. funds that utilize an approach based on informed, independent investment judgment, as opposed to passive management (indexing), which seeks to match the performance of the overall market (or some part of it) by mirroring its composition or by being broadly diversified.
2. the buying and selling of bonds, as opposed to holding them to maturity.

actuarial yield total YIELD on a bond, obtained by equaling the bond's current market value to the discounted cash flows promised by the bond; also called YIELD TO MATURITY (YTM).

adjustable rate preferred stock (ARPS) PREFERRED STOCK that pays dividends that go up and down with the general level of interest rates; also called *floating rate* or *variable rate preferred stock*. The prices of these securities are therefore less volatile than fixed-dividend preferred stock, and they may be a safe haven for investors. YIELDS obtained from adjustable rate preferreds may be lower than debt issues.

adjusted present value (APV) type of NET PRESENT VALUE (NPV) analysis by multinational companies in capital budgeting. A foreign investment project that is financed differently than that of the parent firm could he evaluated using this approach. In APV, operating cash flows are *discounted separately* from (1) the various tax shields provided by the deductibility of interest and other financial charges and (2) the benefits of project-specific concessional financing. Each component cash flow is discounted at a rate appropriate for the risk involved. Typically, the operating cash flows from the project are discounted at the *all-equity rate* plus any financing side effects discounted at the *all-debt rate*.

advance/decline analysis *see* ADVANCE/DECLINE (A/D) RATIO.

advance/decline (A/D) ratio ratio of stocks advancing compared to those declining. It is a barometer of the market's condition; when advancers outnumber decliners, it indicates strength. The general direction of the market can be determined by the steepness of the advance/decline line over time. Minor day-to-day variations are insignificant. It is the direction over a period of time that is significant and important. An extremely steep A/D line is either BULLISH (favorable) or BEARISH (negative), depending on whether the line is increasing or declining.

advance refunding opportunity for one holding bonds due to expire shortly to exchange them for new bonds on favorable terms. This strategy is used by the U.S. Treasury to try to keep its BONDHOLDERS from switching to other securities.

advancing market market in which the ADVANCE/DECLINE line is strongly favorable, indicating that more stocks are advancing than

ADVISORY LETTERS

declining. One theory holds that three consecutive days in which advances lead declines by 1000 issues or more is a very BULLISH signal.

advisory letters any of a series of private financial newsletters written by financial "experts" primarily devoted to advice on STOCK MARKET and MUTUAL FUND investing, but also including advice on COMMODITY and MONEY MARKET fund investing. The advisory letters vary in their services; however, some may provide an 800 "hot line" where a subscriber can call to get the latest investment advice, or the service may call the subscriber directly when it feels an investment opportunity is particularly timely. In the case of commodity market, money market, and mutual fund letters, advice is often given on timing "switches" between commodities or funds, respectively, depending on market developments. Advisory letters are distinct from financial advisers in that they do not take direct responsibility for investing and managing the client's portfolio. Subscribers to advisory letters pay a subscription fee that varies widely with the individual letter and any related services.

advisory services fee-based investing service provided by financial specialists in several areas, including insurance, stocks, and real estate. Services may also include publications devoted to their investment markets, insurance strategies, or particular companies. As with ADVISORY LETTERS, advisory services take no direct responsibility for investing client portfolios and limit their services to investment advice based upon specific research.

after-tax rate of return rate of return after income taxes that an investor can keep out of the CURRENT INCOME and CAPITAL GAINS (OR LOSSES) earned from investments.

against the box description of a transaction in which stock is sold short by the holder of a LONG POSITION in the identical security. *Box* means the securities are retained at the brokerage firm for safekeeping. The shares necessary to cover a sale *against the box* are typically borrowed from the broker. It is used to protect a long position in a stock against price depreciation. It is also used illegally to avoid taxes by recording the SHORT SALE as an actual sale while preserving the original long position in the stock.

aggressive growth mutual fund fund comprised of securities of rapidly growing business entities. Growth companies have past and expected future earnings growth that exceeds the average. Growth companies may be small or large. The primary return for aggressive growth companies is in the form of appreciation in market price of stock instead of dividend income. Dividends paid, if any, are minimal. Growth companies experience more fluctuation in price than the overall market and are more speculative. Growth companies have a percentage increase in stock price significantly more than an overall bull market, but they have a percentage decrease in stock price significantly more than an overall bear market.

AIMR Global Investment Performance Standards   professional standards, set by AIMR (Association for Investment Management Research), that must be applied by its members worldwide. The standards are divided into five sections reflecting the basic elements involved in presenting performance information: input data, calculation methodology, composite construction, disclosures, and presentation and reporting. *See also* GLOBAL INVESTMENT PERFORMANCE STANDARDS.

air pocket stock   stock that declines in value significantly and suddenly, typically when there is negative news such as a lawsuit filed against the business or a negative earnings announcement. This causes investors to sell quickly and, with fewer buyers in the market, the price declines significantly. It is analogous to an airplane dropping sharply in an air pocket.

alien corporation   firm incorporated under the laws and regulations of a foreign country doing business in a country other than the one in which it was incorporated; also called *foreign corporation*.

all-equity beta   BETA associated with the unleveraged cash flows of a capital project or company. Unleveraged cash flows are those not rising from debt financing. To transform the beta into all-equity beta, the effects of debt financing must be separated out. This operation is known as unlevering, or converting a levered equity beta to its unlevered, or all-equity, value. Unlevering can be achieved by using the following approximation:

$$b^* = \frac{b}{1 + (1-t)(DE)}$$

where b = a firm's beta, t = tax rate, and DE = debt-equity ratio.

EXAMPLE:
If the beta of a firm's stock is 1.2, and it has a debt-equity ratio of 60% and an applicable tax rate of 34%, then its all-equity beta, b*, is 0.93:

$$0.93 = 1.3/(1 + 0.66 \times 0.6)$$

all-equity (discount) rate   discount rate that reflects only the business risks of a capital project as separated from the effects of financing. This rate applies directly to a project that is financed entirely with owners' equity. *See also* ALL-EQUITY BETA.

all hands meeting   gathering that occurs during the preparation stage for an INITIAL PUBLIC OFFERING (IPO) that is attended by representatives of the issuer, the underwriters, their respective lawyers, and the issuer's accountants. A public offering typically will involve several all hands meetings to conduct DUE DILIGENCE and to draft the registration statement and prospectus.

ALL OR NONE

all or none
1. situation in which an investor instructs his or her broker to either buy or sell an order of securities or options totally or none at all. This order will not automatically be terminated if the full transaction is not made unless it is specifically identified as FILL-OR-KILL.
2. situation in which there is an offer providing the issuer with the option to cancel the entire issue in the event the underwriting is not completely subscribed to.
3. term referred to by investment banking entities in bidding for underwriting rights. It applies to the decision to either underwrite the whole issue of a company's newly issued securities or not undertake the underwriting at all.

See also BUY ORDER.

alligator spread
1. OPTION SPREAD that causes the customer to be "eaten alive" with commission costs to be executed. It could be a series of put and call option maneuvers that would be unlikely to result in any profit for the client.
2. any option transaction in which the commission costs are higher than potential profits.

all-in rate rate used in charging clientele for accepting BANKER'S ACCEPTANCES that consists of the interest rate for the discount and the commission.

All Ordinaries Index index that tracks 330 of the most actively traded companies listed on the Australia Stock Exchange (ASX).

allotment number of shares given to each participant in the syndicate for the underwriting and sale of a new issue. The allotment notice specifies subscriber responsibilities.

alpha excess return that the portfolio manager is able to earn above an unmanaged portfolio (or market portfolio) that has the same risk. In the context of a mutual fund, an alpha value is the value representing the difference between the return on a fund and a point on the market line, where the market line describes the relationship between excess returns and the portfolio BETA.

$$\text{Alpha} = \text{beta} \times (\text{market return} - \text{risk-free return})$$

Morningstar Inc. (800) 876-5005 offers alpha values of major funds, as does its web site at *www.morningstar.net*.

EXAMPLE 1:
If the market return is 8% and the risk-free rate (such as a rate on a T-bill) is 5%, the market excess return equals 3%. A portfolio with a beta of 1 should expect to earn the market rate of excess returns, or alpha, equal to 3% ($1 \times 3\%$). A fund with a beta of 1.5 should provide excess returns of 4.5% ($1.5 \times 3\%$).

ALTERNATIVE ORDER

Alpha value is used to evaluate the performance of mutual funds. Generally, a positive alpha (excess return) indicates superior performance, while a negative value leads to the opposite conclusion.

EXAMPLE 2:
The fund in Example 1 has a beta of 1.5, which indicates an expected excess return of 4.5% along the market line. Assume that the fund had an actual excess return of only 4.1%. That means the fund has a negative alpha of .4% (4.1% − 4.5%). The fund's performance is therefore inferior to that of the market.

The following presents alphas for some selected international funds:

BETAS FOR SOME SELECTED INTERNATIONAL FUNDS

Company	Ticker Symbol	Alpha
GAM: International	GMMNX	−13.0
Harbor International	HAINX	−1.0
Strong International	STISX	−4.2
Fidelity Overseas	FOSFX	−2.1
Templeton International A	TEGEX	−1.0
Vanguard International Growth	VWIGX	−1.2

Source: MSN Money Central Investor
(*http://moneycentral.msn.com/investor/contents.asp*), April 3, 2001.

Note: A fund's alpha is only reliable when its R-SQUARED is relatively high.
See also JENSEN'S PERFORMANCE MEASURE; BETA FOR A MUTUAL FUND; R-SQUARED (R^2); STANDARD DEVIATION; SHARPE'S RISK-ADJUSTED RETURN.

alteration premise that the stock market usually does not behave exactly the same twice in a row. For example, if a certain kind of top in the market took place last time, it is not likely to do so again.

alternative investment type of investment in which funds are placed in assets that are riskier than savings in the bank, as neither principal nor income is guaranteed.

alternative order order given to a broker to buy or sell stocks depending upon a specified alternative; also called an *either-or order* or a *one-cancels-the-other order*. Once the alternative is met, the order is executed. For example, there may be an integrated buy limit/buy stop order, wherein the buy limit is less than the present market price and the buy stop is higher than the current market price.

American Association for Individual Investors (AAII) based in Chicago, an independent, nonprofit corporation formed in 1978 for the purpose of assisting individuals in becoming effective managers of their own assets through programs of education, information, and research. Its flagship publication is *AAII Journal*.

American Depositary Receipt (ADR) certificate of ownership, issued by a U.S. bank, representing a claim on underlying foreign stocks. ADRs let U.S. residents buy and sell foreign stocks without the hassle of actually owning them. Banks issue ADRs, not the corporation's stock certificate, to an American investor who buys shares of that corporation. The stock certificate is kept at the bank. The process of ADRs works as follows: A foreign company places shares in trust with a U.S. bank, which in turn issues depositary receipts to U.S. investors. The ADRs, then, are claims to shares of stock, and are essentially the same as shares. The depository bank performs all clerical functions—issuing annual reports, keeping a shareholder ledger, paying and maintaining dividend records, and other administrative functions—allowing the ADRs to trade in markets just like domestic securities trade. ADRs are *sponsored* or *unsponsored*. If an ADR is sponsored it means that the original issuing firm has explicitly decided to court U.S. investors. Companies that sponsor ADRs are obligated to supply English-language versions of their corporate shareholder documents. Further, investors have full voting rights, while with unsponsored ADRs, they do not. Unsponsored ADRs are created when a broker or bank detects sufficient U.S. investor interest in a foreign share to make it worthwhile to set up a deposit program. The foreign company is not directly involved. Only sponsored ADRs are traded on the major U.S. STOCK EXCHANGES. Unsponsored ADRs are traded on the non-NASDAQ OTC market or in the PINK SHEETS.

The Bank of New York maintains indexes of how ADRs listed in the United States perform. This information can be retrieved at the Bank of New York Internet site (*www.bankofny.com*). J. P. Morgan also maintains an Internet site providing ADR market performance (*adr.com*). The Bank of New York and Stock City (*www.cyberhost3.com/stockcit/adr/index.html*) provide the name, exchange, and ticker symbol for ADRs. You can download *The Complete Depositary Receipt (DR) Directory* from the Bank of New York web site.

Note: Benefits of ADRs to investors are as follows:

Liquidity. ADRs are as liquid as their underlying securities because they can easily be exchanged for the underlying shares. Since ADRs can be continuously created to meet investor demand, they provide trading liquidity equal to the home market securities they represent.

Convenience. Like all U.S. securities, ADRs are negotiable. They are quoted and pay dividends in U.S. dollars, and, to the extent they can be traded in the United States, they trade exactly like other U.S.

securities. Companies with certain types of Depositary Receipt programs can also establish direct share purchase and sale plans such as Global Buy *DIRECT* as a value-added service for investors.

Cost-Effectiveness. By investing through ADRs, investors eliminate the need to custodize underlying securities in non-U.S. markets, reducing custody charges and other transaction costs typically associated with cross-border investing. Additionally, dividends and other cash distributions are converted into dollars at competitive rates. *See also* BANK OF NEW YORK ADR INDEX.

American option OPTION that can be exercised at any time before expiration; also called *American-type option*.

American shares foreign equities that investors can buy here in the United States, instead of buying foreign stocks overseas. They are traded in the United States typically in two ways: (1) AMERICAN DEPOSITARY RECEIPTS (ADRS) and (2) American shares. American shares are securities certificates issued in the United States by a transfer agent acting on behalf of the foreign issuer. The foreign issuer absorbs part or all of the handling expenses involved. See also AMERICAN DEPOSITARY RECEIPT (ADR); GLOBAL REGISTERED SHARES.

American Stock Exchange Market Value Index market value-weighted (capitalization) index of the AMERICAN STOCK EXCHANGE (AMEX) stocks. It is computed by adding all of the plus net changes and minus net changes above or below previous closing prices. The sum is then divided by the number of issues listed and the result added to or subtracted from the previous close. It is actually more like an average than an index since it does not have a base period. *See also* MARKET INDICES AND AVERAGES.

American terms foreign exchange quotations for the U.S. dollar, expressed as the U.S. dollar price per unit of foreign currency; also called *American basis* or *American quote*. For example, U.S. $0.00909/yen is an American term. American terms are normally used in the interbank market of the U.K. pound sterling, Australian dollar, New Zealand dollar, and Irish punt. Sterling is quoted as the foreign currency price of one pound. The relationship between American terms and EUROPEAN TERMS, on the one hand, and direct and indirect, on the other, can be summarized as follows:

American Terms	European Terms
U.S. dollar price of one unit of foreign currency (for example, US $0.00797/¥)	Foreign currency price of one U.S. dollar (for example, ¥125.52/$)
A direct quote in the U.S.	A direct quote in Europe.
An indirect quote in Europe.	An indirect quote in the U.S.

American terms are used in many retail markets (for example, airports for tourists), on the foreign currency futures market in

analyst research analyst who has expertise in assessing and analyzing investments, and typically is employed by investment banks, brokerage firms, investment advisors, or mutual fund companies; also called a *financial analyst* or *security analyst*. These analysts make buy, sell, and hold recommendations on securities. Most specialize in specific sectors in the economy or specific countries to allow for more thorough research. An analyst will often be a key component in selecting an underwriter since analyst coverage of the company after the public offering helps to generate interest in the company's securities. *See also* CHARTIST.

analytical information available current data in conjunction with projections and recommendations about potential investments.

angel
1. person or entity that provides financing to companies that have progressed beyond the START-UP phase but are not yet ready for venture financing.
2. bond of an investment grade.
3. opposite of a FALLEN ANGEL.

annual percentage rate
1. true measure of the effective cost of credit. It is the ratio of the finance charge to the average amount of credit in use during the life of the loan, and is expressed as a percentage rate per year.
2. true measure of the effective annual rate of return on investments. Different types of investments use different compounding periods. For example, most bonds pay interest semiannually. Some banks pay interest quarterly. If an investor wishes to compare investments with different compounding periods, he needs to put them on a common basis. The annual percentage rate (APR), or effective annual rate, is used for this purpose and is computed as follows:

$$APR = (1+r/m)^m - 1.0$$

where r = the stated, nominal, or quoted rate
       m = the number of compounding periods per year.

EXAMPLE:
Assume that a bank offers 6% interest, compounded quarterly; then the APR is:

$$APR = (1 + .06/4)^4 - 1.0 = (1.015)^4 - 1.0 = 1.0614 - 1.0$$
$$= .0614 = 6.14\%$$

This means that if one bank offered 6% with quarterly compounding, while another offered 6.14% with annual compounding, they would both be paying the same effective rate of interest.

annual report evaluation prepared by companies at the end of the reporting year that might be either on a calendar or fiscal basis. Contained in the annual report are the company's financial statements including footnotes, supplementary schedules, MANAGEMENT DISCUSSION AND ANALYSIS of earnings, president's letter, audit report, and other explanatory data (for example, research and marketing efforts) helpful in evaluating the entity's financial position and operating performance. The annual report is read by stockholders, potential investors, creditors, employees, regulatory bodies, and other interested financial statement users. *See also* 10-Q; 10-K.

annualize
1. switching to an annual basis. For example, a $250 monthly return on a $30,000 investment would be $(250 \times 12)/30,000 = 10\%$ annual return.
2. expressing the terms of a contract on a fixed annual basis. Annualizing is common in financial forecasting.

annualized returns investment returns converted to an annual (yearly) basis; for example, an international fund returning 0.5% a month returns 6% on an annualized (yearly) basis.

anticipated holding period time interval an individual expects to keep a financial asset; for example, you may decide to buy and sell a stock quickly or to hold on to the stock for many years.

anticipatory hedge hedging a cash position that has not yet been taken but is expected to be taken in the near future, in contrast with CASH HEDGE. In other words, it involves buying futures contracts in anticipation of a cash purchase. This is usually referred to as a LONG HEDGE, since the investor is long in futures contracts.

antidilution, full ratchet provisions that apply to the lowest sale price for any shares of common stock (or equivalents) sold by the company after the issuing of an option or CONVERTIBLE SECURITY as being the adjusted option price or conversion ratio for existing shareholders.

EXAMPLE:
If a prior round of financing raised capital at $4 per share with investors receiving full ratchet antidilution protection, and a subsequent round of financing was consummated at $2 per share, the early round investors would have the right to convert their shares at the $2 price, thereby doubling the number of shares they would receive. *See also* ANTIDILUTION, WEIGHTED AVERAGE.

antidilution, weighted average provisions that apply a weighted average formula to adjust the option price or conversion ratio of an early-round investor, based on the sale price and number of common equivalent shares sold by the company after the issuing of the option or CONVERTIBLE SECURITY.

EXAMPLE:
If a first round of financing raised $2 million of capital at $3 per share and the first-round investors received weighted average antidilution protection, and a second round of financing was consummated for another $2 million at $2 per share, then the first-round investors would have the right to convert their shares at a weighted average adjusted price of $2.50 per share. *See also* ANTIDILUTION, FULL RATCHET.

any-and-all bid offer to pay an equal price for all shares tendered by a specified date.

appreciation
1. increase in value of an asset (such as a security). For example, an individual sold a share of ABC Company's stock for $55 that he bought for $30. The amount of appreciation is $25. *See also* CAPITAL GAIN OR LOSS; RETURN; YIELD.
2. APPRECIATION OF THE DOLLAR.

appreciation of the dollar rise in the foreign exchange value of the dollar relative to other currencies; also called *strong dollar, strengthening dollar,* or *revaluation of a dollar*. The opposite of appreciation is weakening, deteriorating, or depreciation of the dollar. Strictly speaking, revaluation refers to a rise in the value of a currency that is pegged to gold or to another currency. A strong dollar makes Americans' cash go further overseas and reduces import prices—generally good for U.S. consumers. If the dollar is overvalued, U.S. products are harder to sell abroad and at home, where they compete with low-cost imports. This helps give the United States its huge trade deficit. A weak dollar can restore competitiveness to American products by making foreign goods comparatively more expensive. But too weak a dollar can spawn inflation, first through higher import prices, then through spiraling prices for all goods. Even worse, a falling dollar can drive foreign investors away from U.S. securities, which lose value along with the dollar. A strong dollar can be induced by raising U.S. interest rates. The following table summarizes the impacts of changes in foreign exchange rates on the multinational company's products and services and foreign investments.

THE IMPACTS OF CHANGES IN FOREIGN EXCHANGE RATES

	Weak Currency (Depreciation/ devaluation)	Strong Currency (Appreciation/ revaluation)
Imports	More expensive	Cheaper
Exports	Cheaper	More expensive
Payables	More expensive	Cheaper
Receivables	Cheaper	More expensive
Inflation	Fuel inflation by making imports more costly.	Low inflation

THE IMPACTS OF CHANGES IN FOREIGN EXCHANGE RATES (cont.)

	Weak Currency (Depreciation/ devaluation)	Strong Currency (Appreciation/ revaluation)
Foreign investment	Discourage foreign investment. Lower return on investments by international investors.	High interest rates could attract foreign investors.
The effect	Raising interest rates could slow down the economy.	Reduced exports could trigger a trade deficit.

The amount of appreciation or depreciation is computed as the fractional increase or decrease in the home currency value of the foreign currency or in the foreign currency value of the home currency:

With *Direct Quotes*:

$$\text{Percent change} = \frac{\text{Ending rate} - \text{beginning rate}}{\text{Beginning rate}} \times 100$$

With *Indirect Quotes*:

$$\text{Percent change} = \frac{\text{Beginning rate} - \text{ending rate}}{\text{Ending rate}} \times 100$$

EXAMPLE:
An increase in the exchange rate from $0.64 (or DM1.5625/$) to $0.68 (or DM1.4705/$) is equivalent to a DM appreciation of 6.25% [($0.68 − $0.64)/$0.64 = 0.0625] or [(DM1.5625 − DM1.4705)/DM1.4705 = 0.0625]. This also means a dollar depreciation of 5.88% [($0.64 − $0.68)/$0.68 = −0.0588].

See also DEPRECIATION; DIRECT QUOTE; INDIRECT QUOTE.

approximate compound yield measure of the annualized compound growth of a long-term investment.

arbitrage simultaneous purchase or sale of a commodity in different markets to profit from unwarranted differences in prices; for example, it involves the purchase of a security or commodity, including foreign exchange, in one market at one price while simultaneously selling that same currency in another market at a more advantageous price, in order to obtain a risk-free profit on the price differential. Profit is the price differential minus the cost. If exchange rates are not equal worldwide, there is profit opportunity for simultaneously buying a currency in one market while selling it in another. This activity would raise the exchange rate in the market where it is too low, because this is the market in which you would buy, and the increased demand for the currency would result in a higher price. The market where the exchange rate is too high is the one in which you would sell, and this increased selling activity would result in a lower price. Arbitrage would continue until the exchange rates in different markets were so close that it would not be worth the costs incurred to do any further buying and selling. When this situation occurs, we say that the rates are "transaction costs close." Any remaining deviation between exchange rates will not cover the costs of additional arbitrage transactions, so the arbitrage activity ceases.

Arbitrage Pricing Model (APM) pricing model that includes multiple risk factors, besides the security's BETA. This is in contrast to the CAPITAL ASSET PRICING MODEL (CAPM), which assumes that required rates of return depend on only one risk factor, the stock's *beta*. The Arbitrage Pricing Model (APM) disputes this and includes any number of risk factors:

$$r = r_f + b_1 RP_1 + b_2 RP_2 + \ldots + b_n RP_n$$

where r = the expected return for a given stock or portfolio, and
r_f = the risk-free rate, and
b_i = the sensitivity (or reaction) of the returns of the stock to unexpected changes in economic forces i (i = 1, ... n), and
RP_i = the market risk premium associated with an unexpected change in the i_{th} economic force, and
n = the number of relevant economic forces.

Roll and Ross suggest the following five economic forces:
1. changes in expected inflation
2. unanticipated changes in inflation
3. unanticipated changes in industrial production
4. unanticipated changes in the yield differential between low- and high-grade bonds (the default-risk premium)
5. unanticipated changes in the yield differential between long-term and short-term bonds (the term structure of interest rates)

EXAMPLE:
Suppose returns required in the market by investors are a function of two economic factors according to the following equation, where the risk-free rate is 7%:

$$r = 0.07 + b_1(0.04) + b_2(0.01)$$

ABC stock has the reaction coefficients to the factors, such that $b_1 = 1.3$ and $b_2 = 0.90$. Then the required rate of return for the ABC stock is

$$r = 0.07 + (1.3)(0.04) + (0.90)(0.01) = 0.113 = 11.3\%$$

Arbitrage Pricing Theory (APT) *see* ARBITRAGE PRICING MODEL (APM).

arithmetic average return simple mean of successive one-period rates of return, defined as: Arithmetic average return = $1/n\ r_t$, where n = the number of time periods, r = the single holding period return in time t, and Σ = summation. *Caution:* The arithmetic average return can be misleading in multiperiod return computations. *See also* COMPOUND (GEOMETRIC) AVERAGE RETURN.

arithmetic mean   *see* AVERAGES.

Arms Index (TRIN)   short-term trading index that offers the day trader as well as the long-term investor a look at how volume—not time—governs stock price changes, developed by Richard W. Arms, Jr. It is also commonly referred to by its quote machine ticker symbols, TRIN and MKDS. The Arms Index is designed to measure the relative strength of the volume associated with advancing stocks versus that of declining stocks. If more volume goes into advancing stocks than declining stocks, the Arms Index will fall to a low level under 1.00. Alternatively, if more volume flows into declining stocks than advancing stocks, the Arms Index will rise to a high level over 1.00. It helps forecast the price changes of market indexes as well as of individual issues. You will find Arms indices for the NYSE, the NASDAQ market, the AMEX, and Giant Arms (a combined index for NASDAQ and AMEX). There is also the Bond Arms Index, which helps forecast interest rates. The Arms Index is calculated by dividing the ratio of the number of advancing issues to the number of declining issues by the ratio of the volume of advancing issues to the volume of declining issues. It is computed separately for the NYSE, the American Stock Exchange, and NASDAQ.

Using the data in the figures given in *Diaries* of *The Wall Street Journal*:

$$\frac{\frac{\text{Advances}}{\text{Declines}}}{\frac{\text{Advance Volume}}{\text{Decline Volume}}} = \frac{1130/775}{166,587/78016} = 0.71$$

It is found in *Barron's* and *The Wall Street Journal* and is reported daily in TV reports such as *Nightly Business Report* and on the CNNFN and CNBC networks.

A figure of less than 1.0 indicates money flowing into stocks (BULLISH sign), while a ratio of greater than 1.0 shows money flowing out of stocks (BEARISH sign).

One variation of the Arms Index that many technicians monitor is the Open 10 TRIN (also known as the Open 10 Trading Index). It is calculated by taking a ratio of a 10-day total for the number of advancing issues to a 10-day total of the number of declining issues, and dividing it by a ratio of a 10-day total of the volume of advancing issues to a 10-day total of the volume of declining issues.

In addition, a 30-day version of the Open 10 TRIN is frequently used.

High readings reflect an oversold condition and are generally considered bullish. Low readings reflect an overbought condition and are generally deemed bearish.

arrearage past-due payments such as cumulative PREFERRED STOCK DIVIDENDS that have been declared but have not been paid on their payment dates. (COMMON STOCK dividends cannot be paid as long as cumulative preferred stock dividends are in arrears.) *See also* ACCUMULATED DIVIDEND.

Artificial Currency Unit (ACU) financial accounting unit created by international agreement and based on a basket of national currencies. Examples are the ASIAN CURRENCY UNIT (ACU), EUROPEAN CURRENCY UNIT (ECU), and SPECIAL DRAWING RIGHT (SDR). ACUs are traded among member nations and for accounts held by major international banks. They cannot be used in private transactions.

ascending term in TECHNICAL ANALYSIS meaning a chart pattern of a stock's closing price over a period of time displaying repeatedly higher peaks. *See also* ASCENDING TOPS.

ascending tops term in TECHNICAL ANALYSIS meaning a series of peaks, each peak higher than the previous one on the stock's chart pattern. This upward movement is considered to be extremely BULLISH by CHARTISTS. The same analysis can be applied to the stock market as a whole. *See also* DESCENDING TOPS.

Asian Currency Unit (ACU) separate accounting entity by which the Asian dollar deposit market was created. The market emerged from a Bank of America proposal. *See also* ARTIFICIAL CURRENCY UNIT; EUROPEAN CURRENCY UNIT (ECU); SPECIAL DRAWING RIGHT (SDR).

Asian Development Bank (ADB) financial institution for supporting economic development in Asia, created in the late 1960s. The Asian Development Bank (ADB) operates on similar lines as the World Bank. Member countries range from Iran to the United States of America. *See also* INTERNATIONAL MONETARY FUND (IMF); WORLD BANK.

Asian dollar market market in Asia in which banks collect deposits and make loans denominated in U.S. dollars.

Asian dollars U.S. dollar-denominated deposits kept in Asian-based banks, similar to Eurodollars.

ask *see* ASKED PRICE.

ask price *see* ASKED PRICE.

asked price
Also called *offering price, ask price, asking price,*
 1. price at which an investment, such as a security, commodity, or real estate, is offered for sale. It is usually the lowest price at which one can purchase the investment.

2. for MUTUAL FUNDS, the current NET ASSET VALUE per share plus sales charges, if any.

asset allocation
   1. apportionment of money invested among different asset classes such as cash, stocks, bonds, precious metals, collectibles, commodities, and real estate. The way assets are allocated will have an effect on expected return and risk.
   2. apportionment of funds invested in different instruments within a particular class. An example is buying stocks within 20 different industry groupings. Another example is buying different kinds of stock such as BLUE CHIPS, GROWTH STOCKS, INCOME STOCKS, and DEFENSIVE STOCKS. Another example is buying different kinds of bonds including U.S. bonds, municipal bonds of states and cities, and corporate bonds.
   3. situation in which a mutual fund manager switches funds among different investment types based on changing market conditions. For example, if the fund manager believes stocks will rise, he or she will switch from MONEY MARKET funds to stocks. If the fund manager believes the U.S. stock market is excessively overvalued, he or she may sell U.S. stocks and buy stocks of foreign companies.
   See also INTERNATIONAL ASSET ALLOCATION; PORTFOLIO DIVERSIFICATION.

asset management account   account at a brokerage firm or bank in which there is a combination of brokerage and banking services. The biggest feature of this account is that it switches cash into a MONEY MARKET (MUTUAL) FUND. Brokerage services include the purchase and sale of securities, margin loans, and receipt of a monthly statement of transactions consummated. Banking services include credit card usage, debit card usage, and checking.

asset manager   money manager who determines which assets an investment will buy and sell at specific times to gain the greatest appreciation (value). *See also* PORTFOLIO MANAGER.

assimilation   absorption of a new issue by investors after all shares have been sold by the issuer's underwriters.

Association for Investment Management Research (AIMR)   U.S. independent, nonprofit organization that awards the Chartered Financial Analyst (CFA) certification and sets professional standards that must be applied by its members worldwide.

at market order   *see* MARKET ORDER.

at or better   order placed with a broker or account representative to buy or sell securities at the price requested by the investor or better; also called *at order* or *better order*. For example, if a stock or bond is being sold, the broker will seek the price asked for or higher. However, if a stock or bond is being bought, the broker will seek to buy it at the price specified by the investor or lower.

at par literally, "equal" to the nominal, FACE VALUE, or maturity value of a security. The most common use of the term is in trading of bonds where a bond trading at par is trading at a price equal to its face value. However, if the bond or security should fall in price, it is trading at a discount. Conversely, a bond or security trading above its PAR VALUE is trading at a premium. A bond would be selling at a discount or premium depending on such factors as the interest rate of the bond relative to the prevailing market interest rate, riskiness of the issue, and the maturity period.

at risk term indicating that the money is exposed to the possibility of loss. Thus, money invested is at risk. Speculative stocks are an extreme example of "at risk" investments.

at the close
1. order to buy or sell stock at the ending price for the trading day. If the stock is traded on more than one stock exchange, clear specification must be made of the exchange it should be executed on. In the event the transaction is not entered into, cancellation of the order occurs.
2. in the options and futures market, it constitutes a transaction to be fulfilled on some exchanges during the closing period.

at the market   *see* MARKET ORDER.

at-the-money term used when the EXERCISE (STRIKE) PRICE of an option is equal or virtually equal to the current market price of the underlying stock.

at the opening
1. market or limit price order to be fulfilled when the opening occurs for the stock on the specified exchange. If the order or part thereof is not consummated, it is cancelled. Because of the tumultuous trading that often occurs at the close, brokers never guarantee that these orders will be executed.
2. in the options and futures market, it is a market order during which a price range exists at the opening.

auction market market in which buyers enter competitive bids and sellers enter competitive offers at the same time. Examples are two-sided auctions (such as NYSE) and Dutch auctions (such as Treasury bills).

auction-market preferred stock (AMPS)   *see* DUTCH AUCTION PREFERRED STOCKS.

Autex system electronic mechanism informing brokers that other brokers desire to purchase or sell large blocks of stock. After there is a match, the trade is executed on the floor of the exchange or OVER-THE-COUNTER.

automatic investment plan investment plan that allows investors to contribute as little as $20 a month. The funds are automatically deducted from the investor's checking/savings account or off his or her paycheck and invested in a retirement account or mutual fund.

average share cost average cost of an investment used for income tax purposes in order to determine a CAPITAL GAIN OR CAPITAL LOSS. *See also* AVERAGE SHARE PRICE.

average share price
1. average price of stock that was purchased at different dates; also called *average share cost*. Example: An individual purchased XYZ Company stock as follows:

Date	Number of shares	Price/Shares	Total
Jan 6	1000	$5	$5000
June 2	200	$6	$1200
Sept. 17	500	$4	$2000
Total	1700		$8200

The average price equals $\dfrac{\text{Total cost}}{\text{Total shares}} = \dfrac{\$8200}{1700} = \$4.82.$

2. calculation on a weighted basis of a basket of stocks indicating the mean share price of those included. One popular measure, the Dow Jones Average, a price-weighted arithmetic average, includes 30 industrial stocks for the industrial index, 20 transportation stocks for the transportation index, and 15 public utility stocks for the utilities index. A composite index, known as the Dow Jones Average, is taken for all 65 stocks. There is also a Dow Jones Bond Average measuring the average value of six groups of bonds, and the Standard & Poor's Composite 500 Index (an index that is capitalization weighted), which includes 425 industrial stocks, 50 utilities, and 25 railroads traded on the New York Stock Exchange.

average up stock trader's strategy of buying shares of stock on a rising market so as to reduce the overall cost. Buying an equal number of shares, say, 200 shares at $12, $13, $14, $15, and $16, for example, will make the average share cost $14, as shown below. *Note:* This strategy does not determine whether the stock is worth purchasing at any of these prices.

PURCHASE OR SALE OF XYZ CORP. STOCK

Shares	Price	Average Cost per Share
200	12	12.00
200	13	12.50
200	14	13.00
200	15	13.50
200	16	14.00

See also DOLLAR COST AVERAGING (DCA).

AVERAGE YIELD BASIS

average yield basis measure of the rate of return on a series of investments over time. In securities, particularly in stock, dividend returns are calculated as a percentage of the purchase price of the stock; however, if the same stock has been purchased at varying prices over time, then the average yield basis is calculated on its TOTAL RETURN including dividends as well as CAPITAL GAINS realized or unrealized. See example below:

AVERAGE YIELD XYZ STOCK

Purchase Date	Purchase Price	Quantity	Total Cost	Dividend Per Share	Total Dividend	Yield
Jan. 1	$15.00	300	$4,500.00	$1.50	$450.00	10.00%
Feb. 23	$18.00	200	$3,600.00	$1.50	$300.00	8.33%
Mar. 15	$23.00	250	$5,750.00	$1.50	$375.00	6.52%
Apr. 16	$19.00	500	$9,500.00	$1.50	$750.00	7.89%
June 25	$21.00	150	$3,150.00	$1.50	$225.00	7.14%
Aug. 14	$14.00	600	$8,400.00	$1.50	$900.00	10.71%
Sept. 16	$12.00	700	$8,400.00	$1.50	$1,050.00	12.50%
Total		2700	$43,300.00		$4,050.00	9.35%

Average Price/Share = $43,300/2,700 = $16.04

12-MONTH AVERAGE YIELD INCLUDING CAPITAL GAINS AND DIVIDENDS

Sales Price	Purchase Cost	Capital Gain	Earned Dividends	Average Yield
$47,775.00	$43,300.00	$4,475.00	$4,050.00	19.69%

averages
1. for a set of numbers, the total of all number values divided by the number of items in the set; also called *arithmetic mean*.
2. number used to measure the general behavior of security prices by reflecting the arithmetic average price of a representative group of securities at a given point in time and comparing it to the arithmetic average price of the same group at a different time.

B

back-end load (deferred sales charge) deferred charges assessed when funds are withdrawn from the fund. These charges are intended to discourage frequent trading in the fund. Deferred sales charges are typically on a scale, which reduces them yearly until they disappear after a predetermined time period. For example, if a holder of a mutual fund exits after being in the fund one year the fee might be 4%, after two years 3%, after three years 2%, after four years 1%, and thereafter, no exit fee. The back-end load charge is subtracted from the selling price to arrive at the net proceeds to be received. An example of a mutual fund having a back-end load is the Kaufmann Fund.

back months months having the longest expiration dates in OPTIONS and FUTURES trading.

back office departments within a brokerage firm handling the bookkeeping of buy and sell trades, dealings between branches, and governmental compliance reporting. The back office does not directly execute buying, selling, or other direct trading activities. Order processing is slowed when trading volume on the stock market is very voluminous.

backspread delta-neutral spread composed of more LONG OPTIONS than SHORT OPTIONS on the same underlying instrument. This position generally profits from a large movement in either direction in the underlying instrument.

backwardation hypothesis that futures prices will tend to rise over the life of a contract.

balance of payments (BOP) systematic record of a country's receipts from, or payments to, other countries. In a way, it is like the balance sheets for businesses, only on a national level. The reference in the media to the BALANCE OF TRADE usually refers to goods within the goods and services category of the current account. It also known as *merchandise* or *visible trade* because it consists of such tangibles as foodstuffs, manufactured goods, and raw materials. "Services," the other part of the category, is known as *invisible trade* and consists of intangibles such as interest or dividends, technology transfers, and others (such as insurance, transportation, financial). When the net result of both the current account and the capital account yields more credits than debits, the country is said to have a surplus in its balance of payments. Figures are reported in seasonally adjusted volumes and dollar amounts. It is the only nonsurvey, nonjudgmental report that appears in *Survey of Current Business*, produced by the Department of Commerce.

BALANCE OF TRADE

balance of trade merchandise exports minus imports; also called *merchandise trade balance* or *visible trade*. Thus, if exports of goods exceed imports the trade balance is said to be "favorable," or to have a trade surplus, while an excess of imports over exports yields an "unfavorable" trade balance or a trade deficit. Visit a web site such as *www.economy.com* for its statistical data. The balance of trade is an important item in calculating balance of payments. *See also* BALANCE OF PAYMENTS.

balance sheet condensed financial statement showing the nature and amount of a company's assets, liabilities, and stockholders' equity as of a given date; also called *financial position statement*; a financial snapshot of what the company owns, what it owes, and the ownership stake.

balanced investment strategy asset allocation and management method aimed at balancing risk and return.

balanced (mutual) fund MUTUAL FUND that combines investments in common stock and bonds and often preferred stock, and attempts to provide income and some capital appreciation. Balanced funds tend to underperform all-stock funds in strong BULL MARKETS.

balloon bond bond that is repaid in a lump sum at maturity. Many bonds, however, are progressively amortized over their maturity through a SINKING FUND provision.

Banca Commerciale Italiana General Index index that includes over 325 Italian companies on the Milan Exchange.

Bangkok Book Club Index index of all the shares listed on the Securities Exchange of Thailand.

Bank of New York ADR Index real-time index to track all Depositary Receipts—AMERICAN DEPOSITARY RECEIPTS (ADR) and GLOBAL DEPOSITARY RECEIPTS (GDR)—traded on the New York Stock Exchange (NYSE), the American Stock Exchange (AMEX), and NASDAQ. The Bank of New York ADR Index is capitalization-weighted and is calculated on a continuous basis throughout the trading day. In addition to the Composite Index, there are three regional indices—The Europe ADR Index, The Asia ADR Index, The Latin America ADR Index and three market indices—The Emerging Markets ADR Index, The Developed Markets ADR Index, and The Euroland ADR Index—as well as various sector and country indices. This information can be retrieved at the Bank of New York Internet site (*www.bankofny.com*). (Refer to the following chart.)

COMPARISON OF THE BANK OF NEW YORK ADR INDICES

Index	High	Low	Close	Prev Close	% Change	Year To Date % Change
ADR Index	112.24	110.30	110.30	111.46	−1.04%	−13.97%
Europe	119.30	117.08	117.08	118.08	−0.85%	−16.57%
Asia	101.16	99.40	99.40	101.16	−1.74%	−7.89%
Latin America	91.90	90.48	90.54	91.19	−0.71%	−0.39%
Emerging Markets	112.00	108.95	108.97	112.00	−2.71%	−5.47%

(data as of March 20, 2001)

banker's acceptance (BA) time draft drawn on a bank by a corporation to pay for merchandise. The draft promises payment of a certain sum of money to its holder at some future date. What makes banker's acceptances (BAs) unique is that by prearrangement a bank accepts them, thereby guaranteeing their payment at the stated time. Most BAs arise in foreign trade transactions. The most common maturity for BAs is three months, although they can have maturities of up to 270 days. Their typical denominations are $500,000 and $1 million. BAs offer the following advantages as an investment vehicle: (1) safety; (2) negotiability; (3) liquidity; (4) several basis points higher yield spread than those of TREASURY BILLS (T-BILLS); (5) smaller investment amount producing a yield similar to that of a CD with comparable face value. BAs are short-term, money market instruments actively traded in the SECONDARY MARKET. Depending on the bank's creditworthiness, the acceptance becomes a financial instrument that can be discounted. In addition to the discount, an acceptance fee (usually 1.5% of the value of the draft) is charged to customers seeking acceptances.

bar chart technical chart on which vertical lines appear at each time period, and the top and bottom of each bar show the high and low prices. A horizontal line across the bar marks the ending price.

BAR CHART

Stock Price

⊢ Closing price
⊢
 ⊢

Month

barbell portfolio   primarily a bond security PORTFOLIO that distributes its bond maturity dates around the normalized distribution concept found in a bell-shaped curve. The portfolio contains more intermediate bonds than short-term bonds or long-term bonds. The portfolio seeks to reduce short- or long-term risk and to HEDGE against FLUCTUATIONS in interest rates.

EXAMPLE:
An investor with $160,000 to invest might structure a barbell portfolio, whereby $40,000 matures in one year, $10,000 matures in each of the next eight years, and $40,000 matures in year ten. As the bonds come due at the end of year one, he might reinvest $30,000 to mature in one year (totaling $40,000), and the remaining $10,000 to mature in year ten (totaling $50,000). He reduces the impact of changing interest rates on the value of his portfolio.

bargain hunter   investor looking to buy shares at reduced prices in a period of market decline.

Barings Emerging Market Indexes (BEMI)   *see* ING BARINGS EMERGING MARKET INDEXES (BEMI).

barrier options   OPTIONS whose payoff depends on whether or not the underlying asset has reached or exceeded a predetermined price.

Barron's   weekly publication by Dow Jones; the second most popular source of financial news behind *The Wall Street Journal*.

Barron's Confidence Index   a corporate bond index published weekly in *BARRON'S* following the trend in investor sentiment. Barron's Confidence Index equals:

$$\frac{\text{Yield on Barron's 10 top-grade corporate bonds}}{\text{Yield on Dow Jones 40 bond average}}$$

The numerator will have a lower yield than the denominator because it consists of higher-quality bonds (rated AAA or AA). Some high-quality bonds are those of AT&T, General Electric, and Procter & Gamble. The lower the risk of DEFAULT, the lower the return rate is.

EXAMPLE:
Assume the Dow Jones yield is 8% and the Barron's yield is 7%. The Confidence Index is

$$\frac{7\%}{8\%} = .875 = 87.5\%$$

Because top-quality bonds have lower yields than lower-grade bonds, the index will be below 100%. Typically, the trading range is between 80% and 95%. When bond investors are BULLISH, yield differences between the high-grade bonds and low-grade bonds will be small. In such cases, the index may be close to 95%. If the feeling is BEARISH, bond market investors will want to hold top-quality issues.

Some investors who continue to put their money in average-quality bonds or lower-quality bonds will want a high yield for the increased risk. The Confidence Index will then decline, since the denominator will be getting larger. If confidence is high, investors are apt to purchase lower-grade bonds. As a result, the yield on high-grade bonds will decrease while the yield on low-grade bonds will increase. When bond traders are ignoring lower-quality bonds, it can be a signal that either the economy is in trouble or a buying opportunity for those lower-quality bonds exists. If an investor knows what bond traders are doing now, he or she may also be able to predict what stock traders will be doing in the future. The lead time between the Confidence Index and economic conditions and stock market performance is considered to be several months. This leaves ample time for an investment decision. If bond traders are bullish, an investor may invest in stocks now before stock prices rise. On the other hand, if bond traders are bearish, an investor would not buy stocks or consider selling current holdings on the expectation that stock prices will fall.

Note: Bond traders may be making the wrong investment decision, which could result in misleading inferences as to stock prices. The Confidence Index has a mixed track record in predicting the future. The index is deficient in that it considers investors' attitudes only on yields (simply, a look at the demand function). It ignores the supply of new bond issues (supply pattern) as they affect yields. A large bond issue by a major corporation, for example, may result in increased high-grade bond yields. Such movement would occur despite heavy demand for single issues but prevailing investor attitudes that yields should be dropping.

basic earnings per share ratio of a company's net income less preferred dividends divided by its outstanding common shares.

EXAMPLE:
If Company X has a net profit of $2,000,000, preferred dividends of $300,000, and outstanding common shares of $1,000,000, its basic earnings per share will be

$$\frac{\$2,000,000 - \$300,000}{1,000,000} = \$1.70 \text{ per share}$$

See also DILUTED EARNINGS PER SHARE.

basis
1. figure or value that is the starting point in computing CAPITAL GAIN OR LOSS. If you bought an ADR for $500 a year ago and sold it today for $1500, the basis is $500 and the profit of $1000 ($1500 − $500) is a capital gain.
2. difference between the FUTURES (or FORWARD) price of an asset and its SPOT (or cash) PRICE. The basis can be expressed as a value or as a percentage of the spot price.

BASIS POINT 26

   3. bond's YIELD TO MATURITY at a given price. A 10% bond selling at 100 has a 10% basis.

basis point unit of measure for the change in interest rates for bonds and notes. One basis point is equal to $1/100^{th}$ of a percentage point, that is, 0.01%. Thus, 100 basis points = 1%.

EXAMPLE:
When something is down 50 basis points, it is down half a percentage point.

basket trade
   1. significant transaction comprised of numerous shares in different companies.
   2. unit of 15 or more stocks used in PROGRAM TRADING.
   3. program trading vehicles offered by the New York Stock Exchange (called *Exchange Stock Portfolio* or *ESP*) and the CHICAGO BOARD OPTIONS EXCHANGE (called *Market Basket*) to institutional investors and index arbitrageurs. Both baskets allow the purchase in one trade of all the stocks making up the Standard & Poor's 500 Composite Index.

bear one who is pessimistic and believes that prices in the security and commodity markets will decline. A bear can profit from a declining stock market by selling a stock SHORT or buying a PUT OPTION. A BULL, the opposite of a bear, thinks prices will rise. *Note*: The term *bear* originates from bearskin jobbers who used to sell bearskins before the bears were captured. Slowly, the term *bear* came to mean speculators who agreed to sell shares they did not own. These bears would agree to sell a stock at a certain price if they felt the price was about to go down. Then they would quickly buy the stock at its lower price and sell it for the previously agreed-on higher price. Apparently, the bears were betting on a price decline. Because bull- and bearbaiting were once popular sports, bulls came to mean the opposite of bears. Bulls were those who bought heavily expecting a stock price to move up.

bear market market declining about 20% or more after reaching a peak. Such a situation may occur when there is an expectation of declining economic activity or higher interest rates. A bear market may last six months to several years, during which time stock prices continue declining. Any upward movement in price is brief. There are typically three phases in a bear market:
   1. Distribution. This begins with the final phase of a BULL MARKET, when farsighted investors deem the market to be overvalued and hasten their selling of shares. Even though there is active trading volume, it diminishes on rallies. The investing public, while still active, is becoming more cautious.
   2. Panic. Buyers thin out and sellers are becoming more worried. There is major downward pressure in stock prices with a huge jump in volume.

3. Washout. This relates to the sale of positions by investors who have held out up to this point. In a bear market, a bottom, the lowest point in a sequence of prices trending downward with occasional brief recoveries, may be reached. Securities bought now will typically do well since they are made at historically low overall stock market levels.

bear raid illegal trading act in which securities are sold short below the last trading price in sufficient volume to depress the stock and result in a trading profit. This can cause wild gyrations in a stock and is considered a form of stock manipulation. The Securities and Exchange Commission (SEC) imposed the so-called UPTICK rule mandating that stocks can be shorted only on the next uptick in the price of the security.

bear spread option strategy that yields maximum profit when the price of the underlying security declines. It involves the acquisition and simultaneous sale of options. Puts or calls can be used. A higher STRIKE PRICE is purchased and a lower strike price is sold. The options should have the same expiration date.

bear squeeze increase in the price of stocks or commodities that forces SHORT sellers to cover their sales by buying securities back. This action results in a squeeze on the short sellers, often incurring a financial loss for them.

bearer bond
  1. unregistered bond (one that does not have the owner's name recorded) that entitles the holder to payments of both principal and interest; also called a *coupon bond* because whoever presents the coupon is entitled to the interest. With respect to transfers, bond endorsement is not a requirement. The detached coupons must be presented to the issuer or paying agent to receive semiannual interest payments. Bearer bonds that may be changed to registered bonds are referred to as *interchangeable bonds*.
  2. time draft by a company whose payment is guaranteed by the bank's acceptance of it.

being long buying securities in the hope that they will go up in value. *See also* LONG POSITION.

bellwether stock stock that indicates the direction of the security market. General Electric is an example because much of it is owned by institutional investors whose trading actions have a pronounced effect on the market price of securities. Further, actions by institutional investors usually influence smaller investors. Bellwether stocks exist for each industry to reflect its performance and directions such as Microsoft as an indicator of the technology sector.

benchmark
  1. standard measurement or metric used to evaluate the performance of a portfolio; for example, an appropriate stock or bond

index can be used to gauge the performance of an investment such as a mutual fund. An example is the EAFE (EUROPE, AUSTRALIA, AND FAR EAST) INDEX, a value-weighted index of the equity performance of major foreign markets, which is often used to evaluate the performance of international mutual funds. A list of benchmarks is presented below.

TYPICAL MARKET INDEXES USED AS PERFORMANCE BENCHMARKS

Funds	Index
Domestic	
Growth	S&P 500
Aggressive Growth	Value Line
Small Company	Russell 2000
Government Bond	Various Lehman Bros. Government/Corporate Bond Indexes
Municipal Bond	Lehman Bros. Municipal Bond Index
International	
Global	Morgan Stanley International World Index; Morgan Stanley Europe, Australia, and the Far East (EAFE) Index
Foreign Bond	Salomon Bros. Non-U.S. Dollar World Bond Index
Global Bond	Shearson World Bond Index

2. *see* BENCHMARK RATES.

benchmark bond bond representative of current market conditions and used for performance comparison. Government bonds are almost always used as benchmark bonds. The 10-year TREASURY BOND is an example.

benchmark rates interest or loan rates that other rates are pegged to. An example is LIBOR, the rate quoted to a top-quality borrower on the EUROCURRENCY MARKET. Another example is the U.S. prime rate on which other loan rates are based.

best efforts *see* BEST EFFORTS UNDERWRITING.

best efforts underwriting agreement in which an underwriter consents only to use its best efforts to sell the securities as the issuer's agent. The underwriter does not purchase the securities itself and has no obligation to purchase any amount not purchased by investors.

best execution official term for the requirement that brokerages obtain the highest price for sellers and the lowest price for buyers.

beta *see* BETA COEFFICIENT.

beta coefficient second letter of the Greek alphabet, used as a statistical measure of risk relative to its BENCHMARK; also simply called *beta*. For equity funds, the market benchmark is the S&P 500 Index. For fixed-income funds, it is TREASURY BILLS. Beta measures volatility. Put another way, it is a measure of a security's return over time to that of the overall market. For example, if ABC's beta is 1.5, it means that if the stock market goes up 10%, ABC's common stock goes up 15%; if the market goes down 10%, ABC goes down 15%. Here is a guide to reading betas:

Beta	What It Means
0	The security's return is independent of the market. An example is a risk-free security such as a T-bill.
0.5	The security is only half as response as the market.
1.0	The security has the same response or risk as the market (for example, average risk). This is the beta value of the market portfolio such as Standard & Poor's 500.
2.0	The security is twice as responsive, or risky, as the market.

Beta of a particular stock is useful in predicting how much the security will go up or down, provided that investors know which way the market will go. Beta helps to figure out risk and expected (required) return.

$$\text{Expected (required) return} = \text{risk-free rate} + \text{beta} \times (\text{market return} - \text{risk-free rate})$$

The higher the beta for a security, the greater the return expected (or demanded) by the investor. *Note*: A low beta, however, does not necessarily mean lower volatility, just that the fund does not have a high correlation with its benchmark. The beta is used for comparative purposes only. It should not be interpreted as a predictor or a guarantee of future performance.

EXAMPLE:

XYZ stock actually returned 9%. Assume that the risk-free rate (for example, return on a T-bill) = 5%, market return (for example, return on the S & P 500) = 10%, and XYZ's beta = 1.5. Then the return on XYZ stock required by investors would be

$$\text{Expected (required) return} = 5\% + 1.5\,(10\% - 5\%)$$
$$= 5\% + 7.5\% = 12.5\%$$

Since the actual return (9%) is less than the required return (12.5%), you would not be willing to buy the stock. Betas for stocks (and MUTUAL FUNDS) are widely available in many investment newsletters and directories. The following table presents betas for some selected multinational companies (MNCs):

BETAS FOR SOME SELECTED MULTINATIONAL CORPORATIONS

Company	Ticker Symbol	Beta
IBM	IBM	1.25
Wal-Mart	WMT	0.95
Microsoft	MSFT	1.77
McDonald's	MCD	0.65
Honda	HMC	0.72
Pfizer	PFE	0.67
Nokia	NOK	1.94

Source: AOL Personal Finance Channel and MSN Money Central Investor (*http://moneycentral.msn.com/investor/contents.asp*), April 3, 2001.

beta for a mutual fund measure of uncontrollable risk that results from forces outside of the MUTUAL FUND'S control. Purchasing power, interest rate, and market risks fall into this category. This type of risk is measured by BETA. In measuring a fund's beta, an indication is needed of the relationship between the fund's return and the market return, such as the return on the Standard & Poor's 500 Stock Composite Index. This relationship is statistically computed, which is not covered here. Betas for mutual (stock) funds are widely available in many investment newsletters and directories. Examples are *S&P's Stock Guide, Money Magazine, Business Week, Forbes, Fortune, The Individual Investor's Guide to No-load Mutual Funds*, and various reports from Morningstar Inc. and Lipper Analytical Service. Financial advisory services such as Morningstar (Internet users can check out *www.morningstar.net*), S&P/Micropal, and Lipper Analytical Service also provide their own risk-adjusted rating systems developed based on beta and return. The following table presents betas for some selected INTERNATIONAL FUNDS:

BETAS FOR SOME SELECTED INTERNATIONAL FUNDS

Company	Ticker Symbol	Beta
GAM: International	GMMNX	0.34
Harbor International	HAINX	0.66
Strong International	STISX	0.78
Fidelity Overseas	FOSFX	0.84
Templeton International A	TEGEX	0.44
Vanguard International Growth	VWIGX	0.65

Source: MSN Money Central Investor (*http://moneycentral.msn.com/investor/contents.asp*), April 3, 2001.

Note: If a fund's R-SQUARED is low, beta is less reliable as a predictor of volatility.

beta for a security *see* BETA COEFFICIENT.

bid highest price a buyer will pay for a security at a given time.

bid and asked   term used in the OVER-THE-COUNTER MARKET to describe unlisted securities. Bid is the highest price an investor is willing to pay, while asked is the lowest price a seller is willing to take. Together, the two prices represent a QUOTATION in a security or commodity. A spread is the difference between the BID PRICE and the ASKED PRICE for the security or commodity. For example, if a stock has a bid and asked price of $5.50 and $6, the spread is $0.50 per share.

bid price
1. price a buyer is willing to pay, or "bid," for a particular security. It is the highest price offered by a dealer to buy a given security traded in the OVER-THE-COUNTER MARKET.
2. price per share that shareholders receive when they cash in (redeem) their shares.

bid-ask spread   difference between the BID (the price a buyer is willing to pay) and the ASK (the price a seller is offering) quoted prices. Generally, the fewer the shares outstanding, the less the demand for shares, and the higher the risk of the issue, the bigger the spread, putting investors at a disadvantage.

big bang
1. deregulation that allowed foreign firms to operate in London's financial markets on Big Bang Day (October 27, 1986).
2. supporting drastic changes in the foreign or economic policies of a country.

Big Board   term used for the New York Stock Exchange.

bilateral exchanges   currencies participating in the *European Economic and Monetary Union (EMU)* expressed in terms of the EURO until January 1, 2002. To convert one currency to another, you must use the following method: Convert the first currency to the euro and then convert that amount in euros to the second currency, using the fixed conversion rates adopted on January 1, 1999 (see below).

FIXED EURO CONVERSION RATES

Country	Currency	Currency Literacy Abbreviation	Rate
Euroland	Euro	EUR	1
Austria	schilling	ATS	13.7603
Belgium	franc	BEF	40.3399
Finland	makka	FIM	5.94573
France	franc	FRF	6.55957
Germany	mark	DEM	1.95583
Ireland	punt	IEP	.787564
Italy	lira	ITL	1,936.27
Luxembourg	franc	LUF	40.3399
Netherlands	guilder	NLG	2.20371
Portugal	escudo	PTE	200.482
Spain	peseta	ESP	166.386

black markets illegal markets in foreign exchange. Developing nations generally do not permit free markets in foreign exchange and impose many restrictions on foreign currency transactions. These restrictions take many forms, such as limiting the amounts of foreign currency to be purchased or government licensing requirements. As a result, illegal markets in foreign exchange develop to satisfy trader demand. In many countries such illegal markets exist openly, with little government intervention.

Black-Scholes Option Pricing Model (OPM) formula for valuing stock options designed in 1973 by Nobel laureates Fischer Black and Myron Scholes. The formula provides the relationship between call option value and the five factors that determine the premium of an option's market value over its expiration value:
1. **Time to maturity**. The longer the option period, the greater the value of the option.
2. **Stock price volatility**. The greater the volatility of the underlying stock's price, the greater its value.
3. **Exercise price**. The lower the exercise price, the greater the value.
4. **Stock price**. The higher the price of the underlying stock, the greater the value.
5. **Risk-free rate**. The higher the risk-free rate, the higher the value.

blank cheque preferred stock authorized preferred stock whose terms are left open under the company's charter, allowing the board of directors to alter the terms without stockholder approval. This is often used as an anti takeover device.

block voluminous number of shares or bonds or dollar amounts attributed thereto owned or traded. An example is the purchase or sale of 10,000 or more shares. Another example is the buying or selling of $100 million bonds.

block trade large-size transaction, usually involving at least 10,000 or more shares of stock or $200,000 or more worth of bonds.

blocked funds funds in one nation's currency that may not be exchanged freely due to *exchange controls* or other reasons.

blowoff steep and rapid increase in price followed by a steep and rapid drop in price; also called *blowup top*.

blue chip
1. common stock of high quality that has a long record of earnings and dividend payments. They are known for excellent management, goods and services, and personnel. They have an excellent reputation. Blue chip stocks are often viewed as long-term investment instruments. They have low risk and provide modest but dependable return. Examples are General Electric and Merck. Blue chip stocks usually have high prices and moderate ratios of dividends to market price per share. They are less vulnerable to

cyclical market changes than other stocks. *Note:* The term originates from the blue chips used in poker—always the most valuable chips.
  2. high-quality bonds that are secure and stable in price and interest payments.

blue chip stock   *see* BLUE CHIP.

blue-sky laws   U.S. state regulations to protect investors against securities fraud. Blue-sky laws require sellers of new issues to register their offerings and provide financial details so that investors can base judgments on trustworthy data.

board minutes   minutes of board of directors meeting. A board of directors establishes corporate management policies and makes decisions on major company issues and when dividends will be paid to stockholders. They are typically written after a board meeting and approved at the subsequent meeting.

boiler room   place having high-pressure brokers calling typically uninformed investors to make unsuitable or even fraudulent speculative investments. Such activities, if not against the law, do violate fair practice rules of the National Association of Securities Dealers (NASD).

Bollinger bands   bands that mark one standard deviation above and below the 30-day price average. The bands represent an envelope of support and resistance levels. A few general behaviors identified follow.
  1. Sharp moves tend to occur after the bands tighten to the average. A move outside the bands calls for a continuation of the trend.
  2. Tops and bottoms made outside the bands, which are followed by tops and bottoms made inside the bands, indicate a trend reversal.
  3. A move originating at one band tends to go to the other band.

Bombay SE Sensitive Index (SENSEX)   capitalization-weighted price index that includes the 30 leading Indian stocks based on market capitalization and activity.

bond   IOU or promissory note of a corporate, municipal, or government debt, expressed in a stipulated FACE VALUE, and a date at which the issuer—U.S. or foreign—will pay the holder the face value of the bond. Investors essentially lend money to these organizations in exchange for IOUs, represented by BOND CERTIFICATES. The borrowers promise to repay the loan by a certain date and to pay interest regularly to the investors in the interim. *See also* BOND TRADING; FOREIGN BOND.

bond aggregate indexes   BENCHMARK bond indexes. They include:
Lehman Brothers Aggregate Bond Index: Benchmark for investment-grade fixed-rate debt issues, including government, corporate, asset-backed, and mortgage-backed securities, with maturities of at least one year.

Lehman Brothers Intermediate Government/Corporate Bond Index: Benchmark for government and corporate fixed-rate debt issues with maturities between one and ten years.

Lehman Brothers One-to-Three-Year Government/Corporate Bond Index: Index that tracks government and corporate fixed-rate debt issues with maturities between one and three years.

bond certificates evidence of debt issued to investors who purchase bonds. The bond certificate includes the names of the issuer and transfer agent, face value of the bond, interest rate, and maturity date.

bond house brokerage firm concentrating on the trading and underwriting of bonds. A bond house may have bond brokers trading for their own accounts on the floor of the exchanges. Bond houses are critical in obtaining financing for corporations and governments, as they are involved in the entire transaction from the original development of the issue to the final marketing and sale. These transactions can be in relatively small amounts.

bond indenture lengthy, legal agreement detailing the issuer's obligations pertaining to a bond issue. It contains the terms of the bond issue as well as any restrictive provisions placed on the firm, known as *restrictive covenants*. The indenture is administered by an independent trustee. The terms of the bond may include the type of bond, amount of issue, collateral, and call provisions. Restrictive covenants may include a sinking fund requirement and maintenance of (1) required levels of working capital; (2) a particular current ratio; and (3) a specified debt ratio.

bond (mutual) fund MUTUAL FUND that emphasizes safety and invests in bonds. The portfolio may consist of various levels of quality of bonds depending on the particular objectives of the specific mutual fund. For example, there may be high-grade bonds, medium-grade bonds, or low-grade bonds (JUNK BONDS). There are three key facts about the bonds in any portfolio.
1. **Quality:** Check the credit rating of the typical bond in the fund. Ratings by Standard & Poor's and MOODY's show the relative danger that an issuer will DEFAULT on interest or principal payments. AAA is the best grade. A rating of BB or lower signifies below investment grade.
2. **Maturity:** The average maturity of the fund's bonds indicates how much an investor stands to lose if interest rates rise. The longer the term of the bonds, the more volatile is the price. For example, a 20-year bond may fluctuate in price more than a four-year issue.
3. **Premium or discount:** Some funds with high current yields hold bonds that trade for more than their face value, or at a premium. Such funds are less vulnerable to losses if rates go up. Funds that hold bonds trading at a discount to face value can lose most.

Note: An investor should keep in mind the following guidelines:
- *Rising interest rates drive down the value of all bond funds.* For this reason, rather than focusing only on CURRENT YIELD, investors should look primarily at TOTAL RETURN (yield plus capital gains from falling interest rates or minus capital losses if rates climb).
- *All bond funds do not benefit equally from tumbling interest rates.* If interest rates are expected to decline and the investor want to increase his or her total return, he or she should buy funds that invest in U.S. Treasuries or top-rated corporate bonds.
- *Unlike bonds, bond funds do not allow the investor to lock in a yield.* A mutual fund with a constantly changing portfolio is not like an individual bond, which one can keep to maturity. If the investor wants steady, secure income over several years or more, he or she should consider, as alternatives to funds, buying individual top-quality bonds or investing in a municipal bond unit trust, which maintains a fixed portfolio.

bond quotation published investment information about a bond including its CURRENT YIELD, daily volume traded, price, and net change for the day. To see how bond quotations are presented in the newspaper, let us look at the data for an IBM bond, a corporate bond.

Bonds	Cur Yld	Vol	High	Low	Close	Net Chg
IBM $9^3/_8$ 04	11	169	$84^5/_8$	84	84	$-1^1/_8$

The numbers immediately following the company name give the bond coupon rate and maturity date. This particular bond carries a 9.375% interest rate and matures in 2004. The next column, labeled "Cur Yld," provides the current yield calculated by dividing the annual interest income ($9^3/_8$%) by the current market price of the bond (a closing price of 84). Thus, the current yield for the IBM bond is 11%. This figure represents the effective, or real, rate of return on the current market price represented by the bond's interest earnings. The "Vol" column indicates the number of bonds traded on the given day (169 bonds). The market price of a bond is usually expressed as a percent of its PAR (FACE) VALUE, which is customarily $1000. Corporate bonds are quoted to the nearest one-eighth of a percent, and a quote of $84^5/_8$ in the above indicates a price of $846.25 or $84^5/_8$% of $1000. U.S. government bonds are highly marketable and deal in keenly competitive markets so they are quoted in thirty-seconds or sixty-fourths rather than eighths. Moreover, decimals are used, rather than fractions, in quoting prices. For example, a quotation of 106.17 for a Treasury bond indicates a price of $1065.31 [$1060 + (17/32 × $10)]. When a plus sign follows the quotation, the Treasury bond is being quoted in a sixty-fourth. We must double the number following the decimal point and add one to determine the fraction of $10 represented in the quote. For example, a quote of 95.16+ indicates a price of $955.16 [$950 + (33/64 × $10)].

BOND RATINGS

Government bonds and tax-exempt bonds are quoted as follows:

Government bonds transfer at par, at a premium over par, or at a discount from par. The par value of a bond is normally $1000. Government notes are quoted with variations at 1/32 of 1% of par, or 1/32 of a point. Treasury bills are quoted with variations of 1/100 of a point.

GOVERNMENT BONDS

A bid of	Means	Or
98.1	98 + 1/32% of $1000	$980.3125
98.9	98 + 9/32% of $1000	$982.8125
98.12	98 + 12/32% of $1000	$983.7500

TAX-EXEMPT BONDS

(1) Agency	(2) Coupon	(3) Mat Date	(4) Bid	(5) Ask	(6) Change	(7) Yield
Jacksonville Electric	$10^{1}/_{2}$	Jan. 21	62	65	+2	3.11

1. Agency issuing bond
2. Coupon rate
3. Maturity date of bond
4. Bid price—sell price
5. Ask price—buy price
6. Change from ending value on prior day
7. Current percentage yield on current price

bond ratings ratings that reflect the probability that a bond issue will go into default. They can influence investors' perceptions of risk and therefore have an impact on the interest rate. Bond investors tend to place more emphasis on independent analysis of quality than do common stock investors. Bond analysis and ratings are done, notably, by Moody's Investors Service, Standard & Poor's, Duff & Phelps/MCM, and Fitch Investors Service. Below is an actual listing of the designations used by these well-known independent agencies. Descriptions of ratings are summarized below. For original versions of descriptions, see Moody's *Bond Record* and Standard & Poor's *Bond Guide*.

DESCRIPTION OF BOND RATINGS*

Moody's	Standard & Poor's	Duff & Phelps/ MCM	Fitch	Quality Indication
Aaa	AAA	AAA	AAA	Highest quality
Aa	AA	AA	AA	High quality
A	A	A	A	Upper medium grade
Baa	BBB	BBB	BBB	Medium grade

DESCRIPTION OF BOND RATINGS* (cont.)

Moody's	Standard & Poor's	Duff & Phelps/ MCM	Fitch	Quality Indication
Ba	BB	BB	BB	Contains speculative elements
B	B	B	B	Outright speculative
Caa	CCC & CC	CCC	CCC & CC	Default definitely possible
Ca	C		C	Default, only partial recovery likely
C	D		D	Default, little recovery likely
	r			Assigned to derivative products

* Ratings may also have + or − sign to show relative standings in class.

Bond investors pay careful attention to ratings since they can affect not only potential market behavior but relative yields as well. Specifically, the higher the rating, the lower the yield of a bond, other things being equal. It should be noted that the ratings do change over time and the rating agencies have "credit watch lists" of various types. *See also* CREDIT RISK; DEFAULT RISK; NOT RATED (NR).

bond rooms scene of the same kind of brisk auction-style trading that occurs on the stock trading floor.

bond trading trading of corporate, government, and municipal bonds usually by institutional investors, banks, and large securities firms. Bond trading is now offered by roughly a dozen e-brokers. And many other web sites provide prices and other bond-specific data that used to be unavailable to the public. Due to the fact that bond trading must take into account many wrinkles such as yield, maturity, credit quality, and call provisions, as well as price, bond trading on-line has lagged behind stock trading. The following table presents of some of the best bond-trading web sites.

THE BEST BOND-TRADING WEB SITES

E-broker	Web Address	Minimum Account
Fidelity	*www.fidelity.com*	$2500
Merrill Lynch	*www.mldirect.com*	$2000
E*Trade	*www.etrade.com*	$1000
Credit Suisse First Boston	*www.csfbdirect.com*	$0
Charles Schwab	*www.schwab.com*	$5000

Note: Some of the sites allow you to search for bonds in a format similar to a stock-screening page.

BOND VALUATION

bond valuation process of determining the price an investor should pay for a bond; or in the case of an issuing corporation, the price it will ask for a bond it is offering to the public. This process takes into account the coupon interest rate that the bond offers the maturity date, and the risk involved compared to other bonds or other similar investments. The process of determining the value of a security such as common stock or bond involves finding the present value of the security's expected future cash flows using the investor's required rate of return. Thus, the basic security valuation model can be defined mathematically as follows:

$$V = \sum_{t=1}^{n} \frac{C_t}{(1+r)^t}$$

where V = intrinsic value or present value of an asset
C_t = expected future cash flows or earnings in period t = 1, ..., n
r = investor's required rate of return

The valuation process for a bond requires a knowledge of three basic elements: (1) the amount of the cash flows to be received by the investor, which is equal to the periodic interest to be received and the par value to be paid at maturity; (2) the maturity date of the loan; and (3) the investor's required rate of return. The periodic interest can be received annually or semiannually. The value of a bond is simply the present value of these cash flows. Two versions of the bond valuation model are presented below:

If the interest payments are made annually, then

$$V = \sum_{t=1}^{n} \frac{I}{(1+r)^t} + \frac{M}{(1+r)^n} = I \cdot T_2(r,n) + M \cdot T_1(r,n)$$

where

I = interest payment each year = coupon interest rate × par value
M = par value, or maturity value, typically $1000
r = the investor's required rate of return
n = number of years to maturity
T_2 = present value interest factor of an annuity of $1 (see Appendix A)
T_1 = present value interest factor of $1 (Table 1 in Appendix A)

EXAMPLE 1:
Consider a bond, maturing in ten years and having a coupon rate of 8%. The PAR VALUE is $1000. You, as an investor, consider 10% to be an appropriate required rate of return in view of the risk level associated with this bond. The annual interest payment is $80 (8% × $1000). The present value of this bond is

$$V = \sum_{t=1}^{n} \frac{I}{(1+r)^t} + \frac{M}{(1+r)^n}$$
$$= I \cdot T_2(r,n) + M \cdot T_1(r,n)$$
$$= \sum_{t=1}^{10} \frac{\$80}{(1+0.1)^t} + \frac{\$1000}{(1+0.1)^{10}}$$
$$= \$80 \cdot T_2(10\%,10) + \$1000 \cdot T_1(10\%,10)$$
$$= \$80(6.145) + \$1000(0.386)$$
$$= \$491.60 + 386.00$$
$$= \$877.60$$

If the interest is paid semiannually, then

$$V = \sum_{t=1}^{2n} \frac{I/2}{(1+2/r)^t} + \frac{M}{(1+r/2)^{2n}}$$
$$= \frac{I}{2} < T_2(r/2, 2n) + M \cdot T_1(r/2, 2n)$$

EXAMPLE 2:
Assume the same data as in Example 1, except the interest is paid semiannually.

$$V = \sum_{t=1}^{2n} \frac{I/2}{(1+2/r)^t} + \frac{M}{(1+r/2)^{2n}}$$
$$= \frac{I}{2} < T_2(r/2, 2n) + M \cdot T_1(r/2, 2n)$$
$$= \sum_{t=1}^{20} \frac{\$40}{(1+0.05)^t} + \frac{\$1000}{(1+0.5)^{20}}$$
$$= \$40 \cdot T_2(5\%, 20) + \$1000 \cdot T_1(5\%, 20)$$
$$= \$40(12.462) + \$1000(0.377)$$
$$= \$498.48 + \$377.00$$
$$= \$875.48$$

bond yield EFFECTIVE RATE OF RETURN on a bond. Bonds are evaluated on many different types of returns including CURRENT YIELD, YIELD TO MATURITY, yield to call, realized yield, and equivalent taxable yield.

current yield: The current yield is the annual interest payment divided by the current price of the bond. The current yield is reported in *The Wall Street Journal*, among others.

EXAMPLE 1:
Assume a 12% COUPON RATE on a $1000 par value bond selling for $960. The current yield is:
$$\$120/\$960 = 12.5\%$$

BOND YIELD

The problem with this measure of return is that it does not take into account the maturity date of the bond. A bond with one year to run and another with fifteen years to run would have the same current yield quote if interest payments were $120 and the price were $960. Clearly, the one-year bond would be preferable under this circumstance because not only would you get $120 in interest, but also a gain of $40 ($1000 − $960) with a one-year time period, and this amount could be reinvested.

yield to maturity: The yield to maturity takes into account the maturity date of the bond. It is the real return to be received from interest income plus capital gain assuming the bond is held to maturity. There are two ways to calculate this measure: the exact method and the approximate method.

The exact method: Under the exact method, a bond's yield to maturity is the INTERNAL RATE OF RETURN on investment in the bond. It is calculated by solving the bond valuation model for r:

$$V = \sum_{t=1}^{n} \frac{I}{(1+r)^t} + \frac{M}{(1+r)^n} = I \cdot T_2(r,n) + M \cdot T_1(r,n)$$

where V is the market price of the bond, I is the interest payment, and M is the maturity value, usually $1000. T_2 and T_1 are found in Appendix A.

Finding the bond's yield, r, involves trial and error. It is best explained by an example.

EXAMPLE 2:

Suppose you are offered a ten-year, 8% coupon, $1000 par value bond at a price of $877.60. The rate of return earned if the bond is bought and held to maturity is computed below.

First, set up the bond valuation model:

$$= \$80 \cdot T_2(10\%, 10) + \$1000 \cdot T_1(10\%, 10)$$
$$= \$80(6.145) + \$1000(0.386)$$
$$= \$491.60 + 386.00$$
$$= \$877.60$$

Since the bond is selling at a discount, the bond's yield is above the going coupon rate of 8%. Therefore, try a rate of 9%. Substituting factors for 9% in the equation, we obtain: V = $80(6.418) + $1000(0.422) = $513.44 + $422.0 = $935.44. The calculated bond value, $935.44, is above the actual market price of $877.60, so the yield is not 9%. To lower the calculated value, the rate must be raised. Trying 10%, we obtain: V = $80(6.145) + $1000(0.386) = $491.60 + $386.00 = $877.60. This calculated value is exactly equal to the market price of the bond; thus, 10% is the bond's yield to maturity.

The approximate method:

$$\text{Yield} = \frac{I + (M - V)/n}{(M + V)/2}$$

where V = the market value of the bond
  I = dollars of interest paid per year
  M = maturity value, usually $1000
  n = number of years to maturity

EXAMPLE 3:
Using the same data as in Example 2,

$$\text{Yield} = \frac{\$80 + (\$1000 - \$877.60)/10}{(\$1000 + \$877.60)/2} = \frac{\$80 + \$12.24}{\$938.80}$$

$$= \frac{\$92.24}{\$938.80} = 9.8\%$$

which came out very close to 10%.

yield to call: Not all bonds are held to maturity. If the bond may be called prior to maturity, the yield to maturity formula will have the call price in place of the par value ($1000).

EXAMPLE 4:
Assume a 20-year bond was initially issued at a 13.5% coupon rate, and after two years, rates have dropped. Assume further that the bond is currently selling for $1180, the yield to maturity on the bond is 11.15%, and the bond can be called in five years after issue at $1090. Thus, if you buy the bond two years after issue, your bond may be called back after three more years at $1090. The yield to call can be calculated as follows:

$$\frac{\$135 + (\$1090 - \$1180)/3}{(\$1090 + \$1180)/2} = \frac{\$135 + (-\$90/3)}{\$1135} = \frac{\$105}{\$1135} = 9.25\%$$

The yield to call figure of 9.25% is 190 basis points less than the yield to maturity of 11.15%. Clearly, the investor needs to be aware of the differential because a lower return is earned.

realized yield: You may trade in and out of a bond long before it matures. You obviously need a measure of return to evaluate the investment appeal of any bonds you intend to buy and sell. Realized yield is used for this purpose. This measure is simply a variation of yield to maturity, as only two variables are changed in the yield to maturity formula. Future price is used in place of par value ($1000), and the length of the HOLDING PERIOD is substituted for the number of years to maturity.

EXAMPLE 5:
In Example 5, assume that you anticipate holding the bond for only three years and that your estimated interest rates will change in the future so that the price of the bond will move to about $925 from its

present level of $877.70. Thus, you will buy the bond today at a market price of $877.70 and sell the issue three years later at a price of $925. Given these assumptions, the realized yield of this bond would be

$$\text{Realized yield} = \frac{\$80 + (\$935 - \$877.70)/3}{(\$920 + \$877.70)/2} = \frac{\$80 + \$15.77}{\$901.35}$$

$$= \frac{\$95.77}{\$901.35} = 10.63\%$$

Fortunately, a bond table is available to find the value for various yield measures. A source is *Thorndike Encyclopedia of Banking and Financial Tables* by Warren, Gorham & Lamont, Boston. *Note*: There are many financial calculators available that contain preprogrammed formulas and perform many yield calculations. Further, spreadsheet software such as Excel has a built-in function for bond yield calculations.

equivalent taxable yield: Yield on a tax-exempt municipal bond needs to be looked at on an equivalent before-tax yield basis, because the interest received is not subject to federal income taxes. The formula used to equate interest on municipals to other investments is:

Equivalent taxable yield = Tax-exempt yield/(1 – tax rate)

EXAMPLE 6:
If you have a marginal tax rate of 28% and are evaluating a municipal bond paying 10% interest, the equivalent before-tax yield on a taxable investment would be

$$10\%(1-.28) = 13.89\%$$

Thus, you could choose between a taxable investment paying 13.89% and a tax-exempt bond paying 10% with no difference between the two. *See also* RATE OF RETURN; YIELD.

bondholder individual who has legal title to a corporate or government bond. He or she is a creditor because money was lent to the issuing entity. A bond may be registered in the name of the owner. If not, it is a bearer bond and the one holding it has the rights to it. Bondholders are entitled to the principal and interest on the bond. Bonds are a unit of debt for a company and bondholders have in bankruptcy a priority claim over the stockholders of the company.

bonus stock
common stock: stock given as an incentive to accept another form of securities, for example, stock given to investors in bonds by a corporation. Such activities are unlawful in most states and the practice has been associated with the term "watered" and "discount" stock.
stock dividend: bonus stock in Britain that refers to a stock dividend issued by a company. Stock dividends serve to increase the total float of the stock.

book to bill semiconductor book to bill ratio. It reports on the amount of semiconductor chips that are booked for delivery as compared with those that companies already have billed for.

book value difference between total tangible assets and total liabilities, less the value of the preferred stock. This gives the book value of the common stockholders' equity. Book value of the net assets of a company may have little or no significant relationship to their market value. It was once used as a proxy for a company's INTRINSIC VALUE. Especially with the NEW ECONOMY, book value is a less relevant measure for a company's fair value for investors. For example, many new economy companies have assets that do not register significantly on their balance sheet, such as intellectual property, employees, strong brand, and market share. Book value per share of a stock *per se* is a company's books based on historical cost. It may differ significantly from current market price per share (as illustrated in the table below). Book value per share of COMMON STOCK equals common stockholders' equity divided by outstanding common shares.

BOOK VALUE AND MARKET VALUE FOR SELECTED COMPANIES

(IN MILLIONS)

(APRIL 17, 2001)

Company	Book Value	Market Value
Microsoft	$28,438	$329,387
IBM	20,511	175,552
Wal-Mart Stores	25,848	219,938
General Electric	42,557	450,454

Source: www.fortune.com, AOL Personal Finance, and *www.moneycentral.msn.com*

book value per share worth of each share of stock on the books of a company based on historical cost. Book value per share is usually less than the current market price per share.

Book value per share equals:

$$\frac{\text{Total stockholders' equity}}{\text{Outsanding shares}}$$

EXAMPLE:
If a company's total stockholders' equity is $800,000,000 and there are 10 million shares outstanding, the book value per share is $80 ($800,000,000/10,000,000).

bottom lowest point or price for a security or index, which is then followed by an advance.

bottom line term referring to the last line in an income statement that reflects a firm's net income (profit) or net loss. Net income equals revenue less total expenses. The term *net* is also used to describe the bottom line.

bottom-fishing seeking bargains among stocks whose prices have recently dropped dramatically.

bottom-up approach investment approach that plays down the significance of economic and market cycles. The attention is paid to the analysis of individual stocks. It tries to identify the specific companies and stocks that will go into the portfolio. This is the point at which if you are using a computer you use "screens," which are nothing more than filters designed to weed out companies that do not clearly fit your investment philosophy—GROWTH INVESTING or VALUE INVESTING. For example, *worldlyinvestor.com* (www.worldlyinvestor.com) has "ADR Screener" that helps you select the criteria you're interested in to find the AMERICAN DEPOSITARY RECEIPTS that meet your investing goals. *See also* TOP-DOWN APPROACH.

bottoming out process in which a long time period of downtrend prices moves in the opposite direction of an UPTREND.

Bourse
1. French term for stock exchange. *See also* PARIS BOURSE.
2. stock exchanges in certain European countries such as Germany.

Bovespa Index index that includes stocks that represent about 85% of all transactions on Brazilian exchanges. Stocks are weighted by their participation in share trading.

Brady bonds U.S. dollar-denominated bonds of developing nations, such as Argentina, exchanged because of a restructuring of defaulted bank loans. The bonds are named after Nicholas Brady, who served as Secretary of the Treasury under George Bush (Senior). There was a pledging of U.S. Treasury ZERO-COUPON BONDS to guarantee principal. Details on Brady bonds and other emerging market bonds are covered in *BradyNet.com* (www.bradynet.com).

breadth *See* BREADTH INDEX.

breadth analysis *See* BREADTH INDEX.

Breadth Index index used in TECHNICAL ANALYSIS that computes for each trading day the net advances or declines in stocks on the NYSE; also called the *advance-decline index*. A strong market exists when there are net advances, while a weak market exists when there are net declines. Of course, the magnitude of strength depends on the excess number of advancing issues versus declining ones. On the other hand, if declining stocks outnumber advancing stocks by 3 to 1, a significant market weakness exists.

$$\text{Breadth Index} = \frac{\text{Number of net advances or declines in securities}}{\text{Number of securities traded}}$$

EXAMPLE:
Assume net advancing issues are 230. Securities traded are 2145. The Breadth Index equals

$$\frac{\text{Net advancing issues}}{\text{Number of securities traded}} = \frac{230}{2145} = +0.107$$

The higher the positive percentage, the better, since *more* stocks are increasing in price relative to those decreasing in price. The Zweig Breadth Advance/Decline Indicator equals

$$\frac{\text{10-day moving average of advancing issues}}{\text{10-day moving average of declining issues}}$$

The Breadth Index may be computed easily by referring to the financial pages of a newspaper. The market diary section of the paper will provide the number of advancing and declining issues along with the number of issues unchanged. The total number of issues traded equals the sum of these and is often provided as well. Some financial advisory publications calculate the index, relieving the investor from performing the computation. Martin Zweig's Breadth Advance/Decline Indicator is published in the *Zweig Forecast*. The financial news program on CNBC reports it daily.

break significant and usually unexpected decline in the price of a particular security. If, for example, on the opening of its trading a stock is several points lower than the previous day's close, then it has suffered a *break*. It is also said to have gapped. Another term for a stock experiencing a break in prices is that it has fallen out of bed. A break may occur when it is announced prior to trading that a company is under investigation by a governmental agency for accounting irregularities or fraudulent activities.

break even
1. sales with no profit or loss; also called *break-even point*.
2. in foreign currency, the amount of currency change that will equate the cost of local currency financing with the cost of home currency (dollar) financing.
3. security transaction in which the return covers only total transaction costs including commissions.
4. break-even stock prices for various option participants, as shown below.

BREAK-EVEN EXCHANGE RATE

Option parties	Break-even market price
A call-holder	the strike price + the premium
A put-holder	the strike price − the premium
A call-writer	the strike price + the premium
A put-writer	the strike price − the premium
A covered call-writer	the original cost of the security − the premium
A covered put-writer (short the stock)	the strike price + the premium

break-even exchange rate future exchange rate such that the return in two bond markets would be even for a given maturity; also called *implied forward exchange rate*.

break out chart pattern used to indicate a rise in a stock's price above its resistance level (such as its previous high price) or fall below its support level (usually the last lowest price).

brick and mortar describing a physical location, a conventional "street-side" business that deals with its customers face-to-face in an office or storefront. It is often compared with web-based businesses that commonly have lower costs and greater flexibility than brick-and-mortar operations.

British pound currency of one of the United States' major allies and trading partners; the British pound is one of the world's most important currencies. Its relationship to the U.S. dollar is a key to the global marketplace and it is seen as a barometer of the United Kingdom's economic strength versus the business climate in the United States. If the pound is at 1.4, that means each U.S. dollar buys 1.4 pounds. To figure out what 1 pound equals in U.S. currency, this formula is used: If $1 buys 1.4 pounds, then 1 pound is equal to $1 divided by 1.4 or 71.4 cents. Currency rates are listed daily in most major metropolitan newspapers as well as national publications such as *The New York Times, The Wall Street Journal,* and *USA Today* and on computer services such as America Online or at a web site on the Internet such as *www.bloomberg.com*.

broad market
  actively traded stock: stock that is normally traded on high volume indicating a very liquid market where large purchases or sales will not noticeably affect its price.
  market: marketplace having large volume and including many stocks, such as the New York Stock Exchange (NYSE).

broker agent who handles the public's orders to buy and sell SECURITIES or COMMODITIES. For this service a commission is charged. Depending on where you do business, a broker may be called by another name. Examples are financial consultant, intuitional salesman, securities salesperson, account executive, investment executive, or portfolio salesman. *See also* SPECIALIST.

broker-dealer securities brokerage firm, usually registered with the SEC, the NASD, and the NYSE, acting as a broker and dealer. It acts as a broker when it buys and sells for its customers and as a dealer when it buys for its own inventory with the likelihood of later sale to clients. Broker-dealers are required to state how they are serving in consummating a transaction.

broker loan rate interest rate on money borrowed by brokers from banks for various uses. It may be used by ODD-LOT DEALERS to help finance inventories of stocks they deal in; by brokerage firms to finance the underwriting of new issues of corporate and municipal securities; and to help finance the purchase of stock for customers who prefer to use margin rather than paying in cash. It is a key MONEY MARKET rate; also called the *call rate* because it is callable on 24-hour notice. *See also* CALL LOAN RATE.

brokerage fee payment charged by a brokerage firm for transacting business for clients. In the case of a retail stock brokerage firm, the fee is determined by the size and price of the securities traded. As the size of the transaction increases, the fee charged is proportionately less. In an underwriting broker situation, brokerage firms set an underwriting spread.

brokerage firm (house) any firm acting as a broker or dealer for securities on the various stock exchanges. Most firms in the United States are members of the New York stock exchanges as well as others. When the firm negotiates and manages the purchase and sale of securities for clients, it is acting as a broker; when it is trading for its own accounts and selling to its clients, it is acting as a dealer. One of the largest brokerage firms in the United States is Merrill Lynch.

brokers' market market for exchange of financial instruments between any two parties using a broker as an intermediary or agent. Along with the *interbank market*, the broker's market provides another area of large-scale foreign exchange dealing in the United States. A good number of foreign exchange brokerage firms make markets for foreign currencies in New York (as well as in London and elsewhere), creating trading in many currencies similar to that in the interbank market. The key differences are that (1) the brokers seek to match buyers and sellers on any given transaction, without taking a position themselves; (2) they deal simultaneously with many banks (and other firms); and (3) they offer both buy and sell positions to clients, where a bank may wish to, operating on only one side of the market at any particular time. Also, the brokers deal "blind," offering rate quotations without naming the potential seller/buyer until a deal has been negotiated.

bubble speculative market or stock in which the values rise very rapidly and then fall sharply. A bubble is a situation in which stock prices are excessively overvalued.

bulge material unanticipated temporary change in overall or specific security or commodity prices.

bull individual or institution that believes a given stock, particular industry, or the stock market in general will experience a price rise. An investor can also be BULLISH (optimistic) about bonds or commodities.

bull market prolonged advancing market that experiences a period of rising prices in securities or commodities; the BULL's horns thrust upward. There is a high trading volume. Bull markets are favorable markets normally associated with investor optimism, economic recovery, and government stimulus.

bull spread OPTION strategy with maximum profit if the underlying security rises in price. Either calls or puts can be used. The lower STRIKE PRICE is purchased and the higher strike price is sold. The options have the same expiration date. See also BEAR SPREAD.

bulldogs Sterling-denominated bonds issued within the United Kingdom by a foreign borrower. They are FOREIGN BONDS sold in the United Kingdom.

bulletin board properly known as the *OTC Bulletin Board*, an electronic quotation service that lists the prices of stocks that don't meet the minimum requirements for listing on a stock exchange or the NASDAQ stock-listing system.

bulletin board stocks OVER-THE-COUNTER (OTC) STOCKS of smaller-capitalization unlisted companies traded via the BULLETIN BOARD, an automated system run by NASDAQ.

bullish describes an investor who believes stock, bond, or commodity prices will increase for an extended time period.

Bund German government bond.

Bundesbank German central bank equivalent to the FEDERAL RESERVE BANK of the United States. Its primary goals are to (1) set the discount rate, known as the LOMBARD RATE; (2) monitor the money supply; and (3) back economic (fiscal and monetary) policies.

burn rate measure of how quickly a company uses up its capital to finance operations before generating positive cash flow from operations; also called *cash burn rate*. This rate is a critical key to survival in the case of small, fast-growing companies that need constant access to capital. Many technology and Internet companies are examples. It is not uncommon for enterprises to lose money in their early goings, but it is important for financial analysts and investors to assess how much money those firms are taking in and using up. The number to examine is FREE CASH FLOW, which is the company's operating cash flows (before interest) minus cash outlays for capital spending. It is the amount available to finance planned expansion of operating capacity. Burn rate is generally used in terms of cash spent per month. A burn rate of 1 million would mean the company is spending 1 million dollars per month. When the burn rate begins to exceed plan or revenue fails to meet expectations, the usual recourse is to reduce the burn rate. In order to stay afloat, the business will have to reduce the staff, cut spending (possibly resulting in slower growth), or raise new capital, probably by taking on debt (resulting in interest expense) or by selling additional equity stock (diluting existing shareholders' ownership stake).

EXAMPLE:
Secure payments provider CyberCash had $26.4 million in cash at the end of March, and at its current burn rate of $7 million to $8 million per quarter, has only enough cash to last through next February. The company generated just $155,000 in revenue in its most recent quarter. Once you get under a year of cash with this type of burn rate, you've got problems.

business cycle recurrent expansion and contraction in the economy. It is the variability in economic activity.

Business Times Index published in Singapore by the *Business Times*, a narrow-based index of 40 companies listed on the Stock Exchange of Singapore. Of the underlying companies, 21 are also components of the STRAITS TIMES INDEX, while 20 companies are also part of the Kuala Lumpur Stock Exchange Composite Index. The index is capitalization-weighted by means of the Passche formula.

buy-and-hold strategy long-term stock purchase strategy in which the investor makes purchases in quality companies over the years and ignores short-term trading patterns. The basic assumption is that a well-managed company will weather the storms and grow over the years. It is a rather passive strategy that does not require day-to-day stock management.

buy in
  1. transaction made when a security purchase fails because of a delivery failure and the purchaser or purchasing broker can obtain the securities elsewhere, charging the additional expense to the seller who failed to make delivery.
  2. method for terminating the responsibility to accept delivery of stock in which the OPTION WRITER buys an option identical to the one he or she previously sold. This is also known as a CLOSING PURCHASE.

buy on bad news practice of an individual or institutional investor of buying a stock that has just fallen off drastically in market price on bad news because it is expected that the stock price has now reached its low and will be increasing in the future as better developments with the company will emerge. Here, it is felt that the low price is temporary and represents an attractive buying opportunity.

BUY ON CLOSE 50

buy on close order to purchase securities or commodities at the ending market price at the end of the trading day.

buy on opening order to purchase securities or commodities at the opeining market price for the trading day.

buy on rumors practice of buying a security based purely on rumors and hearsay regarding earnings surprises and expectations rather than real news on earnings and revenues, in contrast to SELLING ON NEWS.

buy order order entered by the security dealer with the investor's approval for the purpose of purchasing a security.

buy limit order: buy order entered with a specific price to purchase a particular security. You are not obligated to pay more than the price limit, although you could actually pay less if the market conditions favored a lower price. For after-hours trading, most, if not all, brokers require that investors use limit orders. The risk with limit orders is that a stock suddenly jumps, or falls below, the limit price and your order does not get filled.

buy market order: instruction to the broker by the customer to purchase a security at whatever price can be obtained in the open market. The benefit is that you are guaranteed to acquire or unload the stock whenever you would like. The downside is that you have no control over the price at which your orders are filled. *Note:* You can get badly hurt with hot INITIAL PUBLIC OFFERINGS or other fast-moving stocks.

buy minus order: investor's instruction to purchase on DOWNTICKS in the market price of last previous price if that is lower than the previous different price.

buy stop-limit order: this works the same as a stop-loss order, except a LIMIT ORDER rather than a MARKET ORDER is triggered when the stock reaches a certain price. For example, if you had submitted a $60 stop-limit order in the example that follows, the order would not have been filled when the shares tumbled from $60 to $30. *Note*: Some investors prefer to hold on after a steep drop, in the hope that the shares will rebound. The downside risk, though, is that you could lose more, instead of being sold out at $30, if the stock falls further.

buy stop-loss order: customer's instruction that if the market price reaches or exceeds the buy stop limit, the broker is authorized to execute a market buy order at the best obtainable price. Reaching or exceeding the stated price triggers the buy stop order, converting it into a market order. The goal is to limit price on any single stock. For example, you could submit a stop-loss order (simply known as a STOP ORDER) telling a broker to sell your shares if the price of ABC falls to $60. The moment it hits $60, or moves through that point, a market order would automatically be triggered and the stock would be sold at the best available price. *Note:* Despite the name, stop-loss orders apply in the same way to stocks that are rising. If you wanted to buy ABC if the price topped $62 and it "gapped up" to $85, your order would be filled at the best price available, say, $80.

buy the book   investor order (typically from a large institutional investor or professional trader) placed with his or her broker to purchase all available shares of a stock from the specialist in the security or dealer in the stock at the present offer price. The knowledgeable investor is very optimistic about the stock to make such a large investment. The term "book" refers to the record document specialists used to monitor buys and sells prior to the use of computer tracking.

buyback
   1. repurchase of stock by a corporation. Also called *stock buyback*, it suggests that the company thinks its stock is undervalued and inexpensive enough to buy. Many firms have announced or executed stock buybacks in recent years. Buying back shares is also a way for a company to reward its shareholders. When sitting on some profits, a company could use that money to (1) pay down any debt; (2) invest in its growth (buying advertising, building factories, and so on); or (3) choose to pay a cash dividend to shareholders. But with the dividend option, shareholders will be fully taxed on any dividends they receive. By contrast, if a stock buyback helps boost the market price of the shares by increasing earnings per share, long-term CAPITAL GAINS that shareholders realize are taxed at lower rates. Furthermore, buying back shares in essence retires them, resulting in fewer shares outstanding. That means that each shareholder's stake, percentage-wise, in the company is bigger. It is like cutting a pizza into fewer slices; each slice will be larger.
   2. after a SHORT SALE (in which shares are borrowed and then sold), the purchase of an identical amount in order to repay the loan.

buying on margin   buying bonds, commodities, or stock through credit extended by the broker to the customer in a qualified margin account. Margin rules set by the Federal Reserve Board and the participating exchanges for securities generally require a ratio of 50% collateral to cover stock purchases. Margin rules for bonds and commodities vary considerably. *See also* MARGIN BUYING; MARGIN PURCHASE.

buying range   price range in which security analysts recommend buying securities in a BEAR stock market at the suggested prices. The securities may be a good buy because of anticipated future price increases. Security analysts at brokerage firms often note such situations in their analytical research reports.

buyout   acquisition of a controlling interest in a company's stock. A buyout can be previously negotiated or accomplished by a hostile tender offer, resulting in the hot pursuit of the company in the security markets.

C

cable U.S. dollar per British pound CROSS RATE.

CAC 40 Index capitalization-weighted price index of the 40 most actively French traded shares on the Paris stock exchange. CAC stands for Compagnie des Agents de Change.

call
  1. right to buy 100 shares (usually) of a specified stock for a limited length of time (until expiration). *See also* CALL OPTION; OPTION.
  2. process of redeeming a bond or preferred stock issue prior to maturity.

call auction *see* FIXING.

call loan rate interest rate charged on a loan used by brokers to finance purchases of securities. The rate is quoted daily in newspapers as a money market indicator; also called *broker call loan rate*. *See also* BROKER LOAN RATE.

call option right (but not the obligation) to buy 100 shares of a specified stock at a fixed price per share, called the STRIKING PRICE, for up to nine months, depending on the expiration date of the option. The investor who has purchased a call option on a stock has the right to "exercise" the option at any time during the life of the option. This means that, regardless of the current market price of the stock, the investor has the right to buy 100 shares of the stock at the striking price, rather than the current market price. The downside risk of a call option is the invested money.

EXAMPLE:
On February 5, Mr. Guru was convinced that ATT stock, which is trading at $60 a share, will move considerably higher in the next few months, so he buys one call option on ATT stock with a premium of $2 per share. Since this call option involves a block of 100 shares of stock, it costs him a total of $2 times 100 shares or $200. The particular call he selects has a striking price of $65 and expiration date near the end of June. What this means is that for $200 he has the right to buy (1) 100 shares of ATT stock; (2) at $65 a share; and (3) until near the end of June. If ATT stock goes up to $75 a share by the end of June, Mr. Guru would have the right to purchase 100 shares for $6500 ($65 × 100 shares) and to turn right around and sell them for $7500, keeping the difference of $1000, an $800 profit. This works out to 400% profit in less than five months ($800/$200 = 4 = 400%). However, if Mr. Guru is wrong and ATT stock goes down in price, the most he could lose would be his investment money, which is the price of the option, $200.
See also CALL; PUT OPTION.

callable bond issue, all or part of which may be redeemed by the issuing corporation under specified conditions before maturity. The term also applies to preferred shares that may be retired by the issuing corporation.

Canadian Venture Exchange product of the merger of the Vancouver and Alberta Stock Exchanges. The objective of Canadian Venture Exchange (CDNX) is to provide venture companies with effective access to capital while protecting investors. This exchange basically contains small-cap Canadian stocks. The CDNX is home to many PENNY STOCKS.

candlestick charts charting method, originally in seventeenth-century Japan, and only introduced in the United States in the late 1980s, in which the high and low are plotted as a single line and are referred to as *shadows*. Candlestick charts offer a quick, at-a-glance summation of a day's worth of trading information, which many investors prefer to the standard bar chart. The sample chart illustrates how candlestick bodies highlight the opening and closing price and the stock's direction for the day. The overall movement of the stock is easily visible on a chart; more closed bodies (colored red or black) means the stock is headed down, and more open bodies (colored white or green) means the stock is moving up. When the candlesticks display formations or patterns, they can help stock analysts gauge market sentiment, which can be used to anticipate short-term movements in the stock price.

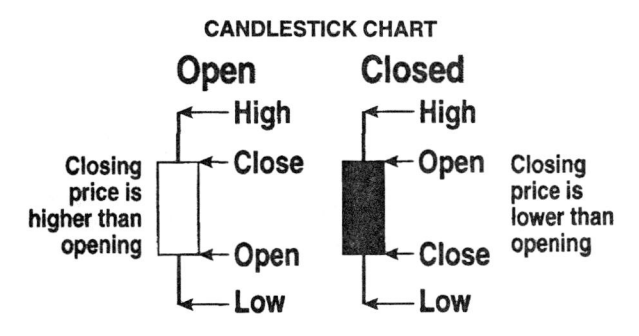

CANDLESTICK CHART

Open — High, Close, Open, Low. Closing price is higher than opening.

Closed — High, Open, Close, Low. Closing price is lower than opening.

cap
1. contract on an interest rate, whereby at periodic payment dates, the writer of the cap pays the difference between the market interest rate and a specified cap rate if, and only if, this difference is positive. This is equivalent to a stream of call options on the interest rate.
2. also used in bonds and mortgages as abbreviation for capitalization, small cap, large cap, and so on.

capital account component of the BALANCE OF PAYMENTS covering all short-term and long-term capital transactions.

Capital Asset Pricing Model (CAPM) model that quantifies the relevant risk of an investment and establishes the trade-off between risk and return, for example, the price of risk. The CAPM states that the expected return on a security is a function of (1) the risk-free rate; (2) the security's systematic risk; and (3) the expected risk premium in the market. The basic message of the model is that risk is priced in a portfolio context. A security risk consists of two components—DIVERSIFIABLE RISK and NONDIVERSIFIABLE (or systematic) RISK. Diversifiable risk, sometimes called controllable risk or unsystematic risk, represents the portion of a security's risk that can be controlled through DIVERSIFICATION. This type of risk is unique to a given security and thus is not priced. Business, LIQUIDITY, and DEFAULT risks fall into this category. Nondiversifiable risk, sometimes referred to as noncontrollable risk or systematic risk, results from forces outside of the firm's control and is therefore not unique to the given security. This type of risk must be priced and hence affects the required return on a project. Purchasing power, interest rate, and market risks fall into this category. Nondiversifiable risk is assessed relative to the risk of a diversified portfolio of securities, or the market portfolio. This type of risk is measured by the BETA COEFFICIENT. The Capital Asset Pricing Model (CAPM) relates the risk measured by beta to the level of expected or required rate of return on a security. The model, also called the *security market line (SML)* (see the figure below), is given as follows: $r_i = r_f + b(r_m - r_f)$ where r_i = the expected (or required) return on security I, r_f = the risk-free security (such as a T-BILL), r_m = the expected return on the market portfolio (such as Standard & Poor's 500 Stock Composite Index), and b = Beta, an index of nondiversifiable (noncontrollable, systematic) risk. In other words, the CAPM (or SML) equation shows that the required (expected) rate of return on a given security (r_i) is equal to the return required for securities that have no risk (r_f) plus a risk premium required by investors for assuming a given level of risk. The higher the degree of systematic risk (b), the higher the return on a given security demanded by investors.

SECURITY MARKET LINE

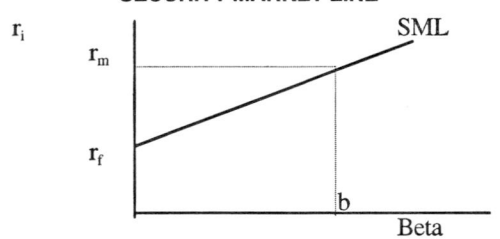

capital gain or capital loss profit or loss from the sale of a capital asset. A capital gain may be either short term (one year or less) or long term (more than one year). The maximum tax rate on long-term capital gains is 20%.

For a stock or a mutual fund, the sales proceeds minus the cost basis of the shares. To calculate gains and losses, you need to determine which shares were sold and the cost basis of those shares. There *can* be two sources of capital gains for a mutual fund shareholder:

The first source is a gain from a sale. If you sell or exchange your mutual fund shares, you must pay tax on any gains arising from the sale, just as you would from a sale of any other securities. Shares held longer than one year are considered long term and shares held for one year or less are considered short term.

The second source is a gain from a distribution. Capital gains are realized by the fund when a security is sold for more than a portfolio manager paid for it. The taxable consequence of that gain is passed through to the shareholders proportionately, according to the number of shares they own on the capital gain distribution record date. These amounts are reported on Form 1099-DIV. (Short-term capital gains are included in Box 1 of Form 1099-DIV. Long-term capital gains are identified as such on Form 1099-DIV Box 2a.)

capital gains distribution income for investors resulting from net long-term profits of a mutual fund realized when portfolio securities are sold at a gain. These profits from sales of securities are passed on by fund managers to shareholders at least once a year. *See also* INCOME DIVIDEND.

capital growth increase in the market value of an individual's investments or an increase in the NET ASSET VALUE (NAV) of mutual fund shares.

capital markets long-term financial markets in which long-term securities such as stocks and bonds are bought and sold.

capital stock EQUITY shares in a corporation authorized by its Articles of Incorporation and issued to stockholders. Such stock may have a PAR VALUE or not. The company presents in its annual report the number of shares authorized and issued, par value or stated value per share, and total par value or stated value. Capital stock may be of two types: common and preferred. If only one class of securities exists, it must be voting common stock. If more than one class of stock exists, the additional classes constitute stock that has some preference or restriction of basic rights.

capitalization total amount of the various securities issued by a corporation. Capitalization may include bonds, debentures, and preferred and common stock. Bonds and debentures are usually carried on the books of the issuing company in terms of their par or face value. Preferred and common shares may be carried in terms of par

CARRYING AMOUNT (VALUE)

or stated value. The capitalized value of common stock equals the outstanding number of shares multiplied by its market price per share. For example, if company X has 3,000,000 shares outstanding at a market price per share of $10, the capitalization is $30,000,000. *See also* MARKET CAPITALIZATION.

carrying amount (value) BOOK VALUE of a security.

cash-and-carry arbitrage arbitrage strategy with a simultaneous spot purchase and forward sale of an asset. The reverse transaction (borrowing the asset, selling it spot, and buying it forward) is known as a reverse cash and carry, or as a carry-and-cash ARBITRAGE. These arbitrages lead to a relation between spot and forward, or futures, prices of the same asset.

cash burn rate *see* BURN RATE.

cash commodity *see* SPOT COMMODITY.

cash equivalent
1. financial instruments of high LIQUIDITY and safety. Examples are a MONEY MARKET FUND and a TREASURY BILL. Cash equivalents are almost as good as cash.
2. short-term, highly liquid investment having an original maturity of three months or less.

cash flow
1. net income plus noncash expenses (for example, depreciation) minus noncash revenue (for example, amortization of deferred revenue) yields cash flow from operations.
2. cash receipts minus cash payments.

cash flow per share ratio of cash earnings divided by number of shares outstanding. Cash earnings equals cash revenue less cash expenses. A high ratio is desirable because that means net income is of higher quality because the earnings are backed up by cash. Cash can be used to meet debt payments, buy fixed assets, and pay dividends.

cash flow return on investment (CFROI) popular financial metric now embraced by multinational companies, along with ECONOMIC VALUE ADDED (EVA). Unlike a traditional measure such as *return on investment (ROI)*, CFROI uses cash flow generated by the firm, rather than income or earnings derived from financial statements, as the "return." The capital base used is also *cash investment*. The formula is

$$\text{CFROI} = \frac{\text{Profit from operations} - \text{Cash taxes} + \text{Depreciation}}{\text{Cash investment}}$$

See also ECONOMIC VALUE ADDED.

cash hedge hedging of an existing position in the spot (cash) market. It generally involves selling FUTURES contracts to cover a cash position and is usually referred to as a SHORT HEDGE. *See also* ANTICIPATORY HEDGE.

cash settlement procedure for settling futures contracts in which the cash difference between the futures price and the SPOT PRICE is paid instead of physical delivery.

cashless exercise exercising your options and selling the resulting shares on the same day. You put no money in and get the cash that remains after paying the exercise price, a small broker's fee, and withholding for taxes.

cats and dogs low-quality and high-risk stocks of companies with an unfavorable track record of revenue, profits, and dividends. These stocks are usually low priced. Typically, these types of securities should be avoided for investment purposes.

CBOE *see* CHICAGO BOARD OPTIONS EXCHANGE.

CBOT *see* CHICAGO BOARD OF TRADE.

CDSC *see* CONTINGENT DEFERRED SALES CHARGE.

Cede & Co. firm that acts as the record owner of securities held in STREET NAME for a large number of major brokerage firms and other financial institutions.

central banks government agencies with authority over the size and growth of the nation's money supply. They commonly regulate commercial banks, act as the government's fiscal agent, and are architects of the nation's monetary policy. Central banks frequently intervene in the foreign exchange markets to smooth fluctuations. For example, the *Federal Reserve System* is the central bank in the United States, while the BUNDESBANK is the central bank of Germany. For the monetary policies and economic performance of central banks, visit the Bank for International Settlements site (*http://www.bis.org/cbanks.htm*).

certified financial planner (CFP) professional designation by the College for Financial Planning. Along with professional financial planning experience, recipients must pass national exams in insurance, investments, taxes, employee benefit plans, and estate planning. *See also* FINANCIAL PLANNER.

CFTC *see* COMMODITY FUTURES TRADING COMMISSION.

changes: up and down listing, usually daily, of the stocks having the highest percentage increase in price and the highest percentage decrease in price for the trading period, in the order of their percentage change. Typically, ten advancing stocks and ten declining stocks are listed separately for the NYSE, AMEX, and NASDAQ. The listing appears in the financial pages of newspapers such as *The Wall Street Journal*.

channel area of the chart between the resistance and support levels. Some guidelines related to channels are

- buy when a security is trading in a channel running significantly upward but is trading close to the low end of that channel, or when a security has been trading in a sideways channel and ultimately trades over its resistance level.
- sell when a security is trading in a downward channel or its price goes below a support level.

Chartered Financial Consultant (ChFC) professional designation awarded by American College. Along with professional financial planning experience, recipients must pass national exams in insurance, investments, taxes, employee benefit plans, estate planning, accounting, management, and economics. *See also* FINANCIAL PLANNER.

charting technique used by TECHNICAL ANALYSTS to appraise the trends in volume and price of securities. In order to interpret charts, one has to detect buy and sell indicators. Some basic charts are line, bar, and point-and-figure. Charts reveal whether the market is in a major upturn or downturn and assist in predicting whether the trend will reverse. The technical analyst may see what price can occur on a given stock or market average. Also, charts aid in predicting the magnitude of a price swing. Standard & Poor's *Trendline* gives charting information on many securities. Other financial services, financial magazines and newspapers, and brokerage research reports also provide charts. The Telescan Analyzer from Telescan Inc. prepares graphs for technical and fundamental indicators. Examples of technical charts are given below. *See also* CHARTIST.

LINE CHART

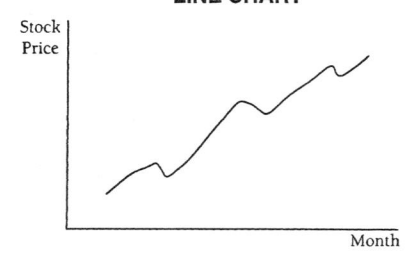

POINT-AND-FIGURE CHART

chartist TECHNICAL ANALYST who charts the direction of securities and commodities to advise on buy, hold, or sell strategies. Chartists try to identify recurring past patterns as a predictor of future prices. *See also* CHARTING.

cheap dollar *see* STRONG DOLLAR.

cheap stock stock that is undervalued and represents a good bargain price. The undervaluation may be due to investor emotional factors resulting in an excessive sell-off of shares, the fact that Wall Street analysts have not recognized the company as being a good buy, and so on.

Chicago Board of Trade (CBOT) world's largest exchange for futures contracts, in terms of the number of contracts traded (243 million in 1997). Founded in 1848, CBOT trades both financial and commodity futures and futures options. U.S. Treasury bond futures are the most frequently traded instruments. Its big rival is the Chicago Mercantile Exchange, which is particularly strong in agricultural futures contracts.

Chicago Board Options Exchange (CBOE) organized national exchange where foreign currency, index, and interest rate options are traded by members for their own accounts and for the accounts of customers.

Chicago Mercantile Exchange (CME) market that trades commodity futures and futures options. Overall the CHICAGO BOARD OF TRADE is probably bigger in number of contracts traded per year, but the CME is bigger when it comes to agricultural futures and OPEN INTEREST contracts.

chief investment officer (CIO) executive responsible for managing and monitoring the company's investment portfolio. The CIO's responsibilities include investment portfolio management, investing surplus funds, pension monies management, maintaining liaison with the investment community, and counseling with financial analysts.

chief operating officer (COO) corporate officer in charge of the daily running of the business. He or she may be the president or executive vice president. The COO reports directly to the chief executive officer.

churning trading done in a customer's account that is excessive. Typically, the customer is in a worse situation because of all the commissions he or she has to pay. Such an illegal practice is prompted by the broker's desire to maximize his or her commissions.

circuit breakers actions used by stock exchanges during large sell-offs. After market indices have fallen a certain percentage, the exchanges halt trading for a certain amount of time, with an objec-

CLEAN PRICE

tive of averting panic selling. Circuit breakers also exist for large advances in market price.

clean price price of a bond obtained by taking the total price of the bond minus accrued interest. Most bonds are traded on the basis of their clean price.

Clearing House Interbank Payments System (CHIPS) a system used by U.S. banks to settle the dollar side of their foreign exchange transactions. CHIPS (*http://www.chips.org*) is a computerized clearing network developed by the New York Clearing House Association (*http://www.theclearinghouse.org*) for transfer of international dollar payments and settlement of interbank foreign exchange obligations, connecting some 150 depository institutions that have offices or affiliates in the City of New York. The transfers account for roughly 90% of all interbank transfers regarding international dollar payments. TARGET is used to settle the EURO side of a transaction.

clearinghouse organization that settles and guarantees trades in some financial markets.

close end of a trading session. The CLOSING PRICE is what's quoted in the newspaper.

close a position
  1. finalize a securities transaction.
  2. sell a security owned from one's portfolio so the investor is no longer involved with the investment.
  3. in commodities FUTURES or OPTIONS trading, traders often end a position through offsetting transactions.

close market market in which there is a narrow difference between the bid and asked prices of a security. A wide difference implies instability. A close market occurs in stocks having high volume.

close to the money situation in which the STRIKE PRICE of a call or put option is near the "going" market price of the related security.

closed-end mutual fund MUTUAL FUND that operates with a fixed number of shares outstanding that trade among individuals in secondary markets such as common stocks. That is, if one wishes to invest in a closed-end fund, he or she must purchase the shares from someone willing to sell them. In the same manner, in order to sell shares, the brokerage house must locate a buyer. Transactions involving closed-end mutual funds are easy to arrange, however, since most of these funds are traded on the New York Stock Exchange or the OVER-THE-COUNTER MARKET. A major point of closed-end funds is the size of discount or premium, which is the difference between their market prices and their NET ASSET VALUES (NAVS). Many funds of this type sell at discounts to the NAV, which enhances their investment appeal. An example of a closed-end mutual fund is Templeton Emerging Markets Fund. COUNTRY FUNDS that represent shares in a specific country or region, such as Italy or France, are often closed-end funds. This chart summarizes the difference between open-end funds, known simply as mutual funds, and closed-end investment companies.

DIFFERENCES BETWEEN OPEN-END AND CLOSED-END FUNDS

	Mutual funds	Closed-end funds
Number of shares	Fluctuates	Fixed
Traded at net asset value (NAV)	Yes	No—a discount or premium from NAV
Liquidity	Almost immediate	3 business days
Dividends and Capital gain	Can be reinvested	Some offer automatic reinvestment
Accessibility	Yes; via a toll-free phone; check-writing privileges	Limited
Method of purchase	Direct from fund or fund salesperson	Stock exchange or OTC
Flexibility	Yes, exchange privileges	No
Commission	Load or no-load	Yes

See also OPEN-END MUTUAL FUND.

closed fund OPEN-END MUTUAL FUND that has decided to stop taking in new money—temporarily or permanently—because its management thinks that the size of its asset base has become more of a burden than an advantage.

closing price ending price of a security for the day; the price for the final transaction of the trading day on the exchange.

closing purchase purchase of an option, by a writer, which has the same terms as an option that has previously been sold. This transaction terminates one's obligations as a writer.

closing quote final bid and offer prices entered by a specialist or market maker at the end of a trading day.

closing range lower and upper amounts of commodity prices within which an order to purchase or sell a commodity can be made during the trading day.

closing sale sale of an OPTION with similar characteristics as an option bought in the past. The options may be in a similar series. The sale of one option similar to that bought in effect cancels each other. For example, the investor may decide to neutralize the buy option because he or she no longer wishes to take possession of the underlying securities.

CME *see* CHICAGO MERCANTILE EXCHANGE.

cold calling   telephoning by a BROKER (usually one recently hired) on an unsolicited basis to individuals to get business such as pushing particular stocks, bonds, mutual funds, or other investment products. Unfortunately, some cold callers are dishonest and may recommend low-quality investments and/or those securities not suitable for the particular investor.

collar
  1. agreement that puts upper and lower limits on the interest rate of an agreement that is binding even if the market rate falls out of this range.
  2. combination of a CAP and a FLOOR.
  3. index level that triggers a CIRCUIT BREAKER.

collateral   assets pledged to secure a debt. The asset will be given up if the borrower defaults on the terms and conditions specified in the debt agreement. An example is pledging inventory to collateralize a bank loan.

collaterized mortgage obligation (CMO)   MORTGAGE-BACKED, PASS-THROUGH SECURITIES that separate mortgage pools into short-, medium-, and long-term time frames. CMOs are an outgrowth of the fact that simple GNMA or FHLMC mortgage-backed securities have uncertain durations (payback of principal and interest factor) because of the possibility of prepayment of the principal amounts remaining on the mortgages. By splitting mortgage pools into different time frames, investors now can buy shares in short-term (such as 5-year) or long-term (such as 20-year) pools. CMOs enjoy LIQUIDITY and a high degree of safety since they are either government-sponsored or otherwise insured. Most of them are sold, however, in minimum amounts of $25,000, which is out of reach for most small investors. *See also* STRIP.

combination bond   bond supported by the credit of the governmental agency issuing it and by the income from the project (for example, a highway) financed by the security. An example is revenue bonds issued by the New York Triborough Bridge and Tunnel Authority.

COMEX *see* COMMODITY EXCHANGE IN NEW YORK.

Commerzbank Index   oldest daily German share index based on 78 BLUE CHIP stocks that represent about 75% of the country's total market value.

commission broker   broker who executes the investor's order for the purchase or sale of securities and commodities.

commission (or round turn)   broker's fee for buying or selling securities.

commodities wheat, eggs, soybeans, silver, pork bellies, and other economic goods.

commodities futures futures contracts on commodities. Commodities futures are used to HEDGE price risks arising from climatic conditions.

Commodity Exchange in New York (COMEX) division of the New York Mercantile Exchange after its merger with NYMEX. It is the main U.S. market for metals futures and options trading in copper, gold, and silver.

Commodity Futures Trading Commission (CFTC) agency (*www.cftc.gov*) that regulates all commodities traded in organized contract markets, established in 1974 by the U.S. Congress. It is to commodity futures as the SEC is to securities markets.

commodity-linked bond bonds that are linked to some commodity prices. Examples are (1) loans with coupons or principal indexed to either the price of a specific good (such as gold) or a global inflation index and (2) inflation-indexed gilts in the U.K. The principal and coupons of these bonds are indexed to British retail prices.

commodity-linked equity stocks that are linked to some commodity prices. Examples are energy company stocks and gold mining stocks.

commodity options OPTIONS on commodities such as oil and precious metals (gold and silver). Portfolio managers use gold options to manage the exposure of their gold-linked assets.

common stock share (or part ownership) in a public or privately held company. It is a security that represents an ownership interest in a corporation. While owners may retain part ownership for a while, they expect to eventually sell to other investors, hopefully at a profit. In the event of liquidation, common stockholders are paid after bondholders and preferred stockholders. The terms *common stock* and *capital stock* are often used interchangeably when the company has no preferred stock. A bond, which is a debt issue, does not represent ownership. The corporation's stockholders have certain rights and privileges including:

1. **Control of the firm:** The stockholders elect the firm's directors, who in turn select officers to manage the business.
2. **Preemptive right:** This is the right to purchase new stock. A preemptive right entitles a common stockholder to maintain his or her proportional ownership by offering the stockholder an opportunity to purchase, on a *pro rata* basis, any new stock being offered or any securities convertible into common stock. This chart summarizes characteristics of common stock.

COMMON STOCK

CHARACTERISTICS OF COMMON STOCK

Voting rights	One vote per share
Income	Dividends; not fixed
Capital gain/loss potential	Yes
Price stability	No
Inflation hedge	Yes
Preemptive right	Yes
Priority of claim	Residual after all other claims paid

Types of Common Stock: Stocks are classified into different categories according to their special characteristics. They are

- **blue chip stocks:** These are common stocks of high quality that have a long and proven record of earnings and dividend payments. These stocks are often viewed as long-term investment instruments, have low risk, and provide modest but dependable return. Examples include AT&T, Exxon, and du Pont.
- **growth stocks:** Growth stocks are issues that have a long record of higher than average earnings than the economy as a whole as well as for the industries of which they are a part. Examples include high-tech stocks.
- **income stocks:** These are issues characterized by higher dividends per share and a high dividend payout ratio. These stocks are for investors who desire CURRENT INCOME (more than future CAPITAL GAINS) with little risk.
- **cyclical stocks:** Cyclical stocks refer to stocks whose earnings and prices move with the BUSINESS CYCLE. Stocks of construction, building materials, airlines, and steel fall into this category.
- **defensive stocks:** These are stocks that tend to be less affected by downswings in the business cycles than the average issue. In other words, they are relatively recession-proof. Utilities, soft drink, and food stocks are examples.
- **speculative stocks:** These stocks generally lack a track record of high earnings and dividends, have uncertain earnings, but have the chance to hit it big in the market. Many of the new issues of oil and gas stocks and cancer-related biotechnology stocks are a sheer gamble. These issues are for investors who are risk oriented, hoping for a big return.

Characteristics of Common Stock: The characteristics that make common stock an attractive investment alternative can be summarized as follows:

- Common stocks provide an ownership feature, as compared with fixed income securities such as bonds, which do not.
- Common stocks provide an income potential not only in terms of current income in the form of dividends but also future capital gain (or loss).
- Common shareholders can participate in the firm's earnings and lay claim to all the residual profits of the entity.
- Common stock can be an INFLATION HEDGE, if the total return from investment in common stock exceeds the rate of inflation.

- Because there is a variety of stocks available, as discussed above, the investor may reduce or eliminate company-specific (unsystematic) risk through DIVERSIFICATION.

common stock valuation process of determining the value of a common stock. It typically involves finding the present value of a stock's expected future income and CAPITAL GAIN, using the investor's required rate of return as the discount rate. A pragmatic approach to valuing a common stock is to use the PRICE/EARNINGS (P/E) RATIO (or multiple). Under this approach, estimated market price can be determined by:
- forecasted price at the end of year = estimated EPS in year t × estimated P/E ratio where EPS = earnings per share and P/E = price/earnings ratio, or earnings multiple. Of course, for this method to be effective in forecasting the future value of a stock, (1) earnings need to be correctly projected and (2) the appropriate P/E multiple must be applied.
- forecasting EPS, which is not an easy task. Some accountants use a simple method of forecasting EPS. They use a sales forecast combined with an after-tax profit margin, as follows:

1. Estimated after-tax earnings in year t =

$$\text{Estimated sales in year t} \times \frac{\text{After-tax profit margin}}{\text{expected in year t}}$$

2. Estimated EPS in year t =

$$\frac{\text{Estimated earnings in year t}}{\text{Number of common shares outstanding in year t}}$$

EXAMPLE:
Assume that a company reported sales of $100 million, and its estimated sales will grow at a 6% annual rate, while the profit margin is about 8%. The company had 2 million shares outstanding. The company's P/E ratio was 15 times earnings and is expected to continue for the next year. Projected sales next year will equal $106 million ($100 million × 1.06).

Estimated after-tax earnings next year are

$$\$106 \text{ million} \times 8\% = \$8.48 \text{ million}$$

Estimated EPS next year = $8.48 million/2 million = $4.24
Then, the company's stock should be trading at a price of $63.60 by the end of next year:

$$\text{Estimated share price next year} = \$4.24 \times 15 = \$63.60$$

Note: If you are looking for an advisory service's estimated EPS for the next year for a company that you are interested in, you can obtain it from publications such as *Value Line Investment Survey*, *First Call*, *Zacks Research*, *Nelson's*, and *I/B/E/S*. These firms constantly poll brokerages for their earnings estimates. From that survey, these companies publish a compilation that includes the high, low, and mean prediction for a company's upcoming quarterly and fiscal year results. Earnings expectations are available on many electronic quotation services such as *Bloomberg Business News*. *The Wall Street Journal* publishes a short list on notable surprises each day along with its daily listings of quarterly corporate results. Many brokerage houses have information available from these two services. On the Internet, Zacks web site at *www.zacks.com* is an excellent free resource.

comparison index
1. index comparing a company's current year's figures (for example, sales of $4,000,000) to a base year or typical year (for example, $5,000,000) to assess relative performances. In this case, the current year's sales Figure is 80% of the company's representative sales.
2. index comparing two competing companies such as by sales or assets. For example, if companies A and B have sales of $6,000,000 and $10,000,000, respectively, relative comparison is company A being 60% of company B in terms of revenue.

composite   universe of portfolios with similar investment objectives.

composite risk   combination of risks, such as business, inflation, market, and liquidity. This allows one to see the overall picture of risk. For example, a corporate bond may have a composite risk consisting of inflation risk, default risk, and interest rate risk. *See also* RISK.

compound (geometric) average return   multiperiod annual return, which is derived as follows:

$$\text{Compound average return} = \sqrt[n]{(1+r_1)(1+r_2)\ldots(1+r_n)} - 1$$

EXAMPLE 1:
Assume the price of a stock doubles in one period and depreciates back to the original price. Dividend income (current income) is nonexistent.

TIME PERIODS

	t = 0	t = 1	t = 2
Price (end of period)	$40	$80	$40
Return	—	100%	−50%

The arithmetic average return is the average of 100% and −50%, or 25%, as indicated below:

$$\frac{100\% + (-50\%)}{2} = 25\%$$

However, the stock bought for $40 and sold for the same price two periods later did not earn 25%; it earned zero. This can be illustrated by determining the compound average return.

Note that $n = 2$, $r_1 = 100\% = 1$, and $r_2 = -50\% = -0.5$
Then,

$$\text{Compound return} = \sqrt{(1+1)(1-0.5)} - 1$$
$$= \sqrt{(2)(0.5)} - 1$$
$$= \sqrt{1} - 1 = 1 - 1 = 0$$

EXAMPLE 2:
Applying the formula to the data below indicates a compound average of 11.63%, somewhat less than the arithmetic average of 26.1%.

(1) Time	(2) Price	(3) Dividend	(4) Total return	(5) Rate of return
0	$100	$-	$-	—
1	60	10	−30(a)	−0.300(b)
2	120	10	70	1.167
3	100	10	−10	−0.083

(a) $10 + ($60 − $100) = $−30.
(b) Return = $−30/$100 = −0.300.

The arithmetic average return is $(−0.300 + 1.167 − 0.083)/3 = .261 = 26.1\%$, but the compound return is $[(1 − 0.300)(1 + 1.167) + (1 + 0.083)]^{1/3} − 1 = 0.1163$, or 11.63%.

See also TOTAL RETURN; RETURN RELATIVE.

conference call
1. phone call by a company to the investment community—financial analysts of brokerage firms—discussing and explaining the company's prospects about future earnings and new products in the pipeline.
2. any call involving three or more participants.

confirmation verification by a brokerage firm that orders have been properly executed according to a customer's instructions.

consolidated balance sheet one that shows the financial position of a related group of companies as though they constituted a single economic unit. The effect of intercompany relationships and the results of intercompany transactions will have been eliminated in the CONSOLIDATION process. The consolidated balance sheet brings together all assets, liabilities, and equity of a parent company and its subsidiaries. Most companies prepare a consolidated balance sheet when they hold more than 50% of the subsidiary's stock. Disclosure is also made of related party transactions.

CONSOLIDATION

consolidation
1. presentation as one economic entity of the earnings of a parent and subsidiary (subsidiaries) subsequent to the date of acquisition. The parent owns more than 50% of the voting common stock of the subsidiary, and is therefore in control. In consolidation, the reporting mechanism is the entire group and not the separate companies. Note that the entities that make up the consolidated group retain their separate legal entity; adjustments and eliminations are for consolidated financial statements only.
2. combining or refinancing loans so as to lower future monthly payments.
3. period when there is a balanced relationship between demand and supply for SECURITIES (stocks, bonds) in which prices move in a narrow range. If the relationship becomes unbalanced, prices will move outside the range.

constant dollar plan investment of a fixed amount of dollars in stocks at periodic times; also called DOLLAR COST AVERAGING. When prices are low, more shares will be bought; however, when prices are high, fewer shares will be purchased.

Consumer Price Index (CPI) average of the prices of various goods and services commonly purchased by families in urban areas. It is frequently referred to as a *cost-of-living index*. The CPI, based at 100 in 1982, is published monthly by the Bureau of Labor Statistics (BLS) of the U.S. Department of Labor. The so-called market basket, covered by the index, includes items such as food, clothing, automobiles, homes, and medical fees. The CPI is the most widely used measure of the purchasing power of the dollar. Consequently, a provision that payments, rents, or wages rise in proportion to the rise in the CPI is written for social security payments and in many lease agreements and collective bargaining agreements. The CPI is widely used by an individual in monitoring inflation. *See also* PRICE INDICES.

consumer stock stock of a company that produces consumer-oriented products such as food, beverages, tobacco, and pharmaceuticals.

continental terms FOREIGN EXCHANGE RATE quotations in foreign currency; the foreign currency price of one U.S. dollar; also called EUROPEAN TERMS. *See also* AMERICAN TERMS.

contingent deferred sales charge (CDSC) BACK-END LOAD that declines over time. For instance, if you sell the mutual fund shares after one year, you may owe a 5% charge, but if you hold for three years, it may decline to 2%.

continuation formation pattern in which demand and supply for a stock are relatively equal. This formation takes place if the stock price approaches from one direction and exits in the same direction.

contract large quantity of a commodity in a futures contract. Examples are as follows:

Commodity	Number of units in one contract	Price per unit	Worth
Japanese Yen	12.5 million yen	$.79 per yen	$9.875 million
Gasoline	42,000 gallons	$1.00 per gallon	$42,000
Sugar	112,000 pounds	$.09 per pound	$10,080

contrarianism investment philosophy based on crowd psychology, which urges investors to do the opposite of what the crowd is doing. *See also* TECHNICAL ANALYSIS.

conversion
1. interchange of one class of corporate security for another. For example, conversion of bonds or preferred stocks for common stocks and the transfer from one mutual fund to another in a single family, called FUND SWITCHING.
2. exchange of one currency for another, called CURRENCY CONVERSION.

conversion charge fee levied against an individual when he or she makes a transfer. For example, a mutual fund may charge a fee when the investor switches between funds, usually in a different family of funds.

conversion feature right to transfer an item, account, or investment into another one. For example, a CONVERTIBLE BOND allows the investor to convert that bond into stock at a later date. Another example is an insurance policy that allows the insured to switch from short-term to permanent life insurance.

conversion hedge HEDGE in a foreign currency when delivery is taken at a later date to protect against a shift in the exchange rate. Assume a $10,000, six-month contract with a French company, payable in francs. To protect against a drop in the exchange rate, the investor may purchase a PUT on francs. If the price of francs goes down, the gain on the put will offset the loss on the contract.

convertible bond, DEBENTURE, or preferred share that may be exchanged by the owner for common stock or another security, usually of the same company, in accordance with the terms of the issue.

convertible bond subordinated DEBENTURE that may be converted, at the holder's option, to either common or preferred shares of the company issuing the bond at a fixed price. Convertible bonds (CVs) are hybrid securities having characteristics of both bonds and common stock in that they provide fixed interest income and potential appreciation through participation in future price increases of the underlying common stock. The pitfall is that the interest of the CV is slightly lower due to the potential capital gain if the stock price goes up.

convertible preferred stock PREFERRED STOCK that can be converted into common stock at the option of the holder.

convertible security PREFERRED STOCK or bond that is convertible into common stock of the issuing corporation at some stated ratio at a later date.

cooling-off period time allowed between filing a prospectus and when securities may be issued by the company to the public. The Securities and Exchange Commission typically provides for a 20-day period.

cornering the market illegal and speculative practice of increasing the price of a security or commodity by buying very large amounts of it. The heavy volume purchase gives the investor great control. As a result, short sellers incur huge losses when they cover their positions at the much higher prices.

corporate bond debt security of a corporation. It represents an agreement that the face value (usually $1000) of the loan will be repaid at maturity and that interest will be paid at regular intervals (usually semiannually). It is a corporate IOU, which is traded on major exchanges. *See also* BOND; ZERO-COUPON BOND.

corporate bond funds mutual funds that seek a high level of income by purchasing primarily bonds of U.S.-based corporations; they may also invest in other FIXED-INCOME SECURITIES such as U.S. TREASURY BONDS.

corporate bond indexes BENCHMARK indexes for corporate bonds. One popular one is the Dow Jones Bond Average, an average of bond prices for major industrial companies and utilities. The bond average is based on 20 bonds and represents an equal number of industrials and utilities. There is also a separate average for each of the industrial and utility bonds (ten each). These indexes are a simple arithmetic average based on ending market prices of the bonds. Some utilities included in the average are Consolidated Edison, Philadelphia Electric, and BellSouth. Some industrials are AT&T, Bethlehem Steel, and IBM. Other corporate bond benchmarks are:

CS First Boston Convertible Securities Index: provides performance coverage of over 250 convertible bonds and preferred stocks rated B-minus or above that have an original PAR VALUE of at least $50 million; preferred stocks must have a minimum of 500,000 shares outstanding. The index also includes U.S. dollar-denominated EUROBONDS issued by U.S.-domiciled companies.

Lehman Brothers Intermediate Corporate Bond Index: provides performance coverage of investment-quality corporate bonds with maturities of one to ten years.

Lehman Brothers Long-Term Corporate Bond Index: tracks investment-grade U.S. corporate bonds with maturities greater than ten years.

Merrill Lynch All-Convertible Securities Index: follows corporate convertible securities that must be convertible only to common stock and have a market value or original par value of at least $50 million.

Merrill Lynch High-Yield Master Index: tracks all domestic and Yankee high-yield bonds. Issues included in the index have maturities of at least one year and have a credit rating lower than BBB-Baa3, but are not in DEFAULT.

Moody's Corporate Bond Index: tracks on a total return, price-weighted basis more than 75 nonconvertible, coupon corporate bonds. These taxable bonds mature in no more than five years.

Standard & Poor's Junk Bond Indexes: track high-risk, high-return corporate bonds. They are considered poor quality with substantial gain potential. There are two Standard & Poor's indexes of junk bonds—BB-rated and B-rated.

corporation   form of business organized as a separate legal entity with ownership evidenced by shares of CAPITAL STOCK. The corporation continues to exist regardless of changes in its ownership. The corporation is formed by the articles of incorporation with the state authority, which returns it with a certificate of incorporation; the two documents together become a corporate charter. Corporations are taxed differently from sole proprietorships and partnerships.

correction   price reaction, usually downward, leading to an adjustment of typically more than 10%, after experiencing a general period of advancing prices. A true correction is then followed by a continued period of advancing prices, which distinguishes it from a major BEARISH turn in the overall direction of the stock or the market.

MARKET CORRECTION

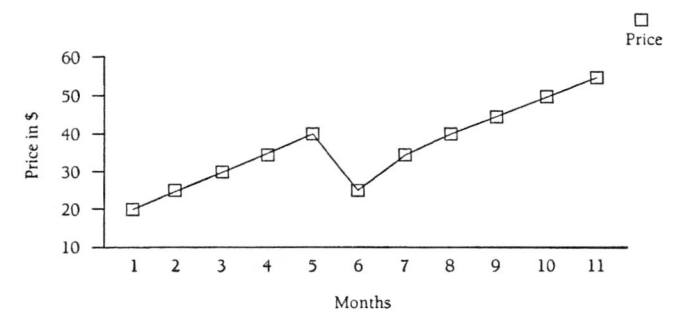

cost basis   initial cost of an investment including its market price and brokerage fees. The difference between its selling price and cost basis is the CAPITAL GAIN OR LOSS for tax purposes. If property is

COST (OF A SECURITY)

inherited, the cost basis is its fair market value at the date of the donor's death.

cost (of a security) initial acquisition price plus incidental costs such as COMMISSIONS.

cost of capital rate of return that is necessary to maintain market value (or stock price) of a firm; also called a *hurdle rate, cutoff rate,* or *minimum required rate of return*. The firm's cost of capital is calculated as a weighted average of the costs of debt and equity funds. It is often called a *weighted average cost of capital (WACC)*. Equity funds include both capital stock (common stock and preferred stock) and retained earnings. These costs are expressed as annual percentage rates. For example, assume the following capital structure and the cost of each source of financing for a multinational company:

Source	Book Value	% of Total Weights	Cost
Debt	$20,000,000	40%	8%
Preferred stock	5,000,000	10	14
Common stock	20,000,000	40	16
Retained earnings	5,000,000	10	15
Totals	$50,000,000	100%	

The overall cost of capital is computed as follows: 8%(.4) + 14%(.1) + 16%(.4) + 15%(.1) = 12.5%. The cost of capital is used for *capital budgeting* purposes. Under the NET PRESENT VALUE method, the cost of capital is used as the discount rate to calculate the present value of future cash inflows. Under the INTERNAL RATE OF RETURN method, it is used to make an accept-or-reject decision by comparing the cost of capital with the internal rate of return on a given project. A project is accepted when the internal rate exceeds the cost of capital.

countercyclical (defensive) stock stock of a company that maintains substantial earnings during a general decline in economic activity because its products are needed. Examples are food and entertainment stocks.

country analysis *see* COUNTRY RISK ANALYSIS.

Country Baskets fund, created by Deutsche Morgan Grenfell, designed to replicate the *Financial Times/Standard & Poor's Actuaries World Indices*. These are available for each of nine countries. Unlike WORLD EQUITY BENCHMARK SHARES (WEBS), which attempt to match the performance of a particular index without owning all of the stocks in the index, Country Baskets owns every stock in the index for that country.

country funds mutual funds that invest in a specific country. Single-country funds are the most focused and therefore by far the most aggressive foreign stock funds. Almost all single-country funds are closed-end funds (exceptions are the Japan Fund and French Fund). This exaggerates their aggressiveness because single-country (and regional) closed-end funds have been known to sell at both *large* discounts and premiums to their net asset value. Thus, closed-end single-country funds are well suited for only the most sophisticated investors who are confident in their ability to assess the potential for a specific market as well as the trends in the fund's stock price versus its net asset value.

country risk analysis   analysis of a country's POLITICAL or SOVEREIGN RISK for the benefit of foreign investors. Political factors are a major determinant of the attractiveness for investment in any country. Examples of political risk are government expropriation of property, currency conversion restrictions, and import barriers. Countries viewed as likely candidates for internal political upheaval or with a pronounced trend toward elimination of the private sector will be unattractive to all investors, foreign and domestic alike. There is no reason to believe that local investors will be systematically optimistic regarding their country's future. When political risks increase significantly, such investors will attempt to diversify from the home market as rapidly as will foreigners.

country risk covering   taking steps to reduce the foreign risk exposure faced by the multinational company such as entering into currency futures contracts to hedge the company's position. *See also* HEDGING.

country risk rating   ratings provided by some prominent rating agencies. Examples are
- *Euromoney Magazine's Country Risk Ratings*, which is published twice a year. The ratings are based on a measure of different countries' access to international credit, trade finance, political risk, and payment record. The rankings are generally confirmed by political risk insurers and top syndicate managers in the EUROMARKETS (*http://www.euromoney.com*).
- *International Country Risk Guide*, published by International Business Communications, Ltd., a London company that offers a COMPOSITE RISK rating, as well as individual ratings for political, financial, and economic risk. The political variable, which makes up half of the composite index, includes factors such as government corruption and how economic expectations diverge from reality. The financial rating looks at such things as the likelihood of losses from exchange controls and loan defaults. Finally, economic ratings consider such factors as inflation and debt-service costs.
- Rating by Economist Intelligence Unit, a New York-based subsidiary of the Economist Group, London, which deals with such factors as external debt and trends in the current account, the consistency of the government policy, foreign-exchange reserves, and the quality of economic management.

coupon detachable certificate attached to a BEARER BOND that has to be presented to the issuing institution or paying agent to receive the payment of semiannual interest on the principal. *See also* COUPON RATE.

coupon bond *see* BEARER BOND.

coupon rate interest rate of a bond as a percent of the FACE VALUE. It is printed on the COUPON of a bond; also called *face rate* or *nominal rate*.

coupon yield *see* COUPON.

cover act of buying a security previously sold short. *See also* SHORT SALE.

covered *see* COVERED OPTION.

covered call option strategy used to increase the yield on a stock or an index holding in a relatively flat market or a falling market. The investor buys BLUE CHIP companies, or a large-cap market index such as the Standard & Poor's 500. He or she then writes (sells) a call option on stock or index he or she owns, thus covering his or her position, and reaps cash flows for the proceeds similar to regular income. Hence, the investor has the cash, and all the risk of the underlying asset—the stocks. Should the call option expire OUT-OF-THE-MONEY, the investor pockets the premium since the call is not exercised. Should the call expire IN-THE-MONEY, the investor must honor the option contract and deliver the stock. Fortunately, the investor with a LONG POSITION does not need to go to the market and purchase the stock first, thus limiting his or her exposure. If the investor wrote the call on stock not owned, he or she would have a NAKED CALL POSITION, which is riskier than a covered call position.

covered interest arbitrage investment in a second currency that is "covered" by a forward sale of that currency to protect against exchange rate fluctuations; also called *covered investment arbitrage*. More specifically, it involves buying or selling securities internationally and using the forward market to eliminate currency risk in order to take advantage of interest (return) differentials. It is a process whereby one earns a risk-free profit by (1) borrowing currency; (2) converting it into another currency where it is invested; (3) selling this other currency for future delivery against the initial original currency; and (4) using the proceeds of forward sale to repay the original loan. The profits in this transaction depend on interest rate differentials *minus* the discount or *plus* the premium on a forward sale.

covered options   options written against stock owned. It is an investment in which all written options are offset with the underlying stock on a share-for-share basis. The loss potential with such a strategy is thereby limited.

covered writing   in the case of call writing, covered means having a holding of shares at least equal to that implied by the short call option position, and in the case of put writing, covered means having a cash sum sufficient to take up the underlying security if assigned on the short put position.

CRB   formerly Commodity Research Bureau, now known as Bridge/CRB.

CRB Bridge Futures Price Index   *see* INFLATION.

CRB Bridge Spot Price Index   *see* INFLATION.

credit risk   possibility that a loss may occur from the failure of another party to perform according to the terms of a contract. For example, credit risk in bond terminology refers to the risk of DEFAULT.

credit spread   value of a sold option exceeding that of the option purchased.

cross hedging   HEDGING across different assets. In a cross hedge, the futures contract used is different from the initial asset to be hedged. Since futures contracts exist for only a few assets, the chance of matching a futures contract to a specific portfolio of bonds or stocks is slim. An example of cross hedges on individual assets is to use U.K. stock index contracts to hedge a specific U.K. stock portfolio.

cross investment   type of FOREIGN DIRECT INVESTMENT (FDI) made, as a defense measure, by oligopolistic companies in each other's home country.

cross rate   exchange rate between two currencies derived by dividing each currency's exchange rate with a third currency. For example, if dollars per pound is \$1.5999/£ and yen per dollar is ¥110.66/\$, the cross rate between Japanese yen and British pounds is as shown below.

$$\text{Cross rate between yen and pound} = \frac{\text{Dollars}}{\text{Pound}} \times \frac{\text{Yen}}{\text{Dollar}} = \frac{\text{Yen}}{\text{Pound}}$$

$$= \$/£ \quad \times ¥/\$ \quad = ¥/£$$

$$= 1.5999 \text{ dollars per pound}$$

$$\times 110.66 \text{ yen per dollar}$$

$$= 177.05 \text{ yen per pound}$$

Because most currencies are quoted against the dollar, it may be necessary to work out the cross rates for currencies other than the dollar. The cross rate is needed to consummate financial transactions between two countries.

KEY CURRENCY CROSS RATES

	British£	Euro	Japanese¥	U.S.$
British£	—	0.6172	0.5653	0.6250
Euro	1.6203	—	0.9153	1.0129
Japanese¥	177.05	109.25	—	110.66
U.S.$	1.5999	0.9873	0.9037	—

Source: Bloomberg L.P. (*http://www.bloomberg.com*).
*Note: Cross currency table calculator can be accessed by *http://www.xe.net/currency/table.htm*. in different countries.

crude oil spot price   market price for a barrel of unrefined petroleum, typically a high-quality grade oil. For example, West Texas intermediate crude oil price is the price of a BENCHMARK grade of crude oil produced in West Texas. Crude oil prices are carefully watched as a barometer of everything from global political tensions to inflation to oil company profits. Rising oil prices ultimately boost prices for gasoline, air travel, shipped products, and petroleum-based products. Investors also can invest directly in oil by buying futures and options contracts. The often-quoted spot price for crude oil is the per-barrel price on the most current Light Sweet Crude futures contracts that trade on the New York Mercantile Exchange. Each futures contract calls for delivery of 1000 barrels of oil but its price is quoted per barrel. The NYMEX, as it is known, also trades futures for crude oil, natural gas, and two refined products—unleaded gasoline and heating oil. The crude oil spot price appears in commodity futures listings in such newspapers as *Barron's, Investor's Business Daily, The New York Times, The Wall Street Journal*, and on computerized databases such as America Online. Or you can check the NYMEX web site at *www.nymex.com*.

cumulative preferred stock   stock having a provision that if one or more dividends are omitted, the omitted dividends must be paid before dividends may be paid on the company's common stock. Nearly all preferred stock is cumulative.

cumulative wealth index   measure or indicator of the total value of money and property owned by an individual or institution.

Curb Exchange   former name of the American Stock Exchange, second largest exchange in the country. The term comes from the market's origin of trading on the streets of downtown New York.

currency arbitrage   form of ARBITRAGE that takes advantage of divergences in exchange rates in different money markets by buying a currency in one market and selling it in another.

currency call option   *see* CURRENCY OPTION.

currency cocktail bond   bond denominated in a blend (or cocktail) of currencies.

currency diversification   practice aimed at slashing the impact of unforeseen currency fluctuations by engaging activities in a portfolio of different currencies. Exposure to a diversified currency portfolio normally results in less CURRENCY RISK than if all of the exposure was in a single foreign currency.

currency futures   futures contracts on foreign currencies, traded much like COMMODITIES.

currency indexes   economic indicators that attempt to measure foreign currencies. Some popular currency indexes are:
- **Federal Reserve Trade-Weighted Dollar**: The index reflects the currency units of more than 50% of the U.S. purchases, principally from trading countries. It measures the currencies of ten foreign countries: the United Kingdom, Germany, Japan, Italy, Canada, France, Sweden, Switzerland, Belgium, and the Netherlands. The index is weighted by each currency's base exchange rate, and then averaged on a geometric basis. This weighting process indicates relative significance in overseas markets. The base year was 1973. The index is published by the Federal Reserve System and is found in its *Federal Reserve Bulletin* or at various Federal Reserve Internet sites such as *http://woodrow.mpls.frb.fed.us/economy*. The trend in this index should be examined to determine foreign exchange risk exposure associated with an investment portfolio and financial positions. Also, the Federal Reserve trade-weighted dollar is the basis for commodity futures on the New York Cotton Exchange.
- **J. P. Morgan Dollar Index**: The index measures the value of currency units versus dollars. The index is a weighted average of 19 currencies including those of France, Italy, the United Kingdom, Germany, Canada, and Japan. The weighting is based on the relative significance of the currencies in world markets. The base of 100 was established for 1980 through 1982. The index highlights the impact of foreign currency units in U.S. dollar terms. The effect of foreign currency conversion can be seen on U.S. dollar investment.

See also BRITISH POUND; GERMAN DEUTSCHE MARK; JAPANESE YEN.

currency option   financial contracts that give the buyer the right, but not the obligation, to buy (or sell) a specified number of units of foreign currency from the option seller at a fixed dollar price, up to the option's expiration date. In return for this right, the buyer pays a premium to the seller of the option. They are similar to foreign currency futures in that the contracts are for fixed quantities of currency to be exchanged at a fixed price in the future. The key difference is that the maturity date for an option is only the last day to carry out the currency exchange; the option may be "exercised," that is, presented for currency exchange, at any time between its issuance and the maturity date, or not at all. Currency options are used as a hedging tool and for speculative purposes.

currency option pricing   based on the work of Black and Scholes and others, the model that yields the OPTION PREMIUM.

currency put option   *see* CURRENCY OPTION.

currency quotations   quotes on foreign currencies. Currency quotes are always given in pairs because a dealing bank usually does not know whether a prospective customer is in the market to buy or to sell a foreign currency. The first rate is the bid, or buy, rate; the second is the sell, ask, or offer rate.

EXAMPLE 1:
Suppose the pound sterling is quoted at $1.5918–29. This quote means that banks are willing to buy pounds at $1.5918 and sell them at $1.5929. Note that the banks will always buy low and sell high. In practice, however, they quote only the last two digits of the decimal. Thus, sterling would be quoted at 18–29 in this example. Note that when AMERICAN TERMS are converted to EUROPEAN TERMS or direct quotations are converted to indirect quotations, bid and ask quotes are reversed; that is, the reciprocal of the American (direct) bid becomes the European (indirect) ask and the reciprocal of the American (direct) ask becomes the European (indirect) bid.

EXAMPLE 2:
So, in Example 1, the reciprocal of the American bid of $1.5918/£ becomes the European ask of £0.6282/$ and the reciprocal of the American ask of $1.5929/£ equals the European bid of £0.6278/$, resulting in a direct quote for the dollar in London of £0.6278–82.

Here is a summary of this result.

DIRECT VERSUS INDIRECT CURRENCY QUOTATIONS

Direct (American)	Indirect (European)
$1.5918–29	£0.6278–82

currency revaluation   rise in a currency's SPOT value that is pegged to other currencies or to gold; also called *appreciation* or *strengthening*. The opposite of revaluation is weakening, deteriorating, DEVALUATION, or depreciation. Strictly speaking, revaluation refers to a rise in the value of a currency that is pegged to gold or to another currency. Revaluation can be achieved by raising the supply of foreign currencies via restriction of imports and promotion of exports.

currency risk   risk that the return on an international security to U.S. investors would be negatively affected by a change in the value of the dollar relative to the foreign currency; also called *foreign exchange risk, exchange rate risk*, or *exchange risk*. A weaker dollar would boost the security's return, since the stronger foreign currency would be exchanged for more U.S. dollars. A stronger dollar would lower the security's return. Since the exchange rates among major currencies have been volatile in recent years, exchange rate uncertainty has often been mentioned as one of the potential barriers to international investment. For example, a strong dollar, meaning that foreign currency buys fewer dollars, would push down foreign returns of the U.S. investor. The following example illustrates how a change in the dollar affects the return on a foreign investment.

EXAMPLE:
You purchased bonds of a German firm paying 12% interest. You will earn that rate, assuming interest is paid and in marks. What if you are paid in dollars? As the following chart shows, you must then convert marks to dollars before the payout has any value to you. Suppose that the dollar appreciated 10% against the mark during the year after purchase. (A currency appreciates when acquiring one of its units requires more units of a foreign currency.) In this example, 1 mark acquired .616 dollars, and later, 1 mark acquired only .554 dollars; at the new exchange rate it would take 1.112 (.616/.554) marks to acquire .616 dollars; thus, the dollar has appreciated while the mark has depreciated. Now your return realized in dollars is only 10.91%. The adverse movement in the foreign exchange rate—the dollar's appreciation—reduced your actual yield.

EXCHANGE RISK AND FOREIGN INVESTMENT YIELD

Transaction	Marks	Exchange Rate: No. of Dollars per 1 Mark	Dollars
On 1/1/20A Purchased one German bond with a 12% coupon rate	500	$.6051	$302.55
On 12/31/20A Expected interest received	60	.6051	36.31
Expected yield	12%		12%
On 12/31/20A Actual interest received	60	.5501*	33.01
Realized yield	12%		10.91%**

* $.6051/(1 + .1) = $.6051/1.1 = $.5501.
** $33.01/$302.55 = .1091 = 10.91%.

Currency risks can be HEDGED by borrowing in the local currency or selling it forward; however, this type of tool is too costly and impractical for individual investors. *Note*: Choosing countries with strong currencies and investing in international mutual funds could be an answer to minimizing currency risk. Note, however, that currency swings work both ways. A weak dollar would boost foreign returns of U.S. investors. This chart is a quick reference to judge how currency swings affect your foreign returns.

CURRENCY CHANGES VS. FOREIGN RETURNS IN U.S. DOLLARS

Foreign returns	Change in Foreign Currency Against the Dollar Return					
		20%	10%	0%	−10%	−20%
	20%	44%	32	20	8	−4
	10	32	21	10	−1	−12
	0	20	10	0	−10	−20
	−10	8	−1	−10	−19	−28
	−20	−4	−12	−20	−28	−36

Note: General Electric Financial Network (*http://www.gefn.com*), for example, has a tool "How do exchange rates affect my foreign fund?" (*http://www.calcbuilder.com/cgi-bin/calcs/MUT12.cgi/gefa*).

This table shows how your international investment returns can change when you convert them from local currency to U.S. dollars.

ANNUAL RETURNS OF THE MSCI EAFE INDEX IN LOCAL CURRENCY AND U.S. DOLLARS
MSCI EAFE INDEX

Year	Local Currency	U.S. Dollars
1998	12.60%	20.33%
1997	13.82	2.06
1996	11.63	6.36
1995	9.83	11.55
1994	−1.78	8.06
1993	29.56	32.94
1992	−5.83	−11.85
1991	9.06	12.50
1990	−29.60	−23.20
1989	21.74	10.80
1988	34.00	28.59

currency risk management practice of managing foreign exchange risk. Foreign exchange rate risk exists when the contract is written in terms of the foreign currency or denominated in the foreign currency. The exchange rate fluctuations increase the riskiness of the investment and incur cash losses. An investor must not only seek the highest return on temporary investments, but must also be concerned about changing values of the currencies invested. One does not necessarily eliminate foreign exchange risk; one may only try to contain it.

currency spread buying an option at one STRIKE PRICE and selling a similar option at a different strike price. Thus, the currency spread limits the option holder's DOWNSIDE RISK on the currency bet but at the cost of limiting the position's upside potential. There are two types of currency spreads:

1. A BULL SPREAD, a spread designed to bet on a currency's appreciation, involves buying a call at one strike price and selling another call at a higher strike price.
2. A BEAR SPREAD, designed to bet on a currency's decline, involves buying a PUT at one strike price and selling another put at a lower strike price.

currency swap temporary exchanges of monies between two parties that do not go through the FOREIGN EXCHANGE MARKET. In *official* swaps, the two parties are central banks. *Private* swaps are between central banks and MNCs. Currency swaps are often used to minimize CURRENCY RISK. *See also* CURRENCY RISK MANAGEMENT; SWAPS.

currency trading selling and buying foreign currency for speculation or investment purposes. Currency traders are always watching for changes in monetary policies and the forces that shape currency trends. The major economic indicators moving today's FOREIGN EXCHANGE MARKETS are trade deficits, GDP, industrial production, inflation rates, and interest rates. Economic factors usually affect a currency by altering the interest rate structure of the country. The interest rate structure of a country could reflect perhaps an even more important structure—the overall monetary health of that country. As these economic indicators rise and fall in each country, their corresponding currencies will appreciate or depreciate. *See also* CURRENCY RISK; FOREIGN EXCHANGE.

current account account in the BALANCE OF PAYMENTS, analogous to the revenues and expenses of a business, the sum of the merchandise, services, investment income, and unilateral transfer accounts. When combined, they provide important insights into a country's international economic performance, just as a firm's profit and loss statement conveys vital information about its performance.

current income fund mutual fund whose investment objective is to produce high current DIVIDEND YIELDS on common stocks.

current return *see* CURRENT INCOME; CURRENT YIELD; RETURN.

current yield measurement of investment return that relates income to the market price. For a bond, its annual interest is divided by its current market price. For a common or preferred stock, it is the ratio of the annual cash dividend income received to the price paid by the investor. For example, a 12% coupon rate $1000 PAR VALUE bond is selling for $960. The current yield of the bond is

$$\$120/\$960 = 12.5\%$$

The problem with this measure of return is that it does not take into account the maturity date of the bond. A bond with one year to run and another with fifteen years to run would have the same current yield quote if interest payments were $120 and the price were $960.

Clearly, the one-year bond would be preferable under this circumstance because the investor would not only get $120 in interest, but also a gain of $40 ($1000 − $960) with a one-year time period, and this amount could be reinvested. *See also* BOND YIELD; YIELD TO MATURITY (YTM).

cushion bond bond that is not as sensitive to interest rate movements because of its early call option, usually one to two years. Its price is artificially suppressed because of the early call, and will not change up or down as other similar bonds with longer call dates.

CUSIP number nine-digit identifier number used to identify all stocks and registered bonds that trade in the United States. CUSIP stands for **C**ommittee on **U**niform **S**ecurities **I**dentification **P**rocedures, which is a committee set up by the American Bankers Association.

CV *see* CONVERTIBLE.

cyber investing type of investing, such as on-line trading on the Internet.

cyberspace originally used in *Neuromancer*, William Gibson's novel of direct brain-computer networking; refers to the collective realms of computer-aided communication.

cycle analysis
1. evaluation and appraisal of BUSINESS CYCLE associated with periods of expansion and contraction in business activity.
2. assessment of a product's life cycle.

cyclical stock stock whose prices are directly and significantly tied to economic conditions. If the economy is improving, stock prices rise, but if the economy is deteriorating, stock prices decline. Cyclical investing is buying or selling securities based on the point in the long-term market cycle. Cyclical stocks are somewhat risky. Examples of cyclical stocks are General Motors, International Paper, American Airlines, and Kaufman Braud. Noncyclical stocks are not as directly affected by economic changes.

D

data book record or account of investment information such as the holdings in a securities' portfolio.

day high highest price that a security was traded for on the trading day.

day low lowest price that a stock, bond, or option was traded for on the trading day.

day order order placed by an investor to purchase or sell securities or commodities that will end if not transacted or cancelled on the trading day. An order is always deemed to be a day order unless noted otherwise. The primary exception is a GOOD-TILL-CANCELLED (GTC) ORDER. However, even this type of order may be fulfilled on the trading day depending on whether certain conditions are met. *See also* BUY ORDER.

day trading purchase and sale of a security on the same day so that the profit or loss is settled by the end of the trading day. Day trading aims at taking advantage of price swings during that day. Due to the popularity of on-line trading, day trading has a significant impact on the stock market in terms of price and volume. Day trading has the disadvantage of high commissions.

dealer individual or a company that owns and offers securities. The dealer acts as a principal rather than as an agent. Typically, dealers buy for their own account and sell to customers from their own inventory, as distinguished from the broker, who acts as the buyer or seller's agent for a fee. Dealers' profit or loss is the difference between the price they pay and the price they receive for the same security. The dealer's confirmation must disclose to the customer that he or she has acted as principal. The same individual or company may function, at different times, either as broker or dealer. For example, specialists on the floor of the New York Stock Exchange act as dealers when they buy or sell stock for their own account to maintain a market. Specialists act as BROKERS when they execute the orders commission brokers have left with them. *See also* NASD; SPECIALIST.

dealer's spread
  1. COMMISSION or markup a dealer makes when offering a new security. The commission is paid by the company offering the new stock rather than by the retail customer.
  2. difference the dealer makes between the bid and asked price.

debenture any bond that is backed only by the good credit of the organization. It is not secured by a lien on specific property. It is a general debt obligation based solely on the borrower's integrity. Because it is unsecured debt, it is issued usually by large, financially strong companies with excellent bond ratings. There are two kinds of debentures: a *senior* issue and a *subordinated (junior)* issue, which has a subordinate lien. The order of a prior claim is set forth in the bond indenture. Typically, in the event of LIQUIDATION, subordinated debentures come after senior debt.

debit spread   difference in the value of two options. The value of the purchased option is more than the value of the sold option.

debt/equity ratio   total debt divided by shareholders' equity. An excessively high ratio indicates RISK.

debt securities   securities that serve as evidence to the existence of a debt, such as bonds, notes, and so on, as opposed to equity securities, such as stocks, which manifest evidence of ownership. *See also* FIXED-INCOME SECURITIES.

declaration   announcement to pay dividends as a result of the board of directors' decision. *See also* DECLARATION DATE.

declaration date   date on which the dividend is voted and declared by the board of directors of a corporation. A dividend becomes a legal liability of the company on the declaration date.

declining market   market in which there are more sellers than buyers, thereby causing prices to fall. Declining markets for securities may be caused by unfavorable business conditions and high interest rates.

deep discount bond   bond selling for a discount of 25% or more than its FACE VALUE, usually because the coupon rate is lower than CURRENT YIELDS on newly issued bonds of the same quality. A deep discount bond is sold when the issuing company is in desperate need of money. It appreciates faster as interest rates decline and falls faster as rates rise. *See also* ORIGINAL ISSUE DISCOUNT.

deep-in-the-money   term used to describe the value of stock or index options that differ significantly from the market price of the underlying security or index. A call option is deep-in-the-money if its STRIKE PRICE is much lower than the market price. Such a call could be written or sold if a stockholder of the underlying securities is BEARISH on the stock and wants to protect the original investment if the stock does indeed fall in price. A put option is deep-in-the-money if its strike price is significantly above the market price of the related security. This put would be desirable to sell by an individual who shorted the underlying stock and is anticipating that it may rise in price. The price increase of the shorted stock would be covered by the proceeds of the put option up to the strike price of the put. Options that are deep-in-the-money have very little premium since their strike price is significantly different from the market price of the underlying security. *See also* AT-THE-MONEY; IN-THE-MONEY; OUT-OF-THE-MONEY.

default   failure to pay principal and/or interest when due.

default risk   likelihood that a bondholder will not receive the promised interest and principal redemption when due. For example, there is a great amount of default risk inherent in the bonds of a company experiencing financial difficulty. This chart presents the degree of default risk for some investment instruments.

DEFAULT RISK AMONG SHORT-TERM INVESTMENT VEHICLES

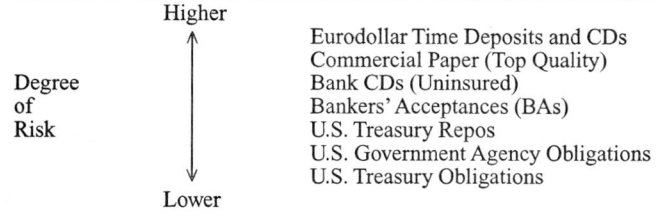

Degree of Risk	Higher ↑ Eurodollar Time Deposits and CDs Commercial Paper (Top Quality) Bank CDs (Uninsured) Bankers' Acceptances (BAs) U.S. Treasury Repos U.S. Government Agency Obligations U.S. Treasury Obligations ↓ Lower

See also BOND RATINGS; RISK.

defensive investment   any investment, domestic or foreign, undertaken principally to insure against loss rather than to make a profit. More often than not, such an investment is made in response to the actions of competitors. For example, in the 1970s the U.S government was encouraging the domestic development of processes to produce petroleum from shale and coal. While such a synthetic fuel probably could never be produced as cheaply as natural petroleum in the Middle East, it represented a defensive investment to help ensure a source of supply.

defensive securities   securities that have relatively stable prices even during business DOWNTURNS and market declines and provide a safe return on invested money. In other words, they are recession-resistant. Examples are government bonds and stocks and bonds of investment grade companies such as public utilities and consumer products. *See also* DEFENSIVE STOCKS.

defensive stocks   common stocks that tend to exhibit price movements contrary to the downward movements of the BUSINESS CYCLE; also called *countercyclical stocks*. The prices of these stocks are expected to remain stable during contractions in business activity. In a BEAR MARKET, defensive stocks perform better than the overall market. They have somewhat lower return but are safe and consistent. They are less affected by RECESSION. Examples of defensive stocks are utilities and consumer product companies. *See also* DEFENSIVE SECURITIES.

defer to wait or postpone an action, such as a payment, until a later date.

deferred sales charges commissions on LOAD and NO-LOAD (MUTUAL) FUNDS. The change may range from 1 to 6% assessed on the investor if the shares are redeemed within a certain time period after purchase.

delisting withdrawal of a particular security from trading on a securities exchange. Stocks can be delisted when the company violates minimum standards of the exchange including failure to maintain a minimum net worth, not having the required number of shareholders, or conviction of certain illegalities. Of course, when a company is merged into another company or is no longer publicly traded, it will be removed from the exchange. This activity should not be confused with delisting in which the company's stock is not permitted to be traded because of nonconformance with basic exchange policies.

delivery transfer of stocks from a seller to a buyer. The certificate representing shares bought *regular way* on the New York Stock Exchange normally is delivered to the purchaser's broker on the fourth business day after the transaction.

delta ratio of change of the option price to a small change in the price of the underlying asset; also equal to the derivative of the option price with respect to the asset price.

delta hedge dynamic hedging strategy using options with continuous adjustment of the number of options used, as a function of the DELTA of the option.

denomination face amount of a bond. Bonds are usually issued in denominations of $1000, $5000, or multiples thereof.

depreciation
1. recovery of the original cost over the estimated life of the fixed assets such as plant and equipment. Depreciation reduces taxable income. It is a noncash expense. The straight-line method results in constant depreciation per year. Accelerated depreciation methods result in more depreciation in the early years and less depreciation in the later years. An example is the sum-of-the-years' digits depreciation method. Variable charge depreciation methods result in depreciation based on the usage of the asset. An example is the units of production method.
2. decline in economic potential of limited life assets originating from wear and tear as well as technological obsolescence.
3. decline in value of a currency; also called cheap (weak) dollar. The depreciation of the dollar is its reduction in value pegged to other currencies or gold.

depressed market state of affairs in a market when the prices of products, services, or securities are in extremely poor demand, and characterized by depressed prices and trading activity. Supply exceeds demand in a depressed market.

derivative financial instrument (DFI)   contract whose value is tied to the return on stocks, bonds, currencies, or commodities. Thus, there may be an underlying interest rate, commodity price, stock price index, foreign exchange rate, or other similar variable.

derivatives   securities bearing a contractual relation to some underlying asset or rate. Options, futures, forward, and swap contracts, as well as many types of bonds, are derivative securities. For example, a call option will increase in price as the underlying stock increases in market value. *See also* DERIVATIVE FINANCIAL INSTRUMENT (DFI).

descending tops   chart pattern showing each new high price for a security lower than the previous high. The downward trend is BEARISH. *See also* ASCENDING TOPS.

descriptive information   factual data on the past behavior of the economy, the stock market, the industry, or a given investment vehicle.

Deutsche Aktienindex (DAX)   index for the 30 largest German companies quoted on the Frankfurt Stock Exchange. The index was launched in 1987 with a base value of 1000 and replaced the Borsen Zeitung Index.

Deutsche Bank Commodity Index (DBCI)   commodity futures price index of five commodities: crude oil, heating oil, aluminum, gold, and silver.

deutsche mark   *see* GERMAN (DEUTSCHE) MARK.

Deutsche Terminborse (DTB)   German derivatives exchange, where the BUND, Euromark futures, and DAX futures and options contracts are traded.

devaluation   deliberate downward adjustment of a country's currency relative to gold and/or currencies of other nations. The opposite is *revaluation*.

diagonal spread   put or call option strategy in which the investor buys and simultaneously sells the same type of option; however, the STRIKING PRICES and maturity dates vary. The exact strategy depends on whether an individual is BULLISH or BEARISH on the underlying security. The immediate objective is to cover at least part of the cost of the overall investment strategy by selling one expiration date of the same class of options to offset the long purchase of the other expiration date of the option.

EXAMPLE:
In a bearish diagonal spread call option strategy, the investor sells a near-term expiration date call option having a striking price near the market price of the stock while simultaneously buying a far-term

DILUTED EARNINGS PER SHARE

OUT-OF-THE-MONEY call option with a future expiration date. The investor hopes the shorted near-term call option will expire if the market price of the underlying stock declines while hedging the strategy by being long on the out-of-the-money call option if the underlying stock rises. Thus, if the market price of the stock rises, the out-of-the-money call option would rise in value, offsetting the loss of the shorted near-term lower striking price call. The profit in the bearish diagonal spread is in the difference between the proceeds of the near-term call option less the cost of the far-term out-of-the-money call option. In the bullish diagonal spread strategy, the investor would sell a near-term expiration date out-of-the-money call option while simultaneously buying a far-term call option with a striking price near the market price. The hope is that the near-term out-of-the-money call option will expire while the market price of the underlying stock rises just short of the list striking price, hedging the strategy by being long on the out-of-the-money call. The sale of the near-term out-of-the-money call would help to offset, but not cover, the purchase price of the far-term call and thus reduce the investment risk. The profit potential is in the rise in value of the far-term call option after the near-term out-of-the-money option expires. It is never possible to short the far-term expiration date option while buying a near-term option, since the earlier expiration date of the purchased option would not provide coverage for the shorted far-term option.

DIAGONAL SPREAD STRATEGY (BEARISH)

Purchase	Striking Price	Cost	Sale	Striking Price	Proceeds	Cost
2 October XYZ Calls	40	$400	2 July XYZ Calls	35	$800	($800–$400)
2 October XYZ Calls	35	$800	2 July XYZ Calls	40	$300	($800–$300)
Net Proceeds		($500)				

diluted earnings per share smallest figure that can be obtained by computing a common stock earnings per share that reflects the possible exercise of all CONVERTIBLE securities. It is based on a broader denominator in the earnings per share fraction than basic earnings per share. Not only does the denominator include the weighted average of common stock outstanding, it also includes those shares that may result from convertible securities and stock options. Diluted earnings per share equals

$$\frac{\text{Net income less preferred dividends}}{\text{Weighted-average common stock outstanding} + \text{diluted securities}}$$

diluted shares number of shares of COMMON STOCK that would be outstanding if all convertible securities were converted to common.

dilution effect of adding to the number of shares outstanding, which reduces the share value to existing shareholders of earnings and assets.

direct foreign investment (DFI) *see* FOREIGN DIRECT INVESTMENT.

direct quote price of a unit of foreign currency expressed in the home country's currency: dollars per pound, dollars per yen, and so on. The direct and indirect quotations are reciprocals.

EXAMPLE:
On April 1, 2001, the direct quote for Japanese yen is $.007967 per yen if the home country is the United States.

$$\text{Direct quote} = \frac{1}{\text{Indirect quote}} = \frac{1}{125.52 \text{ yen}} = \$.007967 \text{ per yen}$$

SPOT (cash) rates, both direct and indirect, for April 1, 2001, are presented the following table.
See also INDIRECT QUOTE; AMERICAN TERMS; EUROPEAN TERMS.

FOREIGN EXCHANGE RATES (APRIL 1, 2001)

Nation	Rates for $1 million minimum $1 in foreign currency	Foreign currency in dollars
Argentina	.9996	1.0004
Australia	2.0542	.4868
Austria	15.706	.0637
Belgium	46.02	.0217
Brazil	2.1620	.4625
Britain	.7055	1.4174
Canada	1.5765	.6343
Chile	593.05	.001686
China	8.2779	.1208
Colombia	2307.50	.000433
Czech Republic	39.04	.0256
Denmark	8.4521	.1183
Dominican Republic	15.70	.0637
Egypt	3.8855	.2574
Euro	1.1409	.87650
Finland	6.7866	.1473
France	7.4847	.1336
Germany	2.2317	.4481
Greece	388.94	.002571
Hong Kong	7.7995	.1282
Hungary	302.01	.0033
India	46.628	.0214
Indonesia	10425.00	.000096

FOREIGN EXCHANGE RATES (APRIL 1, 2001) (cont.)

Nation	Rates for $1 million minimum $1 in foreign currency	Foreign currency in dollars
Ireland	.8990	1.1124
Israel	4.2060	.2378
Italy	2209.35	.000453
Japan	125.52	.007967
Jordan	.70998	1.4085
Lebanon	1513.75	.000661
Malaysia	3.7995	.2632
Mexico	9.4630	.105675
Netherlands	2.5153	.3976
New Zealand	2.4808	.4031
Norway	9.1252	.1096
Pakistan	60.75	.0165
Peru	3.524	.2838
Phillipines	49.42	.0202
Poland	4.08	.2451
Portugal	228.83	.004370
Russia	28.7400	.0348
Saudi Arabia	3.7504	.2666
SDR	.7932	1.26070
Singapore	1.8046	.5541
Slovak Republic	49.36	.0203
South Africa	8.0351	.1245
South Korea	1327.50	.000753
Spain	189.91	.005266
Sweden	10.4225	.0959
Switzerland	1.7416	.5742
Taiwan	32.84	.0305
Thailand	44.80	.02232
Turkey	1042.500	.000001
U.A.E.	3.6727	.2723
Uruguay	12.8080	.0781
Venezuela	707.7500	.0014

dirty price total price of a BOND, including accrued interest.

discount
1. purchase price for a bond bought below its FACE VALUE. *See also* BOND DISCOUNT.
2. manner in which Treasury bills are sold at less than FACE VALUE and are redeemed at face value.
3. taking into account all available good or bad news about the company's prospects in evaluating its current security price. It is called *discounting the news.*

discount bond bond whose current market price is below its FACE VALUE. An example is a bond having a face value of $1000 whose current market price is $980. Each year the investor receives interest on the face of the bond. The yield on this discount bond is calculated on the purchase price of $980 and not on the bond's face value of $1000. The discounted amount of $20 ($1000 − $980) to be received at maturity is included in the yield calculation. *See also* DEEP DISCOUNT BOND; ORIGINAL ISSUE DISCOUNT; ZERO-COUPON BOND; YIELD TO MATURITY.

discount broker broker who charges a reduced commission and does not provide investment advice. *See also* DISCOUNT HOUSE; FULL-SERVICE BROKER.

discount house securities brokerage firm providing basic security transaction services to the public at a lower charge, or discounted commissions. A discount house does not attempt to provide the same services a full-service and full-charge brokerage firm supplies. Thus, a discount house normally does not provide investment advice. Clients are expected to perform their own independent security research.

discount rate amount charged member banks for loans from the Federal Reserve Bank.

discount yield rate of return on investments that are purchased below FACE VALUE with the gain at sale or maturity representing interest income for federal income tax purposes. For example, the annual discount yield on securities such as T-bills is calculated using the formula:

$$\frac{P1 - P0}{P1} \times \frac{360}{n}$$

where P1 = redemption price (usually $10,000), P0 = purchase price, and n = maturity in days. T-bills sold at $9800 and maturing at $10,000 in 90 days give the following discount yield:

$$\frac{\$10,000 - \$9800}{\$10,000} \times \frac{360}{90} = \frac{\$200}{\$10,000} \times 4 = .08 = 8\%$$

discounted cash flow method of estimating the value or asking price of an investment, which emphasizes after-tax cash flows and the return on the invested dollars discounted over time to reflect a discounted yield.

discounting process of finding the present worth of a future sum of money. *See also* DISCOUNTED CASH FLOW; TIME VALUE OF MONEY.

discretionary account account in which the customer gives the broker or someone else discretion, which may be complete or within specific limits, as to the purchase and sale of securities or commodities including selection, timing, and price to be paid or received.

disinflation　　slowing down of the rate of inflation. This condition usually occurs during a RECESSION, when a lack of consumer demand prohibits retailers from passing on higher prices to consumers. *See also* DEFLATION.

disinvestment
1. withdrawal of the capital invested in a company or a foreign country.
2. selling off or closing down all or part of a foreign investment (for example, foreign subsidiaries) for some financial or other reason; also called *divestiture*.
3. sale of fixed assets without replacing them.
4. failure to properly maintain property, plant, and equipment.

distribution
1. selling, over a period of time, of a large block of stock without unduly depressing the market price; also called *professional selling*. A stock is under distribution when volume expands on days when price moves down.
2. payout by MUTUAL FUNDS and CLOSED-END investment companies of realized CAPITAL GAINS on securities contained in the underlying portfolio.
3. return of capital invested such as dividends to distribute part of the net income.
4. redemption from a retirement account.

distribution dates　　key dates related to a stock dividend. They are presented in chronological order.
　declaration date: the day a fund announces a distribution.
　record date: only those who are shareholders at the close of business on this date are entitled to the distribution. For T. Rowe Price funds, the record date is the same day as the declaration date.
　ex-date: the day the amount of the dividend or CAPITAL GAIN to be distributed is deducted from the fund's share price. On this day, the fund's NET ASSET VALUE will drop by the amount of the distribution. Market activity will also affect the fund's price on this day. In newspaper listings, an "x" appears before the fund's closing price on the ex-date.
　　If you reinvest distributions, the number of shares purchased with the distribution is calculated based on this day's share price.
　post date: although distributions are reinvested at the share price on the ex-date, they are not credited to your account until the post date, about three days later.
　pay date: the day when checks are mailed to those who receive distributions in cash.

distribution period　　period of time between the date a stock dividend is declared by the board of directors of a company and the date of record when the stockholder must officially own the stock to be entitled to the dividend.

divergence price of a security, bond, commodity, or index moving significantly in a direction that is either not confirmed or not accompanied by a similar move in a related market indicator. An example is the DJIA reaching a new high but the DOW JONES TRANSPORTATION AVERAGE not doing so.

diversifiable risk that part of the total risk of a security associated with such random events as lawsuits, strikes, winning or losing a major contract, and other events that are unique to a particular company; also called *controllable risk*, *company-specific risk*, or *unsystematic risk*. This type of risk can be diversified away and hence is not priced in a portfolio.

diversification spreading of investment money among many investment vehicles so as to reduce risk. Diversification is also offered by the securities of many individual companies because of the wide range of their activities. Investing in a mutual fund will also accomplish diversification. *See also* ASSET ALLOCATION; PORTFOLIO.

diversification cross investment *see* DIVERSIFICATION; INTERNATIONAL DIVERSIFICATION; PORTFOLIO DIVERSIFICATION.

diversified common stock fund mutual fund that invests in diversified PORTFOLIOS of COMMON STOCK to provide a wide range of income-growth combinations.

dividend distribution of earnings paid to STOCKHOLDERS based on the number of shares owned. The most typical type of dividend is a *cash dividend*. Dividends may be issued in other forms such as stock, property, and STRIP (note). Dividends are customarily paid quarterly. The board of directors of the company decides on how much dividends should be declared and in what form. The investor must include cash dividends received as taxable income.

EXAMPLE:
Company X has 4,000,000 common shares outstanding and declares a $.10 cash dividend per share. Total dividends will be $400,000.

dividend payout ratio dividend payment as a percentage of net earning of a company. It equals dividends per share divided by earnings per share. Generally speaking, newer and smaller companies pay a much lower percentage of earnings in dividends than larger, more mature companies. A company having a relatively large dividend payout ratio may have that much less capital for reinvestment purposes. Utilities commonly have high dividend payout ratios.

EXAMPLE:
If a company's net income is $1,000,000 and the cash dividends are $100,000 with 25,000 common shares, the dividend payout ratio is

$$\text{Dividends per share} = \$100,000/25,000 = \$4$$

$$\text{Earnings per share} = \$1,100,000/25,000 = \$40$$

$$\text{Dividend payout ratio} = \$4/\$40 = 10\%$$

DIVIDEND REINVESTMENT PLAN

dividend reinvestment plan
1. investment plan that allows stockholders to acquire shares through reinvestment of dividends, directly from the corporation and usually free of brokerage commissions. The shares may be available at a discount. In the case of public utilities, tax breaks are available on dividend reinvestment.
2. plan offered by a mutual fund to reinvest dividends without a service charge.

dividend yield   ratio providing an estimate of the return per share on a common or preferred stock investment based on the market price at the end of the reporting period. The ratio equals dividends per share divided by market price per share.

EXAMPLE:
Cash dividends are $80,000, market price per share is $10, and 80,000 shares are outstanding. The dividend yield is .10 ($1/$10).

Dividend yields of stocks are presented in stock tables in financial newspapers such as the *The Wall Street Journal* or *Investors Business Daily*.

Dogs of the Dow theory   investment approach of purchasing ten stocks included in the Dow Jones Industrial Average (DJIA) that have the highest dividend yield. In most cases, investors who bought the ten Dogs of last year outperformed the other twenty stocks in the DJIA in the next year. Dogs of the Dow do better because investors can buy them at depressed prices while receiving a higher DIVIDEND YIELD. Historically, the Dogs do much better the next year. To practice this strategy, the investor can either buy the ten stocks directly or buy a fund or UNIT INVESTMENT TRUST that does it. This approach can also be used in selecting the Dogs in a major index tracking stocks in a foreign country, such as on the LONDON STOCK EXCHANGE.

dollar cost averaging (DCA)   time diversified investment method in which a constant dollar amount of stock is bought at regularly scheduled dates. It is a CONSTANT DOLLAR PLAN. This approach is especially appropriate for BLUE CHIP stocks. Because the same dollar amount of stock is invested in each period, fewer shares are purchased at higher prices and more shares are bought at lower prices. This strategy typically results in a lower average cost per share. Average cost equals

Total investment / total number of shares

Dollar-cost averaging has been most effective for mutual fund investing, whose typically small investment minimums allow investors to implement this strategy easily in a cost-effective way. Many funds and brokerages make this process easy by allowing purchases through direct deductions from investors' checking accounts or paychecks. Investors may unknowingly be using this strategy as part of employer-sponsored savings plans such as 401(k) retirement programs. Many of these benefit plans routinely make equal purchases of assets at set periods, quietly accomplishing dollar-cost averaging. Dollar-cost averaging will work as long as prices of the fund targeted by the strategy rise over the long haul. The first table below shows how dollar-cost averaging works for a NO-LOAD mutual fund and compares it to a hypothetical situation with two other investment strategies: lump-sum up-front investment and lump-sum investment after savings.

DOLLAR-COSTING-BASED MUTUAL FUND PURCHASE PLAN

Period	Amount Invested	Share Price	Shares Purchased
1	$100	$12.50	8
2	100	8.00	12.5
3	100	10.00	10
4	100	8.00	12.5
5	100	10.00	10
6	100	12.50	8
7	100	14.28	7
8	100	12.50	8
9	100	16.67	6
10	100	20.00	5
	$1000	$124.45	87.0

Average share price = $124.45/10 = $12.45
Total shares owned = 87
Average share cost = $1000/87.0 shares = $11.49
Total market value now = 87 shares × $20 = $1740 (assuming a $20 market price per share)

LUMP-SUM UP-FRONT INVESTMENT

Period	Amount Invested	Share Price	Shares Purchased
1	$1000	$12.50	80
2	0	10.00	0
.			
10	0	20.00	0

Average share price = $12.45
Total shares owned = 80
Average share cost = $1000/80 shares = $12.50
Total market value now = 80 shares × $20 = $1600

LUMP-SUM INVESTMENT AFTER $1000 IS SAVED

Period	Amount Invested	Share Price	Shares Purchased
10	$1000	$20.00	50

Average share price = $20.00
Total shares owned = 50
Average share cost = $1000/50 shares = $20.00
Total market value now = 50 shares × $20 = $1000

Note that by the process of dollar-cost averaging, you have purchased 87 shares, now worth $20 apiece, for a total market value of $1740 ($20 × 87 shares). You have invested only $1000 over the period. In other words, your average share cost of $11.49 is lower than the average ($12.45) of the market price of the fund's shares during the periods in which they are accumulated. Therefore, you've actually made money through this process. It works because you bought more shares when they were cheap and fewer shares when they were expensive. Drawbacks to this method are (1) high transaction costs and (2) that it will not work when stock prices are moving in a continuous downward direction.

dollar indexes   measures of the value of the dollar, provided by the Federal Reserve Board (FRB), Morgan Guaranty Trust Company of New York, and Federal Reserve Bank of Dallas; also called CURRENCY INDEXES. They show different movements since they include different countries and are based on different concepts and methodologies. The data are provided in nominal values (market exchange rates) and in real values (purchasing power corrected for inflation). The FRB index is published in a press release and in the monthly *Federal Reserve Bulletin*; the Morgan index is published in the bimonthly *World Financial Markets*; and the FR Dallas index is published monthly in *Trade-Weighted Value of the Dollar*. The FRB and Morgan indexes include 10 and 18 industrial nations, respectively, and the FR Dallas index includes all of the 131 U.S. trading partners.

double bottom   chart pattern used in technical investment analysis when a STOCK or stock market drops to a certain level and then recovers, only to be followed by another drop in price to the same low. The bottom price is interpreted as a support line for the stock or market; however, if this support line is subsequently penetrated, then the analysis for the near-term future would be very BEARISH (see the following chart).

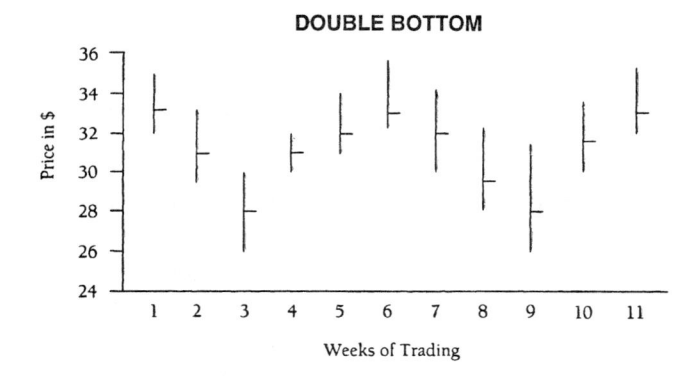

DOUBLE BOTTOM

[Chart showing price bars over 11 weeks of trading, price range $24-$36]

Weeks of Trading

double-digit inflation   yearly rate of INFLATION of 10% or higher.

double top   chart pattern used in technical investment analysis when a stock or security market rises to a certain price level and then falls, only to be followed by a subsequent rise to the previous high price. This double high is interpreted as a RESISTANCE LINE for the stock or market; however, if this price resistance level is penetrated in future trading, then the interpretation for the near term future would be very BULLISH (see the chart below).

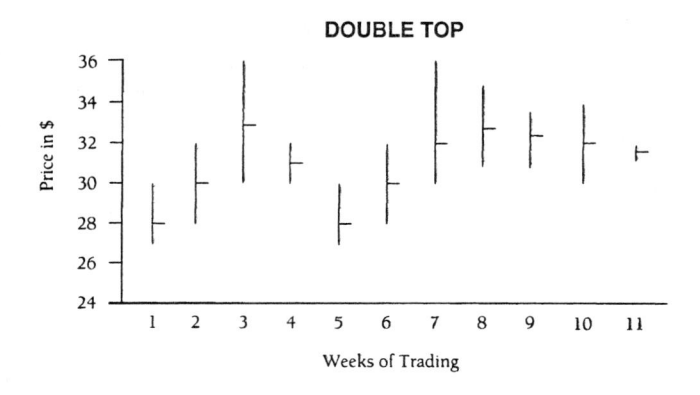

DOUBLE TOP

[Chart showing price bars over 11 weeks of trading, price range $24-$36]

Weeks of Trading

Dow Jones bond averages   mathematical averages of closing prices for groups of utility, industrial, and corporate bonds.

Dow Jones global stock indexes   grouping of indexes tracking stocks around the globe. The biggest index, the *Dow World*, tracks shares in 33 countries. The index is based on an equal weighted average of stock prices. A 100 base value was assigned to the U.S. index on June 30, 1982; a 100 base went to the rest of the world indexes for December 31, 1991. Indexes are tracked in both local currency and in U.S. dollars, though the dollar tracking contains far more analytical data such as a 52-week high and low and year-to-date percentage performance. The index appears daily in *The Wall Street Journal*. The index can be used to examine the difference between performances in various stock markets and BOURSES around the globe. That performance can be used to determine if shares in those countries are good values or poor values. In addition, stock indexes often hint how a country's economy is performing, with rising stock markets typically appearing in healthy economies. *Note:* Currency swings play an important role in calculating investment performance from foreign markets, so if one country's stock market is performing well but its currency is weak versus the dollar, a U.S. investor may still suffer. Conversely, a country with a strong currency and weak stock market may produce profits for U.S. investors despite the rocky climate for equities.

Dow Jones Industrial Average (DJIA) average developed by Charles Dow in 1885 to study market trends. It is the average of the closing prices of 30 representative BLUE CHIP stocks, which have been selected by *The Wall Street Journal* editors. The Dow is often viewed as a proxy for the overall market. DJIA was originally composed of 14 companies (12 railroads and 2 industrials). The rails, by 1897, were separated into their own Average, and 12 industrial companies of the day were selected for the Industrial Average. The number was increased to 20 in 1916, and to 30 in 1928. The stocks included in this Average have been changed from time to time to keep the list up to date, or to accommodate a merger. The only original issue still in the Average is General Electric.

Dow Jones Transportation Average established at the end of the nineteenth century with the new Industrial Average, it was originally called the Rail Average and was composed of 20 railroad companies. With the advent of the airlines industry, the Average was updated in 1970 and the name changed to Transportation Average.

Dow Jones Utility Average Utility Average of 20 companies. In 1929 utility companies were dropped from the Industrial Average. In 1938 the number of issues was reduced to the present 15.

Dow Theory theory of market analysis based upon the performance of the Dow Jones Industrial and Transportation stock price averages. The Theory says that a BULL market is supposed to continue as long as one average continues to make new highs that are "confirmed" by the other. A reversal is signaled when one average does not confirm the other. A BEAR market is supposed to continue as long as one average makes new lows that are confirmed by the other.

downside risk
1. investment RISK evaluation derived by estimating the total loss that could occur in a worst-case scenario. A variety of factors enters into such an evaluation including book value and net earnings as well as general market conditions.
2. company's risk of loss in a DOWNTURN in business activity. For example, an auto manufacturer has downside risk in an economic downturn because it cannot slash its fixed costs, which results from the capital-intensive nature of the industry.

downtick transaction of securities executed at a price below that in the preceding transaction; also called *minus tick*. For example, if a stock has been selling at $23 per share, the next transaction is a downtick if it is at $22.13. *See also* UPTICK.

downturn shift in the stock market cycle from increasing to decreasing. The stock market is in a downturn when it goes from a BULL to a BEAR market. The economy is in a downturn when it goes from expansion to recession.

drag along rights rights that enable a majority shareholder to force a minority shareholder to join in the sale of a company. The majority owner doing the dragging must provide minority shareholders the same price, terms, and conditions for the security being sold as any other seller. The drag along right is intended to protect the majority shareholder. Because some buyers are looking only to have complete control of a company, these rights help to remove minority owners and sell 100% of a company's securities to the buyer.

drag on returns (drag grade) negative impact on returns of three factors: sales charges, annual expenses, and portfolio turnover.

dragon bond U.S. dollar-denominated bond issued in the so-called "Dragon" economies of Asia, such as Hong Kong, Singapore, and Taiwan.

dual currency bond debt instrument in which principal is to be paid in one currency (such as Italian lira) and interest is to be paid in a different currency (such as French francs). The purpose may be to reduce exchange FLUCTUATIONS. Interest might be payable at FIXED EXCHANGE RATES.

dual listing listing of a stock or bond on more than one exchange. An example is a listing of a multinational stock on both a domestic stock exchange and a foreign stock exchange.

dual-purpose fund special type of CLOSED-END FUND. It differs from other investment companies in that it has a limited life and sells two classes of shares to investors. At its inception, equal dollar amounts of income and capital shares are sold, with the proceeds used to purchase a portfolio of assets as usual. However, the *income shareholders* receive all interest and dividends yielded by the assets, and at the termination date of the fund they receive a special redemption value. *Capital shareholders*, on the other hand, are entitled to all assets not received by the income shares; therefore, they receive everything remaining at the termination date.

dual trading facility admission to trading by a stock market or exchange of stock that is already traded on another stock market, and where the company does not raise any capital as part of the further admission process.

EXAMPLE:
When a corporation has raised capital and its shares are traded on NASDAQ, it can apply to EASDAQ for *dual trading facility status*, whereby it does not have to raise any capital on the EASDAQ market and its existing shares can also be traded on the EASDAQ market during the European trading day.

due diligence qualitative assessment of management's character and capability. Due diligence evaluation is similar to "kicking the tires" of the company by conducting plant tours, trade checks, and interviews with competitors, suppliers, customers, and employees. Comprehensive due diligence may also include an examination of the books and records, asset appraisals, reviews of the company's other debt obligations, legal and accounting affairs, internal controls, planned capital expenditures, and other matters that bear on the company's future success and profitability. Due diligence is a legal requirement in dealing with public offerings.

EXAMPLE:
It is a common practice for international fund managers to engage in due diligence for foreign companies through actual visitation.

duration attempt to measure risk in a bond by considering the maturity and the time pattern of cash inflows (for example, interest payments and principal). It is the weighted average of the term to maturity of a bond's cash flows. A simple example below illustrates the duration calculations.

EXAMPLE:
A bond pays a 7% coupon rate annually on its $1000 face value if it has three years until its maturity and has a YIELD TO MATURITY (YTM) of 6%. The computation of duration involves the following three steps:

Step 1: Calculate the present value of the bond for each year.

Step 2: Express present values as proportions of the price of the bond.

Step 3: Multiply proportions by years' digits to obtain the weighted average time.

(1) Year	(2) Cash flow	(3) PV factor @ 6% = T1 from Appendix A	(Step 1) (4) PV of Cash flow	(Step 2) (5) PV as proportion of price of bond	(Step 3) (6) Column (1) × Column (5)
1	$70	.943	$66.01	.0643	.0643
2	70	.890	62.30	.0607	.1214
3	1070	.840	898.80	.8750	2.6250
			$1027.11	1.0000	2.8107

This three-year bond's duration is a little over 2.8 years. Although duration is expressed in years, think of it as a percentage change. Thus, 2.8 years means this particular bond will gain (lose) 2.8% of its value for each 1 percentage drop (rise) in interest rates.

Note: (1) In all cases, a bond's duration is less than or equal to its term to maturity. Only a pure discount bond—that is, one with no coupon or SINKING FUND payments—has duration equal to the maturity; (2) the higher the D value, the greater the interest rate risk, since it implies a longer recovery period; (3) duration will not tell you anything about the credit quality or yield of your bonds, although some bonds (or bond funds) manage to produce top returns without undue risk. For example, Harbor Bond Fund has returned a respectable return—an annualized 11.5% over the past five years. Yet its duration is a middle-of-the-road 5.3 years. While rarely discussed in the media, it is the top figure that professional money managers watch when reviewing a bond portfolio. Owners of BOND FUNDS can get duration figures from the management company. Various reports by fund tracker Morningstar Inc. include duration figures for bond funds.

Note: An investor comparing two bond portfolios with equal yields but different durations might choose the one with the longer duration if he or she believed that interest rates were going to fall. That portfolio would likely produce more capital gains if rates did go lower. However, if an investor thought rates were going to rise, or the investor simply wanted to lower the risk-taking, he or she should choose the portfolio with the shorter duration. *See also* INTEREST RATE ELASTICITY.

Dutch auction   procedure in which a seller gradually lowers his or her price until a bid is met by the purchaser. Treasury bills are sold in this fashion.

Dutch auction preferred stock   ADJUSTABLE RATE PREFERRED STOCK whose dividend is derived every seven weeks in a DUTCH AUCTION of corporate bids. The buys and sells are at the FACE VALUE of the securities.

E

each way brokerage commissions earned on both the sale and purchase of a trade by the same broker.

EAFE (Europe, Australia, and Far East) Index compilation by Morgan Stanley Capital International (MSCI). The index is a value-weighted index of the equity performance of major foreign markets. The EAFE Index (pronounced EE-feh) is, in effect, a non-American world index of moe than 1000 stocks. It is considered the key "rest-of-the-world" index for U.S. investors, much as the DOW JONES INDUSTRIAL AVERAGE is for the American market. The index is used as a guide to the way U.S. shares fare against other markets around the globe. It also serves as a performance benchmark for international mutual funds that hold non-U.S. assets. Morgan Stanley also compiles indexes for most of the world's major stock markets as well as for many smaller, so-called emerging markets. In addition, there are Morgan Stanley indexes for each continent and for the entire globe. The index is quoted two ways: one in local currencies and a second in the U.S. dollar.

earnings announcements company's preliminary results of operations. This includes the most recent quarterly date announced as well as revenue, earnings, and EARNINGS PER SHARE information for that quarter.

earnings growth weighted average of the one-year earnings growth rates of the stocks in the fund. This calculation excludes stocks whose earnings changed from a loss to a gain and stocks whose earnings gains exceeded 999.99%.

earnings multiple *see* PRICE/EARNINGS (P/E) RATIO.

earnings multiplier *see* PRICE/EARNINGS (P/E) RATIO.

earnings per share (EPS) profit accruing to stockholders for each share held. In a simple capital structure, basic earnings per share equals:

$$\frac{\text{Net Income} - \text{Preferred Dividends}}{\text{Weighted-Average Common Stock Outstanding}}$$

In a complex capital structure, basic earnings per share and diluted earnings per share are presented. Diluted earnings per share considers the dilutive effect of stock options, warrants, and convertible securities. As such, diluted earnings per share will be less than basic earnings per share.

EXAMPLE:
Net income is $800,000, preferred dividends are $50,000, and weighted-average common stock outstanding equals 100,000. Basic earnings per share equals:

$$\frac{\$800,000 - \$50,000}{100,000 \text{ shares}} = \$7.50 \text{ per share}$$

See also BASIC EARNINGS PER SHARE.

earnings/price ratio EARNINGS PER SHARE of a security divided by its market price. It is the opposite of the price/earnings ratio; also called EARNINGS YIELD.

If a company has an earnings per share of $10 and a market price per share of $100, the earnings yield is 10% ($10/$100). The ratio is a measure of the yield on the stock. The higher the ratio, the better the yield.

earnings surprises company's announced net income for the reporting period, which is above or below that expected by analysts. Stock price will typically increase if the earnings report is better than anticipated with the opposite effect if the earnings report is less than that expected. In fact, if earnings reported are much lower than that being forecasted by securities' analysts, a drastic falloff in stock price may occur because of the disappointment. An example of a company that closely monitors earnings surprises is First Call Corporation (*www.firstcall.com*).

earnings yield *see* EARNINGS/PRICE RATIO.

easy money increase in the amount of money available for business and individual spending as a result of reduction in the interest rate in the economy. Easy money tends to encourage investment spending and promote economic growth, which can be inflationary. *See also* TIGHT MONEY.

EBIT (earnings before interest and tax) income generated by the company after costs of production (costs of goods sold) and overhead (SG&A or sales, general, and administrative costs) are deducted, but before financing charges or nonoperating gains; also called *operating income*. EBIT is important to look at because it shows the profit of the company from its underlying businesses without contributions (or deductions) from noncore operations (for example, disposals of land or shares), which may not recur, or from financial items (such as taxes), which can be variable. It is worth noting that accounting standards differ from country to country, as does treatment of nonoperating and financial items on an income statement. However, treatment of EBIT or operating income is almost universally the same. Thus, analyzing EBIT accomplishes two goals: (1) It helps to evaluate the strength of a company's core business franchise; and (2) eliminates distortions that may occur from

EBIT margin   EARNINGS BEFORE INTEREST AND TAX (EBIT) divided by revenues. This ratio measures the profitability of a company's core business, before nonoperating and financial items. The net margin (net income divided by revenues) also is a critical measure of profitability, but it can be misleading when comparing international companies because net income is impacted by things such as tax rates and financial income, which are treated differently from country to country.

EBITD (earnings before interest, tax, and depreciation)   same as EARNINGS BEFORE INTEREST AND TAX (EBIT) except it includes DEPRECIATION. Not all companies publish their depreciation figures but when available, analyzing EBITD can be even more useful than EBIT because it helps to smooth yet another potential difference in cross border accounting. Depreciation schedules may vary from country to country and this sometimes distorts income comparisons of international firms. By adding back depreciation to EBIT, we remove this potential distortion and can make more accurate cross border comparisons. In addition, since depreciation is a non-cash charge, EBITD gives us a better picture of the cash being generated by a company's core business than EBIT.

EBITDA (earnings before interest, tax, depreciation, and amortization)   same as EARNINGS BEFORE INTEREST, TAX, AND DEPRECIATION (EBITD) except it also includes amortization. International companies do not always publish amortization figures but they are the best measure to use for evaluating a company's core business rather than EBITD. Amortization also is one of those items that differs from country to country in how it is treated, and by adding it back to EBITD, it removes all potential distortions from this measure of operating income. EBITDA is often used by analysts to measure the cash flow or underlying cash-generating capability of a company.

economic indicators   indicators that attempt to size up where the economy seems to be headed and where it has been. Each month government agencies, including the Federal Reserve, and several economic institutions publish economic indicators. These may be broken down into six broad categories:
1. **Measures of overall economic performance**: These measures include GROSS DOMESTIC PRODUCT (GDP), personal income, plant and equipment expenditures, corporate profits, and inventories.
2. **Price indices**: Indices designed to measure the rate of inflation of the economy. The CONSUMER PRICE INDEX (CPI), the best-known inflation gauge, is used as the cost-of-living index, which labor contracts and social security are tied to. The PRODUCER PRICE INDEX (PPI) covers raw materials and semifinished goods and measures prices at the early stage of the distribution system. It is the one

that signals changes in the general price level, or the CPI, some time before they actually materialize. The GNP implicit deflator, especially personal consumption expenditure deflator, is the third index of inflation that is used to separate price changes in GDP calculations from real changes in economic activity. The fourth, watched closely by the Fed chairman, is the EMPLOYMENT COST INDEX, which measures changes in wages, salaries, and benefits paid by business. This tells the markets if businesses are getting squeezed by higher labor costs, which are bad for profits.

3. **Indices of labor market conditions**: Indicators covering labor market conditions, which are unemployment rate, average workweek of production workers, applications for unemployment compensation, and hourly wage rates.
4. **Money and credit market indicators**: Most widely reported in the media are money supply, consumer credit, the Dow Jones Industrial Average, and the Treasury bill rate.
5. **Index of leading indicators**: This most widely publicized signal caller is made up of 11 data series. They are money supply, business formation, stock prices, vendor performance, average workweek, new orders, contracts, building permits, inventory change, layoff rate, and change in sensitive prices. They monitor certain business activities that can signal a change in the economy.
6. **Measures for major product markets**: Measures designed to be indicators for segments of the economy such as housing, retail sales, steel, and automobile. Examples are ten-day auto sales, advance retail sales, housing starts, and construction permits. It is important to note that indicators are only signals. They tell an investor something about the economic conditions in the country, a particular area, and industry, and, over time, the trends that seem to be shaping up.

Note: Economic indicators can be viewed and downloaded on-line (for example, *www.economy.com*).

See also INFLATION.

economic risk chance of loss due to economic conditions. Economic risks include inflation risk, purchasing power risk, foreign exchange risk, and interest rate risk. *See also* RISK.

economic value added (EVA) the operating profit that a multinational company or its division is able to earn above some minimum rate of return on its assets. A registered trademark of Stern Steward & Company, economic value added (EVA) is one of the two well-known *financial metrics* (measures of performance) of an MNC or its affiliates; also called *residual income*. The other is CASH FLOW RETURN ON INVESTMENT (CFROI). EVA is the value created by a company in excess of the cost of capital for the investment base. It attempts to determine whether management has, in fact, added value to the entity over and above what the providers of capital (both credit and equity holders) to the firm *require*. The formula is:

EVA = Net operating profit after taxes −

(weighted average cost of capital × Capital employed)

Improving EVA can be achieved in three ways: (1) invest capital in high-performing projects; (2) use less capital; (3) increase profit without using more capital.

Economist Commodity Price Index   geometric weighted average based on the significance in international trade of SPOT prices of major commodities. The index is designed to measure inflation pressure in the world's industrial powers. It includes only commodities that freely trade in open markets, eliminating such items as iron and rice. Also, this index does not track precious metal or oil prices. The commodities tracked are weighted by their export volume to developed economies. The index information may be obtained from Reuters News Services or in *The Economist* magazine. The index may be used as a reflection of worldwide commodities prices, enabling the investor to determine the attractiveness of specific commodities. The investor may enter into futures contracts. The indicators also may serve as barometers of global inflation and global interest rates.

EDGAR   *see* ELECTRONIC DATA GATHERING, ANALYSIS, AND RETRIEVAL.

effective interest rate (effective annual yield)

1. YIELD TO MATURITY.
2. The EFFECTIVE ANNUAL YIELD, better known as the ANNUAL PERCENTAGE RATE (APR). Different types of investments use different compounding periods. For example, most bonds pay interest semiannually; banks generally pay interest quarterly. If a financial manager wishes to compare investments with different compounding periods, he or she needs to put them on a common basis. The annual percentage rate (APR), or effective annual rate, is used for this purpose and is computed as follows:

$$APR = \left(1 + \frac{i}{m}\right)^m - 1.0$$

where i = the stated, nominal, or quoted rate, and m = the number of compounding periods per year.

EXAMPLE:
If the nominal rate is 6%, compounded quarterly, the APR is

$$APR = \left(1 + \frac{i}{m}\right)^m - 1.0 = \left(1 + \frac{0.06}{4}\right)^4 - 1.0 = (1.015)^4 - 1.0$$
$$= 1.0614 - 1.0 = 0.0614 = 6.14\%$$

This means that if one bank offered 6% with quarterly compounding, while another offered 6.14% with annual compounding, they would both be paying the same effective rate of interest.

3. Annual percentage rate (APR) also is a measure of the cost of credit, expressed as a yearly rate. It includes interest as well as other financial charges such as loan origination and certain closing fees. The lender is required to disclose the APR. It provides a good basis for comparing the cost of loans, including mortgage plans.

effective rate of return *see* EFFECTIVE INTEREST RATE (EFFECTIVE ANNUAL YIELD).

efficient frontier set of all efficient portfolios for various levels of risk; the investor can receive a maximum return for a given level of risk or a minimum risk for a given level of return.

efficient market market in which all available and relevant information is already reflected in the prices of traded securities. The term is most frequently applied to foreign exchange markets and securities markets. It is very difficult for investors to outperform the market. If competition exists and transaction costs are low, prices tend to respond rapidly to new information, and speculation opportunities quickly dissipate. The efficient market hypotheses have been subjected to numerous empirical tests, but with mixed results. For example, the more recent studies seriously challenge the view of unbiased FORWARD EXCHANGE RATES.

efficient portfolio portfolio that provides the best expected RETURN for a given level of risk. Efficient portfolio is the central gist of Markowitz's PORTFOLIO THEORY. The efficient portfolio theory claims that rational investors behave in a way reflecting their aversion to taking increased risk without being compensated by an adequate increase in expected return. Also, for any given expected return, most investors will prefer a lower risk and, for any given level of risk, prefer a higher return to a lower return.

Electronic Communication Network (ECN) electronic system that brings buyers and sellers together for the electronic execution of trades. It disseminates information to interested parties about the orders entered into the network and allows these orders to be executed.

electronic data gathering, analysis, and retrieval (EDGAR) service that the Securities and Exchange Commission uses to transmit company documents to investors. Those documents, which are available via Smart Edgar service, include 10-Qs (quarterly reports), 8-Ks (significant developments such as the sale of a company unit), and 13-Ds (disclosures by parties who own 5% or more of a company's shares).

Elliott wave analysis named after Ralph Nelson Elliott, an approach to market analysis that is based on repetitive wave patterns and the Fibonacci number sequence. Inspired by the DOW THEORY and by observations found throughout nature, Elliott concluded that the movement of the stock market could be predicted by observing and

EMERGING MARKETS

identifying a repetitive pattern of waves. In fact, Elliott believed that all human activities, not only the stock market, were influenced by these identifiable series of waves. With the help of C. J. Collins, Elliott's ideas received the attention of Wall Street in a series of articles published in *Financial World* magazine in 1939.

emerging markets stock markets of countries whose markets or economies tend to grow at considerably faster rates over the coming years than the economies of industrial nations. Emerging markets attract foreign investors because their potential for rapid economic growth is better than in more mature markets. However, the risks, both economic and political, are high. *Note:* One way to get exposure to emerging markets is through UNIT INVESTMENT TRUSTS or regional funds that specialize in this type of investment.

Employment Cost Index (ECI) most comprehensive and refined measure of underlying trends in employee compensation as a cost of production. It measures the cost of labor and includes changes in wages and salaries and employer costs for employee benefits. ECI tracks wages and bonuses, sick and vacation pay, plus benefits such as insurance, pension, and social security and unemployment taxes from a survey of 18,300 occupations at 4500 sample establishments in private industry and 4200 occupations within about 800 state and local governments. *See also* INFLATION.

entry point at which a trader gets into a position in the market. *See also* EXIT.

EP/ADR earnings per AMERICAN DEPOSITARY RECEIPT (ADR); net income divided by total ADRs outstanding.

equalizing dividend extra distribution the shareholders will receive to make up for a delay, when the customary date of a dividend is altered. An example is when a dividend that is usually paid on July 1 is delayed to August 1.

equipment trust certificate debt instrument used to provide funds for the acquisition of new equipment. The holder of the certificate has a secured interest in the asset in the event of corporate default. The trustee (usually a bank) has title to the equipment until the bond is paid. These certificates are sometimes issued by transportation companies (for example, a shipping company).

equity ownership interest of common and preferred stockholders in a company; also refers to the excess value of securities over the debit balance in a margin account.

equity instrument ownership interest in a business.

equivalent before-tax yield yield on a tax-free bond (such as a municipal bond) on a before-tax basis. It is often computed to see what the yield equivalent would be on a comparable taxable corporate bond.

EXAMPLE:
A triple-tax-free municipal bond has a yield of 6%. The taxpayer has a 40% tax rate combined for federal, state, and city purposes. The equivalent before-tax yield equals

$$\frac{\text{Tax-free interest rate}}{1 - \text{text rate}}$$

$$\frac{.06}{1-.4} = \frac{.06}{.6} = 10\%$$

equivalent bond yield comparison of yields on bonds with coupons and discount yields.

EXAMPLE:
If a 10%, 180-day T-bill with a FACE VALUE of $10,000 costs $9500, the equivalent bond yield is 10.67%, calculated as follows:

$$\frac{\$500}{\$9500} \times \frac{365}{180} = 10.67\%$$

EUREX European Exchange, which is a fully electronic trading system.

EURIBOR interbank offered rate for short-term deposits in EUROS. Euribor is determined by an association of European banks.

euro new currency that is intended to unite 17 European economies. When the euro conversion is complete, perhaps by 2002, investors will notice these changes in Western European investments: (1) Stocks will be priced and settled in euro only; (2) government debt will be quoted in euro only; (3) stock and bond deals, such as mergers, will be stated in euro; (3) financial statements from companies and governments will be in euro.

eurobond bond underwritten by a multinational syndicate of banks and placed outside of the countries of the issuer and of the currency denomination. The issue thus escapes national restrictions.

Euroclear owned and operated by J. P. Morgan from Brussels, an electronic clearing system of EUROBONDS. Euroclear handles about two-thirds of the total eurobond volume.

eurocurrency dollar or other freely convertible currency outside the country of the currency in which funds are denominated. A U.S. dollar-denominated loan, deposit, and bond in Europe is called a EURODOLLAR. There are Eurosterling (British pounds deposited in banks outside the U.K.), Euromarks (Deutschemarks deposited outside Germany), and Euroyen (Japanese yen deposited outside Japan).

eurocurrency market interbank market for short-term borrowing and lending in a currency outside the home country; for example, borrowing and lending of U.S. dollars outside the United States.

Thus, it is an offshore market escaping national regulations. This is the largest money market for the major currencies.

euro-commercial paper (euro-CP or ECP) short-term notes of an MNC or bank, sold on a discount basis in the EUROCURRENCY MARKET. The proceeds of the issuance of euro-commercial papers at a discount by borrowers is computed as follows:

$$\text{Market price} = \frac{\text{Face value}}{1 + \left[\left(\frac{N}{360}\right) \times \left(\frac{Y}{100}\right)\right]}$$

where Y = yield per annum
N = days remaining till maturity

EXAMPLE:
The proceeds from the sale of a $10,000 FACE VALUE 90-day issue of euro-CP priced to yield 8% per annum (reflecting current market yields on similar debt securities for comparable credit ratings) would be:

$$\$10,000 / \{1 + [(90/360) \times (8/100)]\} = \$9,803.90$$

eurodeposit *see* EUROMARKET DEPOSITS.

Euro Depositary Receipt (EDR) as with other depositary receipts, a certificate representing ownership of the issuer's underlying shares. The EDR is denominated and quoted in EUROS.

eurodollar simply a U.S. dollar deposit in a bank outside the United States. Eurodollars are not some strange banknotes. They are so called since they originated in Europe, but eurodollars are really any dollars deposited in any part of the world outside the United States. They represent claims held by foreigners for U.S. dollars. Typically, these are time deposits ranging from a few days up to one year. These deposit accounts are extensively used abroad for financial transactions such as short-term loans, the purchase of dollar certificates of deposit, or the purchase of dollar bonds (called EUROBONDS) often issued by U.S. firms for the benefit of their overseas operations. In effect, eurodollars are an international currency.

eurodollar deposits *see* EUROMARKET DEPOSITS.

euromarket deposits dollars deposited outside of the United States; also called EURODEPOSITS or EURODOLLAR DEPOSITS. Other important eurocurrency deposits include the euroyen, the euromark, the eurofranc, and the eurosterling.

euromarkets offshore money and capital markets in which the currency of denomination is not the official currency of the country where the transaction takes place; also called EUROCURRENCY MARKETS. They are the international markets that are engaged in the lending and borrowing of U.S. dollars and other major currencies outside their countries of origin to finance international trade and investment. The main financial instrument used in the Eurocurrency market for long-term investment purposes is the EUROBOND. Despite its name the market is not restricted to European currencies or financial centers. It began as the eurodollar market in the late 1950s.

euronote short- to medium-term unsecured debt securities issued by multinational companies outside the country of the currency in which it is denominated.

EURO.NM a pan-European grouping of regulated stock markets dedicated to high-growth companies.

EURO.NM All Share Index index (*http://www.euronm.com*) based at 1000 in 1997. EURO.NM member markets are Le Nouveau Marche (Paris Stock Exchange) Neuer Market (Deutsche Borse), EURO.NM Amsterdam (Amsterdam Exchanges), EURO.NM Belgium (Brussels Exchange), and Nuovo Mercata (Italian Exchange).

European Association of Securities Dealers (EASD) association of securities houses, investment banks, VENTURE CAPITAL firms, professional advisors, and others formed to promote the development of securities markets in Europe for growth companies. The creation of the EASDAQ stock market was one of its first initiatives. It is headquartered in Brussels.

European Association of Securities Dealers Automated Quotation (EASDAQ) only pan-European stock market that offers international growth companies and investors seamless cross-border trading, clearing, and settlement within a unified market infrastructure. EASDAQ (*http://www.easdaq.com*) is a fully regulated market, independent of any national exchange. Trading takes place through member firms in 15 countries.

European currency unit (ECU) theoretical currency basket constructed as a weighted average of several European currencies. It is being replaced by the euro.

European Monetary System (EMS) formal association of European countries founded by the Treaty of Rome in 1957; formerly known as the EEC.

European option option that can be exercised only at EXPIRATION; also called *European-type option*.

European terms FOREIGN EXCHANGE quotations for the U.S. dollar, expressed as foreign currency price of one U.S. dollar. For example, 1.50 DM/$ may also be called *German terms*. *See also* AMERICAN TERMS.

European Union (EU) formal arrangement linking some, but not all, of the currencies of the EU.

Eurotop 100 Index index that measures the collective performance of the most actively traded stocks on Europe's major stock exchanges and is designed to be representative of the European stock market as a whole. The index comprises the 100 most actively traded stocks in nine European countries: Belgium, France, Germany, Italy, the Netherlands, Spain, Sweden, Switzerland, and the United Kingdom. The index is weighted based on each country's total stock market capitalization and gross national product, a weighting that determines a country's total number of stocks as well as the number of shares of the stocks represented in the index. The index's aggregate price is in EUROPEAN CURRENCY UNITS (ECUS). Country weightings are based on each nation's exchange capitalization at the end of the previous calendar year. Information on this index can be obtained at *www.amex.com* and information on trading in options tied to this index runs in *The Wall Street Journal*.

even lot standard securities or commodities trading unit; also called ROUND LOT. For example, the standard New York Stock Exchange common stock trading unit is 100 shares, and most trades are in multiples of 100 shares.

event arbitrage fund type of HEDGED FUND that takes bets on some event specific to a company or security. It includes ARBITRAGE in case of mergers and acquisitions (M&A), for example, buying the target company and selling the acquiring company.

ex-rights without the rights.

excess returns *see* ALPHA.

exchange privilege right to transfer investments from one fund to another, generally within the same fund group, at nominal cost; also called *switching privilege*.

exchange risk SEE CURRENCY RISK.

ex-dividend synonym for "without dividend." Stocks and registered bonds have record dates for the payment of dividends and interest. The New York Stock Exchange sets dates a few days ahead of each one to allow for the physical transfer of the securities. Investors who buy stocks before this day receive this dividend; investors who buy after it do not.

exercise actual fulfillment of the terms of the option contract. The specified number of shares of the underlying stock are bought or sold at the price predetermined in the option contract.

exercise price *see* STRIKE PRICE.

exhaustion gap relatively wide gap in the price of a stock or commodity that occurs near the end of a strong directional move in the price. These gaps are quickly closed, most often within two to five days, which helps to distinguish them from *runaway gaps*, which are not usually covered for a considerable length of time.

exit point at which a trader closes out of a trade. *See also* ENTRY.

exit fee   *see* BACK-END LOAD.

expected return
1. rate of return that an investor expects to get on an investment.
2. average of all the predicted returns on an investment.

expense ratio   measure of how much it costs to own a mutual fund. Other than commissions or other sales fees, these costs are not directly billed to the investors, which makes them hard to follow. These expenses, from the fund's legal bills to the manager's profit, are taken out of the fund's NET ASSET VALUE. The ratio reflects the various expenses charged against the value of the assets in a fund. These expenses include management fees paid to the fund company, the cost of running the fund, and added charges for marketing the fund, which are called 12b-1 fees. They are totaled and then divided by the total assets in the fund. The ratio equates to the amount the fund's total return is reduced in comparison to directly owning the same securities. The expense ratio does not include sales commissions or the fund's costs of trading securities. To evaluate a fund, an investor would look at his or her fund's total annual expenses and then compare the costs with the industry-wide averages. For example, the industry-wide ratios as of June 2000 are: Equity funds, 0.93%; Taxable bond funds, 1.03%; Tax-exempt bonds, 0.69%; Money-market funds, 0.60%.

expiration
1. final date stipulated in a letter of credit in which the required documents must be presented to the bank issuing the letter for the purpose of guaranteeing payment.
2. date a contract no longer is effective.
3. last day one can exercise an option. If the option is not exercised, it becomes worthless and the investor has lost his or her entire investment. *Expiration cycle* refers to the expiration dates associated with short-term options trading. Options are traded in three-, six-, and nine-month contracts.

expiration date   *see* EXPIRATION.

expiry   EXPIRATION DATE of a derivative security.

exponential smoothing   mathematical, statistical methodology of forecasting that assumes future price action is a weighted average of past periods; a mathematical series in which greater weight is given to more recent price action. It uses a weighted average of past data as the basis for a forecast. The procedure gives heaviest weight to more recent information and smaller weights to observations in the more distant past. The reason for this is that the future is more dependent upon the recent past than on the distant past.

expropriation   forced takeover of foreign-owned assets by a government without compensation (or with inadequate compensation).

If it is not followed by prompt, adequate, and effective compensation, it is called *confiscation*.

extra   *see* EXTRA DIVIDEND.

extra dividend   bonus dividend paid to shareholders on top of the customary dividend. Such a payment is made after an unusually profitable year. Some companies give the usual dividend in cash, and the extra dividend in stock.

F

face amount *see* FACE VALUE.

face interest rate stated rate of interest due on a bond, note, or mortgage. The face interest rate is calculated on the face amount of the security. It may differ from the effective rate and YIELD TO MATURITY depending on whether the security was purchased at a discount or premium for the face amount. *See also* BOND YIELD; DISCOUNT; EFFECTIVE INTEREST RATE; YIELD.

face value nominal (par) amount of a debt obligation (for example, bond, mortgage, note) or equity security as stated on the instrument or certificate. It excludes interest and dividends. Bonds are typically in denominations of $1000. State and city municipal bonds are usually stated in $5000 face values. The face value of an instrument is often different from its issuance price; for example, a bond may be issued at a bond discount or bond premium. Also, after issuance the going market price of an instrument will typically differ from its face (maturity) value. At maturity, the debt instrument will be redeemed at its face amount. The nominal amount of a share of stock represents its par value or stated value. Interest on a bond is computed based on its face value; for example, a $100,000, 8% bond will pay annual interest of $8000.

fair market value
1. amount that could be received on the sale of a security in the market. There are willing and financially capable buyers and sellers who have informed knowledge. No unusual circumstances exist such as emergencies.
2. appraisal amount derived by an independent appraiser.

fair value
1. price negotiated at *arm's length* between a willing buyer and a willing seller, each acting in his or her own best interest.
2. theoretical value of a security based on current market conditions. The fair value is such that no ARBITRAGE opportunities exist.
3. FAIR MARKET VALUE of a multinational company's activities that is used as a basis to determine the tax.
4. "proper" value of the spread between the Standard & Poor's 500 futures and the actual S&P Index that makes no economic difference to investors whether they own the futures or the actual stocks that make up the S&P 500. Their buy and sell decisions will be driven by other factors. Through a complex formula using current short-term interest rates and the amount of time left until the futures contract expires, one can determine what the spread between the S&P futures and the cash "should" be. The formula for determining the fair value

$$F = S[1+(i-d)t/360]$$

where F = breakeven futures price, S = spot index price, i = interest rate (expressed as a money market yield), d = dividend rate (expressed as a money market yield), and t = number of days from today's spot value date to the value date of the futures contract.

fall out of bed   vernacular term used in the stock market to describe a precipitous decline in the market price of a particular security.

fallen angels   bonds that were at the date of issuance investment grade but have since fallen to below investment grade because of perceived lower quality. An example is a bond that has gone when issued from A to its present rating of C. A BENCHMARK of below investment grade is one that is not higher than BB.

family of funds   group of mutual funds, all with different investment objectives, that are under the same management company. Shareholders can switch between the funds, sometimes at no charge, as their investment objectives and perceptions change.

Federal funds rate   federal or *Fed funds rate* is the rate that bankers charge one another for overnight loans, although the Fed heavily manages this rate as well. The Fed funds rate is the major tool that the nation's central bank, the Federal Reserve, has to manage interest rates. Changing the target for the Fed funds rate is done when the Fed wants to use monetary policy to alter economic patterns.

Federal National Mortgage Association (FNMA)   government-sponsored corporation engaged in the buying and selling of FHA, FHDA, or VA mortgages; also known as *Fannie Mae*.

Federal Reserve trade-weighted dollar   INDEX that measures the currencies of ten foreign countries: the United Kingdom, Germany, Japan, Italy, Canada, France, Sweden, Switzerland, Belgium, and the Netherlands. The index is weighted by each currency's base exchange rate, and then averaged on a geometric basis. This weighting process indicates relative significance in overseas markets. The base year was 1973. The index reflects the currency units of more than 50% of U.S. purchases from principal trading countries. The index is published by the Federal Reserve System and is found in its *Federal Reserve Bulletin* or at various Federal Reserve Internet sites such as *http://woodrow.mpls.frb.fed.us/economy*.

52-week highs   listing and number of stocks that have reached their new high prices in daily trading for the current 52-week period. If new highs significantly exceed new lows, this reflects a positive sign for the stock market.

52-week lows   listing and number of stocks that have reached their new lows in daily trading for the current 52-week period. If new lows significantly exceed new highs, this is a negative indicator for the stock market.

fill   to execute by a broker a client's order to purchase or sell a security. The order is satisfied when such security is supplied. A partial fill occurs if less than the amount of the order is supplied.

fill-or-kill order (FOK)   buy or sell order in the security and commodity market by a client to the broker either to execute the order immediately at the specified price limit or to cancel it entirely. Although fill-or-kill instructions are normally buy orders, they can also be sell orders. Fill-or-kill orders are useful for large-quantity executions in which a market order could cause a measurable price change in the security or commodity being traded. This instruction was more commonly used 10 or 15 years ago. *Note:* Ironically, fill-or-kill orders might slow down the processing of an order, because such orders must be handled "manually" rather than through an automated system that generally fills orders within a few seconds. *See also* ALL OR NONE; DAY ORDER; GOOD-TILL-CANCELLED ORDER; IMMEDIATE-OR-CANCEL ORDER.

financial adviser   professional who gives professional financial advice and may also sell a particular financial and investment product. The financial adviser should be knowledgeable in investments, tax planning, insurance, estate planning, or similar fields. *See also* FINANCIAL PLANNER.

financial analysis   application and transformation of financial data into a form that can be used to monitor and evaluate an entity's financial position, to plan future financing, and to evaluate the size of the entity and its rate of growth. Financial analysis includes the use of financial ratios and the analysis of cash flows. *See also* FUNDAMENTAL ANALYSIS.

financial analyst   *see* ANALYST.

financial asset   cash, receivables, contractual right to exchange other financial instruments, or equity instrument of another company.

financial derivative   *see* DERIVATIVE FINANCIAL INSTRUMENTS.

financial futures   type of futures contract in which the underlying commodities are financial assets such as debt securities, foreign currencies, or market baskets of common stocks.

financial information services   services providing historical, financial, market and economic information, and current stock market prices and financial news. Information is obtained through a diskette or an on-line database with a modem.

financial institutions institutions, such as banks, that serve as intermediaries between suppliers and users of funds. In general, they are wholesalers and retailers of funds. It is in the FINANCIAL MARKET that entities demanding funds are brought together with those having surplus funds.

financial instrument cash, an ownership interest in another company, or a contract to deliver cash or another financial instrument or exchange financial instruments. A financial instrument may be by class, risk, business activity, or other classification appropriate by company policy.

financial intermediaries *see* FINANCIAL INSTITUTIONS; FINANCIAL MARKETS.

financial leverage portion of an entity's assets financed with debt instead of equity and therefore involving contractual interest and principal obligations. Financial leverage benefits investors as long as the borrowed funds generate a return in excess of the cost of borrowing, although the increased risk can offset the general cost of capital. For this reason, financial leverage is popularly called TRADING ON EQUITY.

financial markets markets in which companies demanding funds are brought together with those having surplus funds. Financial markets provide a mechanism through which the financial manager obtains funds from a wide range of sources, including financial institutions. The financial markets are composed of money markets and capital markets. Money markets are the markets for short-term (less than one year) debt securities. Examples of money market securities include U.S. Treasury bills, commercial paper, and negotiable certificates of deposit issued by government, business, and financial institutions. Capital markets are the markets for long-term debt and corporate stocks. The New York Stock Exchange, which handles the stocks of many of the larger corporations, is an example of a major capital market. The American Stock Exchange and the regional stock exchanges are other examples. In addition, securities are traded through the thousands of brokers and dealers on the OVER-THE-COUNTER (OTC) MARKET, a term used to denote all buying and selling activities in securities that do not occur on an organized stock exchange.

financial planner one who is engaged in providing personal financial planning services to individuals. He or she may be an independent professional or may be affiliated with a large investment, insurance, accounting, or other institution. Financial planners come from a variety of backgrounds and therefore may hold a variety of degrees and licenses. Some take specialized training in financial planning and earn credentials such as certified financial planner (CFP) or CHARTERED FINANCIAL CONSULTANT (ChFC). Others may hold degrees or registrations such as attorney (JD), chartered life underwriter (CLU), or certified public accountant (CPA).

To become a CFP, a designation conferred by the Certified Financial Planners Board of Standards (Phone: (303) 830–7500; Web: *www.CFP-Board.org*), a candidate must take a two-year course. The six parts of the course, each capped by a three-hour test, are the following: introduction to financial planning; risk management (insurance); investments; tax planning and management; retirement planning and employee benefits; and estate planning. The candidate must pass a two-day exam covering more than 100 financial planning topics, three to five years of financial planning work experience is also required. Other financial planning and investment designations are described below.

Certified Public Accountant (CPA): CPAs must have a bachelor's degree, pass a national exam, and continually keep up with changing tax laws. They should also belong to the American Institute of Certified Public Accountants. Phone: (888) 777-7077; Web: *www.aicpa.org*.

Chartered Financial Analyst (CFA): The most prestigious designation in financial planning and analysis, it is earned by securities analysts, money managers, and investment advisers who complete a rigorous program and tests on investments and securities. CFAs must pass three tests that require expertise in investing. Emphasis is on financial analysis and portfolio management. They must have a bachelor's degree and three years of experience in the financial sector; awarded by the Association for Investment Management and Research. Phone: (800) 247-8132; Web: *www.aimr.org*.

Chartered Financial Consultant (ChFC): Must have three years of experience in financial services and must complete a ten-course curriculum that focuses on comprehensive financial planning issues; awarded by American College in Bryn Mawr, Pennsylvania. For information, call the Society of Financial Service Professionals. Phone: (610) 526-2500; Web: *www.financialpro.org*.

Chartered Life Underwriter (CLU): Awarded to life insurance agents; must complete ten insurance-related courses. Awarded by American College in Bryn Mawr, Pennsylvania. For information, call the Society of Financial Service Professionals. Phone: (610) 526-2500; Web: *www.financialpro.org*.

Enrolled Agent (EA): Must pass a two-day tax exam and background check, both administered by the Internal Revenue Service, or an individual may become an enrolled agent if he or she has worked for the IRS for at least five years in a job where he or she applied and interpreted IRS provisions, codes, and regulations. The applicant should be a member of the National Association of Enrolled Agents. Phone: (800) 424-4339; Web: *www.naea.org*.

Personal Financial Specialist (PFS): Awarded to CPAs who have at least three years of financial planning experience, pass a six-hour financial planning exam, and complete 72 hours of continuing education every three years. They must be members of the American

Institute of Certified Public Accountants. Phone: (888) 777-7077; Web: *www.aicpa.org*.

Registered Investment Adviser (RIA): Anyone can become an RIA by registering with the Securities and Exchange Commission, filing a form, and paying a fee. An RIA who manages money only in a NO-LOAD (MUTUAL) FUND for a percentage of assets is not required to register with the National Association of Securities Dealers or the state. Phone: (800) 289-9999; Web: *www.nasdr.com*.

Registered Representative: A stockbroker; must pass exams administered by the National Association of Securities Dealers and also must pass any exams required by the state. All registered representatives—including financial planners—who execute, buy, or sell orders for mutual funds, stocks, bonds, commodities, or other securities for clients for compensation must be licensed by the appropriate state securities agency and registered with the NASD. Phone: (800) 289-9999; Web: *www.nasdr.com*.

A financial planner may assist the client in the following ways:
- assess the client's financial history, such as tax returns, investments, retirement plans, wills, and insurance policies.
- help the client decide on a financial plan, based on his or her personal and financial goals, history, and preferences.
- identify financial areas in which the client may need help, such as building up retirement income or improving investment returns.
- prepare a financial plan based on the client's individual situation and discuss it thoroughly with him or her in plain English.
- help the client implement the financial plan, including referring him or her to specialists such as attorneys, investment counselors, bankers, and certified financial planners, if necessary.
- review the client's situation and financial plan periodically and suggest changes in the program when needed.

financial planning process of developing and implementing plans to achieve financial goals.

financial planning software personal finance computer programs that keep track of income and expenses by budget category, reconcile accounts, store tax records, figure net worth, track stocks and bonds, and print checks and financial reports. Some programs are sophisticated enough to generate a detailed, long-term personal financial plan covering planning for college education, investment planning, and retirement planning. Examples of financial planning software are *Quicken* and *Managing Your Money*.

financial position financial health of a person or business entity as presented in the BALANCE SHEET. Financial position is typically expressed in terms of net worth (assets less liabilities).

financial risk
  personal: RISK a person has of running into financial problems and/or incurring financial losses. An example is an individual who has most of his or her funds invested in JUNK BONDS.
  corporate: portion of total risk resulting from using debt. The greater the proportion of debt to equity the firm has, the greater is its financial risk.

financial statement analysis approach used by lenders and investors to appraise the past, current, and projected financial condition and performance of a company. *Ratio analysis* is the most important type of financial analysis. It provides relative measures of a company's financial condition and operating performance. *Horizontal analysis* is used to evaluate the trend in the accounts over the years. *Vertical analysis* (common size analysis) looks at the relationship of an account to a total with the same year such as cost of sales or item sales. It discloses the internal structure of the entity. Vertical analysis reveals the relationship between sales and each income statement account. It represents the mix of assets that generate income and the mix of debt and equity financing. When using financial ratios, comparisons should be made of a company's ratios over the years to identify trends. In determining relative performance, comparisons should also be made between a company's ratios and industry norms (averages), as well as a company's ratios to competing companies in the industry. An example of a financial ratio of interest to an investor is dividend yield equal to dividends per share divided by market price per share.

Financial Times-Stock Exchange 100-Share Index known as the *Footsie*, a capitalized market value index of 100 major companies in the United Kingdom. It is to the British market what the Dow Jones Industrial Average is to American traders. Some companies included in the index are Glaxo, Wellcome, Grand Metropolitan, British Steel, British Petroleum, Barclays Bank, Hanson, Rolls Royce, and Allied-Lyons.

first call research notes and "earnings estimates," gathered by First Call Corporation (*http://www.firstcall.com*) from a large number of brokerage firms, both in the United States and abroad. First Call is occasionally quoted by the financial media for its consensus estimate of a company's earnings. The quarterly estimate is compared to the quarterly reported earnings per share in determining an "earnings surprise."

fiscal year (FY) twelve consecutive months used by a business entity to account for and report in its business operations. Typically, businesses use a fiscal year ending December 31. (The year-end December 31 is referred to as a *calendar year*.) However, many entities use the natural business year, referring to a year-ending at the annual low point in activity or at the end of the season. An example is a fiscal year ending June 30. A company prepares its financial statements and includes them in the annual report at the end of the fiscal year. It is a company's accounting year, which may or may not coincide with a calendar year, either by chance or some peculiarity of the company's business.

Fisher effect theory that nominal interest rates in each country are equal to the required real rate of return to the investor plus compensation for the expected amount of inflation.

fit investment term describing a situation in which a particular investment conforms to an investor's financial requirements and portfolio.

fixed charges expenses that remain constant in total regardless of changes in activity or volume; examples are rent and insurance. Fixed cost per unit changes as volume changes. Fixed expenses are those that have to be met whether the company has earnings or not. The fixed charge coverage ratio may prove enlightening. The ratio equals

$$\frac{\text{Income before fixed charges and taxes}}{\text{Fixed charges}}$$

The ratio indicates how many times fixed charges are covered by before-tax earnings. A higher ratio provides a better margin of safety.

fixed exchange rates system under which the values of currencies in terms of other currencies are fixed by intergovernmental agreement and by governmental intervention in the currency exchange markets.

fixed-income securities investment vehicles that provide a fixed periodic return; examples are debt securities such as bonds.

fixing method for determining the market price of a security by finding the price that balances buyers and sellers; also called a *call auction*. A fixing takes place periodically each day at defined times.

flat describing securities on which interest and perhaps principal may not be paid. Bonds of bankrupt railroads and income bonds that need not pay interest when there are no earnings are traded flat.

flat market securities market in which prices are basically moving horizontally and that often is associated with low volume. In a flat market, prices trade within a narrow range over an extended period, showing only small up or down changes. An example is a stock trading between $90 and $93 for a year.

flat yield return on debt or equity securities that does not include capital appreciation. It equals the annual return (interest income or dividend income) divided by the cost of the investment.

flexible exchange rates *see* FLOATING EXCHANGE RATES.

flexible portfolio funds mutual funds that invest in any one investment class (stocks, bonds, money market instruments, options, futures, or foreign securities) or any combination thereof, depending on the conditions in each market; often called ASSET ALLOCATION FUNDS. Because they do not limit a fund manager's exposure to any one market, these funds provide the greatest flexibility in anticipating or responding to economic changes.

float shares in the public hands out of the total number of shares outstanding. For example, if a corporation has 100 million shares outstanding and insiders hold 35% of them, then the float is the remaining 65%, or 65 million shares. *Note:* The size of float with smaller companies should be noted with special attention, as stocks with smaller floats (referred to as THINLY TRADED) can be very volatile. Any kind of demand can send the stock price soaring when supply is limited. By the same token, a wave of selling can quickly cause such stocks to plummet. *See also* FLOATING AN ISSUE; SHARES OUTSTANDING.

floating an issue offering an ISSUE to the public for companies or governments to raise cash. *See also* FLOAT.

floating exchange rates system under which the exchange rate for converting one currency into another is continuously adjusted depending on the laws of supply and demand.

floating rate note (FRN) bond issued with variable quarterly or semiannual interest rate payments, generally linked to LIBOR. It is an example of INDEX-LINKED BONDS.

floor
1. actual trading floor area of the stock exchange where securities' trading occurs among brokers and traders. Exchange rules allow only members to trade on the floor.
2. price below which a stock must be sold, as in a sell STOP ORDER. If the price penetrates the floor price, it will be "stopped out."
3. contract on an interest rate, whereby the writer of the floor periodically pays the difference between a specified floor rate and the market interest rate if, and only if, this difference is positive. This is equivalent to a stream of put options on the interest rate.

floor broker registered member of a stock exchange who transacts orders for clients on the floor to buy or sell any listed stock. A floor broker is distinguished from a FLOOR TRADER, who trades securities as a principal for his or her account, rather than for clients.

floor trader *see* FLOOR BROKER.

fluctuation
1. variation and change in the form of increases and decreases in stock prices, bond prices, commodity prices, interest rates, and

exchange rates. It is the state of continually varying in an irregular way. The fluctuation trend may be slight or significant.
2. variability in economic conditions.

fluctuation limit upper and lower bounds put on commodity futures prices set by the commodities exchanges. The limits assure that traders will not lose excessive amounts on a specific contract for the trading day. Once a commodity goes to its limit price, trading in that commodity ceases for that trading day.

flurry unanticipated and often intense increase in trading volume of a stock often occurring on news concerning the underlying company or related developments. Flurries of trading activity are often as brief as they are intense.

follow-up action term used to describe the trades an investor makes subsequent to implementing a strategy. Through these trades, the investor transforms one option strategy into a different one in response to price changes in the underlying stock.

foreign bond bond issued by a foreign borrower on a foreign capital market just like any domestic (local) firm. The bond must of course be denominated in a local currency—the currency of the country in which the issue is sold. The terms must conform to local custom and regulations. A foreign bond is the simplest way for a multinational company to raise long-term debt for its foreign expansion. A bond issued by a German corporation, *denominated in dollars*, and sold in the United States in accordance with SEC and applicable state regulations, to U.S. investors by U.S. investment bankers, would be a foreign bond. Except for the foreign origin of the borrower, this bond will be no different from those issued by equivalent U.S. corporations. Foreign bonds have nicknames: foreign bonds sold in the United States are YANKEE BONDS; foreign bonds sold in Japan are SAMURAI BONDS; and foreign bonds sold in the United Kingdom are BULLDOGS. The following specifically reclassifies foreign bonds from a U.S. investor's perspective.

FOREIGN BONDS TO U.S. INVESTORS

		Sales	
		In the United States	In Foreign Countries
Issuer	Domestic	Domestic bonds	Eurobonds
	Foreign	Yankee bonds	Foreign bonds Eurobonds

Note: If you own a foreign bond, you have CURRENCY RISK. If you buy and hold a U.S. Treasury bond to maturity, you face virtually zero risk (except for INFLATION RISK). But with a foreign bond—even the aptly named British government GILTS and the supersafe German government BUNDS—you run the real risk of the dollar rising in value against the

FOREIGN BOND QUOTATIONS

currency in which the bonds are denominated during the time you hold that bond. Additional drawbacks of buying foreign bonds are (1) buying foreign bonds is considerably more expensive than buying U.S. bonds since there exist the currency translation costs; (2) foreign-bond markets are not nearly as liquid as the U.S. market. *Recommendation*: If you are still interested in foreign bonds, consider FOREIGN BOND FUNDS that use some form of currency hedging.

foreign bond funds   international mutual funds—well-diversified portfolios of international bonds of varying duration, from short-term money market-like funds to long-term plays. Unlike the United States, most foreign governments limit their long-term bond issues to 10-year maturities.

foreign bond indexes   indexes that track the performance of bonds in different countries. A number of services issue indexes that track the performance of these bonds. The CBS MarketWatch Internet site (*cbs.marketwatch.com*) provides access to many of these indexes. *Note:* The CBS MartketWatch Ticker Symbols for these indexes can be found in Appendix D.

The subscription services that follow foreign bonds include

- J. P. Morgan Chase issues Government Bond Indexes for the United States and other countries. This information can be accessed free through the CBS MarketWatch Internet site along with the J. P. Morgan web site (*www.jpmorgan.com*). The indexes are followed in both U.S. dollars and the local currency.
- Salomon Smith Barney issues the Salomon Smith Barney World Government Bond Indexes for the United States and 16 other countries. As is true with J. P. Morgan, the indexes are reported in both U.S. dollars and local currency. These indexes can be accessed free through the CBS MarketWatch Internet site.
- UBS Group, a Swiss-based financial institution issues UBS Benchmark Bond indexes for the United States and other countries. These can be accessed free from the CBS MarketWatch Internet site. The indexes are given in local currency and U.S. dollars.

foreign bond market   that portion of the domestic bond market that represents issues floated by foreign companies or governments.

foreign bond quotations   quotes on FOREIGN BONDS. (see example on next page.)

EXPLANATORY NOTES:
1. Exchange. Traded: New York Stock Exchange; American Stock Exchange.
2. Individual Issue Statistics. Descriptions of individual issues. For abbreviations see page 2 of the *Bond Guide*.
3. Interest Dates. Interest dates are indicated by the first letter of alternate six months in which interest is payable. (An) or (Q) precedes dates on which interest is payable either annually or quarterly. Unless otherwise noted, dates are the first day of the

(5) Foreign Bonds (7) ABB-ASI 203

(1) Exchange ↓ BONDS (2) Description, Interest Rate, Due and Interest Dates		(3)	(4) S&P Rating	Redemption Provisions: Regular	Redemption Provisions: For Sinking Fund	Redemption Provisions: Refund Earliest/ Other	(6) Underwriting: Firm	Underwriting: Price	Underwriting: Year	Out-standing Mil-$ This Issue	Price Range 1986-1998: High	Price Range 1986-1998: Low	1999: High	1999: Low	Month End Price Sale(s) or Bid	Yield to Maturity
Abbey Nat'l 1st Capital B.V. ....[1]Sub[2]Notes[3]	6.20s 2004	$aO15	AA−	NC	....	....	M2	99.77	'94	500	113¾	96¾	111⅛	104⅞	105	7.03
Abbey Nat'l plc .... Perp Sub Reset[4]CapSecs	7.35s	$ao15	A+	NC	....	....	S1	99.95	'96	500	110⅝	97½	103¼	96⅝	96⅝	....
Abitibi-Consolidated .... Deb	7.40s 2018	$Ao	BBB−	NC	....	....	G1	99.29	'98	100	103⅛	91	95⅜	88½	89⅝	8.49
Abitibi-Consolidated .... Deb	7⅞s 2028	$Ao	BBB−	NC	....	....	G1	99.18	'98	250	103⅝	90¼	95¼	87	88⅜	8.60
Abitibi-Consolidated .... Notes	6.95s 2008	$Ao	BBB−	NC	....	....	G1	98.81	'98	250	101⅛	97	99¼	93¼	93⅝	7.94
ABN AMRO Bank N.V.[6] ....Sub[2]Notes[7]	7.55s 2006	$Jd28	AA−	NC	....	....		99.99	'96	750	109¾	99⅛	109⅛	100¼	100⅞	7.36
ABN AMRO Bank N.V.[6] ....Global Sub[7]Notes[2]	7⅛s 2007	$Jd18	AA−	NC	....	....		99.95	'97	750	107¼	99⅜	108⅛	98⅝	98⅜	7.33
ABN AMRO Bank N.V.[6] ....Sub[7]Notes[2]	7s 2008	$Ao	AA−	NC	....	....		99.20	'96	250	107⅛	94½	107⅜	97⅝	98⅛	7.29
ABN AMRO Bank N.V.[6] ....Sub[7]Notes[8]	7.30s 2028	$jD	AA−	[9]100	....	....		97.79	'96	400	104	90	102	91⅜	93⅜	7.87
Acindar Industria Argentina ....[2]Notes[10]	11¼s 2004	$Fa15	B+	[11]106.625	....	....	C5	100	'97	100	110⅜	66¼	82½	67	67½	23.19
AEGON N.V. ....Sub Notes[2]	8s 2006	$fA15	AA−	NC	....	....	M5	98.09	'94	400	114⅜	94	113⅜	103⅜	104⅛	7.24

month. The month of maturity is indicated by a capital letter. Symbols following interest dates note foreign issues payable in U.S. funds or currency of issuing country; and issues in default. See page 1 of the *Bond Guide* for explanation.

(4) S&P Debt Rating. Standard & Poor's Debt Rating definitions appear in the front section of the *Bond Guide*.

(5) Redemption Provisions. Regular call price with beginning or ending date. See the *Bond Guide* for additional information. SINKING FUND, if any, is reported together with applicable price and date. Refund restrictions are denoted by the symbol "x"—giving the date at which restriction expires. Redemption provision may include the symbol NC, which mean noncallable, and others (+, Z, *), which are explained on page 1.

(6) Underwriting. It indicates by key to the *Directory of Underwriters*, the original underwriter, usually the head of the syndicate, the price, and the year the issue was originally offered.

(7) Outstanding (Mil. &). The amount of issues outstanding, in millions of dollars, as of the latest available complete BALANCE SHEET.

foreign currency futures   *see* CURRENCY FUTURES.

foreign currency option   option contract that gives the holder the right but not the obligation to exercise it to purchase a given amount of foreign currency at a fixed price during a fixed time period. Contract specifications are similar to those of futures contracts, except that the option requires a premium payment to purchase (and it does not have to be exercised). *See also* CURRENCY OPTION.

foreign currency swaps   *see* CURRENCY SWAP.

foreign currency trading   *see* CURRENCY TRADING.

foreign direct investment (FDI)   purchase of physical assets, such as plant and equipment, or business operations in a foreign country, to be managed by the parent corporation. FDI is in contrast to FOREIGN PORTFOLIO INVESTMENT.

foreign exchange   exchange of the currency of one country for that of another country. Foreign exchange is not simply currency printed by a foreign country's central bank. Rather, it includes such items as cash, checks (or drafts), wire transfers, telephone transfers, and even contracts to sell or buy currency in the future. Foreign exchange is any financial instrument that fulfills payment from one currency to another. The most common form of foreign exchange in transactions between companies is the *draft* (denominated in a foreign currency). The most common form of foreign exchange in transactions between banks is the *telephone transfer*. Foreign exchange is the backbone of all international capital transactions. The FOREX market has vital implications for the economic prospects of the countries concerned and the general prosperity of the free world economy, as some $1.5 trillion worth of international currencies are bought and sold every single trading day (*www.knewmoney.com*). This volume of trade is equivalent to more than two months of trading on the New York Stock Exchange. *Note:* A FOREIGN EXCHANGE MARKET is now available to individual investors for trading foreign exchanges. *See also* CURRENCY TRADING.

foreign exchange arbitrage   use of simultaneous contracts to buy and sell FOREIGN EXCHANGE at different prices or at different times, such that a profit is made and no exchange risk is undertaken.

foreign exchange contract   *see* FUTURES FOREIGN EXCHANGE CONTRACT; FORWARD CONTRACTS.

foreign exchange hedging   protecting against the possible impact of exchange rate changes on the firm's business by balancing foreign currency assets with foreign currency liabilities.

foreign exchange market (FOREX)   market in which foreign exchange transactions take place, that is, where different currencies are bought and sold; or, more broadly, a market for the exchange of financial instruments denominated in different currencies. The most common location for foreign exchange transactions is a commercial bank, which agrees to "make a market" for the purchase and sale of currencies other than the local one. This market is not located in any one place, most transactions being conducted by telephone, wire service, or cable. It is a global network of banks, investment banks, and brokerage houses that comprise an electronically linked infrastructure servicing international corporations, banks, and investment funds. FOREX trading follows the sun around the world; starting in Tokyo, the market activity moves through to London, the last banking center in Europe, before traveling on to New York and finally returning to Japan via Sydney.

The interbank market has three sessions of trading. The first begins on Sunday at 7:00 P.M., EST, which is the Asia session. The second is the European (London) session, which begins at approximately 3:00 A.M., and the third and final session is New York, which begins at approximately 8:00 A.M. and ends at 5:00 P.M. The majority of all trading occurs during the London session and the first half of the New York session. As a result, buyers and sellers are available 24 hours a day. Investors can respond to currency fluctuations caused by economic, social, and political events at the time they occur—day or night. The functions of the foreign exchange market are basically threefold: (1) transfer purchasing power; (2) provide credit; and (3) minimize exchange risk.

foreign exchange parity   FOREIGN EXCHANGE RATE of two currencies that is officially fixed by international agreement.

foreign exchange rate   *exchange rate* for short; specifies the number of units of a given currency that can be purchased with one unit of another currency. Exchange rates appear in the business sections of newspapers each day and financial dailies such as *Investor's Busi-*

ness Daily and *The Wall Street Journal*. Exchange rates are also available at many finance web sites such as the Bloomberg World Currency Values web site (*http://www.bloomberg.com/markets/wcv.html*). The actual exchange rate is determined by the interaction of supply and demand in the FOREIGN EXCHANGE MARKET. Such supply and demand conditions are determined by various economic factors (for example, whether the country's basic BALANCE OF PAYMENTS position is in surplus or deficit). Exchange rates can be quoted in DIRECT or INDIRECT QUOTES and in AMERICAN TERMS or EUROPEAN TERMS. Exchange rates can be fixed at a predetermined level (FIXED EXCHANGE RATE), or they can be flexible to reflect changes in demand (FLOATING EXCHANGE RATE). Foreign exchange refers to the instruments used for international payments. Exchange rates can be SPOT (OR CASH) or FORWARD. Foreign exchange rates are determined in various ways:

1. **Fixed exchange rates**: An international financial arrangement in which governments directly intervene in the FOREIGN EXCHANGE MARKET to prevent exchange rates from deviating more than a very small margin from some central or parity value. From the end of World War II until August 1971, the world was on this system.
2. **Flexible (floating exchange) rates**: An arrangement by which currency prices are allowed to seek their own levels without much government intervention (for example, in response to market demand and supply). Arrangements may vary from free float (that is, absolutely no government intervention) to managed float (that is, limited but sometimes aggressive government intervention in the foreign exchange market).
3. **Forward exchange rate**: The exchange rate in contract for receipt of and payment for foreign currency at a specified date usually 30 days, 90 days, or 180 days in the future, at a specified current or "spot (or cash)" price. By buying and selling forward exchange, importers and exporters can protect themselves against the risks of fluctuations in the current exchange market.

foreign exchange risk   *see* CURRENCY RISK.

foreign exchange risk premium   difference between the forward rate and the expected future spot rate.

foreign market beta   measure of foreign market RISK that is derived from the CAPITAL ASSET PRICING MODEL (CAPM). The formula for the computation is

$$\frac{\text{Standard deviation of foreign market}}{\text{Standard deviation of U.S. market}}$$

EXAMPLE:
If the correlation between the German and U.S. markets is 0.44, and the standard deviations of German and U.S. returns are 20.1% and 12.5%, respectively, then the German market beta is

$$0.71 = \left(0.44 \times \frac{0.201}{0.125}\right).$$

In other words, despite the greater risk of the German market relative to the U.S. market, the low correlation between the two markets leads to a German market beta (.71), which is lower than the U.S. market beta (1.00).

foreign portfolio investment investment by individuals, firms, or public bodies (such as national and local governments) in foreign financial instruments (that is, government bonds, foreign stocks) for the sake of obtaining investment income or CAPITAL GAINS rather than entrepreneurial income, which is the case with FOREIGN DIRECT INVESTMENTS (FDI). *See also* INTERNATIONAL INVESTMENT.

foreign stock indexes indexes for foreign stock markets similar to U.S. indexes. They allow investors to easily gauge the general performance of the foreign markets and their sectors. Major newspapers and the financial media regularly report the changes in these indexes. The following chart shows these listings from the Bloomberg Internet site (*www.bloomberg.com*). The CBS MarketWatch Internet site (*cbs.marketwatch.com*) reports a number of indexes for foreign market indexes and their sectors. *Note:* The TICKER SYMBOLS for these indexes are reported in Appendix D. The ING Barings web site (*www.ingbarings.com/pweb/research/research_frame.htm*) contains an extensive list of links to sites dealing with financial markets in foreign countries.

A number of investment banking firms follow foreign stocks, and many of these firms issue foreign stock indexes that chart the change in the values of foreign stocks in different countries. These include the following:
- FTSE International produces a number of foreign stock indexes. These can be obtained free at their Internet site (*www.ft-se.co.uk*). One of the different families of the FTSE indexes is the FT/S&P indexes, which can be accessed free at the CBS MarketWatch Internet site. *See* Appendix D for ticker symbols.
- ING Barings produces the Barings Emerging Markets Indexes. These can be accessed free from the CBS MarketWatch Internet site. *See* Appendix D for ticker symbols.
- HSBC Holdings Group issues the HSBC James Capel Indexes. These can be accessed free from the CBS MarketWatch Internet site. *See* Appendix D for ticker symbols.
- Morgan Stanley Capital International produces a number of global indexes (including the EAFE INDEX). These indexes can be accessed free from the Morgan Stanley Capital International Internet site (*www.msci.com*) and can also be accessed free from the CBS MarketWatch Internet site. *See* Appendix D for ticker symbols.

- Standard & Poor's issues S&P Global Indexes that can be accessed free from its Internet site (*www.spglobal.com*).
- Stoxx, Ltd., a joint venture between Dow Jones and some European investment banking firms, issues the Dow Jones Stoxx and the Dow Jones Euro Stoxx Indexes. Some of these indexes can be accessed free at the UBS Internet site (*www.ubs.ch*). In addition, the CBS MarketWatch Internet site carries an extensive listing of these indexes. *See* Appendix D for ticker symbols.

World Indices
Fri, 12 Nov 1999, 8:19pm EST

SPONSORED BY Qwest UNLIMITED Internet Access

North/Latin America

Index	Value	Chg	Pct Chg	Date
DOW JONES INDUS AVG (INDU)	10769.32	174.02	1.64%	16:03
S&P 500 INDEX (SPX)	1396.06	14.60	1.06%	16:59
NASDAQ COMB COMPOSITE IX (CCMP)	3221.15	23.86	0.75%	17:15
TSE 300 Index (TS300)	7526.20	37.74	0.50%	17:02
MEXICO BOLSA INDEX (MEXBOL)	5034.76	-51.54	-0.85%	16:02
BRAZIL BOVESPA STOCK IDX (IBOV)	13114.01	-75.26	-0.57%	15:14

Europe/Africa

Index	Value	Chg	Pct Chg	Date
BLOOMBERG EUROPEAN 500 (EURO500)	239.62	-0.32	-0.13%	13:00
FT-SE 100 Index (UKX)	6511.60	-39.80	-0.61%	11:31
CAC 40 INDEX (CAC)	5141.51	9.43	0.18%	11:24
DAX INDEX (DAX)	5791.05	-11.31	-0.19%	11:45
IBEX 35 INDEX (IBEX)	10469.90	-27.20	-0.26%	11:00
MILAN MIB30 INDEX (MIB30)	33930.00	-177.00	-0.52%	11:51
BEL20 INDEX (BEL20)	3354.22	69.80	2.13%	11:01
AMSTERDAM EXCHANGES INDX (AEX)	589.87	-4.93	-0.83%	10:30
SWISS MARKET INDEX (SMI)	7421.20	62.00	0.84%	11/11

Asia/Pacific

Index	Value	Chg	Pct Chg	Date
NIKKEI 225 INDEX (NKY)	18258.55	-68.73	-0.38%	1:05
HANG SENG STOCK INDEX (HSI)	14189.67	83.96	0.60%	3:05
ASX ALL ORDINARIES INDX (AS30)	3010.20	27.40	0.92%	0:07
SING: STRAITS TIMES INDU (STI)	2185.82	32.15	1.49%	4:02

foreign stock quotations quotes on foreign stock prices. Newspapers often provide two listings associated with foreign securities: (1) foreign securities in U.S. dollars; and (2) foreign exchange rates that give the exchange rate between U.S. dollars and foreign currencies in both U.S. dollars and the foreign currency. Typically, the current exchange rate and the rate for the previous trading day are both given.

The rates in the following listings are interbank rates. As a rule of thumb, we add 2% to the interbank rate to determine the rate for stock transactions. To determine a rough price for foreign securities in U.S. dollars, you must multiply the price by the applicable exchange rate.

EXAMPLE 1:
In the case of ANA closing at 1270 yen, we note that for the Japanese yen, the latest exchange rate is $.007605. Two percent added to this gives you an estimated exchange rate of $.007757. Multiplying the price of the stock in foreign currency by the approximate U.S. equivalent of yen we obtain a rough per-share price of the stock in U.S. dollars.

1270 yen (price of stock)

× $.007757 U.S.$ (rough exchange value of $1)

= $9.85 U.S.$ (price of stock in U.S. dollars)

EXAMPLE 2:
Assume that BASF cost 41 German marks. Assume that the rate to exchange German marks into U.S. dollars is $.5497. Two percent added to this gives you an estimated exchange rate of $.560694 ($.5497 + .010994). If you multiply the price of the stock in foreign currency by the approximate U.S. equivalent of yen, you obtain a rough per-share price of the stock in U.S. dollars.

41 marks (price of stock)

× $.560694 U.S.$ (rough exchange value of $1)

$22.988454 U.S.$ (price of stock in U.S. dollars)

FOREX *see* FOREIGN EXCHANGE MARKET.

formula timing buying and selling of securities based on an investment methodology that times such decisions with various indicators, depending upon the theoretical methodology. For example, some investors may turn BULLISH and begin buying stocks when the short interest ratio is extremely high, on the theory that everybody who is going to sell has already done so. Others may time their decisions based on the highs and lows of various securities.

forward contracts contracts similar to futures, however, forward contracts are not uniform or standardized and are not traded on exchanges. In such a contract, goods are actually delivered at a future date or settlement may be in cash. Forward contracts may be on commodities or instruments. The contract fixes the quantity, price, and date of purchase or sale.

forward differential *see* FORWARD PREMIUM OR DISCOUNT.

forward exchange rate   contracted exchange rate for receipt of and payment for foreign currency at a specified date in the future, at a stipulated current or SPOT price. In the forward market, you buy and sell currency for a future delivery date, usually, one, three, or six months in advance. If you know you need to buy or sell currency in the future, you can HEDGE against a loss by selling in the forward market. By buying and selling forward exchange contracts, importers and exporters can protect themselves against the risks of FLUCTUATIONS in the current exchange market. Suppose that the spot and the 90-day forward rate for the British pound are quoted as $1.5685 and $1.5551, respectively. You are required to pay £10,000 in three months to your English supplier. You can purchase £10,000 today by paying $15,551 (10,000 × $1.5551). These pounds will be delivered in 90 days. In the meantime, you have protected yourself. No matter what the exchange rate of pound or U.S. dollar is in 90 days, you are assured delivery at the quoted price. As can be seen in the example, the cost of purchasing pounds in the forward market ($15,551) is less than the price in the spot market ($15,685). This implies that the pound is selling at a *forward discount* relative to the dollar, so you can buy more pounds in the forward market. It could also mean that the U.S. dollar is selling at a *forward premium*. *Note*: It is extremely unlikely that the forward rate quoted today will be exactly the same as the future spot rate. *See also* SPOT EXCHANGE RATE.

forward foreign exchange market   simply called *forward market*, the forward foreign exchange market is the market where foreign exchange dealers can enter into a FORWARD CONTRACT to buy or sell any amount of a currency at any date in the future. Forward contracts are negotiated between the offering bank and the client as to size, maturity, and price. The rationale for forward contracts in currencies is analogous to that for futures contracts in commodities; the firm can lock in a price today to eliminate uncertainty about the value of a future receipt or payment of foreign currency. Such a transaction may be undertaken since the firm has made a previous contract, for example, to pay a certain sum in foreign currency to a supplier in three months for some needed inputs to its operations. This concept is called HEDGING. The principal users of the forward market are currency arbitrageurs, hedgers, importers, exporters, and speculators. Arbitrageurs wish to earn risk-free profits; hedgers, importers, and exporters want to protect the home currency values of various foreign currency-denominated assets and liabilities, and speculators actively expose themselves to exchange risk to benefit from expected movements in exchange rates. It differs from the FUTURES MARKET in many significant ways.

forward market   *see* FORWARD FOREIGN EXCHANGE MARKET.

forward premium or discount   percentage difference between the FORWARD EXCHANGE RATE and the SPOT EXCHANGE RATE (premium if

FORWARD PREMIUM OR DISCOUNT

positive, discount if negative); also called FORWARD-SPOT DIFFERENTIAL, *forward differential*, or *exchange agio*. When quotations are on an indirect basis, a formula for the percent-per-annum forward premium or discount is as follows:

With INDIRECT QUOTES, the formula becomes

Forward premium (+) or discount (−)

$$= \frac{\text{Spot} - \text{Forward}}{\text{Forward}} \times \frac{12}{n} \times 100$$

where n = number of months in the contract.

EXAMPLE:
Assume that the spot exchange rate = ¥110/$ and the one-month forward rate = ¥109.66/$. Since the spot rate is greater than the one-month forward rate (in *indirect quotes*), the yen is selling forward at a premium.

The one-month (30-day) forward premium (discount) is

$$\frac{¥110.19 - ¥109.66}{¥109.66} \times \frac{12}{1} \times 100 = +5.80\%$$

The three-month (90-day) forward premium (discount) is

$$[(¥110.19 - ¥108.55)/¥108.55] \times 12/3 \times 100 = +6.04\%$$

The six-month (180-day) forward premium (discount) is

$$[(¥110.19 - ¥106.83)/¥106.83] \times 12/6 \times 100 = +6.29\%$$

Note: A currency is said to be selling at a premium (discount) if the forward rate expressed in *indirect quotes* is less (greater) than the spot rate.

With DIRECT QUOTES:

$$\text{Forward premium or discount} = \frac{\text{Forward} - \text{Spot}}{\text{Spot}} \times \frac{12}{1} \times 100$$

$$\text{Forward premium or discount} = \frac{\$0.009119 - \$0.009075}{\$0.009075} \times \frac{12}{1} \times 100$$
$$= +5.80\%$$

Note: A currency is said to be selling at a premium (discount) if the forward rate expressed in *direct quotes* is greater (less) than the spot rate.

This table shows forward rate quotations and annualized forward premiums (discounts).

FORWARD RATE QUOTATIONS AND ANNUALIZED FORWARD PREMIUMS (DISCOUNTS)

Quotation		¥/$ (Indirect Quote)	$/¥ (Direct Quote)	% per Annum
Spot Rate		¥110.19	$0.009075	
Forward				
	1 month	109.66	0.009119	+5.80%
	3 month	108.55	0.009212	+6.04%
	6 month	106.83	0.009361	+6.29%

Note: In the Example, since a dollar would buy *fewer* yen in the forward than in the spot market, the forward yen is selling at a PREMIUM.

forward rate   *see* FORWARD EXCHANGE RATE.

forward rate agreement (FRA)   agreement between two parties that will apply to a future national loan or deposit.

forward-spot differential   *see* FORWARD PREMIUM OR DISCOUNT.

founder's stock   stock issued to the founders of a company, usually at a low price in comparison to that paid by investors.

fourth market   trading activity that takes place directly between buyer and seller of securities without the assistance of a broker, eliminating sales commissions. Buyers and sellers are usually large institutional investors, such as insurance companies, MUTUAL FUNDS, or pension funds. Computers, such as a computerized subscriber service called INSTINET, an acronym for Institutional Networks Corporation, aid the fourth market. Among its subscribers are a large number of mutual funds and other institutional investors (and wealthy individuals) linked to each other by computer terminals. The system permits subscribers to display tentative volume interest and bid-ask quotes to others in the system.

Frankfurt Stock Exchange   known as *FWM* (*Frankfurters Wertpapier Borse*), the largest of eight German stock exchanges, with roughly 70% of the volume in German equities. Banks act as brokers on the exchange, and some specialists traditionally had responsibility for setting the price at the periodic auctions and, to some extent, for acting as dealers. The trading system was a call auction and replaced in 1997 by XETRA (eXchange Electronic TRAding). XETRA functions as a pure order-driven trading and settlement system.

free cash flow   cash from operations minus capital expenditures and dividends paid.

free cash flow per share   trailing 12-month free cash flow divided by the trailing 12-month average shares outstanding found on the income statement.

front-end load sales fees or other charges that have to be initially paid besides the cost of the investment itself when making certain investments such as buying shares of some mutual funds. The investor must assess whether the initial sales charge is worth it; for example, is the quality of a mutual fund and its track record such as a front-end fee of, say, 2% justified? As a general rule, the performance from the fund should pay for the sales charge within a relatively short time period. Front-end sales charges may also exist for limited partnerships, life insurance policies, and annuities.

FT-Actuaries World Nordic Index *Financial Times of London*'s market value-weighted barometer of over 90 company issues traded in four Scandinavian markets.

FT-All Shares Index *Financial Times of London*'s market value-weighted barometer of over 750 company issues traded in the U.K. market.

FT Eurotop 300 index of the share prices of the 300 largest European companies, by market capitalization.

FT-SE "Footsie" 100 (U.K) Stock Index FINANCIAL TIMES-STOCK EXCHANGE 100-SHARE INDEX, a capitalized market value index of 100 major companies in the United Kingdom. It is to the British market what the Dow Jones Industrial Average is to American traders. *The Financial Times*-Stock Exchange 100-Share Index (known as the Footsie) is a narrow capitalized-weighted index of the market prices of the 100 most capitalized shares on the exchange. Some companies included in the index are Glaxo, Wellcome, Grand Metropolitan, British Steel, British Petroleum, Barclays Bank, Hanson, Rolls Royce, and Allied-Lyons. Index information appears in major local and national newspapers and business dailies. Early risers can find live coverage of European markets on financial TV shows. This index can also be tracked by on-line databases such as America Online and on the Internet at web sites such as *www.bloomberg.com*

FT-SE 100 *see* FT-SE "FOOTSIE" 100 (U.K) STOCK INDEX.

full-service broker broker providing a wide range of services to clients. Unlike discount brokers, full-service brokers provide buy and sell advice on stocks, bonds, options, commodities, and mutual funds. A full-service broker may offer research services, asset management accounts, tax shelters, and limited partnerships as well as allowing participation in new security issues.

full trading authorization permission given to a broker by a customer for a third party, such as an investment adviser, to execute buy and sell orders in his or her account; also called *full discretionary account*. In addition, funds or stocks may be withdrawn from the account.

fully valued   when a stock's price is considered to be what the entity's earning power and financial condition justifies. It may be considered fully valued when it matches the consensus of securities analysts. A stock price in excess of the consensus price is overvalued, while it is undervalued when the stock price is below the consensus price.

fund of funds   a mutual fund or UNIT TRUST that invests in other funds or unit trusts, providing the investor with double diversification. Often a fund or funds will also invest in funds and trusts run by the same group, but some of them will also invest in funds run by other groups.

fund switching   practice of moving assets from one type of a mutual fund to another within the same family of funds to take advantage of timely investment opportunities. For example, one might move money from a fund specializing in American equities to a fund investing primarily in a specific foreign country when the comparative opportunity for an increased investment return became greater in the foreign country.

fundamental analysis
1. appraisal based in economic theory and models to forecast exchange rate movements. The factors to consider are money supply, inflation rate, interest rate, and BALANCE OF PAYMENTS.
2. predicting economic direction by examining such conditions as GROSS DOMESTIC PRODUCT, inventory levels, and unemployment.
3. evaluation of a company's stock based on an examination of the firm's financial statements. It considers overall financial health (such as SOLVENCY, earning potential, revenue generation, rate of return on assets, earnings quality), economic and political conditions, industry factors, marketing aspects, management quality, and future outlook of the company. The analysis attempts to ascertain whether stock is overpriced, underpriced, or priced in proportion to its market value. We want to find the intrinsic value of the stock. Further, fundamental analysis seeks to determine if the company is fairly priced. Fundamental analysis provides much of the data needed to forecast earnings and dividends. Its tools include ratio and trend analysis, which give a relative measure of the operating performance and financial condition of the company. Fundamental analysis considers the company's liquidity, solvency, rate of return on assets, profitability, earning power, return on investment, revenue generation, and dividend-paying ability. A company's ratios are compared to industry averages and to ratios of major competitors. We also look at the trend in the company's ratios over the years. With respect to the economy, consideration is given to budget, trade deficits, production indexes, scarcity of commodities, and consumer spending. A ratio compares the relative strength of two indicators or measures. For example, the performance of a particular stock or industry

FUNDAMENTAL ANALYSIS

can be compared to an overall market measure (for example, Standard & Poor's 500). How is the individual stock or industry doing compared to the overall market? An analysis of the ratio trend may reveal several points. In looking at industry factors, note that it may make less sense to invest in a strong stock in a sick industry than to invest in a weak stock in a strong industry. To obtain useful conclusions from the ratios, you must make two comparisons:

- *Industry comparison*: This will allow you to answer the question "how does a business fare in the industry?" You must compare the company's ratios to those of competing companies in the industry or with industry standards (averages). You can obtain industry norms from financial services such as Value Line, Dun & Bradstreet, Philadelphia-based Risk Management Association (RMA), and Standard & Poor's. Numerous on-line services such as AOL and MSN Money Central, to name two, also provide these data. For example, RMA has been compiling statistical data on financial statements for more than 75 years. The RMA Annual Statement Studies provide statistical data from more than 150,000 actual companies on many key financial ratios, such as gross margin, operating margins, and return on equity and assets. If you're looking to put real authority into the "industry average" numbers that your company is beating, use the Statement Studies. They're organized by SIC codes, and you can buy the financial statement studies for your industry for $59.95 in report form or over the Internet (*www.rmahq.org*).
- *Trend analysis*: To see how the business is doing over time, you will compare a given ratio for one company over several years to see the direction of financial health or operational performance.

Note: A deficiency of fundamental analysis is that it looks to the appraisal of stock information. However, the market is interested in looking ahead. Some investors integrate fundamental and TECHNICAL ANALYSIS. An example is using the fundamental approach to select a given stock and then using charts for timing decisions of when to buy or sell. This flow chart summarizes the basic structure of fundamental analysis.

FUNDAMENTAL ANALYSIS

Economic Analysis
(Assessing the Future Performance
of the Overall Economy)

Business Cycles, Monetary Fiscal Policy, Economic Indicators, Government Policy, World Events and Foreign Trade, Public Attitudes of Optimism or Pessimism, Domestic Legislation, Inflation, GNP Growth, Unemployment, Productivity, Capacity Utilization, Interest Rates, and More

↓

Industry Analysis
(Based on the Economic and Market)
Analysis, Determining the Business Cycle's
Impact on Specific Industries, and
Evaluating Industry Characteristics)

Business Cycle Exposure, Industry Structure, Growth of the Industry, Competition, Product Quality, Cost Elements, Government Regulations, Labor Position, Technological Development, Financial Norms and Standards

↓

Company Analysis
(Analyzing how Specific Companies
Perform in Terms of Their Operating and
Financial Features Given Industry
Changes and the Economy)

Growth of Sales, Earnings, Dividends, Quality of Earnings, Position in the Industry, Discount Rates, Fundamental Analysis (Balance Sheet Analysis, Income Statement Analysis, Cash Flow Analysis), Analysis of Accounting Policy and Footnotes, Management, Research and Development, Return and Risk, Brands, Patents, Goodwill, and Diversification

---

See also TECHNICAL ANALYSIS.

FUNDAMENTAL FORECASTING

fundamental forecasting forecasting currency rates based on fundamental relationships between economic variables (such as exchange rates, inflation rates, and interest rates). Given current values of these variables along with their historical impact on a currency's value, investors can develop exchange rate projections.

future return RETURN (earnings and CAPITAL GAIN) on investment expected for a future period of time. Future return, not historical or past return, is the one that determines the current value of an investment.

futures contract to purchase or sell a given amount of an item for a given price by a certain date (in the future—thus the name *futures market*). *Note:* It is similar to deals made now to take place in the future. The seller of a futures contract agrees to deliver the item to the buyer of the contract, who agrees to purchase the item. The contract specifies the amount, valuation, method, quality, month and means of delivery, and exchange to be traded in. The month of delivery is the expiration date; in other words, the date on which the commodity or financial instrument must be delivered. Commodity contracts are guarantees by a seller to deliver a commodity (such as cocoa or cotton). Financial contracts are a commitment by the seller to deliver a financial instrument (for example, a Treasury bill) or a specific amount of foreign currency. Futures can by risky; to invest in them, you will need specialized knowledge and great caution. Futures differs from forward contracts in many ways:

FUTURES VERSUS FORWARD CONTRACTS

Futures Contracts	Forward Contracts
1. Standardized contracts in terms of size and delivery dates.	**1.** Customized contracts in terms of size and delivery dates.
2. Standardized contract between a customer and a clearinghouse.	**2.** Private contracts between two parties.
3. Contract may be freely traded on the market.	**3.** Impossible to reverse a contract.
4. All contracts are marked to market; profits and losses are realized immediately.	**4.** Profit or loss on a position is realized only on the delivery date.
5. Margins must be maintained to reflect price movements.	**5.** Margins are set once, on the day of the initial transaction.

This chart shows the advantages and disadvantages of using futures rather than forwards.

PROS AND CONS OF FUTURES

Advantages	Disadvantages
1. Because of the institutional arrangements, the default risk is low.	1. Futures exist for only a few high-turnover (large-volume) exchange rates.
2. Because of standardization, transaction costs or commissions are low.	2. Because of standardization, a hedger may have to settle for an imperfect but inexpensive hedge in terms of the size or the amount.
3. Due to the liquidity nature of futures, futures position can be closed out early.	3. Futures is available only for short maturities.
	4. Futures contracts involve cash flow and interest rate risk.

Futures and forwards appear to cater to two different clienteles. As a general rule, forward markets are used primarily by corporate hedgers, whereas futures tend be preferred by speculators. *See also* FOREIGN CURRENCY FUTURES.

futures contract standardized contract to buy or sell a given COMMODITY on a future date for a predetermined price. It requires delivery of a specific quantity of a commodity to the buyer of the contract at the date of EXPIRATION. The contract specifies the amount, method, quality, valuation, month and means of delivery, and commodity exchange to be traded in. Futures exist for commodities, debt instruments, composite stock indexes, foreign currencies, and so on. *See also* FUTURES.

futures foreign exchange contract legal contract similar to a forward contract, except that it is traded on a securities exchange, and has fixed specifications such as maturity date, contract size, and trading limitations during the contract's life.

futures market commodity market that trades futures contracts; also called *futures exchange*. It is a self-regulating body whose aim is to decide the conditions for acceptance of members, their trading terms, and their behavior in trading. The following table presents futures exchanges and commodities they trade. The second table is a summary of how to get in and out of the futures market.

THE U.S. FUTURES EXCHANGES

Chicago		
	Chicago Board of Trade (CBT)	Corn, oats, and other grains
	Chicago Mercantile Exchange (CME)	Meat and livestock
	International Monetary Market (IMM)	Treasury bonds and notes, currencies, precious metals, financial indexes
	Chicago Rice and Cotton Exchange	Rice and cotton
	Mid America Commodity Exchange	Financial futures
Philadelphia		
	Philadelphia Board of Trade	Foreign currencies
New York		
	COMEX	Precious metals, copper
	New York Cotton Exchange	Cotton, etc.
	Coffee, Sugar and Cocoa Exchange	Coffee, sugar, cocoa, etc.
	NYFE	Commodity and stock indexes
	New York Mercantile Exchange	Petroleum, precious metals

ENTERING AND LEAVING THE FUTURES MARKET

To get into the market	which means	To get out of the market	which means
Go *long*	Take a position as a *buyer*	Go *short*	Offsetting contracts cancel each other.
Go *short*	Take a position as a *seller*	Go *long*	Leaves no more obligations—you are out of the market

futures options   options on futures contracts such as currency futures. The advantage of a futures option contract over a futures contract is that with a futures contract, the holder must deliver one currency against the other or reverse the contract, regardless of whether this move is profitable. On the contrary, with the futures option contract, the holder is protected against an adverse movement in the exchange rate but may allow the option to expire unexercised if it would be more profitable to use the SPOT MARKET.

FY   *see* FISCAL YEAR.

G

gap risk that type of INTEREST RATE RISK in which the timing of maturities is mismatched.

general mortgage debt relating to a borrower's general real property. Since it is not a specific property, it has a lower priority claim if a company is in LIQUIDATION.

generally accepted accounting principles (GAAP) standards, conventions, guidelines, rules, and procedures accountants follow in recording and summarizing transactions, and in the preparation of financial statements. GAAP is based on authoritative accounting pronouncements such as American Institute of Certified Public Accountants' Opinions, Financial Accounting Standards Board Statements, industry practice, and accounting literature in the form of books and articles. In the audit report, the CPA must indicate that the client has followed GAAP on a consistent basis.

generic *see* PLAIN-VANILLA.

geometric average return *see* COMPOUND RETURN.

German (Deutsche) mark unit of currency in Germany (100 pfennig = 1 mark). As Germany has been Europe's economic powerhouse, the mark has become one of the world's most important currencies. Its relationship to the U.S. dollar was once a key to the global marketplace and was seen as a barometer of Germany's economic strength versus that of the United States. Now that Germany has joined the European Union and its currency is linked to the euro, the mark's importance is dwindling. Marks will be used as the German currency until 2002, so, while its relationship to other currencies will be fixed as a ratio to the new EURO CURRENCY, it will still be quoted in newspapers and financial reports on television and radio in terms of its relationship to the U.S. dollar. If the mark is at 60, that means that each mark is worth 60 U.S. cents. To figure out what $1 equals in German currency, investors use this formula: If 1 mark buys 60 cents, then $1 is equal to 1 divided by .60, or 1.67 marks.

For American investors buying German securities, the mark's movement is a key part of the profit potential of the investment. If the mark rises after an investment in German securities is made, the value of those stocks or bonds to a U.S. investor will get a boost from the currency because when the investment is sold, the stronger mark will generate more dollars when the proceeds are converted to the U.S. currency. Conversely, a weak mark will be a negative to a German investment for a U.S. investor. In some cases, the movement of the mark also can be viewed as an indicator of German economic health. This will greatly change in coming years as the new euro takes hold in Europe and its investors' psyche. Still, a strong mark can signal a buoyant European economy, a possible indication to buy German stocks. The mark's strength, however, must be verified not only against the U.S. dollar but against other major currencies outside of the euro circle. *Note:* Widely quoted currency rates are typically for transactions of $1 million or more. Consumers looking to use such figures to determine currency rates for foreign travel and investment should expect to get somewhat less favorable exchange rates.

German Share Index (Frankfurt DAX) INDEX of the market prices of shares of German companies traded on the Frankfurt Stock Exchange. It is Germany's version of the Dow Jones Industrial Average. It is a narrowly determined capitalization-weighted index of 30 of the most active issues. The index is updated continuously on a daily basis. It comprises about 75% of German equity value. Some major stocks listed are Bayer, Deutsche Bank, Daimler-Benz, Volkswagen, and Schering. Index information appears in major local and national newspapers and business dailies. Early risers can find live coverage of European markets on financial TV shows. This index can also be tracked by on-line databases such as America Online.

gilt market market for fixed-income bonds and INDEX-LINKED BONDS issued by the British government.

gilts fixed income or INDEX-LINKED BONDS issued by the British government. When you buy a gilt, you are lending the government money in return for regular interest payments and the promise that the nominal value of the gilt will be repaid (redeemed) on a specified later date. The rate of interest will be in the name of the gilt. For example, an 8% Treasury 2021 is a gilt issued by the Treasury, which pays 8% interest per annum and is repayable in 2021. You don't have to hold a gilt until its redemption, however, as they are tradable instruments just like shares. Since they are tradable, their prices continually move in line with supply and demand, and the main influences on prices are the market's view of future interest rates and inflation.

Ginnie Mae *see* GOVERNMENT NATIONAL MORTGAGE ASSOCIATION (GNMA).

GIPS *see* GLOBAL INVESTMENT PERFORMANCE STANDARDS (GIPS).

glamor stock stock widely held in the market by individual and institutional investors. Such stocks have a track record of consistently growing revenue and earnings. In a BULL MARKET, glamor stocks usually increase in price faster than the overall market averages.

global bond funds funds seeking a high level of income by investing in the DEBT SECURITIES of companies and countries worldwide, including issuers in the United States. The funds' money managers deal with varied currencies, laws, and regulations. Because of these factors, although global funds provide added diversification, they are also subject to more risk than domestic bond funds.

global bond indexes BENCHMARK indexes for global bonds. Today, investors do not have to settle only for the U.S. bond market to get fixed-income results. The J. P. MORGAN GOVERNMENT BOND INDEX is considered to be the most widely used benchmark for measuring performance and quantifying risk across international fixed-income bond markets. The index and its underlying subindices measure the total, principal, and interest returns in each of 13 countries and can be reported in 19 different currencies. The index limits inclusion to markets and issues that are available to international investors, to provide a more realistic measure of market performance.

Other global bond indexes include
- **J. P. Morgan Emerging Markets Bond Index Plus**: Total return index of U.S. dollar and other external currency denominated BRADY BONDS, loans, EUROBONDS, and local market debt instruments traded in emerging markets.
- **Salomon Smith Barney World Government Bond Index**: Tracks debt issues traded in 14 world government bond markets. Issues included in the index have fixed-rate coupons and maturities of at least one year. While finding bond yields is relatively easy, locating bond index results can be trickier. *The Wall Street Journal* and *Barron's* have extensive bond index coverage. Business news cable TV channels such as CNBC and CNNfn also track these indexes. Internet users can check web sites such as *http://www.bloomberg.com* or *http://www.bondsonline.com* for bond index results.

global depositary receipt (GDR) negotiable security that is issued by a U.S. commercial bank and represents shares of a non-U.S. company. Unlike ADRs, GDRs are simultaneously listed on several national markets. These GDRs give the firms access to a larger base to raise new capital. GDRs are priced and pay DIVIDENDS in dollars, and allow investors to buy and sell shares of non-U.S. companies in exactly the same way as they purchase or sell shares of U.S. companies. GDRs as well as ADRs are a popular method of investing in non-U.S. companies for those investors who aim to diversify their portfolios internationally. *See also* AMERICAN DEPOSITARY RECEIPT (ADR).

global (equity) funds mutual fund that invests globally, in both U.S. and foreign securities. Unlike an international fund, it invests anywhere in the world, including the United States. However, most global funds keep the majority of their assets in foreign markets.

global funds funds seeking capital appreciation (a rise in share price) by investing in both U.S. and non-U.S. securities traded worldwide, including issuers in the United States. These funds provide added DIVERSIFICATION but also added risk—a different risk profile (such as currency risk) from that provided by domestic funds. Global funds tend to keep a minimum of 25% of their assets in the United States. For example, in one recent year, Templeton World Fund had over 60% of its assets in the United States, and small positions in Australia and Canada.

Global Investment Performance Standards (GIPS) set of detailed, ethical principles intended to promote full disclosure and fair representation by investment managers worldwide in reporting their investment results to existing and prospective clients. GIPS is a *worldwide* standard for the calculation and presentation of investment performance in a fair, comparable format with full disclosure. It was adopted in 1999 by the ASSOCIATION FOR INVESTMENT MANAGEMENT RESEARCH (AIMR) and mandated for international portfolio managers worldwide.

global/macro fund type of HEDGE fund taking bets on the direction of a market, a currency, an interest rate, a commodity, or any macroeconomic variable. It tends to use heavily derivative products.

global registered shares EQUITY shares that are registered and traded in many foreign equity markets. They contrast with AMERICAN DEPOSITARY RECEIPTS (ADRS), which are foreign company shares placed in trust with a U.S. bank, which in turn issues depositary receipts to U.S. investors. For quotations on global shares, log on to *www.adr.com* by J. P. Morgan. *See also* AMERICAN SHARES.

global-scanning capability investor's ability to identify stocks worldwide worthy of investment.

go-go fund *see* PERFORMANCE FUND.

gold mutual fund mutual fund that invests in gold stocks. An example is Lexington Gold Fund.

golden handcuffs contractual agreement almost virtually assuring that the STOCKBROKER will stay with the brokerage firm for a specified time period. The incentive may be in the form of high commission rates, bonuses, participation in a forthcoming INITIAL PUBLIC OFFERING (IPO) of the brokerage firm itself, or other attractive fringe benefits. The contract may specify a penalty the broker will incur such as forfeiting past commissions if he or she leaves the brokerage firm before a specified date.

golden parachute highly lucrative contract giving a senior corporate executive monetary or other benefits if his or her job is lost in a merger or acquisition. Examples of benefits are generous severance pay, bonus, and stock option.

Goldman Sachs Commodity Index (GSCI) commodity futures price index that was launched in 1991 and comprises some 26 individual commodities (six energy products, nine metals, and eleven agricultural products). Each commodity is weighted according to an assessment of its importance in the world economic production. The GSCI does not include less active futures contracts, such as lumber and coal, which are included in the Bridge/CRB indexes. In 1992 the CHICAGO MERCANTILE EXCHANGE introduced futures and option contracts on the GSCI.

good funds monies that have been through the clearing procedure and are unconditionally and freely available for use.

good-this-month (GTM) order investor order to purchase or sell securities that continues in effect until month-end. Such order typically is at the investor's specified limit price or STOP PRICE.

good-this-week (GTW) order investor order to buy or sell securities that remains active until the end of the week.

good-till-cancelled (GTC) order investor's order to a broker to buy or sell a security or option at a given price. The order continues in effect until it is executed or cancelled by the investor. In the event the GTC order has not been executed for an extended time period, the broker will typically contact the investor to ascertain whether he or she still wants to keep the order open. *See also* BUY ORDER.

government (agency) securities securities issued by U.S. government agencies, such as the Federal Home Loan Bank (FHLB); also called *agency securities*. Most of these securities are not secured by the federal government, unlike Treasury securities.

government bond indexes BENCHMARK indexes for U.S. government bonds, especially U.S. Treasuries. One popular index that tracks this niche is the Lehman Brothers Treasury Bond Index. This index has two components, the Intermediate Treasury Index and the Long Treasury Index. The former consists of U.S. Treasury issues with maturities of less than ten years, while the latter is comprised of issues with maturities of ten years or more.

Other indexes that track Treasury bonds as well as other government bonds including mortgage securities are

Lehman Brothers Government Bond Index: Benchmark for U.S. government and government agency securities (other than mortgage securities) with maturities of one year or more.

Lehman Brothers 1/5 Year U.S. Government Bond Index: Benchmark for government fixed-rate debt issues with maturities between one and five years.

Lehman Brothers Mortgage-Backed Securities Index: Provides performance coverage of 15- and 30-year fixed-rate securities backed by mortgage pools of the Government National Mortgage Association (GNMA or "Ginnie Mae"), Fannie Mae, and Freddie Mac.

Ryan Treasury Index: Tracks total return of the most recently auctioned Treasury notes and bonds with maturities of two years to thirty years. It was developed by the Ryan Financial Strategies Group and is made up of the current 2-, 3-, 4-, 5-, 7-, 10-, and

GOVERNMENT BONDS

30-year issues that are auctioned by the Treasury on a periodic schedule.

Salomon Smith Barney GNMA Index: Provides performance coverage of 15- and 30-year fixed-rate securities backed by mortgage pools of the GNMA.

Salomon Smith Barney Mortgage Index: Provides performance coverage of 15- and 30-year fixed-rate securities backed by mortgage pools of the GNMA, Fannie Mae, and Freddie Mac.

Salomon Smith Barney Three-Month T-Bill Index: Tracks the average of T-bill rates for each of the prior three months, adjusted to a bond equivalent basis.

Salomon Smith Barney Treasury/Agency Index: Provides performance coverage of U.S. Treasury and U.S. government agency securities with fixed-rate coupons and weighted-average lives of at least one year.

Standard & Poor's Government Bond Indexes and Averages: Tracks U.S. Treasury bonds in terms of yield and price. Long-term issues for the yield average and price index are 10 years and 15 years, respectively. Intermediate-term issues for the yield average and price index are 6 to 9 years and 7.5 years, respectively. Short-term issues for the yield average and price index are 2 to 4 years and 3.5 years, respectively. The yield average is the arithmetic average of four typical issues.

government bonds obligations of the U.S. government, regarded as the highest grade issues in existence.

Government National Mortgage Association (GNMA) government-owned corporation, nicknamed Ginnie Mae. GNMA primarily issues PASS-THROUGH SECURITIES. These pass through all payments of interest and principal received on a pool of federally insured mortgage loans. GNMA guarantees that all payments of principal and interest will be made on the mortgages on a timely basis. Since many mortgages are repaid before maturity, investors in GNMA pools usually recover most of their principal investment well ahead of schedule. Ginnie Mae is considered an excellent investment. The higher yields, coupled with the U.S. government guarantee, provide a competitive edge over other intermediate-term to long-term securities issued by the U.S. government and other agencies. *See also* MORTGAGE-BACKED SECURITIES.

gray market sale of stocks or bonds not yet officially issued by a company that is not a participant in the UNDERWRITING syndicate. By examining the trading activities in the when-issued market we can gauge how much demand may exist for a forthcoming new stock or bond issue.

greater fool theory investment strategy in which it doesn't matter what you pay for a stock, because a bigger fool will come along and buy the shares at an even higher price. Aggressive growth managers consider the stock "cheap" since they believe this theory.

green shoe provision in an UNDERWRITING contract specifying that if unusual and unexpected demand exists, the issuer will provide more shares to be distributed by the syndicate.

greenmail payoff given to a potential acquirer by a company targeted for a takeover. For example, this premium payment may be made to the raider due to a PROXY contest. In most cases, the targeted company buys back its shares at a significantly higher price. In reciprocation for selling the stock back, the suitor agrees to end the attempted takeover. Sometimes management pays this exorbitant price to protect its position. The premium may be made to thwart the takeover if the raider concurs not to purchase additional shares or to otherwise pursue the takeover for a stipulated number of years.

gross domestic product (GDP) measure of the value of all goods and services produced by the economy within its boundaries; it is the nation's broadest gauge of economic health. Gross domestic product (GDP) is normally stated in annual terms, though data are compiled and released quarterly. The Department of Commerce compiles GDP. It is reported as a "real" figure, that is, economic growth minus the impact of INFLATION. The figure is tabulated on a quarterly basis, coming out in the month after a quarter has ended. It is then revised at least twice, with those revisions being reported once in each of the months following the original release. GDP reports appear in most daily newspapers and on-line at services such as America Online. Also visit the Federal Government Statistics web site on the Internet at *http://www.fedstats.gov/*

Group of Seven (G-7) seven leading countries (Canada, France, Germany, Italy, Japan, the United Kingdom, and the United States) that meet periodically to enhance cooperative action on international economic matters. The G-5 is made up of France, Germany, Japan, the United Kingdom, and the United States and assumes a similar role.

growth and income fund mutual fund that seeks both current dividend income and capital gains. The goal of the fund is to provide long-term growth without much variation in share value. An example is Fidelity Investors' Growth and Income Fund.

growth fund mutual fund that seeks to maximize its return through capital gains. It typically invests in the stocks of potential companies that are expected to rise in value faster than inflation. These stocks are best for an individual desiring steady growth over a long-term period but feeling little need for income in the meantime. An example is T. Rowe Price Capital Appreciation Fund.

growth investing strategy used by many well-known money managers, such as Fidelity Magellan Fund's former boss Peter Lynch and Twentieth-Century Investors. It is associated with stocks of fast-growing companies. "Growth" issues are often considered risky because their share prices trade at high PRICE/EARNINGS RATIOS compared to other shares in the market. Growth-oriented portfolios traditionally contain stocks that have higher-than-average sales and growth rates. Investors seeking growth investments must obtain these or other ratios of growth for the investment they are reviewing as well as key market BENCHMARK or peer securities. *Note:* International growth investors look for companies that are growing faster than the economy in which they operate. *See also* VALUE INVESTING.

growth rate
in general: percentage change in EARNINGS PER SHARE, dividends per share, sales, market price of stock, or total assets, compared to a base year amount.
securities: compounded annual rate at which a security appreciates (depreciates). *See also* TIME VALUE OF MONEY.
economics: periodic growth rate in GROSS DOMESTIC PRODUCT (GDP) of the economy, expressed as a percentage over the preceding year or quarter. The growth rate generally signifies the state of the economy—prosperity or RECESSION.

growth stock stock, usually paying a small or no dividend that puts a priority on EARNINGS PER SHARE growth, often the stock of a young company with little or no earnings history. The company is valued on the basis of anticipated future significant earnings and thus has a high price/earnings ratio. The growth company generally grows faster than the economy as a whole and also faster than the industry of which it is a part, but may also vacillate more in price. Such a company is risky because capital gains are speculative, especially in the case of young companies in new industries. An example of a growth company is a high-tech company. *Note:* Growth stocks are more popular with investors who desire capital appreciation instead of dividend income. *See also* COMMON STOCK.

GTC order *see* GOOD-TILL-CANCELLED ORDER.

guilder shares (New York shares) Dutch regulations do not permit their companies to issue ADRs linked to active home-country shares, even if those shares are held by a depository bank, which is the normal procedure. Instead, the appropriate quantity of underlying home-country shares are cancelled and the equivalent amount of New York Shares (guilder shares) are issued.

gun jumping
1. buying or selling stock based on significant information prior to it being made public. This may be illegal.
2. soliciting buy orders in an underwriting prior to the finalization of an SEC registration. This practice is against the law.

H

hammering the market aggressive selling of security positions in expectation of a large sell-off in the market. Speculators anticipating this soon-to-be eventuality will hammer the market by selling short. In selling short, individuals sell securities (stocks and bonds), commodities, foreign exchange, or other ASSETS that they do not actually own, hoping to buy them back at a lower price than they sold them at.

Hang Seng Index market value-weighted barometer of the company issues of the 33 largest companies that represent about 70% of the total market capitalization in the Hong Kong market. *See also* HONG KONG INDEX.

hard currency
  1. gold or coin rather than paper currency, which is referred to as soft currency.
  2. currency in which there is strong confidence such as that of the United States. This is better for investment purposes since investors have confidence in that country.

hard landing *see* SOFT LANDING.

hardening market
  1. situation in which prices of items are starting to increase.
  2. upward movement in securities prices.

head and shoulders chart pattern for a stock or stock market in which the highest point of the stock, or stock market, is preceded and followed by intermediate highs. When the pattern is graphed, it has the characteristic look of a head atop a pair of shoulders, hence the name. It is considered BEARISH when a head-and-shoulder formation is completed and moves to the right shoulder. According to classic CHARTIST interpretations, the next leg would then be down. However, an inverted head-and-shoulder formation is considered to be BULLISH since the completion of the chart's right shoulder normally precedes an upward movement (see below).

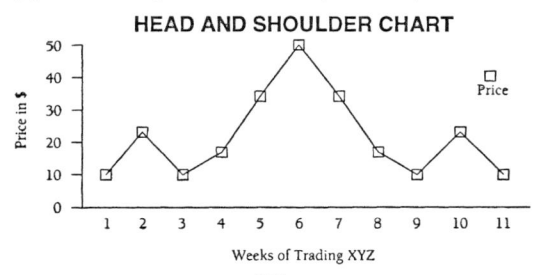

HEAD AND SHOULDER CHART

Weeks of Trading XYZ

151

head-and-shoulders pattern   *see* HEAD AND SHOULDERS.

heavy market   situation in which supply is significantly more than demand, resulting in a drop in prices of goods or services.

hedge   any strategy used to offset an investment risk. While a perfect hedge would eliminate all investment risk, it would also eliminate any possible investment gain.

stocks: in stock investment, there are several possible hedges. An investor having a LONG POSITION in a stock can follow several strategies. First, the investor could buy a put option that could be exercised should the stock fall. For example, if the stock is purchased at $50, the investor could hedge the position by also purchasing a $50 put option. If the stock fell to $40, the put could be exercised and the stock sold at $50. The expense would be the commission cost of buying the put option and exercising it as well as the STRIKING PRICE premium. However, if the stock stayed at substantially the same price, or rose in price, the investor would lose the cost of the put option plus the purchase commission. Another alternative is to sell a call option to cover the DOWNSIDE RISK for the amount received from the option. However, if the stock fell lower than the option proceeds, then the investor would incur the loss. Additionally, if the stock appreciated more than the striking price of the call option, the option would be exercised, with the investor incurring a stock appreciation opportunity cost. Another hedge technique for an investor seeking to preserve capital gains against any possible loss is to sell short AGAINST THE BOX by shorting an equal number of shares of a stock that is owned long.

inflation: investors seeking to insulate themselves against inflation have sought investment hedges in real estate and gold since both assets tend to rise in value during inflationary periods.

international investing and trade: international commercial transactions in which monetary fluctuations that can have a significant impact on the value of the contract can be hedged by either buying or selling the futures of the currencies involved. For example, if you sell a product to an international company that expects payment in that nation's currency, the value of the transaction can be hedged by selling the currency's futures. *See also* HEDGING.

hedge ratio   percentage of the position in an asset that is hedged with DERIVATIVES.

hedged funds
1. limited partnership of investors that invests in speculative stocks.
2. mutual funds that seek to make money betting on a particular bond market, currency movements, or directional movements based on certain events such as mergers and acquisitions. It attempts to HEDGE in order to minimize an exposure to currency risk. In general, international short-term bond funds usually

hedge most of the currency risk while longer-term funds have substantial exposure. Funds use currency options, futures, convertible bond arbitrage, merger arbitrage, and elaborate cross-currency hedges, but the most effective hedges are expensive. Among the most successful hedge fund strategies in recent years has been convertible bond arbitrage. Hedge funds buy convertible bonds, which carry a low coupon but can be exchanged for equity at a certain price. They then take short position against the company's stock, trading on the relationship between the company's stock and bond prices.
3. mutual funds that hedge their risk by buying or selling options to protect their positions against MARKET RISK. For example, a fund specializing in government debt securities may hedge its position by selling call options against its position to protect it against downside risk. Contrary to popular opinion, a hedge fund constructively uses options to protect investment positions and is pursuing an extremely conservative investment philosophy.

hedging process of reducing the uncertainty of the future value of a portfolio by taking positions in various DERIVATIVES (for example, forward and futures contracts). The aim is to protect oneself against wide market swings by taking both buy and sell positions in a security or commodity. *Note:* There are fairly powerful arguments against hedging: (1) for long-term investors, currency moves tend to cancel themselves out; (2) a diversified international portfolio may be exposed to 25 or more different currencies, some of which will fall against the dollar while others rise; (3) hedging costs money and eats into your ultimate returns; (4) currency moves are unpredictable; (5) an adverse currency move may be beneficial in the long run. When a currency weakens against the dollar (hurting your conversion of foreign returns into dollars), the move often helps the country's own economy through cheap exports, ultimately boosting corporate earnings and stock prices. *See also* HEDGED FUNDS.

Hersatt risk settlement risk, named after a German bank that went bankrupt after losing a huge sum of money on foreign currencies. *See also* SETTLEMENT RISK.

Herzfeld Closed-End Average index that tracks 20 CLOSED-END MUTUAL FUNDS traded on the stock exchange. The average is compiled by Thomas J. Herzfeld Advisors and presents the capitalized market value of closed-end funds emphasizing investment in U.S. companies. It equals about 50% of the value of all the funds. It is assumed that the same amount is invested in each of the funds with capital gains reinvested in new shares. There is no assumed dividend reinvestment. It is published in *Barron's*. The investor can follow the performance of closed-end mutual funds by examining the trend in the average. An upward trend is a positive sign in a BULLISH market.

HIDDEN LOAD

hidden load annual undeclared charge by a mutual fund of 1 to 1.25% annually, which pays for marketing and distribution fees.

high
1. relative term describing appreciated prices or values compared to similar items or assets at any market point.
2. greatest price for a stock or debt instrument in a particular trading period or during its history of being publicly traded. Annual security trading ranges showing the high and low price are published in the daily price quotations.

high coupon interest rate on a DEBT SECURITY that is high compared to the maturity amount of the instrument.

high current income fund mutual fund whose investment objective is to produce relatively high cash dividends to its owners. An example might be a fund that invests in high-yielding utility stocks. Most generally, this term has been applied to JUNK BOND funds over the past several years.

high flyer stock stock whose price has been increasing or decreasing rapidly relative to other stocks during the recent past. It is a high-priced speculative security that has increased sharply in price in a short time period. An example is an unproven new high-tech company.

high-grade security stocks and bonds having very high investment quality ratings, usually A or better, by the three major security rating services: Fitch's, Moody's, and Standard & Poor's. The investment rating is reached after considering the corporation's assets, liabilities, quality of earnings, dividend record, and management as well as other factors. Government bonds are rated based on the unit of government, types of government guarantees, the revenue and debt of the governmental entity, and previous credit history. While government agencies consistently have the highest rating, state and local bonds also have high ratings based on their credit history and particular types of revenue guarantees.

high-risk bonds bonds that yield greater potential for gain, but pose a higher risk; commonly referred to as *high-yield bonds*, or JUNK BONDS.

high-tech stock stock of companies involved in advanced technology fields, such as biotechnology, robotics, or computers. *See also* COMMON STOCK; GROWTH STOCK.

high-yield bond funds mutual funds that invest in the debt securities issued by noninvestment grade companies and municipalities (those rated Baa or lower by Moody's rating service, and BBB or lower by Standard & Poor's rating service). Because of the possibility of higher DEFAULT RISK, especially in an economic downturn, high-yield bond funds pay higher yields. *See also* BOND RATINGS.

hold
1. practice of a long-term investor buying and retaining a security over an extended period of time; this allows the earnings of the company to grow, resulting in a concomitant increase in the stock's market value.
2. analyst's recommendation on a stock between accumulate and sell.

holder of record person whose name is recorded by the issuing company or transfer agent as the purchaser and owner of a security at a particular time. This is important for dividend declarations, which are always given to the holder of record at a particular date.

holding company
1. any corporation, partnership, trust, association, or organized group of persons owning or controlling 10% or more of the outstanding voting shares of a company.
2. corporation that exercises control over other companies through title to their securities, primarily voting issues.

holding period time interval for which an investor holds an investment. The return on a given investment depends primarily on this period of time. The period is used for income tax purposes to determine whether a profit earned or loss incurred is treated as short- or long-term CAPITAL GAINS OR CAPITAL LOSSES.

holding period return (HPR)
1. TOTAL RETURN earned from holding an investment for the holding period of time.
2. in the case of a MUTUAL FUND, the return is distributed in three ways: dividends, capital gains distribution, and price APPRECIATION. The annual rate of return, or the holding period return (HPR) in a mutual fund is calculated incorporating all these three, as follows:

$$HPR = \frac{(\text{Dividends} + \text{capital gain distributions} + (\text{ending NAV} - \text{beginning NAV}))}{\text{Beginning NAV}}$$

where NAV = net asset value and (ending NAV − beginning NAV) represents price appreciation. For example, assume that a mutual fund paid dividends of \$.50 and capital gain distributions of \$.35 per share over the course of the year, and had a price (NAV) at the beginning of the year of \$6.50 that rose to \$7.50 per share by the end of the year. The holding period return (HPR) is:

$$HPR = \frac{(\$.50 + \$.35 + (\$7.50 - \$6.50))}{\$6.50} = \frac{\$1.85}{\$6.50} = 28.46\%$$

See also RETURN.

holding the market   attempt to stabilize the falling price of a security that is being sold in abundance. Purchase orders are entered into to accomplish this objective. While this is against the law, an underwriter of a new issue may do this to stabilize the price. This practice must be approved by the Securities and Exchange Commission.

Hong Kong Index   narrow base of 49 companies that represents approximately 75% of the total market capitalization in the Hong Kong Stock Exchange. *See also* HANG SENG INDEX.

horizontal spread   purchase and sale of an equal number of option contracts having the same STRIKE PRICE but with varying maturity dates; also called *calendar spread*. The purpose of the horizontal spread is to offset the risk of the furthest option contract by selling a nearer term option contract.

HORIZONTAL SPREAD

	Debit	Credit
Buy 5XYZ July 60 striking price Call Options @ $600 per contract	$3,000.00	
Sell 5 XYZ April 60 striking price Call Options @ $300 per contract		$1,500.00
Net Cost	$1,500.00	

The purchased option contract with the latest expiration date covers the shorted near-term option contract. It is never possible, therefore, to collateralize a far-term option contract with a near-term option contract.

hot issue   new (INITIAL PUBLIC OFFERING) SEC-registered public offering having higher demand than supply when coming to market. It therefore sells at a premium price.

hot money   money that moves internationally from one currency to another either for SPECULATION or because of *interest rate differentials*, and swings away immediately when the interest difference evaporates. An investor is likely to withdraw funds from a foreign country having currency problems.

hot stock   stock having a great deal of investor interest with subsequent high trading volume and rapid increases in price. For example, a publicly traded company announces it is about to be taken over by another company at a substantially higher price than the current market price. Under these circumstances, the stock experiences a very rapid rise in price together with heavy trading volume.

hung up   term that describes an investor who has suffered significant holding losses on his or her securities portfolio, and who as a result would be very reluctant to sell them now at the currently depressed prices.

hybrid foreign currency options purchase of a put option and the simultaneous sale of a CALL—or vice versa—so that the overall cost is less than the cost of a straight option.

hybrid security security that has features of both common stock and a corporate bond. An example is preferred stock. It is like common stock in that it represents equity ownership and is issued without stated maturity dates. It is also like a corporate bond in that its dividend is fixed for the life of the issue.

I

IBEX 35 Index index of the 35 most traded stocks of the four Spanish exchanges.

I-bond *see* U.S. SERIES I SAVINGS BOND.

IFC Emerging Markets Index index covering 32 emerging markets. For each country, the target aggregate market capitalization of the index is from 60% to 70% of the total capitalization of all listed shares on the local stock exchange. Each stock enters the index in proportion to its market capitalization.

immediate-or-cancel order order (typically large) placed with a broker to execute all or part of the order. The part of the order that is not transacted is automatically terminated. For example, an investor places a buy order for 100,000 shares of Company XYZ stock at $70 per share or less. The broker enters the order but is only able to buy 70,000 shares at that price. As a result, the other 30,000 shares are cancelled.

implied forward exchange rate *see* BREAK-EVEN EXCHANGE RATE.

implied volatility volatility of an asset that is implicit in the current market price of an option (using a standard BLACK-SCHOLES formula).

import and export price indexes measure of price changes in agricultural, mineral, and manufactured products for goods bought from and sold to foreigners. They represent increases and decreases in prices of internationally traded goods due to changes in the value of the dollar and changes in the markets for the items. Import and export price indexes are provided monthly by the Bureau of Labor Statistics in the U.S. Department of Labor.

in and out description of the action of an option or stock trader who purchases and quickly sells options or stocks with the purpose of making rapid profits. An in-and-out trader has a very short-term time perspective.

in the tank
1. slang term meaning that market prices of securities are down significantly.
2. slang term referring to the rapid decline in stock market prices at the conclusion of a trading day.
3. street slang used to describe a situation in which your investment is in a deep hole; in other words, it is doing poorly.

imbalance of orders situation in which orders to either buy or sell a security are excessive. An example is buy orders without matching sales orders. If the imbalance is very significant, especially before the trading day opens, trading in the stock may be delayed. The specialist attempts to make an orderly market.

income bond DEBT SECURITY promising to repay PRINCIPAL at the maturity date but the payment of interest is required only when earnings are available. Typically, interest that is bypassed does not accumulate. Income bonds are traded with no accrued interest. They are commonly used during the reorganization of a failing or failed business firm. Often the issuer agrees to add any unpaid interest to the face amount of the income bond when it is paid off.

income bond funds mutual funds seeking a high level of income by investing in a mixture of corporate and government bonds.

income equity funds mutual funds seeking a high level of income by investing primarily in stocks of companies with a consistent history of dividend payments.

income fund mutual fund that invests for income rather than capital growth. *See also* MUTUAL FUND; INCOME BOND FUNDS; INCOME EQUITY FUNDS; INCOME-MIXED FUNDS.

income-mixed funds mutual funds seeking a high level of current income by investing in income-producing securities, including both equities and debt instruments.

income stock stock that pays a regular sizable dividend to stockholders. Income stocks have a stable profit stream. A high-quality income stock is one with a history of periodically increasing its dividends. Of course, dividends received are taxable to investors. Income stocks provide above-average returns. They are suitable for individuals wanting less risk and high current income rather than capital growth. It is for investors who want to satisfy their current living requirements. Examples of income stocks are Con Edison and J. P. Morgan.

indenture formal agreement, also termed a deed of trust, between a bond issuer and BONDHOLDER detailing (1) the type of bond; (2) amount of the issue; (3) collateralized property (unless a DEBENTURE); (4) covenants; (5) working capital and the current ratio; and (6) call privileges or redemption rights. The indenture also provides for a trustee for all holders of the bond issue.

independent (outside) director member of the board of directors of an entity who is an outsider, meaning he or she is not an employee of that entity. An example is a broker sitting on the board of a client company. Such directors are important because they bring unbiased opinions regarding the company's decisions and diverse experience to the company's decisionmaking process. In order not to have a conflict of interest, independent directors should not participate on the boards of directly competing businesses. Directors are typically compensated based on a standard fee for each board meeting.

index statistical yardstick expressed in terms of percentages of a base year or years. For instance, the Department of Commerce's CONSUMER PRICE INDEX (CPI) is based on 1982–84 as 100. In April 1990, the index stood at 128.9, which meant that CPI that month was almost 29% higher that in the base period. An index is not an average. The index differs from an average in that it weighs changes in prices by the size for the companies affected. The STANDARD & POOR'S INDEX of 500 stocks calculates changes in prices as if all the shares of each company were sold each day, thus giving a giant such as General Motors its due influence. *See also* MARKET INDICES AND AVERAGES; PRICE INDEXES.

index arbitrage purchase of a stock-index future in one market and sale of the stocks that constitute that index in another market, or vice versa, in order to profit from temporary price differences in the two markets. Index arbitrage is the most widely used form of program trading.

index bond bond in which the principal and/or interest will be paid, taking into account the change in purchasing power of the dollar or foreign currency. The bond may be linked, for example, to the CONSUMER PRICE INDEX or to the exchange rate of the British pound. The purpose is to assure that the investor receives the real value of money at the payment date. For example, if price levels rise, the rate of bond interest is adjusted accordingly. Since the principal grows with inflation, the investor is guaranteed that the real purchasing power will keep pace with the rate of inflation.

index fund mutual fund that has as its primary objective the matching of the performance of a particular stock index such as the Morgan Stanley EAFE INDEX. The beauty of index funds is twofold:
1. They minimize costs. All the fund company has to do is construct a portfolio out of the stocks in a chosen index. The fund is passively managed, with changes being made only to fine-tune the fund's performance to match more closely the index's results. The alternative is an actively managed fund, which even sounds more expensive.
2. The index funds eliminate your need to work so hard and worry too much. You can be fairly assured that your performance will be as good—or as bad—as the overall performance of the market or markets you select. Drawbacks to index funds are:
    (a) since the index is made of the stocks of large, well-known, and highly regarded companies, they can miss out on the opportunity of superior stock-price appreciation that some small companies often provide;
    (b) regional indexes tend to be made up of stocks from the various countries in the region in the same proportions as the

market capitalization of these countries' stock markets. For example, Japan has a market weighting of 85% of some Asian regional index funds, and any prolonged decline in Japan's market is reflected in those funds no matter what the other countries are doing.

See also REGIONAL FUNDS.

index-linked bond bond whose interest rate payments and/or redemption value are contractually linked to some specified index (such as a COMMODITY price, or some variable interest rate). *See also* FLOATING RATE NOTE (FRN); GILTS.

Index of Bearish Sentiment index based on a reversal of the recommendations of investment advisory services as contained in their market letters. Such services are considered to be proxy for "majority" opinion. This index operates according to the contrary opinion rule: Whatever the investment advisory services recommend, the investor should do the opposite. It is a technical investment analysis tool, published by *Investors Intelligence* (New Rochelle, New York 10801). It can be found in *Barron's*. The index was originally developed by A. W. Cohen of Chartcraft. *Investors Intelligence* believes that advisory services are trend followers rather than anticipators. They recommend equities at market bottoms and offer selling advice at market tops. The index is:

$$\text{Index} = \frac{\text{Bearish investment advisory services}}{\text{Total investment advisory services}}$$

Investors Intelligence believes that when 42% or more of the advisory services are BEARISH, the market will go up. On the other hand, when 17% or fewer of the services are bearish, the market will go down.

index options call or put option contracts purchased and sold on the Standard & Poor's (S&P) 100 Index, STANDARD & POOR'S 500 STOCK COMPOSITE, major market index, international market index, computer technology index, oil index, and institutional index. Essentially, the investor is risking a specified amount of money, the price of the option contract, on the possibility that the selected index will move up, in the case of the call option, or down, in the case of the put option, sufficiently for the investor to make a profit by selling the option prior to the expiration date of the contract. All options are short term in nature and the time value of their premiums depreciates over their life. Thus, index options are an extremely speculative investment, but do not have as much leverage or risk as a futures contract.

indirect quote price of a unit of a home currency, expressed in terms of a foreign currency. For example, in the United States, a quotation of 110 yen per dollar is an indirect quote for the Japanese yen. Indirect and DIRECT QUOTES are reciprocals.

$$\text{Indirect quote} = \frac{1}{\text{Direct quote}} = \frac{1}{\$0.00909} = 110 \text{ yen}$$

An indirect quote is the general method used in the OVER-THE-COUNTER MARKET. Exceptions to this rule include British pounds, Irish punts, Australian dollars, and New Zealand dollars, which are quoted via direct quote for historical reasons (for example, 1 pound sterling = $1.68). In their foreign exchange activities, however, U.S. banks follow the European method of direct quote. *See also* DIRECT QUOTE; AMERICAN TERMS; EUROPEAN TERMS.

individual investor   individual as opposed to an institutional investor such as a mutual fund or pension fund.

inflation   general rise in prices of consumer goods and services. The federal government measures inflation with four key indices: CONSUMER PRICE INDEX (CPI), PRODUCER PRICE INDEX (PPI), GROSS DOMESTIC PRODUCT (GDP) DEFLATOR, and EMPLOYMENT COST INDEX (ECI). Price indices are designed to measure the rate of inflation of the economy. Various price indices are used to measure living costs, price level changes, and inflation. They are

- **Consumer Price Index:** The Consumer Price Index (CPI), the best-known inflation gauge, is used as the cost-of-living index, which labor contracts and social security are tied to. The CPI measures the cost of buying a fixed basket of goods (some 400 consumer goods and services), representative of the purchase of the typical working-class urban family. The fixed basket is divided into the following categories: food and beverages, housing, apparel, transportation, medical care, entertainment, and other. Generally referred to as a *cost-of-living index*, it is published by the Bureau of Labor Statistics of the U.S. Department of Labor. The CPI is widely used for escalation clauses. The base year for the CPI index was 1982–1984 at which time it was assigned 100.

- **Producer Price Index:** Like the CPI, the PPI is a measure of the cost of a given basket of goods priced in wholesale markets, including raw materials, semifinished goods, and finished goods at the early stage of the distribution system. The PPI is published monthly by the Bureau of Labor Statistics of the Department of Commerce. It signals changes in the general price level, or the CPI, some time before they actually materialize. (Since the PPI does not include services, caution should be exercised when the principal cause of INFLATION is service prices.) For this reason, the PPI and especially some of its subindexes, such as the index of sensitive materials, serve as one of the leading indicators that are closely watched by policy makers. It is the one that signals changes in the general price level, or the CPI, some time before they actually materialize.

- **GDP Deflator:** The index of inflation is used to separate price changes in GDP calculations from real changes in economic activity. The Deflator is a weighted average of the price indexes used to deflate GDP so true economic growth can be separated from inflationary growth. Thus, it reflects price changes for goods and services bought by consumers, businesses, and governments. Because it covers a broader group of goods and services than the CPI and PPI, the GDP Deflator is a very widely used price index that is frequently used to measure inflation. The GDP deflator, unlike the CPI and PPI, is available only quarterly, not monthly. It is also published by the U.S. Department of Commerce.

- **Employment Cost Index:** This is the most comprehensive and refined measure of underlying trends in employee compensation as a cost of production. It measures the cost of labor and includes changes in wages and salaries and employer costs for employee benefits. ECI tracks wages and bonuses, sick and vacation pay, plus benefits such as insurance, pension, and social security and unemployment taxes from a survey of 18,300 occupations at 4500 sample establishments in private industry and 4200 occupations within about 800 state and local governments.
- **CRB Bridge Spot Price Index and CRB Bridge Futures Price Index:** The two widely watched BENCHMARKS for commodity prices are by Bridge/CRB, formerly Commodity Research Bureau (CRB). The CRB Spot Price Index is based on prices of 23 different commodities, representing livestock and products, fats and oils, metals, and textiles and fibers, and it serves as an indicator of inflation. Higher commodity prices, for example, can signal inflation, which in turn can lead to higher interest rates and yields. The CRB Futures Price Index is the composite index of futures prices that tracks the volatile behavior of commodity prices. As the best-known commodity index, the CRB Index, produced by Bridge Information Systems, was designed to monitor broad changes in the commodity markets. The CRB Index consists of 21 commodities. In addition to the CRB Futures Index, nine subindexes are maintained for baskets of commodities representing currencies, energy, interest rates, imported commodities, industrial commodities, grains, oil-seeds, livestock and meats, and precious metals. All indexes have a base level of 100 as of 1967, except the currencies, energy, and interest rates indexes, which were set at 100 as of 1977.
- *The Economist* **Commodities Index:** This index is the gauge of commodity SPOT PRICES and their movements. The index is a geometric weighted average based on the significance in international trade of spot prices of major commodities. The index is designed to measure inflation pressure in the world's industrial powers. It includes only commodities that freely trade in open markets, eliminating such items as iron and rice. Also, this index does not track precious metal or oil prices. The commodities tracked are weighted by their export volume to developed economies. The index information may be obtained from Reuters

INFLATION RISK

News Services or in *The Economist* magazine. The index may be used as a reflection of worldwide commodities prices, enabling the investor to determine the attractiveness of specific commodities. The indicators also may serve as barometers of global inflation and global interest rates.

Price indexes get major coverage appearing in daily newspapers and business dailies, on business TV programs such as on CNN and CNBC and on Internet financial news services. Government Internet web sites *http://www.stats.bls.gov* and *http://www.census.gov/econ/* also provide this data. You can download a variety of inflation data from *www.economy.com*.

A Word of Caution: Inflation results in an increase in all prices, but relative price changes indicate that not all prices move together. Some prices increase more rapidly than others, and some go up while others go down. Inflation is similar to an elevator carrying a load of tennis balls, which represent the prices of individual goods. As inflation continues, the balls are carried higher by the elevator, which means that all prices are increasing, but as the inflation continues and the elevator rises, the balls, or individual prices, are bouncing up and down. So, while the elevator lifts all the balls inside, the balls do not bounce up and down together. The balls bouncing up have their prices rising relative to the balls going down. *See also* PURCHASING POWER PARITY; PRICE INDEXES; PURCHASING POWER RISK.

inflation risk risk that the value of an investment will not increase at least as rapidly as the rate of inflation. *See also* PURCHASING POWER RISK.

information ratio (IR) ratio of the excess return from the BENCHMARK divided by the TRACKING ERROR relative to the benchmark. A money manager trying to beat a benchmark takes some active bets and hence incurs tracking errors. The information ratio (IR) measures whether the EXCESS RETURN (often called ALPHA) is large relative to the tracking error incurred.

information risk lack of information that makes investing somewhat more risky. International investing is riskier than investing at home due to this type of risk. It is simply harder to find what is going on in another country, whether in politics, economics, markets, or individual companies. Also, the lack of transparency and international accounting standards makes foreign investing more risky.

ING Barings Emerging Markets Indexes (BEMI) emerging markets indexes covering over 30 countries on a daily basis. ING Barings Emerging Markets Indexes (BEMI) consider only major stocks that are available to foreign investors. Each national index consists of some 10 to 50 stocks weighted in proportion to their market capitalization. ING Barings also publishes a BEMI world index and regional indexes. Foreign investment restrictions are reflected in the world weightings. Some 600 stocks, from 26 countries, were included in 1999. Some equally weighted indexes are also available. All series are calculated on a price-only and a total-return basis, in local currency and in U.S. dollar terms. BEMI indexes have been available since July 1992.

initial margin   partial payment required by an investor to a broker when he or she buys securities with the remainder on credit. The broker retains the securities as collateral and charges the investor interest on the money owed. The Federal Reserve Board determines margin requirements. The initial margin requirement for stocks is higher than that for bonds because of greater risk. Assume that with an initial margin requirement of 50% (present requirement for stocks and convertible bonds), 100 shares of Company XYZ stock are bought at $100 per share. The actual amount invested is $5000, with a margin of $5000 on credit. The current initial margin requirement on a short sale is 50% of the proceeds.

initial margin requirement   legal requirement that investors deposit a minimum amount of money in securities or in FUTURES CONTRACTS in their account with the broker before they start trading in that account. This margin constitutes a certain percentage of the purchase price of the securities or contracts. Under REGULATION T of the Federal Reserve Board, the initial margin is $2000 plus 50% of the purchase price or 50% of the proceeds of a SHORT SALE.

initial performance bond   *see* INITIAL MARGIN.

initial price
  1. first offering price of an item.
  2. first price of a stock after all buy and sell orders have been received and matched.

initial public offering (IPO)   corporation's first offering of stock to the public. It is typically an opportunity for the present investors, participating venture capitalists, and entrepreneurs to make big profits, since for the first time their shares will be given a market value reflecting expectations for the company's future growth.

inside information   privileged information obtained regarding material business results and pending security transactions that will not be made public until a certain date. Taking advantage of inside information for the purpose of making a profit is illegal.

insider trading
  1. buying and selling of a company's securities based on material information relating to the company that has not been made public. Insider trading according to this definition is against the law in most countries.
  2. buying and selling of shares of a public company by its officers, directors, and stockholders who own more than 10% of the company's stock. In the United States such transactions must be reported monthly to the SEC under Section 16 of the Securities

Exchange Act of 1934: reporting rules for similar trading may also exist in different countries or markets.

insiders directors, officers, key employees, and any other persons privy to material nonpublic information relating to a company. This may be further defined in different countries or markets.

Instinet owned by Reuters, an electronic trading network, part of the FOURTH MARKET. Instinet has become the largest computerized brokerage, with over 5400 terminals worldwide. It is a system designed only for brokers and institutions that pay commissions of about one cent per share and also receive free proprietary terminals. Instinet is always open for trading stocks on any of the 16 exchanges worldwide to which Instinet belongs. It offers anonymous trading, allowing large traders to bypass brokers with their often attendant leaks on who is transacting. Trades are often less than 10,000 shares each, and an institution can do multiple trades to get into or out of a position in a stock without others knowing.

institutional investor institution such as a mutual fund, bank, insurance company, or pension fund, operating on behalf of a broad client base that trades large blocks of securities.

institutional obstacles attempts by institutional investors to stand in the way of certain proposed actions by a company's management they do not agree with.

insuring undertaking RISK MANAGEMENT program for global risk exposure.

intellectual property patents, copyrights, trademarks, trade secrets, and similar rights in ideas, concepts, and so on.

interbank offered rate rate of interest at which banks lend to other major banks. Terms are established for the length of the loan and individual foreign currencies. A number of financial centers offer an IBOR, including: Abu Dhabi (DIBOR), Bahrain (BIBOR), Brussels (BRIBOR), Hong Kong (HKIBOR), London (LIBOR), Luxembourg (LUXIBOR), Madrid (MIBOR), Paris (PIBOR), Saudi Arabia (SAIBOR), Singapore (SIBOR), and Zurich (ZIBOR). *See also* LONDON INTERBANK OFFERED RATE.

intercommodity spread spread between the long and short positions in different but related commodities. For example, you may be long in silver futures but short in gold futures. You expect to have a net gain from the changing prices in these commodities.

interdelivery spread futures or options trading strategy that involves buying one month of a contract and selling another month on the same contract hoping to profit from the widening or narrowing of the price difference between the contracts. An example is an investor who simultaneously buys an August cotton contract and sells a November cotton contract.

interest arbitrage exchange arbitrage across maturities; also called *intertemporal arbitrage* or *covered investment arbitrage*. It involves buying foreign exchange in the spot market, investing in a foreign currency asset, and converting back to the initial currency through a FORWARD CONTRACT. It is similar to two-way or three-way (*triangular*) arbitrage, in that it requires starting and ending with the same currency and incurring no exchange rate risk. In this case, profits are made by exploiting *interest rate differentials* as well as exchange rate differentials. In other words, this works when *the interest parity theory* is not valid. Also, an interest arbitrageur must utilize funds for the time period between contract maturities, while the two- and three-way arbitrageurs need funds only on the delivery date. *See also* COVERED INTEREST ARBITRAGE.

interest rate elasticity percentage change in bond price divided by percentage change in YIELD TO MATURITY (YTM). Since bond prices and YTMs move inversely, the elasticity will always be a negative number. Any bond's elasticity can be determined directly with the above formula. Knowing the DURATION coefficient (D), we can calculate the elasticity (E) using the following simple formula:

$$(-1)E = D \frac{YTM}{(1+YTM)}$$

EXAMPLE:
A bond pays a 7% COUPON RATE annually on its $1000 FACE VALUE if it has three years until its maturity and has a yield to maturity (YTM) of 6%. The duration coefficient (D) is 2.8107. Then the elasticity is calculated as follows:

$$(-1)E = 2.8107\,[0.06/(1.06)],\ E = -0.1591$$

which means that bonds (and bond funds) will lose or gain 15.91% of principal value for each 1 percentage point move in interest rates.

interest rate futures contract in which the holder commits to take delivery of a specified amount of the applicable debt security at a subsequent date. Typically, it is no more than three years in maturity. Futures may be in Treasury bills and notes, commercial paper, certificates of deposit, or others. Interest rate futures are stated as a percentage of the PAR VALUE of the related debt obligation. The value of the contract is directly tied to interest rates. For instance, if interest rates rise, the value of the contract decreases. If the price of the contract drops, the purchaser of the contract suffers a loss while the seller gains. A change of one basis point in interest rates results in a price change. The holder of the interest rate future typically does not take possession of the financial instrument. The contract may be used to HEDGE or to speculate on future interest rates and security prices. A speculator will find a financial future attractive because of its potential significant return on a minimal investment from the low deposit; however, interest rate futures contracts are very risky.

interest rate options   put and call options written on FIXED-INCOME SECURITIES.

interest rate parity   theory stating that investors should expect to earn the same return in all countries after adjusting for risk. It recognizes that when you invest in a country other than your home country, you are affected by two forces—returns on the investment itself, and changes in the exchange rate. It follows that your overall return will be higher than that investment's stated return if the currency your investment is denominated in appreciates relative to your home currency. By the same token, your overall return will be lower if the overseas currency you are holding declines in value.

interest (rate) risk   possibility that the market value of an asset will change adversely as interest rates change. For example, when market interest rates rise, the prices of fixed-income securities such as bonds fall. *See also* RISK.

interest rate swap   exchange by two parties of interest rates on borrowings made in the two markets—fixed for floating and floating for fixed. Consequently, each party obtains the type of liability it prefers and at a more attractive rate. The advantages to interest rate swaps are as follows: (1) The swap contract is simple and straightforward; (2) swaps provide alternative sources of financing; (3) swaps give the corporation the flexibility to convert floating-rate debt to fixed-rate, and vice versa; (4) there are potential interest rate savings; (5) swaps may be based on outstanding debt and may thus avoid increasing liabilities; (6) swaps are private transactions; (7) rating agencies, such as Moody's and S&P, take a neutral to positive position on corporate swaps; (8) tax treatment on swaps is uncomplicated, as there are no withholding taxes levied on interest payments to overseas swap partners, and the interest expense of the fixed-rate payer is treated as though it were on a fixed-rate obligation. One major drawback to swaps is the risk that one swap partner may fail to make the agreed payments to the other swap partner. It is a growing trend that MNCs will use swaps to match assets to liabilities and to protect investments in capital assets, such as plant and equipment, from floating rate interest fluctuations. Financial institutions also see swaps as a way to match receivables (loans made) to liabilities (investors' deposits). *See also* SWAPS.

interest rates   cost of money. Interest rates take many different forms. They are as follows

- **Fed funds, discount, and prime rates:** These are three key interest rates closely tied to the banking system. The discount rate is the rate the Federal Reserve Board charges on loans to banks that belong to the Fed system. The federal or Fed funds rate is the rate that bankers charge one another for very short-term loans, although the Fed heavily manages this rate as well. The prime rate is the much discussed BENCHMARK rate that bankers charge customers. The three rates, at times, work in tandem. The Fed funds rate is the major tool that the nation's central bank, the Federal Reserve, has to manage interest rates. Changing the target for the Fed funds rate is done when the Fed wants to use monetary policy to alter economic patterns. The discount rate was once the Fed's key tool. Now it takes a backseat as a largely ceremonial nudge to markets made often after Fed funds changes are implemented. The prime rate is a heavily tracked rate although it isn't as widely used as a corporate loan benchmark as it has been in the past. The prime is set by bankers to vary loan rates to smaller businesses and on consumers' home equity loans and credit cards.

- **10-Year Treasury Bonds:** The most widely watched interest rate in the world, the security known as the "T-bond" is seen as the daily barometer of how the bond market is performing. The 10-year Treasury bond is a fixed-rate direct obligation of the U.S. government. There are no call provisions on Treasury bonds. Traders watch the price of the U.S. Treasury's most recently issued 10-year bond, often called the "bellwether." The price is decided by a series of dealers who own the exclusive right to make markets in the bonds in U.S. markets. (The bond trades around the clock in foreign markets.) Bond yields are derived from the current trading price and its fixed coupon rate. Because of its long-term nature, the T-bond is especially sensitive to inflation that could ravage the buying power of its fixed-rate payouts. Thus, the T-bond market also is watched as an indicator of where inflation may be headed. Also, T-bond rates somewhat impact fixed-rate mortgages. Still, the T-bond yield is also seen as a barometer for the housing industry, a key leading indicator for the economy.

- **Three-Month Treasury Bills:** The Treasury bill rate is a widely watched rate for secure cash investments. In turbulent times the rate can be volatile and can be viewed as a signal of the economy's health. T-bills, both three-month and six-month issues, are auctioned every Monday by the U.S. Treasury through the Federal Reserve. The T-bill rate shows what can be expected to be earned on no-risk investments. Historically, T-bills have returned little more than the inflation rate. Many conservative investors buy T-bills directly from the government. T-bill rates approximate rates on MONEY MARKET MUTUAL FUNDS or statement savings accounts, also popular savings tools for the small investor.

interest subsidy grant of money to pay interest, as from a government to a private enterprise.

intermarket trading system (ITS) electronic trading system designed to have the order executed on another market that displays a better quote.

internal rate of return (IRR) real effective annual return on an investment. The IRR is a recommended procedure for calculating annual return when there have been multiple purchases of a stock or an ADR over time. It is the rate that equates the cash invested with the present value of cash returns from an investment. For example, the YIELD TO MATURITY (YTM) on a bond is the IRR.

EXAMPLE:
Suppose you invest $1000 and it grows to $2000 in one year, then your holdings advanced 100%. If you invest $1000, though, then add $500 midyear, then end the year with $2000, your holdings did not appreciate by 100%. Part of that gain is from the midyear cash infusion.

Calculating the IRR can be complicated. However, it can be easily computed by using (1) any financial calculator on the market; (2) the IRR function on your spreadsheet software such as Excel, or entering your portfolio into an on-line portfolio tracker that calculates IRR, such as *http://www.portfolio.fool.com* and *http://www.moneycentral.msn.com*

internalization close corollary of PAYMENT FOR ORDER FLOW. Instead of selling orders to an outside firm, an on-line brokerage transfers them to another division of its firm for execution, thus keeping the profit in house.

international asset allocation practice of creating your own international investment portfolio. It involves spreading your investments internationally—by countries and by regions. You may do this yourself or seek help from a professional, either through mutual funds or from professional money management firms. This allocation plan is based on your financial goals, your own risk tolerance, and your investment time horizon—the time you have to reach those goals before embarking on any investment program. To build your international investment portfolio that meets your goals, you must have a good understanding of the rewards and risks (especially CURRENCY RISK) of global investing. *Note:* Without a proper understanding, you might be better off buying international INDEX FUNDS, which provide maximum diversification and minimum expense and trouble.

international banking facility (IBF) authorized in December 1981, a separate banking operation within a domestic U.S. bank, created to allow that bank to accept EUROCURRENCY deposits from foreign residents without the need for domestic reserve requirements, interest rate regulations, or deposit insurance premiums applicable to normal U.S. banking. IBFs simply require a different set of books to receive deposit from, and make loans to, nonresidents of the United States, or other IBFs. IBFs are not institutions in the organizational sense, but accounting entities that represent a separate set of asset and liability accounts of their establishing offices. They are actually a set of asset and liability accounts segregated on the books of the establishing institutions. IBFs are allowed to conduct international banking operations that, for the most part, are exempt from U.S. regulation. Deposits, which can be accepted only from non-U.S. residents or other IBFs and must be at least $100,000, are exempt from reserve requirements and interest rate ceilings. The deposits obtained cannot be used domestically; they must be used for making foreign loans. In fact, to ensure that U.S.-based firms and individuals comply with this requirement, borrowers must sign a statement agreeing to this stipulation when taking out the loan.

international bond funds bond funds that invest in foreign bonds, as opposed to international stock funds. They are limited in the number of available funds as well as in the performance history. In selecting international bond funds, consider the following factors: open-end versus closed-end, average maturity, country focus, and currency risk. It is often suggested that you should stay short-term (typically, four years or less) and locate a fund that HEDGES some of the foreign exchange risk and invests in countries with currencies that move with the U.S. dollar.

international capital asset pricing model (ICAPM) international version of the CAPITAL ASSET PRICING MODEL (CAPM). It differs from a domestic CAPM in two respects: (1) the relevant market risk is world market risk, not domestic market risk; (2) additional risk premium is linked to an asset's sensitivity to currency movements. The ICAPM can be used to estimate the required return on foreign projects, taking into account the world market risk.

International Corporate 1000 published by Monitor Publishing Co. with annual updating, a source that provides addresses, phone numbers, areas of business, officers, directors, and financial data on foreign companies. *See also* INTERNATIONAL DIRECTORY OF CORPORATE AFFILIATIONS; MOODY'S INTERNATIONAL MANUAL.

International Country Risk Guide guide, published by a U.S. division of International Business Communications, Ltd., London, that offers a COMPOSITE RISK rating, as well as individual ratings for political, financial, and economic risk. The political variable, which makes up half of the composite index, includes factors such as government corruption and how economic expectations diverge from reality. The financial rating looks at such things as the likelihood of losses from exchange controls and loan defaults. Finally, economic ratings consider such factors as inflation and debt-service costs.

International Depositary Receipts (IDRs) depositary receipts that include AMERICAN DEPOSITARY RECEIPTS (ADRS) and GLOBAL DEPOSITARY RECEIPTS (GDRS). They are a popular method of investing in non-U.S. companies for those investors who aim to diversify their portfolios internationally.

International Directory of Corporate Affiliations published twice a year by National Register Publishing Co., a source that provides addresses, phone numbers, areas of business, officers, directors, and financial data on foreign companies. *See also* INTERNATIONAL CORPORATE 1000; MOODY'S INTERNATIONAL MANUAL.

international diversification attempt to reduce the investor's risk by investing in more than one country, thus lowering the *country risk*. By diversifying across nations whose BUSINESS CYCLES do not move in tandem, investors can typically reduce the variability of their returns. Adding international investments to a portfolio of U.S. securities diversifies and reduces the risk. This reduction of risk will be enhanced because international investments are much less influenced by the U.S. economy, and the correlation to U.S. investments is much less. Foreign markets sometimes follow different cycles than the U.S. market, and from each other. Although foreign stocks can be riskier than domestic issues, supplementing a domestic portfolio with a foreign component can actually reduce your portfolio's overall volatility. The reason is that by being diversified across many different economies that are at different points in the economic cycle, DOWNTURNS in some markets may be offset by superior performance in others. There is considerable evidence that global diversification reduces systematic risk (BETA) because of the relatively low correlation between returns on U.S. and foreign securities. The risk reduction graph illustrates this, comparing the risk reduction through diversification within the United States to that obtainable through global diversification. A fully diversified U.S. portfolio is only 27% as risky as a typical individual stock, while a globally diversified portfolio appears to be about 12% as risky as a typical individual stock. This represents about 44% less than the U.S. figure. The second graph demonstrates the effect over the past ten years. Notice how adding a small percentage of foreign stocks to a domestic portfolio actually decreased its overall risk while increasing the overall return. The lowest level of volatility came from a portfolio with about 30% foreign stocks and 70% U.S. stocks, and, in fact, a portfolio with 60% foreign holdings and only 40% U.S. holdings actually approximated the risk of a 100% domestic portfolio, yet the average annual return was over two percentage points greater.
See also INTERNATIONAL ASSET ALLOCATION.

INTERNATIONAL DIVERSIFICATION

RISK REDUCTION FROM INTERNATIONAL DIVERSIFICATION

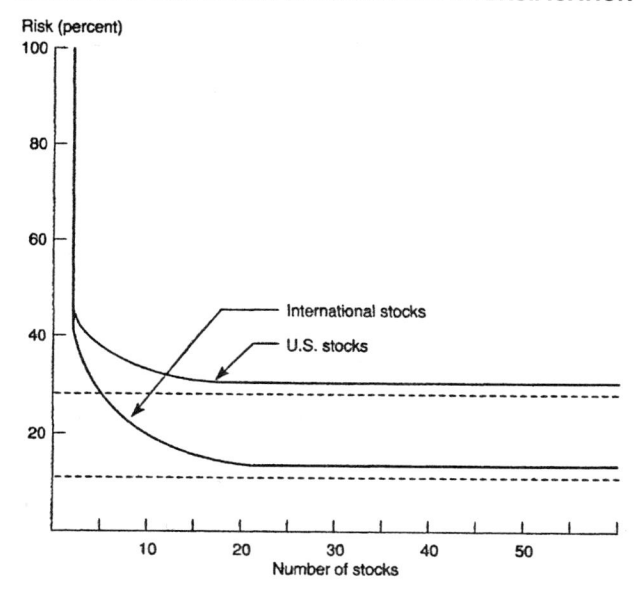

HOW FOREIGN STOCKS HAVE BENEFITTED A DOMESTIC PORTFOLIO

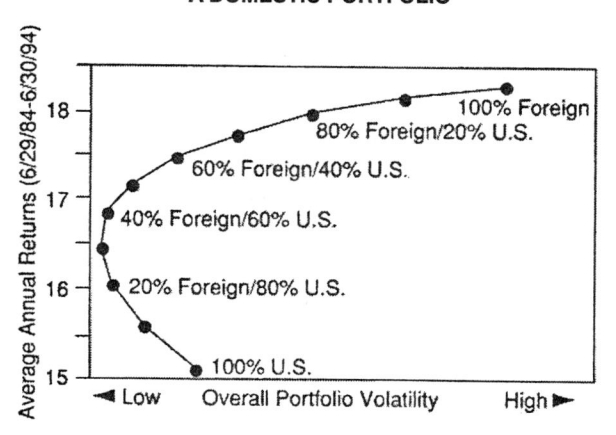

INTERNATIONAL FINANCE CORPORATION (IFC)

International Finance Corporation (IFC)   member of the World Bank Group (*www.worldbank.org*). The IFC publishes monthly emerging stock market indexes, which allows portfolio managers to measure the performance of their portfolios invested in developing countries. The IFC calculates indexes for more than 50 emerging countries—an IFC global composite index of all emerging markets, as well as three regional indexes (Latin America, Asia, and Europe, Middle East and Africa). *See also* IFC EMERGING MARKETS INDEX.

international Fisher effect   theory stating that the difference in interest rates between two countries is explained by the difference in the price level (their inflation differentials); often called *Fisher-open*.

international fund   Mutual fund that invests only in foreign stock or bond markets; also called *a foreign fund* or *an overseas fund*. Because these funds focus only on foreign markets, they allow investors to control the portion of their personal portfolio they want to allocate to non-U.S. stocks. International funds may be open end or closed end, equity or bond, small cap or large cap. Listed below are a group of international funds as reported in *The Financial Times* (*www.ft.com*). CURRENCY RISK exists associated with international fund investing. International funds make significant gains when the dollar is falling and foreign stock prices are rising. Some funds invest in many overseas markets, while others concentrate only on specific foreign areas. *Note:* General Electric Financial Network (*www.gefn.com*), for example, has a tool "How do exchange rates affect my foreign fund?" (*www.calcbuilder.com/cgi-bin/calcs/MUT12.cgi/gefa*). *See also* GLOBAL FUNDS.

INTERNATIONAL FUNDS

Open-end Funds

>China Region Funds
>Japanese Funds
>Pacific (ex. Japan) Funds
>Pacific Region Funds
>European Region Funds
>Canadian Funds
>Latin American Funds
>Emerging Markets Funds
>Global Funds
>Global Small-Cap Funds
>International Funds
>International Small-Cap Funds
>International Income Funds
>Global Income Funds
>Gold Oriented Funds
>Short World Multi-Market Income Funds

INTERNATIONAL FUNDS (cont.)

Closed-end Funds
        Pacific Region Funds
        Western European Funds
        Pacific (ex. Japan) Funds
        Western European Funds
        Eastern European Funds
        Latin American Funds
        Emerging Markets Funds
        Misc. Country/Region Funds
        Global Funds

international investing liquidity marketability of foreign securities owned. For example, high-quality foreign stocks of developed nations have a much greater base of sale than speculative foreign stocks of emerging countries.

international investment investment in foreign stocks and bonds, which contrasts with global investing, which involves investing in both domestic and foreign securities. International investing offers opportunities (1) to put your money where economies or sectors may be growing more rapidly than those at home and (2) to add total returns capitalizing on currency fluctuations. Problems with foreign investing, however, include lack of transparency on financial data; government regulation; added transaction costs; taxes, high minimum purchase requirements, illiquidity; and more importantly, political and currency risks. *See also* CURRENCY RISK; FOREIGN PORTFOLIO INVESTMENT.

International Monetary Fund (IMF) international financial institution, created in 1946 after the 1944 *Bretton Woods Conference*. International Monetary Fund (IMF) (*http://www.imf.org*) aims at promoting international monetary harmony, monitoring the exchange rate and monetary policies of member nations, and providing credit for member countries that experience temporary BALANCE OF PAYMENTS deficits. Each member has a quota, expressed in SPECIAL DRAWING RIGHTS, which reflects both the relative size of the member's economy and that member's voting power in the Fund. Quotas also determine members' access to the financial resources of, and their shares in the allocation of special drawing rights by, the Fund. The IMF, funded through members' quotas, may supplement resources through borrowing.

International Monetary Market (IMM) division of the Chicago Mercantile Exchange where currency futures contracts, patterned after grain and commodity contracts, are traded. Futures contracts are currently traded in the British pound, Canadian dollar, German mark, Swiss franc, French franc, Japanese yen, and Australian dollar. Most recently, the IMM has introduced a cross current futures contract (for example, DM/¥).

international money market   market for international short-term financial claims. A well-developed money market is able to attract savings and channel them to their most efficient uses, making funds more cheaply and freely available to the business sector. Every country that has banks that accept short-term deposits (time deposits) has a money market of sorts. As the economy grows, there would appear a demand for a wider range of financial instruments, such as commercial paper, acceptances, and government securities, and these would be traded in a secondary market where financial claims could be freely bought and sold. As the economy becomes open through international transactions, the national money market became linked to international money markets just as the national capital market has its linkages with international capital markets. The international money market is the EUROCURRENCY market and its linkages with other segments of national markets for credit. One unique feature of the international money market is the diversity of its participants, the wide range of borrowers and lenders that compete with one another on the same basis. It is simultaneously an *interbank market*, a market where governments raise funds, and a lending and deposit market for corporations. The market is extremely homogeneous in its treatment of borrowers and lenders. While in national markets there is invariably credit rationing during periods of tight credit, often mandated by government, in the EUROMARKETS the funds are always available for those willing and able to pay the price. Equally important, the market's size assures that the marginal cost of funds is less. Another advantage to borrowers is that funds raised in the international money market have no restrictions attached as to where they can be deployed. And third, the Euromarkets provide corporate borrowers with flexibility as to terms, conditions, covenants, and even currencies. The international money market parallels the FOREIGN EXCHANGE MARKET. It is located in the same centers as its foreign exchange counterpart. The market operates only in those currencies for which the forward exchange market exists and that are easily convertible and available in sufficient quantity.

international money market funds   money market funds that invest in international money market securities. International money market funds are a relatively recent phenomenon. Many funds invest only in dollar-denominated foreign money market instruments, thereby eliminating the CURRENCY RISK. If you are a currency risk-averse investor, you should put your money in international money market funds.

international portfolio   mix of foreign stocks and bonds. *See also* INTERNATIONAL ASSET ALLOCATION.

international returns   returns in international investments. When investors buy and sell assets in other countries, they must consider exchange rate risk. This risk can convert a gain from an investment into a loss or a loss from an investment into a gain. An investment denominated in an appreciating currency relative to the investor's domestic currency will experience a gain from the currency movement, while an investment denominated in a depreciating currency relative to the investor's domestic currency will experience a decrease in the return because of the currency movement. To calculate the return from an investment in a foreign country, we use the following formula:

$$\text{Total return (TR) in domestic terms} = \text{Return relative (RR)} \times \frac{\text{Ending value of foreign currency}}{\text{Beginning value of foreign currency}} - 1.0$$

The foreign currency is stated in *direct* terms; that is, the amount of domestic currency necessary to purchase one unit of the foreign currency.

EXAMPLE:
Consider a U.S. investor who invests in UniMex at 175.86 pesos when the value of the peso stated in dollars is $0.29. One year later UniMex is at 195.24 pesos, and the stock did not pay a dividend. The peso is now at $0.27, which means that the dollar *appreciated* against the peso.
Return relative for UniMex = 195.24 / 175.86 = 1.11
Total return to the U.S. investor after currency adjustment is

$$\begin{aligned}
\text{TR denominated in \$} &= \left(1.11 \times \frac{\$0.27}{\$0.29}\right) - 1.0 \\
&= [1.11 \times 0.931] - 1.0 \\
&= 1.0334 - 1.0 \\
&= .0334 \text{ or } 3.34\%
\end{aligned}$$

In this example, the U.S. investor earned an 11% total return denominated in Mexican currency, but only 3.34% denominated in dollars because the peso declined in value against the U.S. dollar. With the strengthening of the dollar, the pesos from the investment in UniMex buy fewer U.S. dollars when the investment is converted back from pesos, pushing down the 11% return a Mexican investor would earn to only 3.34% for a U.S. investor.

International Securities Market Association (ISMA)   an association formed in 1969 to establish uniform trading procedures in the international bond markets. Formerly named AIBD.

International Standard (ISO) Code   internationally agreed-upon standard codes for foreign currencies created by the International Standards Organization (ISO—*http://www.xe.net/currency/iso_4217.htm*). Here are the commonly used symbols for several international currencies and their international standard (ISO) code.

INTERNATIONAL SWAP & DERIVATIVES ASSOCIATION

Country	Currency	Symbol	ISO Code
Australia	Dollar	A$	AUD
Austria	Schilling	Sch	ATS
Belgium	Franc	BFr	BEF
Canada	Dollar	C$	CAD
Denmark	Krone	DKr	DKK
Finland	Markka	FM	FIM
France	Franc	FF	FRF
Germany	Deutsche mark	DM	DEM
Greece	Drachma	Dr	GRD
India	Rupee	Rs	INR
Iran	Rial	RI	IRR
Italy	Lira	Lit	ITL
Japan	Yen	¥	JPY
Kuwait	Dinar	KD	KWD
Mexico	Peso	Ps	MXP
Netherlands	Guilder	FL	NLG
Norway	Krone	NKr	NOK
Saudi Arabia	Riyal	SR	SAR
Singapore	Dollar	S$	SGD
South Africa	Rand	R	ZAR
Spain	Peseta	Pta	ESP
Sweden	Kronar	SKr	SEK
Switzerland	Franc	SF	CHF
United Kingdom	Pound	£	GBP
United States	Dollar	$	USD

International Swap and Derivatives Association (ISDA) association of swap dealers formed in 1985 to promote uniform practices in the writing, trading, and settlement procedures of swaps and other derivatives.

international underwriting syndicate group of INVESTMENT BANKERS engaged in PUBLIC OFFERINGS of debt issues such as EUROBONDS. The offering procedure for Eurobonds is much like that of a domestic issue. The offering is preceded by a prospectus and is then marketed by an international underwriting syndicate.

international yield curves graphical presentation of the TERM STRUCTURE OF INTEREST RATES—YIELD TO MATURITY—for each currency, typically the yield curves for government bonds. International interest rate differentials are caused by a variety of factors, such as differences in national monetary and fiscal policies, and inflationary and foreign exchange expectations. This graph shows sample yield curves for various countries.

YIELD CURVES FOR VARIOUS CURRENCIES
BASED ON EUROBOND YIELDS

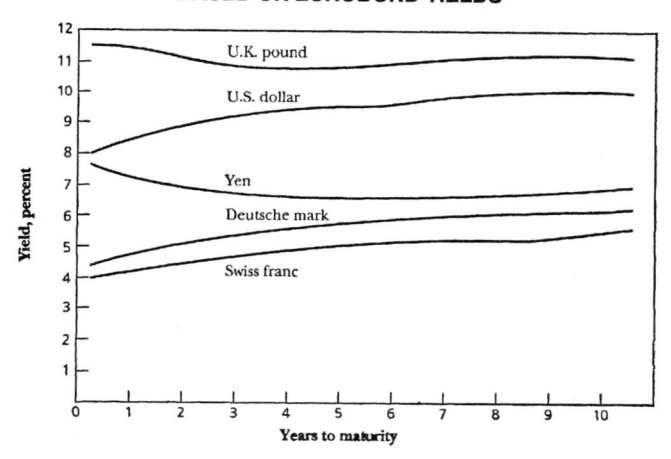

[Chart showing yield curves for U.K. pound (~11%), U.S. dollar (rising from ~7.5% to ~10%), Yen (rising from ~4.5% to ~6%), Deutsche mark (~6%), and Swiss franc (~4.5% to 5.5%) plotted against years to maturity from 0 to 10]

in-the-money term describing the current market price of a call option that is higher than the exercise (STRIKE) of the related stock (if not, it is considered to be under water); a put option with an exercise price greater than the market price of the underlying security. For example, a 50 calls option on a stock selling at 53 is in the money. A 50 put option on a stock selling at 48 would also be in the money. There are two reasons for buying or selling in-the-money options: (1) if an investor is selling a covered put or call option, more money would be realized, giving greater downside price protection on the underlying stock; (2) in-the-money options trade with less premium because they are not trading at the exercise price, causing their prices to move more directly with market prices.

intrinsic value
  1. basic theoretical value of a call or put option. It is the amount by which the option is IN-THE-MONEY; that is, the spot price *minus* the STRIKE (or exercise) price. *See also* CURRENCY OPTION; OPTION.
  2. present value of expected future cash flows of a security. *See also* VALUATION.

investment use of money for the purpose of making more money, to gain income or increased capital, or both. Safety of principal is an important consideration.

investment banker professional who specializes in marketing primary offerings of securities. Investment bankers buy new securities (equity or debt issues) from issuers and resell them publicly, that is, they underwrite the risk of distributing the securities at a satisfactory price; also known as an *underwriter*. They can also perform other financial functions, such as (1) advising clients about the types of securities to be sold, the number of shares or units of distribution, and the timing of the sale; (2) negotiating mergers and acquisitions; and (3) selling secondary offerings. Most investment bankers function as broker-dealers and offer a growing variety of financial products and services to their wholesale and retail clients. Investment bankers typically form an INTERNATIONAL UNDERWRITING SYNDICATE in order to handle a large volume of EUROBOND issues.

investment climate
  1. laws, conditions, and restrictions that are present in a country that impact the opportunity for investment in a foreign country.
  2. economic and political factors, among others, impacting investment performance.

investment club group of individuals joining together for the purpose of sharing security investment ideas. Normally, an investment club develops a pool of capital contributed by its members, which is subsequently invested in securities. Additional money is also contributed at monthly or quarterly intervals, depending on the wishes of the members. Investment decisions are made through a vote of the membership.

investment company company owning a diversified PORTFOLIO of securities that are professionally chosen and managed on the basis of certain investment criteria. The most common type of investment company is the MUTUAL FUND.

investment counselor one who is professionally engaged in rendering investment advisory and supervisory services.

investment grade
  1. highly rated bonds that are purchased by institutional investors because they are very marketable, and hence carry less risk. Standard & Poor's considers investment grade items to be from AAA through BBB-minus, whereas Moody's considers them to be rated from AAA to Baa-3. *See also* BOND RATINGS; JUNK BOND.
  2. investment situation in which a company has a strong BALANCE SHEET, considerable CAPITALIZATION, and continuous DIVIDENDS, and is recognized as a leader in its industry.

investment letters newsletters that provide, on a subscription basis, the analyses and recommendations of various experts in different aspects of investment vehicles.

investment life cycle period of time between acquiring an investment and disposing of it. A good way to measure the return from an investment is over its entire life. For example, if an investment was bought on January 15, 20X1, and later sold on January 15, 20X3, its life cycle is two years.

investment objective individual financial objectives determining subsequent financial investment decisions. For example, a younger man may have a certain disposable income that he wishes to invest for the purposes of growth. He is willing and able to absorb any loss in capital that may result. Suitable investments would include investments in growth companies paying a minimal dividend. An older person seeks to preserve capital as well as to maximize income. Suitable income would include any of several secure, highly rated investments including high-quality bonds, money market funds, and utility stocks paying a stable dividend.

investment philosophy general term describing one's view of the best investments to make for maximizing individual investment objectives. For example, the investment philosophy of some investors may be that real estate has far more investment potential and security than stocks or bonds. Other elements of investment philosophy include the timing of investments and the degree of acceptable risk. Others may be significantly affected by fundamental economic conditions, while still others may rely extensively on chart positions in making investment decisions.

investment planning process of formulating an investment strategy based on an individual's goals and financial characteristics. Investment planning should aim at arriving at a good mix of risk and reward. It should first outline the types of investments available, including their return potential and riskiness. It should take into account the general risks of investing including those related to stock market price variability, inflation, and money market conditions. Investing is an integral part of all personal FINANCIAL PLANNING (see the investment planning flow chart). Realistically, it can be done only with money left over after paying expenses, having proper insurance, and making pension contributions. The person with capital has a wide choice of investment options.

types of investments: Investments can be classified into two forms: fixed and variable. Simply stated, fixed-income investments promise the investor a stated amount of income periodically. These include corporate bonds and preferred stocks, U.S. government securities, municipal bonds, and other savings instruments (savings account, certificates of deposit). On the other hand, variable investments are those in which neither the principal nor the income is contractually set in advance in terms of dollars. That is, both the value and income of variable-dollar investments can change in dollar amount, either up or down, with changes in internal or external economic conditions. These include common stocks, mutual funds, real estate, variable annuities, and other tax-sheltered investments. Factors to be considered in investment planning decisions are safety, return rate, stability of income and dividends, and liquidity.

security of principal: degree of risk involved in a particular investment. There should not be a loss of part or all of the initial investment. For example, foreign investing is exposed to a special type of risk—CURRENCY RISK.

rate of return: the primary purpose of investing is to earn a return on the investor's capital in the form of interest, dividends, rental income, and capital appreciation. However, increasing total investment returns would entail greater investment risks. Thus, yield and degree of risk are directly related. An investor has to choose the priority that fits his or her circumstances and objective.

stability of income: when steady income is an important consideration, bond interest or stock dividends should be emphasized. This might be the situation for retired people or individuals who need to supplement their earned income on a regular basis with income from their outside investment.

marketability and liquidity: ability of an investor to find a ready market to dispose of the investment at the right price. *See also* FINANCIAL PLANNING.

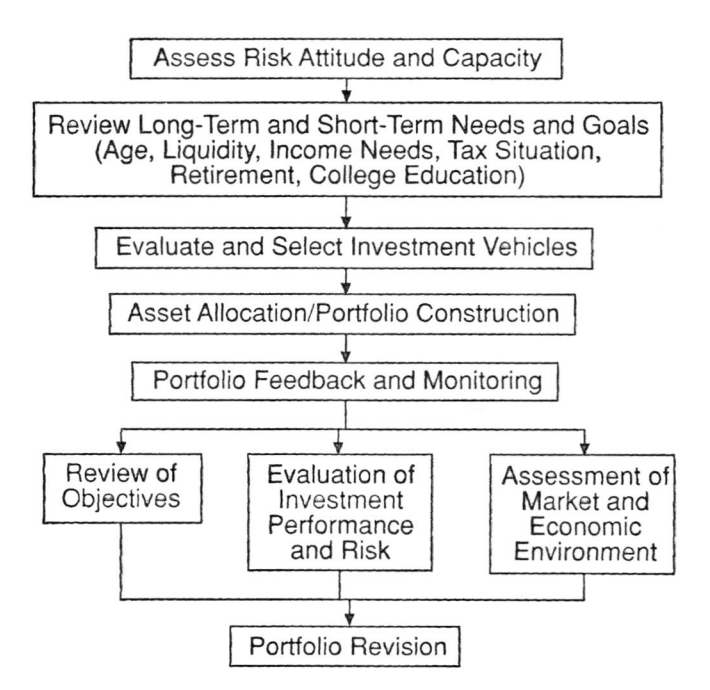

```
┌─────────────────────────────────────────┐
│      Assess Risk Attitude and Capacity  │
└─────────────────────────────────────────┘
                    │
                    ▼
┌─────────────────────────────────────────┐
│ Review Long-Term and Short-Term Needs   │
│ and Goals (Age, Liquidity, Income Needs,│
│ Tax Situation, Retirement, College      │
│ Education)                              │
└─────────────────────────────────────────┘
                    │
                    ▼
┌─────────────────────────────────────────┐
│   Evaluate and Select Investment Vehicles│
└─────────────────────────────────────────┘
                    │
                    ▼
┌─────────────────────────────────────────┐
│   Asset Allocation/Portfolio Construction│
└─────────────────────────────────────────┘
                    │
                    ▼
┌─────────────────────────────────────────┐
│   Portfolio Feedback and Monitoring     │
└─────────────────────────────────────────┘
         │          │          │
         ▼          ▼          ▼
    ┌────────┐ ┌──────────┐ ┌────────────┐
    │Review  │ │Evaluation│ │Assessment  │
    │of      │ │of        │ │of Market   │
    │Object- │ │Investment│ │and Economic│
    │ives    │ │Performance│ │Environment │
    │        │ │and Risk  │ │            │
    └────────┘ └──────────┘ └────────────┘
                    │
                    ▼
            ┌──────────────────┐
            │Portfolio Revision│
            └──────────────────┘
```

investment risks possibility of a capital loss as well as the incurring of legal liability as the result of an investment. For example, a person's direct investment in a business either as an active or silent partner could result in loss of the original investment capital as well as a lawsuit for negligence or other legal matter. *See also* RISK.

investment software computer program keeping a record and analysis of investments in shares, cost, and income. Some packages have price and dividend history of companies. Comparisons may be made of market averages and indices. The program updates the market value of the securities, shows unrealized gains or losses, presents accumulated dividends, and so on. Some packages reveal the tax effects of investment decisions. Numerous on-line services (such as *AOL Personal Finance, www.CNBC.com, www.moneycentral.MSN.com,* and others) track your investment portfolio.

investment strategy plan to allocate funds among stocks, bonds, commodities, real estate, and other assets. An investor's strategy should take into account his or her tax status, age, risk tolerance, amount of liquid funds, and time horizon, among other factors such as economic factors (such as inflation, economic cycle, recession, interest rates) and political concerns. In general, a BUY-AND-HOLD STRATEGY does well in a BULL MARKET. Further, the rate of return on a stock often exceeds the inflation rate long term. Many stocks experience a long-term advance interrupted by minor corrections. For example, a particular stock that has lost value toward the end of a BEAR MARKET will be in a solid technical position for an upward advance. The opposite is also true: A company at the top of a bull market may be ready for a long-term decline in price when the downward trend commences. Therefore, life cycles and the characterization of companies must be taken into account in identifying trends in price. PYRAMIDING is adding further positions to stock, bonds, or commodities as the market continues in the right direction. The buy or sell signals take place on the first signal.

Some other investment strategies are to

- buy the stocks of well-known companies; however, stocks that receive a lot of attention from the mass media may be overpriced.
- buy leading stocks or groups. Buying a leading stock or group of stocks at the beginning of a bull market usually is quite profitable. Further, there is a tendency in an upward market for certain groups of stocks to outperform the market averages at various stages of a bull market.
- buy stocks in an OUT-OF-FAVOR INDUSTRY or company. Out-of-favor stocks may be bought cheap. When their earnings pick up, stock prices will rise. An example is buying interest-sensitive stocks such as banks when interest rates are increasing, if you expect future declining interest rates to benefit financial institutions.
- invest in undervalued companies.

- invest in companies that are doing well financially but not being followed by analysts. SLEEPERS have potential to gain in price once they are recognized by Wall Street.
- fish at the bottom. This may allow you to buy a security at a low price; however, what may appear to be a low price often falls even further, and there may be a valid reason for a steep decline in the price of the stock. A reversal formation at the bottom may reveal that the stock will be on its way up. Is the stock in a turnaround situation in which price has been lowered so much that any good news to come out about the company will cause a drastic price increase?
- do what the "smart money" is doing, since they have expertise and know best. This includes following insider transactions and tracking program trades.

investment trust investment company that uses its capital to invest in various investment vehicles. There are two principal types: the CLOSED-END and the OPEN-END investment company. The shares in closed-end investment trusts are readily transferable in the open market and are bought and sold like other shares. CAPITALIZATION of those companies is fixed. Open-end funds sell their own new shares to investors, stand ready to buy back their old shares, and are not listed. Open-end funds are so called because their capitalization is not fixed since they issue more shares as people want them. *See also* MUTUAL FUND.

IPC (Indice de Precios y Cotizaciones) capitalization-weighted price index that includes the 40 representative Mexican stocks based upon trading value and volume as well as capitalization.

iron law of risk and return direct positive relationship between risk and return. *See also* RISK-RETURN TRADE-OFF.

issue
  1. floating a new public or private securities issuance, such as stocks and bonds. The issuer may be a corporation or governmental agency.
  2. stocks and bonds that are to be or have been sold.

J

J. P. Morgan Commodity Index (JPMCI) index representing a diversified, liquid, investable commodity futures portfolio that historically provides positive correlation to inflation and growth and acts as a HEDGE for stock and bond portfolios. The JPMCI basket includes base metals, energy, and precious metals. In addition to the JPMCI basket, the JPMCI family of indices (*www.jpmorgan.com/MarketDataInd/CommodityIndex/JPMCI. HTM*) include energy, metals, and food baskets, as well as individual indices on each of 15 different investable commodities. The JPMCI is designed to be an efficient hedge for a financial asset portfolio. Hedges should not be broadly diversified in the same way as financial asset portfolios. Negatively correlated hedges, since they provide the greatest diversification benefit to the portfolio, should be as efficient as possible. Oil and metals provide the most efficient hedging benefits. As baskets add more and more commodities, although the basket themselves are becoming more diversified, they are also becoming less volatile and less efficient at hedging per unit of hedge used.

J. P. Morgan Currency Index index that measures one country's currency strength relative to 18 other industrial-country currencies, for example, the U.S. index measures the dollar's strength against a basket consisting of Canada, Japan, Germany, France, Italy, the U.K., Australia, Belgium, Denmark, Finland, the Netherlands, Norway, Spain, Sweden, Switzerland, Greece, Austria, and Portugal. These indices are weighted to reflect the global pattern of bilateral trade in manufactures in 1990 and based to the average of 1990 = 100.

J. P. Morgan Dollar Index weighted-average of 19 currencies including that of France, Italy, the United Kingdom, Germany, Canada, and Japan. The weighting is based on the relative significance of the currencies in world markets. The base of 100 was established for 1980 through 1982. The index appears in *The Wall Street Journal*. The index highlights the impact of foreign currency units in U.S. dollar terms. The investor can see the effect of foreign currency conversion on U.S. dollar investment.

J. P. Morgan Emerging Local Markets Index (ELMI) index that tracks total returns for local currency-denominated MONEY MARKET instruments in the emerging markets. The instruments include Treasury bills, foreign exchange forwards, and deposits. Ten countries are currently included in the ELMI (*www.jpmorgan.com/ MarketDataInd/EMBI/elmi.html*)—Argentina, Mexico, Indonesia,

Malaysia, the Philippines, Thailand, the Czech Republic, Poland, Turkey, and South Africa.

J. P. Morgan Emerging Markets Bond Index Plus total return index of U.S. dollar and other external currency-denominated BRADY BONDS, loans, EUROBONDS, and local market debt instruments traded in emerging markets.

J. P. Morgan Government Bond Index index considered to be the most widely used BENCHMARK for measuring performance and quantifying risk across international fixed-income bond markets. The index and its underlying subindices measure the total, principal, and interest returns in each of 13 countries and can be reported in 19 different currencies. The index limits inclusion to markets and issues that are available to international investors, to provide a more realistic measure of market performance.

January barometer theory suggesting that there is a tendency for the stock market to be higher at year-end if stock prices increase during January, and lower if they decrease; also called *January cycle*. In other words, look at January to determine how stocks will fare for the year.

January effect observed tendency for stock returns to be higher in January than in other months. Much of the abnormal returns for small firms occur in the month of January, possibly because tax-induced sales in December temporarily depress prices, which then recover in January.

Japanese term Japanese yen rate of one U.S. dollar, generally known as EUROPEAN TERMS. A Japanese yen quote of ¥105.65/$ is called "Japanese terms."

Japanese yen Japanese currency. Its relationship to the U.S. dollar is a key to the global marketplace and is seen as a barometer of Japan's economic strength versus that of the United States. It is typically quoted in newspapers and financial reports on television and radio in terms of its relationship to the U.S. dollar. If the yen is at 135, that means that each U.S. dollar buys 135 yen. To figure out what 1 yen equals in U.S. currency, investors use this formula: 1 yen = $1U.S./Yen-to-dollar rate.

EXAMPLE:
If $1 buys 135 yen, then 1 yen is equal to $1 divided by 135 or $.00741.

Currency rates are listed daily in most major metropolitan newspapers as well as national publications such as *The New York Times*, *USA Today*, and *The Wall Street Journal* and on on-line services such as America Online.

Jensen's performance measure measure of a security's excess return; also called ALPHA. A positive alpha means that the asset performed better than the market (for example, STANDARD & POOR'S 500 STOCK COMPOSITE) in risk-adjusted terms. A negative alpha means the opposite. If alpha is zero there is equality of return between the asset and the market on a risk-adjusted basis.

JSE gold index   index tracking leading mining companies on the Johannesburg Exchange in South Africa.

junk bond   low-quality, high-risk but high-yield bond having a credit rating of BB or less. Issues of junk bonds are from companies with poor credit standing and may have a history of poor revenue and profitability. A junk bond may be used in assisting in financing a takeover. Junk bonds experience volatility in price. The investment in junk bonds is highly speculative. The investor is willing to take a high risk to get a high yield.

K

kangaroo bonds   Australian dollar-denominated bonds issued within Australia by a foreign company.

Keefe's domestic and foreign bank ratings   ratings based upon a quantitative analysis of all segments of the organization including, where applicable, HOLDING COMPANY, member banks or associations, and other subsidiaries. Keefe BankWatch (more recently known as Thomson BankWatch) assigns only one rating to each company, based on consolidated financials. While the ratings are intended to be equally applicable to all operating entities of the organization, there may, in certain cases, be more LIQUIDITY and/or credit risk associated with doing business with one segment of the company versus another (for example, a holding company versus a bank). It should be further understood that Keefe BankWatch ratings are not merely an assessment of the likelihood of receiving payment of principal and interest on a timely basis. The ratings incorporate Keefe's opinion as to the vulnerability of the company to adverse developments that may impact the market's perception of the company, thereby affecting the marketability of its securities.

knockout option   option that is cancelled (knocked out) if the exchange rate crosses, even momentarily, a predefined level called the *outstrike*; also known as *barrier option*. If the exchange rate breaks this barrier, the holder cannot exercise this option, although it ends up IN-THE-MONEY. This type of option is obviously less expensive that the standard option because of the risk of early termination.

Korea Composite Index   index that tracks all stocks listed on the Seoul Exchange in South Korea.

L

laddered portfolio strategy for investing in bonds to build a variety of portfolios with different maturities, usually staggered evenly over time to provide regular CASH FLOW.

EXAMPLE:
You might invest $100,000 in equal amounts of $10,000 that mature in each of ten years. As your principal comes due, you reinvest the amount to mature in ten years. Because funds become available for reinvestment each year, this smoothes out the effects of interest rate fluctuations: If interest rates rise, you invest your principal at higher rates; if rates fall, you still have most of your portfolio invested in longer-term, higher-rate bonds.

lagging indicators economic series of indicators that follow or trail behind aggregate economic activity. There are currently six lagging indicators published by the government comprising of unemployment rate, business expenditures, labor cost per unit, loans outstanding, bank interest rates, and book value of manufacturing and trade inventories.

large block ratio sentiment indicator showing trades in large blocks (10,000 shares or more) relative to the total volume traded on a stock exchange (for example, the NEW YORK STOCK EXCHANGE). The ratio equals

$$\frac{\text{Number of large blocks}}{\text{Total volume traded}}$$

The higher the ratio, the more active the institutional investors. A very high ratio may reveal a market top or bottom since institutional investors (who represent smart money) make substantial trades during extreme overvaluation or undervaluation in equity markets. Hence, the ratio may aid in identifying major reversal points.

last most recent trade of a security.

lead manager bank in charge of organizing a syndicated bank credit or a bond issue.

LEAPS *see* LONG-TERM EQUITY ANTICIPATION SECURITIES.

leg down downward price trend of a security or commodity depicted on a chart. See below.
See also LEG UP.

LEG DOWN

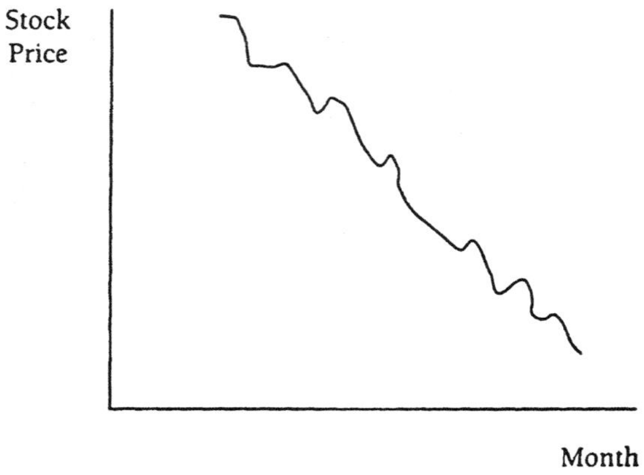
Stock
Price
Month

leg up upward price trend of a security or commodity depicted on a chart. See below. *See also* LEG DOWN.

LEG UP

Stock
Price
Month

Lehman formula compensation formula initiated by Lehman Brothers for investment banking activities, originally structured as follows: 5% of the first million dollars involved in the transaction; 4% of the second million; 3% of the third million; 2% of the fourth million; and 1% of everything thereafter (that is, above $4 million). As a result of INFLATION, investment bankers often seek some multiple of the original Lehman formula.

letter stock   stock or bond issued by a company before being registered with the SEC; also called *letter security*. When a company sells securities directly to the public, it can avoid registering them if the investor writes a letter of intent stating that his or her purpose is to buy the security as an investment rather than to sell it. The necessity of writing a letter to investors for purchasing this form of security is the origin of the terms letter security, letter stock, and letter bond.

leverage

in general: use of borrowed money to magnify potential returns. It is hoped that the investment through leverage will earn a rate of return greater than the after-tax costs of borrowing. *See also* FINANCIAL LEVERAGE.

securities:
1. ratio of dollars controlled in an investment to dollars invested. Buying a stock on MARGIN, for example, allows an investor to borrow up to half the price of the stock. The ratio of dollars controlled to dollars invested in that case would be 2:1.
2. practice of putting a larger sum at risk that one has in hand by using margin loans, warrants, or puts and calls. These tools multiply one's chances of gain or loss as the market moves.

LIBMEAN   *see* LONDON INTERBANK MEAN RATE.

limit
1. upper or lower boundary of a range. It is a point not to be passed.
2. limit move is a price change in a contract that exceeds the limit set for it on the exchange.
3. LIMIT ORDER by which a specific price is placed on either buying or selling a security.

limit or market on close   securities instruction in which a FLOOR BROKER seeks to buy or sell a security at a set price, and if this is not achieved during the trading day, the order becomes a MARKET ORDER on the close of the day's trading. This strategy is useful for individuals who must buy or sell a security on a particular day and wish to do so at a predetermined price; however, the market on close order ensures that the trade will be completed, at whatever the market price is, within the same trading day.

limit order   order to purchase or sell a stock, bond, or commodity at a particular price or better. The trade will occur only if the investor's price limitations are satisfied. For example, an investor places a limit order to buy AT&T at $20 when the stock is at $21. Even if the stock went down to $20 $1/4$ the buy will not occur. If an investor places a limit order to sell AT&T at $22 when the price is $21, the trade will not take place until the stock reaches $22. A higher commission is typically charged for a limit order. A limit order may be appropriate when market prices fluctuate or uncertainty exists. *See also* BUY ORDER.

limit price price specified in a LIMIT ORDER. The investor informs the broker either to buy at a specified limit price or below, or to sell at the limit price or above. For example, an investor places a limit order to sell shares at $60 or to buy shares at $55. The broker transacts the order at the limit price or better.

line charts price charts that connect the *closing* prices of a given market over a span of time. The result is a curving line on the chart. This type of chart is most useful with overlay or comparison charts that are commonly employed in intermarket analysis.

Lipper mutual fund indexes daily BENCHMARKS for stock mutual funds compiled by Lipper Analytical Services of New Jersey. These indexes show the value of (or lack thereof) various mutual fund portfolios. Each member fund contributes an equal weighting to its respective index. As of November 1998, Lipper compiled 61 fund indexes in four broad categories:
1. general equity, including growth and S&P 500 Index funds (8 indexes).
2. specialized equity, including utility and international funds (12 indexes).
3. other equity, including convertible securities and balanced funds (5 indexes).
4. fixed income, including Treasury, corporate, and muni-bond funds (36 indexes).

Daily readings of these indexes are in some newspapers. A weekly summation is found in *Barron's*.

Lipper mutual fund rankings widely watched measures of how mutual funds perform against each other both on an industry-wide and peer-group basis, as compiled by Lipper Analytical Services of New Jersey. Lipper issues reports weekly, monthly, and quarterly. Its long-term rankings with track records of 1 to 15 years are the most quoted. Lipper tracks more than 8000 funds: stock funds, bond funds, and MONEY MARKETS. The Lipper rankings are based strictly on total return, which is price appreciation or depreciation plus dividends paid out. No further analysis is done. That's unlike rankings by Morningstar Inc., which consider funds for both return, consistency of that return, and risk-taking. Lipper then splits funds into various categories that range from broad ones (stocks, bonds, money funds) to extremely narrow ones (international stock funds by specific country). Lipper results are the basis for many newspapers' weekly and quarterly coverage of the fund industry. Every business day, *The Wall Street Journal* uses Lipper data to highlight the best and worst funds in a specific fund category. Lipper's report on the quarterly performance of stock funds is issued within a week of a quarter's end and gets nationwide media coverage. The Lipper performance numbers also frequently appear in mutual fund advertising.

liquidation process of converting securities or other property into cash, or the dissolution of a company, with cash remaining after sale of its assets and payment of all indebtedness being distributed to the shareholders.

liquidity
1. ability of current assets to pay current liabilities when due. The degree of liquidity of an asset is the period of time anticipated to elapse until the asset is realized or is otherwise converted into cash. A liquid company has less risk of being unable to meet debt than an illiquid one. Also, a liquid business generally has more financial flexibility to take on new investment opportunities. A company with poor liquidity will have higher financing cost and difficulty in paying bills and dividends. Liquidity risk may be evaluated by computing a multinational company's current ratio (current assets divided by current liabilities), quick ratio (cash plus trading securities plus accounts receivable divided by current liabilities), working capital (current assets less current liabilities), accounts receivable turnover (credit sales divided by average accounts receivable), collection period (360/accounts receivable turnover), inventory turnover (cost of sales divided by average inventory), age of inventory (360 divided by inventory turnover), and operating cycle (collection period plus age of inventory).
2. immediate convertibility of assets into cash without significant loss of value. For example, trading securities (including equity and debt) are more liquid than fixed assets, because securities are actively traded in an organized market.
3. ability to buy or sell an asset fast and in significant volume without materially impacting prices. For example, large BLUE CHIP stocks such as Procter & Gamble and Merck are liquid since their active trading will not cause a significant change in price from a few buy or sell orders. Real estate, which depends on market conditions and getting a willing buyer, is less liquid.
4. small companies having few outstanding shares, inactivity, or lack of marketability are not liquid because a significant buy or sell order will have a sharp affect on stock price. For example, an order to sell voluminous shares in a thinly traded stock will cause a significant falloff in stock price.

listed firm any firm whose stock is approved by the SEC and traded on any of the recognized stock exchanges such as the NEW YORK STOCK EXCHANGE (NYSE) and the AMERICAN STOCK EXCHANGE (AMEX); also called *listed security*. The term also indicates that the stock meets the ongoing minimum listing qualifications. Stocks that do not meet the exchange's minimum qualifications are delisted.

LISTED OPTION

listed option CALL or PUT OPTION that has been approved for trading on an exchange.

listed securities securities such as stocks and bonds of a company that are traded on a national securities exchange and for which a listing application and a registration statement, giving detailed information about the company and its activities, have been filed with the Securities and Exchange Commission and the exchange itself. Listing requirements vary with the particular stock exchange. Of course, the listing requirements on the New York Stock Exchange are the most rigorous. Among the listing requirements are size of the company, number of years in business, earnings record, number of shares outstanding, and market value of shares. Listed securities include common stock, preferred stock, bonds, options, warrants, and rights. There are many advantages for a company to have its shares listed including: having LIQUIDITY, timely and accurate reporting on sales and quotations, orderly marketplace, fair prices in the market, availability of information to the public, and safeguards to assure that stockholders are not deceived. Listed securities are distinguished from unlisted securities, which are traded in the OVER-THE-COUNTER MARKET.

load sales charge assessed by a mutual fund to buy shares (FRONT-END LOAD) or sell shares (BACK-END LOAD). A NO-LOAD mutual fund is one that does not assess a fee when buying or redeeming shares in the mutual fund. Typically, the front-end load ranges from 1% to 8% of the initial investment. For example, if a mutual fund has a 2% front-end load and you invest $5000, then $4900 would go into the fund. The load charge is added to the NET ASSET VALUE per share when determining the offer price. *Note*: The absence of a sales charge in no way affects the performance of the fund's management, and eventually, the return on investment.

load (mutual) fund mutual fund sold to the public that charges sales commissions, usually called a FRONT-END LOAD when purchased.

locked in
1. term to describe a situation where you have a profit on a security you own but do not sell because your profit would immediately become subject to the CAPITAL GAINS tax.
2. rate of return that has been secured for a specified time period through an investment such as a certificate of deposit (CD) or a fixed rate bond.
3. mortgage rate guaranteed during the grace period.
4. profits or YIELDS on securities or commodities that have been shielded through HEDGING.
5. commodities position in which you cannot get in or out of the market, because the market has an up or down limit day.

Lombard rate rate used to regulate the MONEY MARKET. The Lombard rate is one of the formal interest rates in Germany. Other countries use the term Lombard to describe rates that function somewhat like the Lombard rate. The Swiss, for example, have their own Lombard rate. In France, it is called the Central Bank Intervention rate but performs the same function.

London Interbank Bid Rate (LIBID) rate quoted to a top-quality lender on the London interbank market.

London Interbank Mean Rate (LIBMEAN) average of LIBID and LIBOR.

London Interbank Offered Rate (LIBOR) rate at which international banks lend on the EUROCURRENCY market. This is the rate quoted to a top-quality borrower. The most common maturities are one-month, three-month, and six-month. There is a LIBOR for the U.S. dollar and a few other major currencies. LIBOR is determined by the British Banking Association in London. *See* also EURIBOR.

London International Financial Futures and Options Exchange (LIFFE) futures and options exchange, located in London, that originally dealt only in financial instruments including equities (shares), government bonds, indices (such as the FT-SE 100 index) interest rates, and a wide range of currencies. In 1996 LIFFE merged with the London Commodity Exchange with unified administration and exchange systems. All trades of the merged exchange are guaranteed by the London Clearing House (LCH). LIFFE is a recognized investment exchange (RIE), regulated by the Financial Services Authority (FSA).

London Market Information Link (LMIL) LONDON STOCK EXCHANGE's main source of U.K. financial data for market professionals and information vendors.

London Securities and Derivatives Exchange (OMLX) integrated exchange and clearinghouse for futures and options derivatives based mainly on the Swedish and Norwegian equity markets. Products include futures and options on the OMX Swedish equity index (the 30 most liquid shares traded on the Stockholm Stock Exchange), the OBX Norwegian equity index (the 25 most traded stocks on the Oslo Stock Exchange), Swedish equity futures and options, and Norwegian equity futures and options.

London Stock Exchange (LSE) largest stock exchange in Europe. In 1997 it introduced a new electronic settlement system called CREST, in which all trades are settled within five days. In the same year, it also installed an order-driven electronic trading system called SETS (Stock Exchange Trading Service).

long signifying ownership of securities. It means that the investor has bought a particular investment instrument; for example, "I am long 100 IBM" means "I own 100 shares in that company." This term is the opposite of being SHORT on an investment.

LONG HEDGE

long hedge   hedge involving buying futures contracts in anticipation of a cash purchase; also called ANTICIPATORY HEDGE. *See also* SHORT HEDGE.

long position
1. purchase of a stock in order to benefit from appreciation in market price and the receipt of dividends.
2. ownership position taken when an individual buys something for future delivery. This may be done in expecting that the security or commodity bought will rise in price. For example, an investor who is "long 100 Coca-Cola" owns 100 shares in that company. This is different from a short position because that person does not own the 100 shares.
3. taking a position to HEDGE a currency risk.

long-term equity anticipation securities (LEAPS)   long-term (two to five years) options traded on exchanges and the OVER-THE-COUNTER MARKET. They usually run for one year or more and are available on several U.S. exchanges. While these options are exchange listed, there is little trading volume for a specific option once it has been written. To get out of the option, you must get it priced by a MARKET MAKER. You can trade in the LEAPS of many large companies such as General Electric.

long-term investor   one who invests for a period exceeding five years. For example, a long-term investor may choose an investment portfolio to prepare for retirement in ten years. Many long-term investors choose conservative investments, such as BLUE CHIP stocks, federal securities, or municipal tax-free bonds.

long-term national financial markets   markets for long-term capital markets trading stocks and bonds in different nations. Many countries allow the company to issue its own securities (stocks and bonds) or invest in the securities of other firms. *See also* SHORT-TERM NATIONAL FINANCIAL MARKETS.

long-term planning   planning for five years or more. Long-term planning seeks to improve one's future status through current and intermediate term actions. An example of a long-term plan that will be accomplished in steps is to be a multimillionaire at age 65.

low grade   a quality rating meeting minimum qualifications. A low-grade quality rating is a poor one. Securities are rated as to qualify by UNDERWRITING houses including Fitch's, Moody's, and Standard & Poor's. A low-grade security would be one rated B or lower. D indicates DEFAULT. A low-grade debt security will be forced to pay a higher rate of interest because of the high risk associated with it. Low-grade equity issues are normally not kept in the portfolios of institutions investing large sums of money in securities. *See also* BOND RATINGS; PREFERRED STOCK RATINGS; STOCK RATINGS.

low-load fund mutual fund that charges low sales commissions on the purchase of its shares, such as 1% to 2%.

low par one- or two-dollar PAR VALUE for a common stock.

low price day's lowest price of a security that has changed hands between a buyer and a seller.

M

M abbreviation for 1000. It is used to specify the face value of a bond.

Macaulay's duration coefficient *see* DURATION.

maintenance margin minimum amount of equity that investors must carry in their margin account at all times. It is used to protect the brokerage houses in margin transactions. If the balance falls below the maintenance margin, for example, because of losses on the foreign currency futures contract, a MARGIN CALL is issued. Enough new money must be added to the account balance to avoid the margin call. The amount of margin is always measured in terms of its relative amount of equity, which is considered the investor's COLLATERAL.

maintenance margin requirement minimum percentage equity an investor must maintain in a stock or bond purchased using borrowed funds, as required by the New York Stock Exchange (NYSE), the National Association of Securities Dealers (NASD), and brokerage firms; also called *minimum maintenance* or *maintenance requirement.* The NYSE and NASD both require a maintenance margin equal to 25% of the market value of securities in margin accounts. Many brokerage firms require more—typically 30%. *See also* INITIAL MARGIN REQUIREMENT; MARGIN BUYING; REGULATION T; SHORT SALE.

maintenance requirement *see* MAINTENANCE MARGIN REQUIREMENT.

making a market act of a security dealer who maintains firm bid and asked ROUND LOT quotes for publicly traded securities as part of his or her obligation to maintain an orderly market. Such a dealer is termed a market maker in the OVER-THE-COUNTER MARKET.

management board of directors, elected by the stockholders, and the officers of the corporation, appointed by the board of directors.

management buyin buying a significant interest in a company by an outside investor group that typically takes a controlling interest. The outside group elects to keep current management because of their expertise and experience. The acquisition is often prompted because of the business entity's quality products and services that have growth potential. The outside investor group is typically made up of venture capitalists who for their own protection put their own representatives on the company's board of directors.

management buyout buying all the publicly held shares of a company by current management. As a result, the once public company is now privately held. In order to entice public shareholders to sell, management will have to give the public shareholders a premium over the present market price per share. In the event management takes out significant debt to raise the funds for the buyout, we have a LEVERAGED buyout situation. Management might want to take over the company for several possible reasons: (1) to avoid public scrutiny; (2) to make more money for themselves because they believe the company has tremendous prospects; and (3) to prevent the takeover by a raider who will change management.

management discussion and analysis (MD&A) required part of the disclosure in a registration statement under the U.S. Securities Act of 1933 or Form 10-K or 10-Q under the U.S. Securities Exchange Act of 1934, where management of the issuer explains, in narrative form, the financial results of operations and financial liquidity of a company. *See also* ANNUAL REPORT.

management fee
1. annual fee (delineated by the fund's expense ratio) assessed to shareholders of a mutual fund for its management, administration, and shareholder relations. The mutual fund may be an open or closed one. The management fee is a constant percentage (for example, 1%) of the fund's NET ASSET VALUE. The management fee reduces the shareholders' assets once a year. The SEC requires full disclosure by the mutual fund of its management fee in the prospectus.
2. fee charged to an investor by a stockbroker or financial advisor for managing an investor's portfolio for a specified time period.
3. fee charged by a real estate management company to manage real estate property.

managing underwriters underwriters whose names appear on the cover page of the prospectus, who assist the company in preparation of the prospectus and the ROAD SHOW, and who form the syndicate of underwriters to sell the securities. The name of the *lead underwriter* will be printed on the left-hand side of the prospectus cover.

manipulation illegal operation. Buying or selling a security for the purpose of creating false or misleading appearance of active trading or for the purpose of raising or depressing the price to induce purchase or sale by others

MAOF index index that covers the 25 largest Israeli shares on the Tel Aviv Exchange.

margin
1. amount of equity used (down payment given) for buying a security or futures contract with the balance being on credit; also called PERFORMANCE BOND. If you use 25% margin, for example, it means that 25% of the investment position is being financed with your own capital and the balance (75%) with borrowed money. Simply put, BUYING ON MARGIN is borrowing money—most often using the secu-

rity you already own as COLLATERAL—to purchase more shares. Essentially, you are taking out a loan to make an investment. The advantage is that you have more buying power for stocks and bonds (with no late-payment charges as in a credit card), and it is quicker than borrowing from a bank. The bad news is that buying stocks on margin brings a lot of risk. For example, while doubling your investment and increasing your opportunity for profits, you may also double your potential losses. *See also* INITIAL MARGIN; MAINTENANCE MARGIN; MARGIN BUYING; MARGIN TRADING.

2. difference between the FORWARD RATE and the SPOT RATE for a foreign currency.

margin buying buying securities on credit. An investor opening a margin account signs a margin agreement, similar to an agreement signed to obtain a bank loan; also called MARGIN TRADING. This document states the annual rate of interest, its method of computation, and specific conditions under which interest rates can be charged. The Federal Reserve Board sets rules specifying the minimum percentage of the purchase price that a margin customer must pay in cash, known as the INITIAL MARGIN REQUIREMENT. This requirement is currently at least 50% of the current market value of the security. (Some securities may not be purchased on margin.) A 60% margin requirement means that 100 shares of a stock selling for $200 a share can be purchased by putting up, in cash, only 60% of the total purchase price, that is, $12,000, and borrowing the remaining $8000. The stockbroker lends the margin purchaser the money at interest, retaining custody of the stock as COLLATERAL. This is a form of LEVERAGE that, whether used in a LONG POSITION or a SHORT POSITION, magnifies the gains and losses from a given percentage of price fluctuation in securities.

margin call demand from the broker asking the investor to put up additional funds or collateral in the form of stocks or bonds into his or her margin account. A margin call occurs when the equity in a customer's margin account goes below a specified minimum amount established by an exchange or by the brokerage firm. This takes place when the market value of assets collateralizing the customer's account unexpectedly falls. The margin call occurs when the value of the investment falls below 75% of its original value. Brokerage firms may set their own margin levels, but not less than 75%.

EXAMPLE:
Suppose that your stock value slips from $1000 to less than $750—to $700—the stock is now less than 75% of its original value. Your broker will call and ask you to deposit at least another $250 ($2.50 × 100 shares) to bring the margin back to its minimum level—to put enough cash into your account to cover your debt. If you don't want to meet the margin call, you must sell the stock, pay back the broker in full, and take the loss. Or your broker can sell your investment or portion of it without your permission. *Note:* The purchase of secu-

margin deposit amount of cash or securities that must be deposited as guarantee on a futures position. The margin is a returnable deposit. *See also* INITIAL MARGIN REQUIREMENT; MAINTENANCE MARGIN REQUIREMENT; MARGIN BUYING.

margin purchase *see* MARGIN BUYING.

margin rate amount of cash collateral needed to buy stock in a margin account. Under Federal Reserve REGULATION T, stock investors are permitted to borrow up to 50% of the price of a stock in a stock margin account, but they do not have to pay what they borrow until the stock is old. Regulation T is subject to modification at the discretion of the Federal Reserve. *See also* MARGIN; MARGIN BUYING; MARGIN PURCHASE; MARGIN REQUIREMENT.

margin requirement amount that must be paid by the investor when purchasing securities on credit. *See also* INITIAL MARGIN REQUIREMENT; MAINTENANCE MARGIN REQUIREMENT; MARGIN BUYING.

margin trading use of borrowed funds (financial leverage or debt) to buy securities. It can magnify returns by reducing the amount of capital that must be put up by the investor. The risk of loss is also magnified when the price of the security falls. The following example illustrates how margin trading can magnify investment returns (ignoring dividends and brokerage commissions) and losses as well.

EXAMPLE:
Jack and Jill both have $4000 to invest. They want to buy shares in the XYZ Company. XYZ trades at $40 per share. Jill pays for her shares straight out of her pocket. Jack who has a bigger appetite for risk, buys on margin.

	Jack (On Margin)	Jill (No Margin)
Deposits	$4000	$4000
Borrows	$4000	$0
Invests	$8000 (200 shares)	$4000 (100 shares)

One week later, XYZ Company is trading at $45. Jack's profits are twice Jill's, less whatever interest he owes his broker on the margin loan.

	Jack (On Margin)	Jill (No Margin)
Original Investment	$8000 (200 shares)	$4000 (100 shares)
Value at $45 per share	$9000	$4500
Profit/Loss	$1000	$500

Another week passes and XYZ unexpectedly drops to $35 per share. Jack's losses now not only double Jill's, but he still has to cover the interest on the original value of the loan he got from his broker.

	Jack (On Margin)	Jill (No Margin)
Original Investment	$8000 (200 shares)	$4000 (100 shares)
Value at $35 per share	$7000	$3500
Profit/Loss	($1000)	($500)

On top of this, when the value of the stock in Jack's account falls below half the value of the margin loan, a MARGIN CALL will be issued. If Jack doesn't deposit cash or more marginable securities into the account immediately, his broker can go ahead and sell Jack's stock in order to repay the loan. *Note*: Margin trading is a double-edged sword. Ultimately, only those investors who have a high tolerance for risk should be buying on margin. *Recommendation:* Most experts recommend that margin buyers start by risking a maximum of 5% to 10% of their marginable securities while closely monitoring their positions. *See also* INITIAL MARGIN REQUIREMENT; MAINTENANCE MARGIN REQUIREMENT; MARGIN BUYING.

markdown
1. amount subtracted from the selling price, when a customer sells securities to a dealer in the OVER-THE-COUNTER MARKET. Had the securities been purchased from the dealer, the customer would have paid a MARKUP, or an amount added to the purchase price.
2. reduction in the price at which the underwriters offer municipal bonds after the market has shown a lack of interest at the original price.
3. downward adjustment of the value of securities by banks and investment firms, based on a decline in market quotations.

marked-to-market
1. daily adjustment of margin accounts to reflect profits and losses. At the end of each day, the futures contracts are settled and the resulting profits or losses paid.
2. valuing a trading security or available-for-sale security at its market value at the end of the reporting period. The security is presented at its market value whether it is below or above cost.

market analysis research on the stock market and individual securities as well as DEBT SECURITIES to determine future trends and directions. There are two schools of market analysis: technical and fundamental analysis. *See also* FUNDAMENTAL ANALYSIS; TECHNICAL ANALYSIS.

market bottom or top lowest or highest price for a market index in a specified time frame.

MARKET INDICES (INDEXES) AND AVERAGES

market breadth analysis of the stock market's performance by comparing the number of stocks that rose as opposed to those that fell. The greater the number of stocks that went up as opposed to those that fell, the more BULLISH is the indicator. Conversely, the larger the number of stocks falling as opposed to those rising, the more BEARISH is the indicator.

market cap (market capitalization) value of a business entity equal to its outstanding shares multiplied by the current market price per share. For example, if 5,000,000 shares are issued and outstanding and the market price per share is $10, the company's market CAPITALIZATION is $50,000,000. Institutional investors including insurance companies, pension plans, and so on will not invest in a company unless its market capitalization is a minimum amount (such as $100 million) predetermined by them. Higher market capitalization reflects a larger and higher quality company, which is probably more widely held and actively traded. *See also* BOOK VALUE.

market efficiency theory that all relevant information is quickly reflected in both the securities markets. In efficient markets, investors would not try to beat the market and rather, resort to passive management strategies focusing on RISK MANAGEMENT. *See also* EFFICIENT MARKET.

market if touched order (MIT) instruction to buy or sell a security or commodity once a predetermined market price occurs, at which time it translates into a MARKET ORDER. For example, a stock is currently at $50 per share. An investor may place an order to buy at $45 per share. When the market price drops to $45, the stock is bought at whatever market price exists when the order is executed.

market imperfections markets that are inefficient and segmented such that investors attempt to beat the market to maximize returns.

market indices *see* MARKET INDICES AND AVERAGES.

market indices (indexes) and averages market gauges used to track performance for stocks and bonds. In theory, an average is the simple arithmetic mean, while an index is an average expressed relative to a preestablished market value. In practice, the distinction is not all that clear. There are many stock market indices and averages available. Each market has several indices published by Dow Jones, Standard & Poor's, and other financial services. Different investors prefer different indices. Indices and averages are also used as the underlying value of index futures and index options.
Dow Jones Averages: Dow Jones averages are the most widely used and watched market indices published by *The Wall Street Journal*. The Dow Jones Industrial Average (DJIA) is one of the four stock averages compiled by the *Journal*. This average consists of 30 large companies and is considered a BLUE CHIP index (stocks of very high

MARKET INDICES (INDEXES) AND AVERAGES

quality). The DJIA represents about 20% of the market value of the New York Stock Exchange (NYSE) stocks. There are three other Dow Jones Averages: the transportation, composed of 20 transportation issues, the 15 utilities, and a composite of the total 65 stocks. The DJIA would be a price-weighted simple average of 30 blue chip stocks but when a firm splits its stock price, the average has to be adjusted in some manner. In fact, the divisor is changed from time to time to maintain continuity of the average. The Dow Jones Averages are designed to serve as indicators of broad movements in the securities markets. The Dow Jones Composite, also called 65 Stock Average, combines all three Dow Jones averages.

***Barron's* Indices:** *Barron's*, which is also a publication of Dow Jones, compiles Barron's 50 Stock Average and an index of low-priced securities that meets the needs of small investors. *Barron's* also publishes a weekly average called *Barron's* Group Stock Averages covering 32 industry groups.

Standard & Poor's Indices: Standard & Poor's Corporation publishes several indices, including two most widely used indices—the S&P 400 Industrials and the S&P 500 Stock Index. The S&P 400 is composed of 400 industrial common stocks of companies listed on the New York Stock Exchange and the S&P 500 Stock Index consists of the 400 industrials and utilities and transportation stocks. They are used as broad measures of the market direction. They are also frequently used as proxies for market return when computing the systematic risk measure (BETA) of individual stocks and portfolios. The S&P 500 Stock Index is one of the U.S. Commerce Department's Index of 11 Leading Economic Indicators. This index represents some 80% of the market value of all issues traded on the NYSE. The Standard & Poor's 100 Stock Index consists of stocks for which options are listed on the Chicago Board Options Exchange (CBOE). S&P Indices are all market-value weighted.

Value Line Composite Average: The Value Line Composite Average is an equally weighted geometric average of 1685 companies from the NYSE and the OVER-THE-COUNTER MARKET.

Other Market Indices: Different exchanges publish their market indices. The NYSE publishes a composite index as well as industrial, utility, transportation, and financial index. The American Stock Exchange (AMEX) compiles two major indices—the AMEX Market Value Index (AMVI) and the AMEX Major Market Index. The National Association of Securities Dealers also publishes several indices to represent the companies in the OVER-THE-COUNTER MARKET. It publishes the NASDAQ OTC composite, insurance, industrial, and banking indices.

Wilshire 5000 Equity Index: The index is published by the Wilshire Associates of Santa Monica, California and represents the market value of 5000 NYSE, AMEX, and OVER-THE-COUNTER issues.

Bond Averages: *Barron's* publishes an index of 20 bonds, 10 utility bonds, and 10 industrial bonds as an average of the bond market. Dow Jones publishes two major bond averages—the Dow Jones 40

Bond Average, representative of six different bond groups, and the Dow Jones Municipal Bond Yield Average.

Mutual Fund Averages: Lipper Analytical Services compiles the Lipper Mutual Fund Investment Performance Averages. It publishes three basic fund indices for growth funds, growth-income funds, and balanced funds.

There are also indexes and averages associated with foreign equity and bond markets. *See also* BANK OF NEW YORK ADR INDEX; CORPORATE BOND INDEXES; GLOBAL STOCK INDEXES; FOREIGN BOND INDEXES.

market letter letter or brief statement sent to security investors by brokerage firms and market authorities, often for a fee, giving an expert market analyst's point of view about current market conditions suggesting particular investment strategies, often including specific buy and sell recommendations, to follow; also called INVESTMENT LETTER. Some market letters issue recommendations causing spectacular advances or declines in the stock market. Market letters are only advisory in nature and take no specific responsibility for directly managing an investor's assets.

market maker dealer in the OVER-THE-COUNTER MARKET who makes the bid and offer prices in specified securities by buying or selling ROUND LOTS at prevailing quoted market prices. The purpose of the market maker is to maintain an orderly market for the security over the long term. The one making a market for a security on an organized stock exchange (such as the NEW YORK STOCK EXCHANGE) is referred to as a SPECIALIST.

market-neutral funds mutual funds that allocate half their portfolio to LONG positions and the other half to SHORT positions. The portfolio managers of market-neutral funds will invest undervalued stocks in the hope that the funds will go up, and short stocks that are overvalued in the hope that they will go down. The assumption is that during a BULL market, the long positions will do well, and during a BEAR market, the short positions will outperform. The Rosenberg Value Market-Neutral Fund (BRMIX) is an example.

market-on-the-close order order to buy or sell securities on the market as near as is practical to the close of trading. Often this type of order is issued if a LIMIT day order was unsuccessful and the trade must be completed before the end of the trading session.

market opening time at which trading first starts. Trading may not begin simultaneously for all securities as there may be an imbalance of buy or sell orders and the floor broker is trying to match up the order with available securities.

market order order to purchase or sell a stock or bond at the best available market price when the order reaches the trading floor. Most orders placed by investors are of this type. *See also* BUY ORDER.

MARKET OVERHANG

market overhang depressive effect on the market price of a publicly traded security when the market knows that there is a substantial number of shares that are freely tradable and there is reason to believe the holders may sell in the foreseeable future.

market price
1. price at which the seller and the buyer agree to trade on the open market based on the demand/supply relationship for a security or commodity.
2. last reported price a stock, bond, or commodity was transacted for on an exchange. In the case of OVER-THE-COUNTER securities, market price represents the combined bid and offer prices available at a specific time from dealers in the stock.

market return average return on all stocks, such as those in the S&P 500 Stock Composite Index. *See also* BETA COEFFICIENT; CAPITAL ASSET PRICING MODEL (CAPM).

market risk extent to which the possibility of financial loss can arise from any unfavorable market forces such as changes in interest rates, currency rates, equity prices, or commodity prices. Prices of all securities are correlated to some degree with broad swings in the stock market. Market risk refers to changes in a firm's security's price resulting from changes in the stock or bond market as a whole, regardless of the fundamental change in the firm's earning power; *also called* SYSTEMATIC RISK.

market risk premium extra return exceeding that offered on T-bills, to justify for taking on certain risks expressed by BETA. The higher a stock's beta, the greater the return expected (or required) by the investor.

Expected return = risk-free rate + beta × market risk premium
= risk-free rate + beta (market return
− risk-free rate)

EXAMPLE:
Assume a risk-free rate = 5.5%, expected market return = 12%. If a beta is 2.0, the risk premium equals: 2.0 × (12% − 5.5%) = 2.0 × 6.5% = 13%. The investor would want an extra 13% (risk premium) on the security besides the risk-free return of 5.5%. Hence, the expected return is 5.5% + 13% = 18.5%.

EXPECTED RETURN AND BETA

Risk and Return

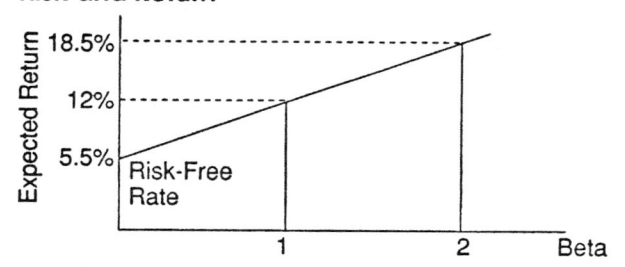

A chart plotting Expected Return against Beta. The Risk-Free Rate is 5.5%. At Beta = 1, Expected Return is 12%. At Beta = 2, Expected Return is 18.5%.

See also BETA COEFFICIENT; CAPITAL ASSET PRICING MODEL (CAPM).

market sentiment feeling or tone of a market shown by the activity and price movement of the securities. A BULLISH market sentiment would be indicated by rising prices, while a BEARISH sentiment would be indicated by falling prices.

market specialist member of a stock or commodities exchange who represents a specific security or group of securities. This individual's responsibility is to maintain an orderly market during particularly turbulent periods by buying and selling securities into his or her own account and providing liquidity. The market specialist also maintains the book where all buy and sell orders are entered and matched together to make a sale. *See also* MARKET MAKER; SPECIALIST.

market technicians those who adhere to the technical analysis school of MARKET ANALYSIS. Market technicians perform technical analysis whereby future security price movements are based on past price fluctuations. Adherents to this field of thought anticipate that past price patterns will reproduce themselves in the future, allowing elaborate technical analyses of current price movements to be projected into the near and intermediate term. Market technicians disregard fundamental analysis and examine market charts exclusively to detect patterns foretelling future price movements. The various stock price patterns that market technicians analyze are termed technical indicators.

market timer professional money manager or investor who analyzes the appropriate time in which to buy or sell an investment. *See also* MARKET TIMING; PORTFOLIO MANAGER.

market timing attempt to predict future market movements, and basing buy and sell decisions on those predications. It uses a variety of analytical tools to devise ENTRY and EXIT methods. The objective of market timing is to avoid major market declines. By avoiding significant DOWNTURNS in the market with market timing, you can achieve superior returns over a BUY-AND-HOLD STRATEGY.

market value policy management policies developed to support the market value of its equity and debt securities. There are many alternative policies management might choose, including selling certain subsidiaries and distributing the proceeds to the shareholders, raising the dividend, or streamlining the company in order to increase profits.

marking to market *see* MARKED-TO-MARKET.

markup *see* MARKDOWN.

matched and lost term for two orders of the same quantity and price for the sale of a stock going the exchange floor at the same time. Both bids are considered to be on an equal basis so the two bidders flip a coin to decide who buys the stock—and who has "matched and lost." The term also applies to offers to sell.

material information
1. financial data that if not disclosed would mislead a reader of the financial statements.
2. important event or data that has a significant effect on the market price of a company's stock. An example is a pending takeover attempt of the company that would most likely increase the market price of the stock. The investor needs to have knowledge of the information to make an informed decision.

maturity
1. due date of a debt (bond, loan) at which time the principal and final interest must be paid.
2. age, experience, and how well established a company is.

McClellan Oscillator index based on New York Stock Exchange net advances over declines. It provides a measure of such conditions as overbought/oversold and market direction on a short- to intermediate-term basis. The McClellan Oscillator measures a Bear Market Selling Climax when registering a very negative reading, such as −150. A sharp buying pulse in the market is indicated by a very positive reading, well above 100.

mean simple arithmetic average of amounts. It is calculated by adding all values in the sample divided by the total observations. *See also* ARITHMETIC AVERAGE RETURN; COMPOUND (GEOMETRIC) AVERAGE RETURN; MOVING AVERAGE.

megafunds collection of funds that invest in mutual funds themselves, diversifying among funds rather than particular stocks or bonds.

member firm securities BROKERAGE FIRM having at least one member who belongs to a major stock exchange such as the New York

Stock Exchange. By exchange rules, the membership must be held by an individual and not a firm.

merchant bank bank (European or part of an American bank) that offers a range of services to corporate clients including advice on such matters as investment banking, international trading, mergers and acquisitions, and flotations, new issues, and capital restructuring.

Merrill Lynch Enmet Index commodity futures price index that includes only six energy and metal ("Enmet") commodities: crude oil, natural gas, aluminum, copper, gold, and silver.

mezzanine financing or round financing round in venture capital-backed companies occurring after the company has completed its product development and after it is an operating company, but before the company is ready for a PUBLIC OFFERING or to be acquired.

misery index index that tracks economic conditions including inflation and unemployment. It was particularly referred to in the economically depressed period of 1977 through 1981 in the United States. The inflation rate was in the double digits at that time. Misery index = inflation rate + unemployment rate + prime rate. The index typically is negatively correlated to the current condition of the stock market. The misery index has little value as a predictor of future stock prices. The index may be found in the Bureau of Labor Statistics publications and *The Wall Street Journal*.

mispricings options that can be overvalued or undervalued. These are temporary, market-driven deviations from the fair value of option premiums. They are usually corrected within a few seconds to a few days through ARBITRAGE and other normal market forces.

modified duration measure of a bond's price sensitivity to interest rate movements. Equal to the duration of a bond divided by one plus its YIELD TO MATURITY.

modified internal rate of return (MIRR) discount rate at which the present value of a project's cost is equal to the present value of its terminal value, where the terminal value is found as the sum of the future values of the cash flows, compounded at the firm's cost of capital. The MIRR is a modified version of the INTERNAL RATE OF RETURN (IRR) and a better indicator of relative profitability, hence better for use in capital budgeting.

momentum
1. measure of how fast a market or stock is rising or falling, incorporating both price levels and trading volumes.
2. technique used to construct an overbought/oversold oscillator. *Momentum* measures price *differences* over a selected span of time. To construct a ten-day momentum line, the closing price ten days earlier is subtracted from the latest price. The resulting positive or negative value is plotted above or below a zero line.

3. underlying power or thrust behind all upward or downward price movement. Momentum is represented on a graph as a line that is continually fluctuating above and below a horizontal equilibrium level that represents the halfway point between extreme readings. Momentum is a generic term embracing many different indicators, such as rate of change (ROC), relative strength indicators (RSIs), and STOCHASTICS INDEX.
4. rate of acceleration of an economic, price, or volume movement. An economy with strong growth that is likely to continue is said to have momentum.

momentum player investor or professional money manager who tries to predict the direction of stock prices or markets by studying MOMENTUMS and trends in buying and selling. Momentum players are essentially technicians or CHARTISTS. *Note:* Very few international money managers use this method due to a lack of historical data by which to judge previous market trend patterns, especially in EMERGING MARKETS. *See also* MARKET TIMER; PORTFOLIO MANAGER.

monetary indicators economic indicators that tell about money and credit market conditions. Most widely reported in the media are money supply, consumer credit, the DOW JONES INDUSTRIAL AVERAGE, and the TREASURY BILL rate. *See also* ECONOMIC INDICATORS.

money flow index index that measures the MOMENTUM (strength) in the market by determining how many funds are going into and out of the market. The indicator accounts for VOLUME. The following steps are required in computing the money flow index:
1. Compute the usual price equal to: (high price + low price + closing price) ÷ 3.
2. Compute the money flow equal to the usual price multiplied by volume.
3. Determine positive or negative money flow over a specified time period.
4. Compute the money ratio equal to the positive money flow divided by the negative money flow.
5. Calculate the money flow index as follows: 100 − [100/(1 + money ratio)]

If there is a decline in the index coupled with increasing security prices, this divergence signals a forthcoming reversal in the market. If the index is more than 80, a market top may exist. If the index is less than 20, a market bottom may exist.

money manager *see* PORTFOLIO MANAGER.

money market
1. marketplace for short-term securities, such as U.S. TREASURY BILLS, bankers' acceptances, commercial paper, and negotiable certificates of deposit. *See also* FINANCIAL INSTITUTIONS; FINANCIAL MARKETS.
2. dealers and their network who trade short-term, relatively risk-free securities.

money-market hedge HEDGE in which the exposed position in a foreign currency is offset by borrowing or lending in the money market; also called *credit market hedge*. It basically calls for matching the exposed asset (accounts receivable) with a liability (loan payable) in the same currency. A firm borrows in one currency, invests in the money market, and converts the proceeds into another currency. Funds to repay the loan may be generated from business operations, in which case the hedge is *covered*, or funds to repay the loan may be purchased in the foreign exchange market at the SPOT RATE when the loan matures, which is called an *uncovered* or open edge. The cost of the money market hedge is determined by differential interest rates.

money market (mutual) funds open-end mutual fund that pools the deposits of many investors and invests exclusively in short-term debt securities (maturing within one year) such as U.S. government securities, commercial paper, and certificates of deposit. These funds provide more safety of principal than other mutual funds since NET ASSET VALUE (NAV) never fluctuates. Typically, shares are quoted at $1 each. (Each share has a net asset value of $1.) Through a unique accounting treatment, all returns are paid as interest so the share price does not change. The yield, however, fluctuates daily. Examples are Fidelity Spartan Money Market Fund and Merrill Lynch CMA Money Fund. The advantages are (1) low-risk, cash equivalent investment; (2) on average, lower fees than stock or bond funds; (3) in many cases, low investment minimum, as little as $250 (if you want to buy short-term securities, a minimum purchase is at least $10,000); (4) check-writing privileges; (5) interest is earned daily; (6) funds can be used as a "parking place" in which to put money while waiting to make another investment; (7) tax-free options; (8) transactions by telephone, mail, or wire; (9) typically, higher yields than bank money market accounts.

The disadvantages are (1) limits on check size and number of checks allowed; (2) the deposit in these funds not insured as it is in a money market deposit account (MMDA) or other federally insured deposits in banks; (3) money market funds can be risky when they invest heavily in commercial paper that does not get the top two credit ratings by Moody's and Standard & Poor's; (4) not for long-term investing—may not outpace INFLATION; (5) for taxable funds, must pay local, state, and federal taxes on interest earned. The Vanguard Prime Money Market Fund and Fidelity Cash Reserves Fund are two of the largest money funds available. *Note:* For money market fund and money market account information, check out *www.imoneynet.com* and *www.bankrate.com*.

money supply stock of money in the economy, consisting of currency in circulation and deposits in checking and savings accounts. The nation's money supply is divided into the categories: M1, M2, M3, and L.

- M1 = narrowest measure of basic money supply, immediately spendable forms: traveler's checks; other checkable deposits (NOW, share draft, and other accounts); demand deposits; currency.
- M2 = M1 + money that cannot be used directly for payments but can be converted easily into spendable forms: savings (time) deposits; repurchase agreements (overnight); money market mutual fund shares; EURODOLLARS (overnight).
- M3 = broader measure of money supply = M1 and M2 plus the financial instruments of large institutions, which are not converted easily into spendable forms: large-denomination time deposits; term repurchase agreements.
- L = M3 + open liquid assets (such as Treasury bills and bonds and term eurodollars)

monitoring the portfolio process of supervising the financial performance of an investment portfolio in order to make buy or sell recommendations regarding certain investments to achieve a maximum financial return on the total assets. The investment return of certain investments could be higher than others, and unless the portfolio is continuously monitored, these opportunities cannot be utilized.

monthly investment plan (MIP) investment strategy whereby an investor invests a particular sum of money each month. In security investments, this is a form of DOLLAR COST AVERAGING and assumes that the long-term direction of the investments is up. The investor is able to reduce the average unit cost of the investment with increased financial returns. Many mutual funds have a monthly investment plan available for investors.

Moody's International Manual published by MOODY'S INVESTORS SERVICE annually in two volumes with weekly updating, a source that provides addresses, phone numbers, areas of business, officers, directors, and financial data on foreign companies.

Moody's Investors Services company that publishes a variety of investment reference manuals, including *Moody's Manuals.* Moody's (*www.moodys.com*) is probably one of the best-known investment rating services, with Standard & Poor's being the other. Moody's rates corporate as well as governmental securities with ratings ranging from AAA for highest investment quality to D for default.

Morningstar mutual fund rankings RISK measurement system for comparing more than 2000 mutual funds' long-term performance. It is available from Chicago-based Morningstar Inc. The system rates stock and bond funds from five stars (the best) to no stars (the worst or unrated). Morningstar uses a proprietary system that measures a mutual fund's price and dividend performance as well as the risks taken by the fund management to get those results. The rankings are then made from comparing a fund both in its own category and against the industry as a whole, thus the best performing fund in a category that has been a weak market sector might get only two or three stars. Morningstar assigns the top 10% of an asset class (international equity, domestic equity, taxable bond, or municipal bond) with five stars (highest). Those falling in the next 22.5% receive four stars (above average); a place in the middle 35% earns three stars (neutral); those in the next 22.5%, receive two stars (below average); and the bottom 10% get one star (lowest). Morningstar also now offers so-called "style reviews" of funds, putting them in one of nine categories designated by what they own, not what their marketing department says the fund is. The nine categories, called "style boxes," for stock funds combine both a fund's investment methodology and the size of the companies in which it invests. The nine categories are: small cap, medium cap, or large cap, each divided into growth, value, or blend slices. The equity style box measures the size of the companies held in a fund's portfolio by median market capitalization and classifies funds as small cap, medium cap, or large cap. A small cap fund's median market capitalization must be less than $1 billion; median market caps, $1 billion to $5 billion; median market caps greater than $5 billion are classified as large cap. To track "investment methodologies," Morningstar divides the average PRICE/EARNINGS RATIO and price/book ratios of a fund by those of the S&P 500 and adds the results. Funds with a total less than 1.75 are classified as value-oriented; blend-oriented funds have a total between 1.75 and 2.25; and growth-oriented funds are greater than 2.25. (The S&P 500's sum is 2.00.)

For bond funds, the nine style categories are sliced by maturity (short-term, intermediate-term, and long-term), credit-quality (high, medium, and low) to provide a snapshot of risk. So, a fixed-income fund in the short maturity/high-quality style should be among the safest, while funds in the long maturity/low-quality style would be the riskiest.

mortgage-backed securities share in an organized pool of residential mortgages. Some are PASS-THROUGH SECURITIES where the principal and interest payments on them are passed through to shareholders, usually monthly. There are several kinds of mortgage-backed securities:

Collaterized mortgage obligations (CMOs): CMOs are mortgage-backed securities that separate mortgage pools into short-, medium-, and long-term portions. Investors can choose between short-term pools (such as 5-year pools) and long-term pools (such as 20-year pools). Mortgage-backed securities enjoy liquidity and a high degree of safety since they are either government-sponsored or otherwise insured.

Federal Home Loan Mortgage Corporation (FHLMC—Freddie Mac) securities: Freddie Mac was established to provide a secondary market for conventional mortgages. It can purchase conventional mortgages for its own portfolio. Freddie Mac also issues

MOVING AVERAGE (MA)

pass-through securities—called participation certificates (PCs)—and guaranteed mortgage certificates (GMCs) that resemble bonds. Freddie Mac securities do not carry direct government guarantees and are subject to state and federal income tax.

Federal National Mortgage Association (FNMA—Fannie Mae) securities: The FNMA is a publicly held corporation whose goal is to provide a secondary market for government-guaranteed mortgages. It does so by financing its purchase by selling DEBENTURES with maturities of several years and short-term discount notes from 30 to 360 days to private investors. The FNMA securities are not government guaranteed and are an unsecured obligation of the issuer. For this reason, they often provide considerably higher yields than Treasury securities.

Government National Mortgage Association (GNMA—Ginnie Mae) securities: GNMA primarily issues pass-through securities, which pass through all payments of interest and principal received on a pool of federally insured mortgage loans. GNMA guarantees that all payments of principal and interest will be made on the mortgages on a timely basis. Since many mortgages are repaid before maturity, investors in GNMA pools usually recover most of their principal investment well ahead of schedule. Ginnie Mae is considered an excellent investment. The higher yields, coupled with the U.S. government guarantee, provide a competitive edge over other intermediate-term to long-term securities issued by the U.S. government and other agencies.

moving average (MA) technique to filter out phenomena not reflective of general sentiment and to uncover TRENDS. The average is calculated by adding a set of data, then dividing the sum by the period. The result is a smoothed version of a trend. With the moving average, a series of calculations is made by taking the arithmetic MEAN, of a consecutive number of items, then discarding the first item and adding the latest item, and continuing the process, so that the number of items in the series remains constant. There are three popular types: 14-day (short-term), 50-day (intermediate), and 200-day (long-term) moving averages. For example, a 14-day moving average price of a security includes prices for the past 14 days. Each day, the oldest price is dropped from the average and the latest day's price is included in the calculation. The moving average is used to predict future market prices and/or volume. Moving averages can be used to produce buy and sell signals for stock trading. For example:
- when a stock crosses the moving average going up it is considered a buy signal.
- When the moving average crosses the moving average in a down move, a sell signal is given.

Moving averages often indicate levels of support or resistance for a security. Numerous on-line services (such as *www.moneycentral.msn.com* or *www.finance.yahoo.com*) provide moving average charts.

moving average convergence/divergence (MACD) price MOMENTUM indicator based on the difference between two MOVING AVERAGES (MA) of the closing price. The horizontal equilibrium line represents the point where both the 10-day and 30-day MAs converge. Plots below the horizontal line mean the short-term MA moved below the long-term MA and vice versa.

MSCI Morgan Stanley's Capital International group.

MSCI Emerging Markets Free Index emerging market index that excludes all stocks that cannot be purchased by foreign investors.

MSCI Emerging Markets Free/Latin America Index market value-weighted barometer of approximately 170 company issues traded in seven Latin American markets.

MSCI Emerging Markets Index market value-weighted barometer of over 850 company issues traded in 22 world markets.

MSCI Europe Index market value-weighted barometer of over 550 company issues traded in 14 European markets.

MSCI Far East Ex-Japan Free Index market value-weighted barometer of over 450 company issues traded in eight Asian markets, excluding Japan.

MSCI France Index unmanaged index of over 75 foreign stock prices, converted into U.S. dollars, assuming reinvestment of all dividends paid.

MSCI Germany Index unmanaged index of over 75 foreign stock prices, converted into U.S. dollars, assuming reinvestment of all dividends.

MSCI Hong Kong Index unmanaged index of over 38 foreign stock prices, converted into U.S. dollars, assuming reinvestment of all dividends paid.

MSCI Japan Index unmanaged index of over 317 foreign stock prices, converted into U.S. dollars, assuming reinvestment of all dividends paid.

MSCI Nordic Countries Free Index unmanaged index of over 95 foreign stock prices, converted into U.S. dollars, assuming reinvestment of all dividends.

MSCI Pacific Index market value-weighted barometer of over 400 company issues traded in six Pacific-region markets.

MSCI United Kingdom Index unmanaged index of over 143 foreign stock prices, converted into U.S. dollars, assuming reinvestment of all dividends paid.

MSCI World Index market value-weighted equity index of over 1500 company issues traded in 22 world markets.

MULTIPERIOD RETURNS

multiperiod returns   *see* ARITHMETIC AVERAGE RETURN versus COMPOUND (GEOMETRIC) AVERAGE RETURN.

municipal bond indexes   BENCHMARK indexes for municipal bonds. Two widely watched municipal bond benchmarks come from *The Bond Buyer*, a daily newspaper that principally covers the municipal bond market. It publishes several benchmark averages for the municipal bond market; the two best-known indexes are its "40" and "20" indexes. The *Bond Buyer 40* consists of 40 actively traded, higher-rated general obligation, municipal bonds of varying maturities. Each bond's price is converted through a complex formula to find at what price the bond would yield 8%. The 40 converted prices are then averaged and put through another "conversion" designed to account for changes made in the index over the years. The *Bond Buyer 20* is an index that tracks the average prices of 20 higher-rated municipal bonds that have 20-year maturities.

Other municipal indexes include

Dow Jones Municipal Bond Yield Average: Shows the weighted-average yield on tax-free municipal bonds. This is an average of the yields of low-coupon bonds in five states and fifteen major cities.

Lehman Brothers California Municipal Bond Index: Market capitalization-weighted index of California investment-grade bonds with maturities of one year or more.

Lehman Brothers Insured Municipal Bond Index: Total return performance benchmark for municipal bonds that are backed by insurers with top-shelf, Triple-A ratings and have maturities of at least one year.

Lehman Brothers Massachusetts Enhanced Municipal Bond Index: Index of Massachusetts investment-grade municipal bonds with maturities of one year or more.

Lehman Brothers Municipal Bond Index: Provides performance coverage of investment-grade municipal bonds with maturities of one year or more.

Lehman Brothers New York Insured Municipal Bond Index: Total return performance benchmark for New York investment-grade municipal bonds with maturities of at least one year.

Standard & Poor's Municipal Bond Price Index: Based on high-quality (AAA to A) municipal bonds having a maturity of about 20 years. Yield to maturity is translated to an equivalent selling price to a 20-year, 4% bond. An average yield is then determined for the bonds.

Standard & Poor's Municipal Bond Yield Index: Determined from 15 highly rated (AAA to A) municipal bonds. The index is an arithmetic average of the effective interest rate.

municipal bonds   BONDS issued by local governments and their agencies on which interest is exempt from federal income taxation provided they qualify as public purpose bonds; simply called *munis*. Interest may also be exempt from state and local income taxation in the state of issue. *Note:* you may consider municipal bonds for tax or income reasons. If you do, you may face three investment choices for diversification: (1) buying them on your own; (2) muni UNIT INVESTMENT TRUST (UIT); and (3) muni mutual funds. If the preservation of capital is of primary importance, the UIT may be a better investment than a mutual fund. This table compares aspects of the three approaches.

INVESTING IN MUNICIPAL BONDS; THREE CHOICES

	Direct Purchase	UIT	Mutual Fund
Portfolio policy and management	Your own selection	Passive; no management	Active management
Payments	Twice a year	Monthly	Monthly or automatic investment
Commissions	Usually some percent buy-sell spread	Some percent buy-sell spread plus front-end load	Load or no-load
Investor profile	Experienced with sizable funds	Long-term (10 years)	Smaller and short-term
Interest rate risk	High	Low	Medium
Capital gain/loss potential	High	Low	Medium

municipal bonds (tax-exempt) fund   a mutual fund that aims at earning current tax-exempt income by investing solely in municipal bonds.

municipal securities   *see* MUNICIPAL BONDS.

munies   *see* MUNICIPAL BONDS.

mutual fund   portfolio of securities professionally managed by the sponsoring management company or investment company that issues shares to investors. Ownership is in the form of proportionate shares. Mutual fund investing is characterized by
- **diversification**: Your investment money may be used to buy a broad range of equity, debt, and other securities. Diversification reduces your risk.
- **automatic reinvestment**: Dividends, interest, and CAPITAL GAINS may be reinvested into the fund, usually at no charge.
- **automatic withdrawals:** Funds may be withdrawn, usually at no charge.
- **liquidity**: You can redeem your shares at any time.
- **switching**: You can go from one fund type to another in a family of funds.
- **small minimum investment**: Some mutual funds can be bought into initially for less than $1000.

A major reason for the attractiveness of mutual funds is the many convenient services offered to their shareholders. Some can be used in your investment strategy. The first table summarizes stocks and mutual funds. Common services are summarized in the second.

MUTUAL FUND

DIFFERENCE BETWEEN STOCKS AND MUTUAL FUNDS

	Stocks	*Mutual funds*
Ownership	Shares of a single company	Shares in the fund; fractional ownership of a group of assets
Voting rights	Yes	No
Value	Per share price	Net asset value (NAV)
Professional management	No	Yes
Diversification	No	Yes
Liquidity	3 business days	Almost immediate
Dividends and Capital gain	Direct	Can be reinvested
Investment decision	by yourself	Fund manager
Choice of investment goals	No	Yes
Accessibility	Via broker or online	Yes; via a toll-free phone
Flexibility	No	Yes, exchange privileges; check-writing services
Commission	Full or discount	Load or no-load

MAJOR SERVICES OF MUTUAL FUNDS

1. Accounting and reporting for tax purposes
2. Safekeeping and custodial
3. Automatic reinvestment
4. Exchange privileges
5. Periodic withdrawals
6. Checking privileges
7. Acceptance of small investments
8. Tax-sheltered plan (such as IRA and Keogh)
9. Guardianship under the Uniform Gifts to Minors Act
10. Preauthorized check plan

How Is Net Asset Value (NAV) Determined?

The price of a mutual fund share is stated as NET ASSET VALUE (NAV). It is computed as follows:

$$\frac{\text{Fund's total assets} - \text{debt}}{\text{Number of shares outstanding in the fund}}$$

EXAMPLE 1:

Assume on a given date, the market values in a fund follow. The fund has liabilities of $4500. Then NAV of the fund is calculated below.

(a) GE—$100 per share × 200 shares	=	$20,000
(b) Westinghouse—$50 per share × 300 shares	=	15,000
(c) CBS—$75 per share × 100 shares	=	7500
Total assets		$42,500
(d) Liabilities		4500
(e) Net asset value of the fund's portfolio		$38,000
(f) Number of shares outstanding in the fund		1000
(g) Net assets value (NAV) per share = (E)/(F)		$38

Assume you own 3% of the fund. Your investment is worth:

3% × 1000 shares = 30 shares; 30 shares × $38 = $1140

How Do You Make Money in a Mutual Fund?

You make money from the change in net asset value, dividends, and capital gains.

Dividends. Mutual funds typically pay out a large percentage of their income. You are fully taxed on dividends.

Capital Gains Distribution. Capital gains are distributed each year to fund holders. You are taxed at the maximum long-term capital gains rate of 20%. *Note:* Do not just consider NAV. It only shows the current market value of your portfolio. Look at the number of shares you own and total value. Your shares will increase over time from dividends and capital gains reinvestment into more shares.

Multiply the number of shares you own by the net asset value per share to determine value.

What Is the Total Return on the Mutual Fund?

Total return equals

(dividends + capital gains distributed + price appreciation in fund).

The percentage return equals

$$\frac{\text{Dividends} + \text{capital gain distributions} + (\text{ending NAV} - \text{beginning NAV})}{\text{Beginning NAV}}$$

where (ending NAV − beginning NAV) is price appreciation.

Example 2:

Your mutual fund paid dividends of $1.00 per share and capital gain distributions of $.40 per share this year. NAV is at the beginning of the year of $10.00 and $12 per share at the year-end. Percentage return equals

$$\frac{\$1.00 + \$.40 + (\$12 - \$10)}{\$10} = \frac{\$3.40}{\$10} = 34\%$$

How Much Will Mutual Funds Charge You?

If you invest in a mutual fund, there will be some kind of fee. When shopping for funds, you should take a close look at these charges. The charges may be classified as follows: load, management fee, 12b-1 fees, back-end loads, deferred loads, and reinvestment loads.

Load. A load is the fee to buy shares as a form of sales charge. Such charge may range from 1% to 8.5% (maximum legal limit) of the amount invested. That means that if you invested $1000 in a fund with an 8.5% load, only $915 would go into the fund. Mutual fund prices are stated in bid and ask form. The bid is the price the fund will buy back its shares (at the NAV). The ask or offer is the price the investor must pay to buy shares. The difference between the offer and bid is the load. No-load mutual funds have no sales fees so there is the same bid and ask prices. *Note:* A sales fee does not mean better performance of the fund. The fee will reduce your net return rate. Load funds do not perform better than no-load funds.

Management and Expense Fees. All funds (no load or load) charge a fee to pay a portfolio manager. It typically ranges from 0.5% to 1% of the fund's assets.

12b-1 Fees. These charges are for advertising and promotion. They typically range from 0.25% to 0.30%, but some run as high as 1.25%.

Back-End Loads, or Redemption Fees. These are charged when you sell your shares. They are based on a percentage of the shares' net asset value, so steep back-end loads can reduce your profits or increase your loss.

Deferred Load, or Contingent Deferred Sales Fees. These are deducted from your original investment if you sell shares before a specified period.

Reinvestment Loads. These fees are taken out of reinvested interest, dividends, and capital gains; for example, if you receive a capital-gains distribution of $150 and the reinvestment fee is 7%, the fund will keep $10.50 and reinvest $139.50.

What Kinds of Mutual Funds Exist?

Mutual funds are categorized by type depending on purpose, structure, fees, switching privileges, return potential, and risk. You can virtually invest in any type of fund based on your investment goals. There are two basic types of funds: open-end funds, commonly called mutual funds, which can sell an unlimited number of ownership shares, and closed-end funds, which can issue only a limited (fixed) number.

What Is the Difference Between Open-End and Closed-End Funds?

In open-end funds, you purchase from and sell shares back to the fund. You can redeem shares when you so desire. Shares are bought at NAV plus service fee, and redeemed at NAV less a commission. In closed-end funds, there is a fixed number of shares traded on the STOCK EXCHANGE or OVER-THE-COUNTER MARKET. Share price is determined independently of NAV by factors of supply and demand. Management fees are assessed by all funds. Some closed-end funds, called *dual-purpose funds*, convert to open-end funds at expiration by vote of shareholders.

What Are the Types of Mutual Funds?

Mutual funds may be categorized as follows:

- **Aggressive growth (capital appreciation) funds**: Funds taking greater risk for high capital appreciation. Dividend income is secondary. They concentrate on new, high-tech businesses. They offer the greatest potential for growth, but also greater risk. *Note*: These funds are appropriate if you are not especially worried about near-term variability in return but with long-term appreciation. Aggressive strategies taken may consist of leverage purchases, short selling, call options, put options, and buying stock.
- **Balanced funds**: Balanced funds seek preservation of capital while seeking growth and income. The aim of these funds is to balance the portfolio with the best ratio of stocks and bonds within the funds' investment objective guidelines. This is done to adjust to prevailing market conditions. Balanced funds tend to underperform all-stock funds in strong BULL MARKETS.
- **Growth funds**: Growth funds want high return via capital gains. They usually invest in companies with growth exceeding the inflation rate. The stocks have constant long-term current income. Like other growth investments, the aim of these funds is to increase share value, not pay dividends.
- **Growth and income funds**: Growth and income funds emphasize current dividend or interest and capital appreciation. They offer moderate growth potential and moderate risk. The objective is long-term growth. Share value should be stable.
- **Income funds**: Income funds generate current income through investments in securities that pay interest or a cash dividend. These securities include dividend-paying stocks, corporate bonds, and a variety of government securities. Generally, the higher the income sought, the riskier the underlying investments. They offer current income with low to high risk.
- **Index funds**: Index funds invest in a broad group of stocks based on an index such as the Standard & Poor's 500. Vanguard Index Trust Fund matches the stock index.
- **International funds**: International funds invest in securities of overseas (foreign) companies. Some international funds invest in one geographic area, such as Fidelity Canada Fund and Vanguard Trustees Commingled International Portfolio. Fund value increases if the dollar decreases due to exchange rates.
- **Money market funds**: Money market funds invest solely in short-term debt securities. The price of the fund is constant, so it is very conservative. You can buy and sell shares at $1.00. Money market funds provide high-interest income with safe principal.
- **Municipal tax-exempt funds**: Tax-free funds seek current, tax-free income by investing for the most part in tax-exempt bonds issued by municipalities to build schools, highways, and public projects. They offer current tax-exempt income with low to high risk depending on the yield sought and individual investments.
- **Sector (specialized) funds**: Sector funds invest by industry (ies). High risk exists because the fortunes of the fund depend on the

MUTUAL FUND PRICE QUOTATIONS

performance of the specific industry. If an industry takes a hit such as can happen with pharmaceuticals, huge losses will ensue.

Note: In selecting a mutual fund, you should consider your return/risk preferences. A mutual fund investor should consider the timing of when to make a purchase or sale depending on the conditions in the financial markets, economic factors, and political aspects.

See also ALPHA; BENCHMARK; BETA FOR A MUTUAL FUND; R-SQUARED; STANDARD DEVIATION.

mutual fund price quotations   Below are quotations of mutual funds shown in a newspaper.

SAMPLE MUTUAL FUND QUOTATIONS

Fund (1)	NAV (2)	Offer Price (3)	NAV Change (4)
ABT Midwest Funds:			
Emerg Gr	10.00	10.93	−0.04
Growth	13.62	14.89	−0.10
Int Gov't	10.63	N.L. **(5)**	+0.04

(1) the fund's name abbreviated. Several names under one heading indicates a fund family. Emerg Gr. and Growth are load funds.

(2) the net asset value (NAV) of a share at the close of the preceding business day. The NAV column may also be called *sell* or *bid*. This is the price you would have received (less any end-load fee or redemption charge) if you sold your shares back to the mutual fund on that business day. You can figure the most recent value of your holdings by multiplying the NAV by the number of shares you own.

(3) the offering price, also called *buy* or *asked*. It is the price you would have paid to buy shares at the close of the preceding business day.

(4) change from the previous day; Emerg Gr was down 4 cents per share.

(5) N. L. indicates a no-load fund.

N

naked   *see* NAKED OPTION.

naked option   uncovered OPTION strategy. It is an investment in which the written options are not matched with a LONG stock position or a long option position that expires no earlier than the written options. The loss potential with such a strategy is thereby unlimited.

narrow market
1. security having relatively few shares outstanding with a small number of investors. This type of a security normally has low volume and is subject to wide price movements as it is traded in this narrow market. The market is not capable of managing higher trading volume, as the impact on price would be exaggerated.
2. security trading with a very small difference between the bid and asked prices.

NASDAQ indexes   measures of current price behavior of securities sold in the OVER-THE COUNTER (OTC) MARKET.

NASDAQ National Market   largest and highest quality of the three markets run by the NASDAQ, and regulated by the NASD. The NASDAQ National Market is now the second largest stock market in the world in terms of volume of shares traded. The NASDAQ markets are not physical stock exchanges in the traditional sense and do not have an exchange floor, but instead use computer-based trading and trade support systems. NASDAQ is headquartered in Washington, D.C.

National Association of Securities Dealers (NASD)   self-regulatory organization that has jurisdiction over broker-dealers who handle OVER-THE-COUNTER (OTC) securities. The NASD requires member broker-dealers to register, and conducts examinations for compliance with net capital requirements and other regulations.

National Association of Securities Dealers Automated Quotations (NASDAQ)   stock market subsidiary of the NASD that facilitates the trading of approximately 5000 most active OTC stock issues through an electronically connected network. The NASDAQ stock market is composed of three markets: the National Market, the SmallCap market, and the OTC Bulletin Board.

national municipal bond funds—long-term   mutual funds that buy primarily bonds issued by states and municipalities to finance schools, highways, hospitals, airports, bridges, water and sewer works, and other public projects. In most cases, income earned on these securities is not taxed by the federal government, and may or

nearbys months of options or future contracts that are closest to expiration in the case of options or delivery in the case of futures. For example, in April, option contracts settling in June would be the nearbuys. Typically, nearby contracts are much more actively traded than contracts for more future out months.

negative yield curve condition in which interest rates on short-term debt securities are higher than interest rates on long-term debt securities; *also called inverted yield curve. See also* YIELD CURVE.

negotiable refers to a security, title to which, when properly endorsed by the owner, is transferable by DELIVERY.

net asset value (NAV)
1. measure of the market value of a mutual fund share, which reveals what each share of the mutual fund is worth. Net asset value equals:

$$\frac{\text{Fund's total assets less total liabilities}}{\text{Number of shares outstanding in the fund}}$$

NAV is computed by most funds after the close of the exchanges each day. The number of shares outstanding can change each day based on how many buys and redemptions there are.

EXAMPLE:
Assume that a fund owns 500 shares each of Coca-Cola, Procter & Gamble, and Merck. Assume also that on a specific day, the market values listed below occurred. The NAV of the fund is computed as follows (an assumption is made that there are no liabilities):

(a) Coca-Cola ($70 per share × 500 shares)	$35,000
(b) Procter & Gamble ($80 × 500 shares)	40,000
(c) Merck ($100 per share × 500 shares)	50,000
(d) Value of the fund's portfolio	$125,000
(e) Number of shares outstanding in the fund	10,000
(f) Net asset value per share (d)/(e)	$12.50

If an investor owns 10% of the fund's outstanding shares, or 1000 shares (10% × 10,000), then the value of the investment is $12,500 ($12.50 × 1000). NAV constitutes one element of the return on mutual fund investments. An investor also receives capital gains and dividends. Thus, the performance of a mutual fund must be appraised on the basis of these three returns.

The net asset value only indicates the current market value of the underlying portfolio. You must know how many shares you have in order to compute the total value of your holdings.

2. book value of a company's different classes of securities such as net book value per common share.

net change difference in the closing price of a security, commodity, or mutual fund from one trading day to the next. The net change for stocks is shown usually as the last figure in a stock price list in the financial pages of newspapers. For example, a net change of +3 for Company XYZ indicates that the stock increased $3 from the final price of the last day to the current day. In the case of NASDAQ stocks, net changes in prices typically reflect the difference between bid prices from one day to the next. For a stock entitled to a dividend on one day but traded EX-DIVIDEND the next, the dividend is taken into account in computing the change. For example, if the ending market price of a stock on Wednesday—the last day it was entitled to receive a $1 dividend—was $50, and $49 at the close of the next day, when it was ex-dividend the price would be deemed unchanged. With a stock split, a stock having a market price of $60 the day prior to a 2-for-1 split and trading the next day at $30 would likewise be considered unchanged. If it is sold at $31.50, it would be considered up $1.50.

net present value (NPV) excess of the PRESENT VALUE (PV) of cash inflows generated by the project over the amount of the initial investment.

net profit
1. difference between the total price you paid for a security, with the brokerage commission you paid, and the net proceeds from sale. It will show either a profit or a loss.
2. sales revenue minus total expenses; also called *earnings* or *net income*.

net transaction securities transaction in which a fee or commission is not charged for the seller and buyer. For example, no commission is charged the buyer when purchasing a new issue. If the stock is offered at $30 a share, the investor pays that exact or issue price.

Neuer Markt Germany's junior stock market (*www.neuermarkt.de*), equivalent to the LSE's AIM and Tech-MARK, which was launched in 1997 to provide means for smaller companies, especially technology companies, to raise capital and list their shares.

neutral expectation that the price of a stock or the market in general will remain relatively unchanged.

new economy new, digital economy driven by industrial information technology, much of which is related to telecommunications such as the Internet—a technology that, many argue, has a huge potential to transform the engineering industry. In the new economy, production and distribution systems are automated, computer-based systems. The old economy, classical or traditional, is undergoing sweeping changes through the speed and efficiency brought by applications of information technology and the Internet.

NEW HIGHS/NEW LOWS

new highs/new lows stock prices that have reached the highest or lowest prices in the last 52-week period. The designation to each stock hitting a new high shown in the newspaper is "u" while a stock with a new low is "d." The total of new highs and new lows each trading day are listed separately for those listed on the New York Stock Exchange, American Stock Exchange, and NASDAQ Stock Market. New highs and new lows are listed in daily financial newspapers such as *The Wall Street Journal* and *Investor's Business Daily*. It is a BULLISH sign when the number of new highs is growing; however, it is a BEARISH indicator when the number of new lows is increasing. The trend in the ratio of the number of new highs to the number of new lows reveals the general direction of the stock market and degree of momentum. An index exceeding 1 shows that the number of stocks reaching new highs is more than those making new lows. A ratio of 10 is bullish, while a low ratio is bearish.

EXAMPLE:
Three issues have reached new highs and 15 have hit new lows. The ratio of .20 is low, a bearish indicator. The number of new highs to the number of new lows is a very low ratio just prior to a major market bottom. This may point to a buying opportunity. On the other hand, a very high ratio of new highs to new lows takes place at market ceilings. This may signal selling. In the event overall market indices are going to new highs but fewer and fewer stocks are reaching new highs, this infers a weak uptrend, a bearish divergence that may reveal a future downward price trend. A positive ratio of new highs to new lows indicates a bullish condition while a negative ratio is bearish. Hence, an uptrend in the ratio of new highs to new lows is a bullish sign for the stock market, while a downtrend is bearish. *Note*: In general, an increasing trend of new highs to new lows is consistent with increases in major market indices. However, if the new highs/new lows indicator goes in the opposite direction to market indices, the divergence implies a possible reversal in the overall market. For example, if new highs/new lows significantly declines while the market indices are increasing, the overall market will likely decline.

new issue first PUBLIC OFFERING of a stock or bond issue. A prospectus normally accompanies most new issues that detail the financial and business aspects of the company disclosing information vital to the success of the issue. For a new issue to trade on the stock exchange, it must have received approval from the SEC. *See also* INITIAL PUBLIC OFFERING; SECONDARY DISTRIBUTION.

New York Mercantile Exchange (NYMEX) merged with the Commodity Exchange (COMEX) in 1994. The exchange now operates two divisions: NYMEX, which deals in futures and options on a number of products including crude oil, heating oil and platinum; and COMEX, which deals in futures and options on copper, gold, and silver.

New York shares foreign stocks traded on American exchanges without being converted into ADRs; also called *direct shares*. They came from countries like the Netherlands, Israel, Italy, or Bolivia, that don't restrict the trading of their stocks on other nations' exchanges. U.S. securities law restricts the trading of American shares on foreign markets.

New York Stock Exchange (NYSE) largest and most prestigious organized securities exchange; also called *Big Board*. It handles a majority of the dollar volume of securities transactions and a high percentage of the total annual share volume on organized securities exchanges. Its listing requirements are the most restrictive. For example, for a company to be listed on the NYSE for the first time, the corporation must have 2000 stockholders owning 100 shares and its aggregate market value must be at least $18 million.

New York Stock Exchange (NYSE) Index a daily index of stock prices that includes all the stocks traded on the New York Stock Exchange. *See also* MARKET INDICES AND AVERAGES.

news ticker news medium employed in brokerage firms that transmits late-breaking market information including corporate earnings reports and news developments, government rulings, trading figures, and economic data; also called *wire*.

nifty-fifty 50 stocks most favored by institutional investors. The mix of this group is constantly changing, although companies that continue to produce stable earnings growth over a long time tend to remain favorites of institutional investors.

Nikkei Golf Membership Index weekly index that tracks the average price of golf membership in the 400 leading clubs in Japan against a base of 100 set up on January 1, 1982. In Japan, business executives like to play golf. Before 1985 the index was a lagging indicator of stock prices on the TOKYO STOCK EXCHANGE. After the stock crash of 1985, memberships were sold to meet margin calls and cover stock market losses. The index is known to give signals about the stock market in Japan.

Nikkei Stock Average most widely watched barometer of Japan's stock market, the world's second largest behind the United States. The index, first published in May 1949, is to Japanese shares what the Dow Jones Industrial Average is to U.S. issues. The Nikkei 225 Stock Average is an average of prices of 225 stocks listed in the prestigious First Section of the TOKYO STOCK EXCHANGE. The companion is the Nikkei 500 Stock Average. Companies included are Asahi Breweries, Fuji Film, Nippon Steel, and Yamaha. Index information appears in major local and national newspapers and business dailies. Thanks to the international date line, *USA Today* can put afternoon Nikkei index results on the front page of its morning paper, and this index can also be tracked by on-line databases such as America Online.

no-load   no sales charge or commission. *See also* MUTUAL FUND.

no-load fund   commission-free mutual fund that sells its shares at NET ASSET VALUE, either directly to the public or through an affiliated distributor, without the addition of a sales charge. Most no-load funds permit switching money among its funds with no transfer fee. In the financial newspaper, the designation of a no-load fund is NL.

no-load (mutual) fund   mutual fund that does not charge a sales commission. Sales strategy includes advertisements and (800) toll-free telephone orders, so that an investor buys shares directly from the fund rather than through a broker, as is the case with LOAD mutual funds.

noncumulative preferred stock   PREFERRED STOCK whose dividends, if not paid in a given period, cease. In other words, there is no accrual for unpaid dividends.

nondiversifiable risk   part of a security's risk that cannot be diversified away; also called UNSYSTEMATIC RISK or *uncontrollable risk*. It includes MARKET RISK that comes from factors systematically affecting most firms (such as inflation, recessions, political events, and high interest rates). *See also* CAPITAL ASSET PRICING MODEL (CAPM).

nonparticipating preferred stock   PREFERRED STOCK paying only stipulated dividends with no possibility of increases because of an increase in corporate profits. Nonparticipating preferred stockholders do not receive a proportionate share in excess dividends of the company over stated rates.

nonvoting stock   equity security that does not give the holder the right to vote in company matters, such as electing the board of directors. Preferred stock is typically nonvoting. Some companies have different classes of common stock to restrict voting. For example, class A may be controlled by management and be voting, while class B may be nonvoting.

normal market size (NMS)   When shares are traded on the LONDON STOCK EXCHANGE, the market makers have to quote a bid price and offer price at which they will deal, but the prices they quote, which are disseminated to brokers via the SEAQ system, have to be honored only up to a certain size of order. The normal market size defines what that figure is for each company and it is based on a percentage of the share's average daily turnover in the previous year. *See also* STOCK EXCHANGE AUTOMATED QUOTATION SERVICE (SEAQ).

normal return   income on an investment at a normal rate of interest. This normal interest rate can be the risk-free interest rate (such as rates on Treasury bills, notes, or bonds) plus a premium for the risk of a given investment.

normal trading unit   standard size of an order for a given security. For example, stocks typically have a trading unit of 100 shares, called a ROUND LOT. Stock units of fewer than 100 shares are termed ODD LOTS.

not-held order (NH) securities trading order directive to a broker either for a LIMIT or MARKET ORDER giving the broker time and price latitude in executing the transaction. In effect, it allows the broker to back away from the crowd until he or she feels conditions are more favorable for the trade. In a not-held order, the client agrees not to hold the broker accountable for fulfilling the order within a particular time period.

not rated (NR) indication that a security has not been rated by one of the securities rating agencies such as Moody's, Standard & Poor's, Duff/Phelps/MCM, or Fitch. It carries no positive or negative investment connotations. *See also* BOND RATINGS; PREFERRED STOCK RATINGS.

(le) Nouveau Marche France's junior market for smaller companies whose members tend to be drawn from the high-tech sector.

NTR short for "not trading related"—part of the standard terminology used on BULLETIN BOARDS.

number of shares number of stock shares that a company has outstanding.

O

October effect perception that the stock market tends to do poorly in October. Although historically there has been a slight underperformance in October, which most observers attribute to chance, the psychological effects of a few serious market crashes in October have kept the perception alive.

odd lot any exception to the standard trading unit of a security. For example, with minor exceptions a standard or ROUND LOT of stock is 100 shares, so any amount bought or sold other than 100 shares or multiples thereof would be an odd lot. (However, inactive stocks typically trade in round lots of 10 shares.) The commission rate on an odd-lot transaction usually includes an odd-lot differential, typically .125 of a point. For example, an investor purchasing 100 shares of a company at $50 a share would pay $50 per share plus commission. An investor buying just 25 shares would pay $50.125 a share plus commission. Thus, the commission rate on an odd-lot transaction is relatively higher than on a round-lot transaction. The cost of odd-lot trading is proportionately less on higher-priced issues. For example, an extra quarter point is not as significant with a stock trading at $100. Stocks having a low market price (such as $15) should preferably be purchased in a round lot (100 shares) particularly if the security is being bought for short-term purchases. Odd-lot activity shows investment decisions by small, inexperienced individual investors.

odd-lot broker *see* ODD-LOT DEALER.

odd-lot dealer broker who handles odd lots of stock. The odd-lot retail investor does pay a higher commission for an odd-lot purchase to the broker. While commission rates can vary, a typical odd lot commission would be 12.5 cents or one-eighth of a point. Thus, buying 40 shares of a stock trading at $12 per share would cost $12.125 per share for an odd-lot purchase.

odd-lot theory theory that the timing of the small investor buying or selling small odd-lot shares of stock is usually wrong and therefore opposite of market movements. Thus, when a measurable increase in odd-lot buying occurs, the market is positioned for a downward CORRECTION. Conversely, a measurable increase in odd-lot selling is interpreted to mean that the market is positioned for an upward reversal. However, research has not validated odd-lot theory, showing instead that the timing of odd-lot buyers is fairly accurate, and rather closely matches the performance of the market. Thus, odd-lot theory is out of favor today, and no longer given credence.

off board
1. trade occurring in the OVER-THE-COUNTER MARKET or an execution of a listed security not consummated on a national stock exchange.
2. block of stock traded among clients of a brokerage house, or between the client and the brokerage firm itself, with the latter purchasing or disposing of securities it holds.

offer price at which a person is ready to sell; also called *ask* or *sell*. Opposed to *bid*, it is the price at which one is ready to buy.

off-floor order order to purchase or sell a security originating outside the exchange. These orders represent client orders starting with brokers, rather than orders of floor members (on-floor orders) for their accounts. Off-floor orders must be transacted prior to on-floor ones.

offer price price at which a market maker is willing to sell a security; also called *ask price*.

offering date first day a stock or bond issue will be available for purchase by the public.

official reserves amount of reserves owned by the central bank of a government in the form of gold, SPECIAL DRAWING RIGHTS, and foreign cash or marketable securities.

offset counteractive action to balance or compensate such as buying a put option on a stock you have a long position on if you expect a temporary downward movement in stock prices.

offsetting trade having an opposite trade effect such as the purchase of a call option and then buying a put option on the same stock.

offshore
1. term to describe a financial institution (such as a bank) headquartered outside of the country in question. For example, a U.S. company having an account in a bank in another country would say it has offshore deposits. Another example is a U.S. mutual fund having a legal domicile in the Cayman Islands. Major reasons for offshore deposits or other transactions is to save on taxes in a lower (or no) tax area or to circumvent stringent regulation in the United States. A mutual fund legally domiciled outside of the United States must follow all federal and state laws to operate in the United States.
2. offshore finance subsidiary of a company located outside the United States to conduct financing, banking, or some other financial related function.

offshore (mutual) fund mutual fund that is managed and resides out of a foreign country, usually outside the United States.

OLD ECONOMY

old economy   *see* NEW ECONOMY.

old economy stocks   stocks in sectors unrelated to telecommunications, the Internet, software, or any other technology-driven industry. NEW ECONOMY stocks are seen as offering the most potential for capital growth. An example of an old economy stock is Colgate Palmolive.

on balance volume   TECHNICAL ANALYSIS technique used to determine when a security or commodity is being heavily bought into or sold out of, by comparing volume to price over time.

on-line database   a service, such as Dow Jones News/Retrieval, AOL, or Yahoo (*www.finance.yahoo.com*), providing historical, financial, market, and economic information, or current stock market prices and financial news obtained via modem.

open   price at which a security opens the trading day. Generally, the opening price reflects the previous day's close, unless extraordinary news or demand to buy or sell have occurred before the market opens.

open buy order   any unexecuted buy order. The term *open buy order* is often used synonymously to mean an order that is GOOD-TILL-CANCELLED (GTC). Technically, however, the order could also be a DAY ORDER.

open contract   futures contract that has not yet been closed out. The contract is closed when it is sold or when the commodities are received.

open-end investment companies   *see* OPEN-END (MUTUAL) FUNDS.

open-end investment trust   *see* INVESTMENT TRUST; OPEN-END (MUTUAL) FUND.

open-end (mutual) fund   mutual fund that an investor buys shares from and then sells shares back to the fund itself. This type of fund offers to sell and redeem shares on a continual basis for an indefinite time period. Shares are purchased at NET ASSET VALUE (NAV) plus commission (if any), and redeemed at NAV less a service charge (if any).

open interest   total amount of exercisable contracts that were purchased in the futures and options markets. Until such time as the futures or options expire or are exercised, they will remain on the records of the clearinghouse as open interest.

open order   buy or sell order for a stock or bond at a specified price that has not been transacted yet or cancelled by the investor. While an open order can be just a DAY ORDER, often the term is used to mean GOOD-TILL-CANCELLED (GTC).

open outcry   trading practice in the commodity exchange by which dealers stand in a pit on the trading floor and yell out bid and offer prices for commodities.

opening
1. order to buy a stock at the beginning of the trading day.
2. opening price.

opening price   MARKET PRICE of a security at the start of the trading day.

opportunity cost   cost of giving up one financial option for another. For example, the opportunity cost of investing in a risky business venture is the risk-free return of, say, 8% on the TREASURY BILL.

option   contract giving you the right, *not the obligation*, to buy or sell a specified number of shares of an asset at a set price for a given time period. The value of an option is typically a minor percentage of the underlying value of the asset. It has three basic features. It allows an investor to reserve the right to buy or sell (1) a specified number of shares of stock; (2) at a fixed price per share; (3) for a limited length of time. There are two types of option contracts: call options and put options. This table summarizes the kinds of options.

CALL AND PUT OPTIONS

	Call	Put
Buy (long)	The right to buy (without obligation) the stock or futures contract at a fixed price until expiration.	The right to sell (without obligation) the stock or futures contract at a fixed price until expiration.
Sell (short)	Selling the right to buy the stock or futures contract until expiration; known as *writing a call*.	Selling the right to sell the stock or futures contract until expiration; known as *writing a put*.

option account   account established in a brokerage firm allowing a client to buy and sell stock options. In order to establish the account, the client must first complete an option agreement. This agreement is used by the brokerage firm to determine that the client qualifies for the firm's financial ability limitations. *See also* OPTION AGREEMENT.

option agreement   form required to be completed by clients of a brokerage firm in order to obtain an OPTION ACCOUNT; also called *option account agreement form*. In addition to obtaining financial information to determine the client's financial qualifications, prior investing experience is also sought as well as the client's agreement to comply with the requirements of the Option Clearing Corporation (OCC) and of the exchange on which the option is traded.

Option Clearing Corporation (OCC)   body that clears options transactions. Founded in 1973, OCC (*www.optionsclearing.com*) is

OPTION COLLAR

the largest clearing organization in the world for financial derivatives instruments. Operating under the jurisdiction of the Securities and Exchange Commission, OCC is the issuer and registered clearing facility for all U.S. exchange-listed securities options. OCC issues put and call options on several types of underlying assets including common stocks and other equity issues, stock indexes, foreign currencies and interest rate composites.

option collar *see* COLLAR.

option holder individual who has purchased and still retains a call or put option.

option mutual fund mutual fund that purchases and/or sells options to enhance the worth of the fund's shares. An aggressive or conservative approach may be practiced. An aggressive option growth fund may buy calls and puts in selected stocks that are expected to change in price significantly either upward or downward. If such significant price change materializes, substantial returns will be earned. However, if the fund manager is wrong, the entire premium will be lost since the options will expire. On the other hand, a conservative option income fund may profit from the premium obtained by selling calls and put options on securities included in the fund's investment portfolio.

option premium excess of the STRIKING PRICE of a call or put option over the price at which the underlying security is trading. For example, if XYZ stock is trading at $52 per share, and the 50 call option, expiring in July, is selling at $6 per call, then the option premium equals the price of the call minus the price of the underlying security minus striking price. Thus, the option premium would be $4 = [$6 − ($52 − $50)]. *See also* OPTION PRICE.

option price market price at which a stock option is selling. All option prices are for a single option on one share of stock, but option contracts are sold in ROUND LOTS of 100. For example, if the option price is $4, the price of the option contract is $400. The option price is the difference between the STRIKING PRICE of a call or put option and the price at which the underlying security is trading plus any PREMIUM, unless the option is trading at a DISCOUNT prior to its expiration. *See also* OPTION PREMIUM.

option spread any combination of numerous option investing strategies in which stock options for the same underlying security, often using two different time periods, are HEDGED against each other to reduce risk while still taking advantage of price movements in the underlying security. If properly used, option spreads can be very effective in reducing risk and exploiting profit opportunities; however, the commission costs associated with an option spread can be substantial. Examples of option spreads include butterfly, HORIZONTAL, DIAGONAL, sandwich, and VERTICAL.

option strategy any of a series of option tactics by which an investor seeks to increase investment return while reducing the risk. These tactics include HEDGING stock investments by writing covered call options; buying put options to offset risk in the purchase of the underlying security; buying put options to offset SHORT SALES of the underlying security; buying call or put options to take advantage of anticipated short-term trading opportunities; developing option SPREAD strategies; and selling NAKED OPTIONS. *See also* OPTION SPREAD.

option writer person or institution selling an option and therefore granting the right to exercise it to the buyer of the option.

option writing situation in which the writer of a call agrees to sell shares at the STRIKE PRICE paid for the call option. Call option writers do the opposite of what buyers do. An option is written because the writer believes that a price increase in the stock will be less than what the call purchaser anticipates. The writer may even expect a flat or decreasing price in the security. Option writers receive the option premium less related transaction costs. If the option is not exercised, the writer earns the price paid for it. If the option is exercised, the writer incurs a loss, which may be significant.

optional dividend dividend of a company giving the recipient an option as to the type of dividend to be received, typically in cash and/or shares.

order imbalance situation in which there are too many buy orders for a particular stock and not enough sell orders—or vice versa. When this occurs, stock exchanges may halt trading temporarily to allow more of the other kind of order to come in. This permits better matching of buyers and sellers and can lessen volatility in the stock.

ordinary shares foreign shares traded on foreign markets. A good broker will check the bid-asked spread on an ADR to make sure it is not out of line with that of the ordinary share.

organized securities exchange institution in which listed securities such as stock are traded by exchange members on a floor organized according to different types of securities. The largest and most prestigious example is the New York Stock Exchange.

organized stock exchange *see* ORGANIZED SECURITIES EXCHANGE.

original issue discount (OID) discount from PAR VALUE when a bond is first issued. The most extreme version of an original issue discount (OID) is a ZERO-COUPON BOND that is issued at a substantial discount from its maturity value. No interest is paid to the holder of the bond while held; rather, the bond is paid in full at maturity. The gain is the difference between the purchase price and the maturity value.

Oslo SE Total Index yield index that includes dividend payments for all Norwegian companies on Oslo Exchange's main list.

out-of-favor industry or stocks industry or stock that is not at the current time attractive to investors. As a result, the stock price of companies in the industry languishes. An industry such as hotels may be unpopular, for example, because of a recession restricting spending.

out of line stock that is priced excessively high or low relative to similar stocks in the market. Such a determination may be based on the PRICE/EARNINGS RATIOS. If all other similar companies had price/earnings ratios of 12, while company XYZ had a price/earnings ratio of 20, the company is probably overpriced.

out-of-the-money term used when the STRIKE PRICE of an option is less than the market price of the underlying stock for a call option, or greater than the price of the underlying stock for a put option.

outright quotation exchange rate quotation in terms of the full price, in one currency, per unit of another currency.

outright rate actual forward rate expressed in dollars per unit of a currency, or vice versa. Commercial customers are quoted this way. *See also* FORWARD EXCHANGE RATE; SWAP RATE.

overbought (overvalued) outcome of excessive buying of a security or commodity resulting in a sharp increase in price sometimes occurring in a short time period. There will be downward market pressure on the stock or commodity price because of the ensuing efficiency of remaining buyers. In consequence, the price of the security or commodity becomes unstable and vulnerable to a price decrease. After the stock has been overbought, few buyers remain to push prices up. An overbought situation can apply to the overall market where stock prices have unexpectedly sharply risen leaving the market susceptible to a correction. In an overbought stock or overall market, the prudent thing to do is sell. *See also* OVERSOLD.

overhang existence of an unusually large amount of inventory in the hands of a potential seller such as stocks, bonds, currency, commodities, real estate, and so on, that has the ability to significantly reduce the price of the item when it is sold on the open market. The potential seller may be an institutional investor, dealer, and so on. There might be a pending secondary distribution of securities. Overhang represents buying activities that might result in increasing prices.

overnight LONG or SHORT position of a broker-dealer in a stock or bond at the close of the trading day.

Overseas Private Investment Corporation (OPIC) established in 1971, a self-sustaining federal agency responsible for insuring direct U.S. investments in foreign countries against the risks of expropriation, currency inconvertibility, and other political uncertainties, such as damages from wars and revolutions.

oversold (undervalued) security or overall market that has unexpectedly had a significant decline in price and is therefore apt to have a forthcoming increase in price. In an oversold market, selling of securities has been excessive. It is theorized that if all investors who desired to sell these stocks have done so, no sellers remain, and in consequence, price should increase. Hence, buying securities is suggested at the depressed prices. *See also* OVERBOUGHT.

oversubscribed term used to describe the UNDERWRITING of a security issue when there are more buyers than shares available. In such an event, when the issue is made public, the price would normally rise rapidly as those not having the opportunity to buy shares at the initial offering will now bid the market price up in an effort to obtain shares. On occasion, when an oversubscribed condition exists early in the initial offering of a security, it may be possible to issue additional shares to satisfy demand. *See also* HOT ISSUE.

over-the-counter (OTC) see OVER-THE-COUNTER (OTC) STOCKS.

over-the-counter (OTC) market trading of securities through a broker-dealer, usually over the telephone, without using the facilities of an exchange. The securities may or may not be listed on an exchange. OTC stocks include those listed on the NASDAQ systems as well as the OTC BULLETIN BOARD (*www.otcbb.com*).

over-the-counter (OTC) stocks stocks traded electronically via a network of dealers across the nation. OTC stands for over the counter, but these days over-the-computer would be more appropriate. Stocks listed on exchanges are traded face to face at one location, such as the New York Stock Exchange (NYSE). All others are OTC stocks. The NASDAQ stock market is the OTC system in the U.S., listing over 5000 companies. In the United States, OTC usually applies to smaller or newer companies that do not meet the stringent listing requirements of one of the major stock exchanges such as the AMEX or NYSE. In recent years, however, this has changed as many companies have elected to keep their shares trading on NASDAQ even after they have grown large, rather than moving to an exchange. A good example of this is Microsoft. As for foreign companies, ADRs are largely available to U.S. investors.

overwriting action of a speculative option writer who is of the opinion that a stock is overpriced or underpriced and sells voluminous calls or puts on the stock anticipating that they will not be exercised. If the option writer is wrong, he or she will likely experience significant loss.

P

Pacific Exchange (PCX) marketplace where individual and institutional investors, professional broker-dealers, and registered member firms meet to buy and sell more than 1800 stocks, bonds, and other securities issued by publicly traded companies, as well as options on more than 800 stocks. The PCX (*www.pacificex.com*) is the third largest stock options exchange in the world. It is the only stock market in the world with trading floors in two cities—San Francisco and Los Angeles. The Pacific trades the most active stocks and bonds listed on the New York and American Stock Exchanges, as well as many growth companies that are too young or too small to meet New York listing requirements. The bulk of its activity, by far, is in the New York Stock Exchange's BLUE CHIP issues. The PCX is the world's technology market for stock options. The Pacific's San Francisco options floor averages around 420,000 contracts per day, with Microsoft, Compaq, Sun Microsystems, MCI Worldcom, Micron Technology, AOL, 3Com, Applied Materials, and Advanced Micro Devices topping the list of the most active issues. LEAPS (extended term options) are available on most active options listings. The *PSE Tech 100* is the leading BENCHMARK for the broad-based technology sector.

paper profit or loss unrealized profit or loss on a security still held. A paper (unrealized) profit occurs when the market price of a security exceeds the original purchase price, while an unrealized loss occurs when the market price of a security declines from the initial purchase price. Such profits or losses have no tax effect except upon the actual sale of the security when it becomes a realized profit or loss.

par value
1. amount arbitrarily assigned by the corporate charter to one share of stock and printed on the stock certificate. The par value represents the legal capital per share. There can be no dividend declared that would cause the stockholders' equity to go below the par value of outstanding shares. Par value may be a minimum cushion of equity capital existing for creditor protection. The par value is the amount per share entered in the capital stock account. It is usually significantly lower than the market price per share.
2. for preferred issues, the value on which the issuer promises to pay dividends. Preferred dividends are typically expressed as a percentage of the preferred stock. For example, a 12%, $500,000 par value stock would pay annual dividends of $60,000.
3. nominal, face value, maturity value of a bond. For example, the face value of a bond is in $1000 denominations. Interest paid on a

bond is the nominal (stated, coupon) interest rate multiplied by the face value of the bond.

4. for a country's currency, the value established by the government for it relative to other currencies.

par yield curve yield curve drawn for straight bonds of different maturities that are priced at PAR.

pari passu equably, rateably, without preference; generally used to describe securities that are to be treated as being of equal priority or preference.

Paris Bourse Paris stock exchange.

participating preferred stock entitled to receive a stated dividend before the common stock and part of any dividend thereafter declared on the common stock.

passed dividend omission of a regular or scheduled dividend.

passive investment
1. type of investment mimicking a BENCHMARK index. *See also* PASSIVELY MANAGEMENT FUNDS.
2. a U.S. tax term meaning the investor does *not* materially participate in the trade or business.

passively managed country funds mutual fund in which the fund manager does *not* actively trade in the stocks of the foreign countries. It typically mimics a BENCHMARK country fund index. The stocks are basically bought and held.

passively management funds funds that might follow an index, a formula, or, in some cases, not changing holdings at all. They simply buy and hold shares of investments found in a BENCHMARK, such as the EAFE INDEX or the STANDARD & POOR'S 500 STOCK COMPOSITE.

pass-through securities securities backed by a pool of mortgages. The principal and interest payments made monthly on the mortgages in this pool are passed through to the investors who purchased the MORTGAGE-BACKED SECURITY. Examples of pass-through securities are the mortgage-backed securities guaranteed by the GNMA and Freddie Mac. The Freddie Mac securities do not carry a federal guarantee.

pay date date on which a declared stock dividend or a bond interest payment is scheduled to be paid.

pay up when an investor wants to own a stock at a particular price and hesitates, and the price begins to increase. Instead of bypassing the purchase, the investor "pays up," buying the shares at the higher prevailing prices.

payment for order flow widespread practice in which on-line brokerages sell customer orders to outside firms that execute the trades. Brokers claim that the payments allow them to charge low commissions. Others argue that many brokerages send orders to firms that pay them the most but that give poor executions to customers. *See also* INTERNALIZATION.

penny stock   stock usually selling for less than $1 a share but which may rise above it after being promoted. Companies issuing penny stocks usually have low revenue and profitability, short lives, or past instability in operations. As such, the companies are financially weak and very speculative. These stocks typically experience volatility in price relative to the stocks of established companies on the major stock exchanges. Many brokerage firms are very careful when they recommend penny stocks because the Securities and Exchange Commission mandates that they should be bought only by investors who are financially and intelligently suited for these high-risk securities. Many brokerage houses will ask for written statements from investors that they are aware of the high speculation and the investors find the penny stocks suitable for them. Most penny stocks are traded in the OVER-THE-COUNTER MARKET.

percent change   percentage change in the price of a security from the previous trading day's closing price.

performance bond   surety bond given by one individual or company to another so as to safeguard the second party from loss if the contractual provisions are not carried out. The surety company is mainly responsible with the principal (contractor) if nonperformance occurs. For example, a company having a new office constructed may ask for a performance bond from the contractor so that the company would be compensated if the office is improperly built within the specified time provided for.

performance bond call   demand for additional funds because of adverse price movement; also referred to as MARGIN CALL. *See also* MAINTENANCE MARGIN.

performance (growth) stock   high-growth security that is expected to materially increase in price. A growth stock pays no dividend or a minimal dividend. Growth companies usually reinvest the earnings into the business instead of paying them out in dividends so as to have funding for fast growth.

perpetual bond   bond without a maturity date that pays interest indefinitely.

Philadelphia Stock Exchange (PHLX)   founded in 1790, as the first securities exchange in the United States. As one of North America's primary marketplaces for the trading of stocks, equity options, index options, and currency options, the PHLX (*http://www.phlx.com*) continues to be a leader in the development and introduction of innovative new products and services. The PHLX trades more than 2300 stocks, 780 equity options, 10 index options, and 100 currency pairs. On the equity floor, PHLX's PACE

(Philadelphia Automated Communication and Execution) system was one of the first automated equity trading systems on any exchange. The PHLX's Oil Service Sector (OSX) Index Option is the most actively traded index option offered by any exchange, serving as a widely quoted benchmark of the oil industry. Similarly, the PHLX's Gold/Silver Sector (XAU), Semiconductor Sector (SOX), KBW Bank Sector (BKX), and Utility Sector (UTY) are well established as leading industry indicators. The PHLX's TheStreet.com Internet Sector (DOT), which is the most actively traded Internet index option, offers investors a way to ride one of the most exciting and volatile sectors in today's marketplace without having to select individual stocks. It reflects the movement of 20 companies involved in Internet commerce, service, and software. In perhaps one of the most important innovations since listed currency options themselves, the PHLX has created a unique market structure for the trading of currency options. Unprecedented flexibility is provided for with the availability of both standardized and customized currency options. Customized currency options offer choice of expiration date, STRIKE (exercise) price, and premium payment.

pink sheet stocks smallest of small OVER-THE-COUNTER STOCKS that do not meet NASDAQ's listing requirements. Their prices are listed just once daily. So named because prices are available only by subscription to a publication originally printed on thin sheets of pink paper. *Note:* Almost all unsponsored ADRs are traded along with all the other non-exchange-traded sponsored ADRs on the non-NASDAQ OTC market or in the pink sheets. *See also* AMERICAN DEPOSITARY RECEIPT (ADR).

pink sheets publication put out for each trading day published by the national quotation bureau listing bid and asked prices of OVER-THE-COUNTER STOCKS not shown in the financial newspapers for the NASDAQ Stock Market including the national NASDAQ and small capitalization NASDAQ listings. The pink sheets present the current prices of NASDAQ stocks not listed along with their market makers. Generally, the companies listed are very small and extremely risky. *Note*: YELLOW SHEETS are used to list debt securities.

pip one hundredth of a basis point.

placement agent agent handling the sale of a new issue of securities to the public or in private.

plain-vanilla security, especially a bond or a swap, issued with standard features; also called *generic*.

point
1. in the case of shares of stock, a point means $1; for example, if Xerox shares rise 2 points, each share has risen $2.
2. in the case of bonds, a point means $10, since a bond is quoted as a percentage of $1000. A bond that rises 2 points gains 2% of $1000 or $20 in value.

POINTS QUOTATION

3. in the case of market averages, the word *point* means merely that and no more. It is not equivalent to any fixed sum of money.

points quotation   a FORWARD EXCHANGE RATE quotation expressed only as the number of decimal points.

poison pill   move by a company about to be bought by another company in which it seeks to block the acquisition by taking some step such as issuing excessive preferred stock or borrowing heavily to be less attractive financially. An objective is to make the cost of the acquisition prohibitive to deter the takeover bid. A threat sometimes used to block the acquisition is that the whole management team threatens to resign immediately if the acquisition becomes effective.

political risk   exposure to potential actions by a host government that would threaten the value of an investment; also called SOVEREIGN RISK. It is the risk associated with political or sovereign uncertainty. Clearly, political factors are a major determinant of the attractiveness for investment in any country. There is no reason to believe that local investors will be systematically optimistic regarding their country's future. When political risks increase significantly, such investors will attempt to diversify from the home market as rapidly as will foreigners. As a result, prices will fall until someone will be satisfied to hold the securities of a risky country. Political instability, limited track records, and poor statistics all make gauging risk a risky business.

political risk insurance   insurance policy to reduce the possible adverse effect of the risk of operating in foreign countries. An example is a policy to reimburse the MNC if its assets are expropriated by a foreign government.

portfolio   holdings of various investment vehicles to reduce risk by DIVERSIFICATION. A portfolio may contain bonds, preferred stocks, common stocks of various types of enterprises, and other investment instruments. *See also* ASSET ALLOCATION.

portfolio diversification   process of selecting alternative investment instruments that have dissimilar risk-return characteristics. The rationale behind portfolio diversification is the reduction of risk. The main method of reducing the risk of a portfolio is the combining of assets that are not perfectly positively correlated in their returns. *See also* ASSET ALLOCATION; PORTFOLIO.

portfolio investments   investing in a variety of assets to reduce risk by diversification. An example of a portfolio is a mutual fund that consists of a mix of assets that are professionally managed. Investors can own a variety of securities with a minimal capital investment. Since mutual funds are professionally managed, they tend to involve less risk. To reduce risk, securities in a portfolio should have negative or no correlations to each other. *See also* DIVERSIFICATION;

EFFICIENT PORTFOLIO; INTERNATIONAL DIVERSIFICATION; PORTFOLIO THEORY.

portfolio manager professional responsible for the management of a portfolio of various investment vehicles on behalf of an individual or institutional investor; broadly known as MONEY MANAGER or *professional money manager*. A portfolio manager may work for a mutual fund, pension fund, profit-sharing plan, bank trust department, or insurance company, as well as private investors. For a fee, the manager has the fiduciary responsibility to manage the investment assets prudently and make sure the funds grow as much as possible for a given amount of RISK. Professional money managers, whether *domestic* or *international*, invariably have a philosophy of investing and a system to implement it. They may be growth managers or value managers, market timers, momentum players, or money-flow investors. They may do their research from the top down or the bottom up. They have different philosophies and methods to screen securities and for determining when to buy and sell. *See also* PORTFOLIO THEORY.

portfolio theory theory advanced by H. Markowitz in an attempt to construct a well-diversified portfolio. The central theme of the theory is that rational investors behave in a way that reflects their aversion to taking increased risk without being compensated by an adequate increase in expected return. Also, for any given expected return, most investors will prefer a lower risk, and for any given level of risk, they will prefer a higher return to a lower return.

position specific instance of a chosen STRATEGY. An option position is an investment comprised of one or more options.

Pratt's Guide directory of VENTURE CAPITAL firms, the types of investments that they typically make, and the industries in which they specialize.

precious metals tangible assets such as gold, silver, and platinum.

precious metals/gold funds mutual funds seeking capital appreciation (a rise in share price) by investing at least two-thirds of fund assets in securities associated with gold, silver, and other precious metals.

preemptive right right of a current stockholder to maintain the percentage ownership interest in the company by buying new shares on a pro rata basis before they are issued to the public. It prevents existing stockholders from dilution in value or control. The typical procedure is that each existing stockholder receives a subscription warrant indicating how many shares can be bought. Usually, the new shares are issued to the current stockholder at a lower price than the going market price so they are attractive to exercise. In addition, brokerage commissions do not have to be paid. For example, if an individual owns 2% of the shares of a company that is coming out

PREFERRED SHARES

with a new issue of 100,000 shares, the individual is entitled to buy 2000 shares at a favorable price to maintain the proportionate interest. Many states allow companies to pay off stockholders to waive their preemptive rights.

preferred shares   *see* PREFERRED STOCK.

preferred stock   class of capital stock generally issued at its PAR VALUE that has preference over common stock in the event of corporate LIQUIDATION and in the distribution of earnings. However, in liquidation, corporate bondholders come before preferred stockholders. Preferred stockholders represent a pseudoequity interest in the corporation, but their risk of loss is limited to the liquidation value of the preferred stock in the event the company declares bankruptcy and makes a distribution of the corporate assets. Preferred stock is considered a hybrid security because it has features of both common stock and corporate bonds. It is like common stock because it represents equity ownership and is issued without stated maturity dates, and it pays dividends. Preferred stock does have certain risks, preferences, or restrictions not existent with common stock. Preferred stock is also like a CORPORATE BOND in that it provides for previous claims on profit and assets, its dividend is fixed for the life of the issue, and it can carry call and convertible features and SINKING FUND provisions. The preferred dividend is stated in dollars per share, or as a percentage of par (stated) value of the stock. For example, 6% preferred stock means that the dividend equals 6% of the total par value of the outstanding shares.

EXAMPLE 1:
A company declares a 5% preferred dividend on outstanding preferred stock having a par value of $1,000,000. The preferred dividend will be $50,000.

The expected return from preferred stock may be computed as follows:

Current yield = Dividends per share/market price per share

EXAMPLE 2:
The annual dividend per share is $5 and the market price per share is $50. The current yield is 10% ($5/$50).

Even though the stock has a fixed dividend return, that dividend is not guaranteed to stockholders. It becomes guaranteed and irrevocable only when it is declared by the board of directors. Except in unusual instances, no voting rights exist; thus, preferred stockholders have no control in formulating corporate business policy or activities. Types of preferred stock include cumulative preferred stock and participating preferred stock.

In the case of cumulative preferred stock, the fixed dividend is never lost. If the preferred stock dividend in a particular year is not declared on cumulative preferred stock, then it becomes a dividend

ARREARAGE of the company and must be disclosed. The common stockholder may not receive any dividends until the cumulative preferred stockholders have received their dividends in arrears in addition to their current year dividend.

Participating preferred stock allows holders to share in earnings above and beyond the declared dividend along with common stockholders usually based on total par value.

Adjustable preferred stock varies the dividend on some basis such as change in the prime interest rate. This is done periodically, typically quarterly.

Some preferred stock is convertible at the option of the preferred stockholders at a specified price over a predetermined time period.

Most preferred stock is redeemable at the issuing company's option; thus, when the issuer decides to call its preferred stock outstanding, the preferred stockholder must turn over his or her shares into the corporation for the share's indicated call price.

Preferred stocks listed on organized exchanges are reported in the same newspaper section as common stocks.

Advantages of owning preferred stock include the following:
- There is a lower unit cost ($10 to $25 per share).
- They provide high predictable current income.

Disadvantages of owning preferred stock include the following:
- They lack significant capital gain potential.
- They are vulnerable to inflation and high interest rates.

Here are the major features of preferred stock.

CHARACTERISTICS OF PREFERRED STOCK

Voting rights	No, unless dividend not paid
Income	Fixed as long as dividend paid
Capital gain/loss potential	Only if interest rates change or company's preferred stock rating changes
Inflation hedge	No except for adjustable
Preemptive right	No
Priority of claim	Prior to common stock

preferred stock fund   mutual fund that invests in PREFERRED STOCK with the emphasis on income rather than growth.

preferred stock ratings   like BOND RATINGS, ratings given by Standard & Poor's and Moody's for the investment quality of PREFERRED STOCKS. S&P uses basically the same rating system as they do with bonds, except that triple A ratings are not given to preferred stocks. Moody's uses a slightly different system, which is given below. These ratings are intended to provide an indication of the quality of the issue and are based largely on an assessment of the firm's ability to pay preferred dividends in a prompt and timely fashion. Note, however, that preferred stock ratings should not be compared with bond ratings as they are not equivalent.

PREMIUM

MOODY'S PREFERRED STOCK RATING SYSTEM

Rating Symbol	Definition
aaa	Top quality
aa	High grade
a	Upper medium grade
baa	Lower medium grade
ba	Speculative type
b	Little assurance of future dividends
caa	Likely to be already in arrears

See also BOND RATINGS.

premium
1. purchase price of a bond or preferred issue higher than the par or face value.
2. purchasing or selling price of an option contract.
3. amount in excess of market value of an entity in a tender offer.
4. fee paid by a short seller to the lender of a security that is sold SHORT.
5. amount at which a CLOSED-END fund trades above its NET ASSET VALUE.

present value (PV) current worth of a future sum or stream—annuity or mixed—of dollars discounted at a specified rate. The process of finding present value is the inverse of finding future value (the compounding process). *See also* TIME VALUE OF MONEY.

price/earnings (P/E) ratio statistic that equals market price per share divided by current year earnings per share.

EXAMPLE:
If market price per share is $50 and earnings per share is $10, the price/earnings ratio equals 5. The P/E ratio may also be computed using an analysts' expected earnings per share for next year (referred to as forward P/E). The higher the P/E ratio the better, because more earnings growth is expected.

The P/E ratio is good to use in evaluating the investment possibility of a company. A steady decrease in the P/E ratio reflects decreasing investor confidence in the growth potential of the entity. Some companies have high P/E multiples reflecting high earnings growth expectations. Young, fast-growing companies often have high P/E ratios with multiples over 20. However, new, quickly growing companies are much more speculative than low P/E stocks because of the high growth expectations. Also, young, inexperienced companies may suffer significant declines in stock price. Low price-earnings stocks are usually in low-growth or mature industries, industry groupings out of favor, BLUE CHIP companies with established stability in financial position and operating performance, and older and established companies. High P/E stocks usually pay no or minimal dividends. In most cases, low P/E stocks have higher yields relative to high P/E stocks. A company's P/E ratio (multiple) depends on many factors such as risk, earnings trend, management quality, industry conditions, and economic factors.

price improvement term for a situation in which a customer receives a better price than the QUOTED PRICE.

price indexes (indices) various price indices that are used to measure living costs, price-level changes, and inflation. They include Consumer Price Index (CPI), Producer Price Index (PPI), GNP Deflator (Implicit Price Index), and Employment Cost Index.

price patterns regular movements of security prices. By examining the pattern, you can better predict the trend in future prices based on past performances.

price to sales ratio current price divided by the sales per share for the trailing 12 months. If there is a preliminary earnings announcement for a quarter that has recently ended, the revenue (sales) values from this announcement will be used in calculating the trailing 12-month revenue per share.

pricing call discussion between the company and the underwriters of a PUBLIC OFFERING during which the price of the securities to be sold is determined. This discussion typically occurs the afternoon or evening immediately after the registration statement has been declared effective and immediately preceding the date on which the securities are to be publicly sold.

primary distribution (offering) new issuance of securities (for example, stocks, bonds) to the public. It is distinguished from a SECONDARY DISTRIBUTION that applies to securities that have been previously sold.

primary market market that trades new issues of securities, as distinguished from the SECONDARY MARKET, where securities of old issues are traded. The term also applies to auctions of government securities such as Treasury bills. *See also* FOURTH MARKET; THIRD MARKET.

prime rate loan rate charged by commercial banks to their best customers. The borrowers are large, well-known firms with high credit ratings. These companies often have access to the commercial paper market and often can often borrow below the prime interest rate. *See also* INTEREST RATES.

principal
 1. person for whom a broker executes an order, or a dealer buying or selling for his own account.
 2. face amount of a bond.
 3. basic amount invested.
 4. owner of a privately held business.
 5. any major party of a transaction.

private (financing) placement raising of capital for a business venture via private rather than public placement, resulting in the sale of securities to a relatively few number of investors. Such investments do not have to be registered with the SEC because no PUBLIC OFFERING is involved.

Producer Price Index (PPI) measure of the cost of a given basket of goods priced in wholesale markets, including raw materials, semifinished goods, and finished goods. The PPI is published monthly by the Bureau of Labor Statistics of the Department of Commerce. *See also* INFLATION; PRICE INDICES.

profit diagram graph showing the relationship between the price of a stock and the corresponding profit or loss to an investor.

profit margin ratio of income to sales:
1. Net profit margin equals net income divided by net sales. If a company's net income was $800,000 and its sales were $8,000,000, the profit margin would be 10%. It indicates the entity's ability to generate earnings at a particular sales level. By examining a company's profit margin relative to previous years and to industry norms, one can evaluate the company's operating efficiency and pricing strategy as well as its competitive status with other companies in the industry.
2. Gross profit margin equals gross profit divided by net sales. Net sales equals gross sales less sales returns and allowances. Gross profit equals net sales less cost of goods sold. A high gross profit margin is desirable since it indicates the company is earning a good return over the cost of its merchandise sold.

profit table table showing the relationship between the price of a stock and corresponding profit or loss to an investor.

profit taking situation in which an investor having a gain on an investment decides to take it either because he or she believes the price of the security will decline or is satisfied with the gain earned so far. It is often applicable to a short-term trader of securities or commodities who wishes to lock in the gain due to a significant increase in price.

program trading term used to describe the use of computer-based buying or selling programs. The software has built-in guidelines that instantaneously trigger buy and sell orders when differences in the prices of the securities are great enough to produce profit. Program trading is used by institutional investors who place buy and sell orders in large blocks of 10,000 or more units. This type of large trade tends to significantly impact the prices of securities in the market. Sometimes, the program trading orders reach the trading floors from a number of firms. This impact can be seen most readily during what is called *triple witching hour*. The triple witching hour occurs four times annually in the hour prior to the moment (4:15 P.M. EST, on the third Friday of March, June, September, and December) when STOCK OPTIONS, STOCK INDEX OPTIONS, and STOCK INDEX FUTURES all expire at once. During this hour, the Dow Jones Industrial Average and other indices have been known to change drastically. For example, there may be a drop by 2 to 5%, respectively, a steep decline in so short a time period. Fortunately, the market usually recovers within a week or so, but if you wanted to sell during one of these drops you could find yourself taking an anticipated loss. For the small investor, it might be best to stay out of the market on the days immediately before the triple witching hour. On the other hand, the speculative investor might choose this as an opportune time to act.

prospectus circular, required by the Securities Act of 1933, that describes securities being offered for sale. Its purpose is full disclosure, especially of any adverse prospects for the issuer. It discloses facts regarding the issuer's operations, including the experience of its management, its financial status, any anticipated legal matters that could affect the company, and potential risks of investing in the corporation. It must be provided to the original purchaser no later than the date of confirmation of their purchase. *See also* PROXY STATEMENT.

proxy written authorization given by a shareholder to someone else to represent him or her and vote his or her shares at a shareholders' meeting. It is like an absentee ballot, which is mailed before each stockholders' annual meeting.

proxy statement written document that the Securities and Exchange Commission requires to be provided to shareholders before they vote by PROXY on corporate matters. (A proxy refers to the authority given to another to act on one's behalf. An example is a power of attorney by which a stockholder transfers his or her voting rights to another party.) It typically contains proposed members of the board of directors, inside director's compensation, resolutions of minority stockholders and of management, and data regarding option plans and bonuses.

prudent man rule investment standard. In some states, the law requires that a fiduciary, such as a trustee, may invest the fund's money only in a list of securities, called the legal list, designated by the state. A reasonable degree of safety and return are expected. In other states, the trustee may invest in a security if a prudent man of discretion and intelligence, who is seeking a reasonable income and preservation of capital, would buy it

public offering
1. offering new securities to the investing public after registration requirements have been filed with the SEC.
2. sale of a limited partnership. It is registered with the SEC and required to meet specified SEC restrictions.

pullback/throwback *pullback*: situation that occurs when the overall market or a particular security falls back in price from a previous high.

throwback: return of the price of a particular stock or overall market to the downside after an upside breakout.

pump-and-dump scare in which a marginal firm's stock is hyped by phone or on the Internet until its price soars, whereupon the scamsters sell out, causing the stock price to crash.

purchasing power
1. dollar amount of goods and services an investor can buy after adjusting for inflation. Purchasing power can be measured by comparing a price index (such as the CONSUMER PRICE INDEX) for a given base period to the one of the present period.
2. amount of credit available to an investor in his or her margin account for the purchase of additional securities. For example, an investor with purchasing power of $10,000 in his or her brokerage account can purchase $20,000 worth of securities under a 50% MARGIN REQUIREMENT.

purchasing power parity (PPP) thesis stating that exchange rates adjust to inflation differentials between two countries. There are two versions of this theory:
- *Absolute PPP:* The price of internationally traded commodities should be the same in every country, that is, one unit of home currency should have the same purchasing power worldwide. The absolute version is popularly called the *law of one price.*
- *Relative PPP:* The relative version of purchasing power parity says that the exchange rate of one currency against another will adjust to reflect changes in the price levels of the two countries.

purchasing power risk risk resulting from possible changes in price levels in the economy that can have a significant effect on the prices of securities; also called *inflation risk.*

put right to sell 100 shares (usually) of a specified stock at a fixed price per share (the STRIKE PRICE) for a limited length of time (until expiration).

put-call parity theoretical relation between a put and a call option with the same STRIKE PRICE and expiration.

put option contract giving the right to sell an asset at a specified price, on or before a specified date.

puts and calls options that give the right to buy or sell a fixed amount of a certain stock at a specified price within a specified time. A put gives the holder the right to sell the stock, a call the right to buy the stock. Puts are purchased by those who think a stock may go down. A put obligates the seller of the contract to take delivery of the stock and pay the specified price to the owner of the option within the time limit of the contract. The price specified in a put or call is usually close to the market price of the stock at the time the contract is made. Calls are purchased by those who think a stock may rise. A call gives the holder the right to buy the stock from the seller of the contract at the specified price within a fixed period of time. Put and call contracts are written for 30, 60, or 90 days, or longer. If the purchaser of a put or call does not wish to exercise the option, the price he paid for the option becomes a loss.

pyramiding
1. adding further positions to stocks, bonds, or commodities as the market continues in the right direction.
2. financial pyramid is a structure of low-, medium-, and high-risk investments. In a financial pyramid, money is invested from most to least as follows: liquid and safe investments, income and long-term growth investments, and speculative and high-risk investments.
3. holding gains from a securities or commodities position as COLLATERAL to buy additional positions with funds borrowed from a broker. The use of leverage results in higher profits in a BULL MARKET, but in a BEAR MARKET there is potential for larger losses arising from margin calls.

Q

quality stock fund mutual fund that invests only in the stock of companies with a track record of strong performance.

quant individual with computer and operations research knowledge who furnishes mathematical and evaluative assistance in the securities industry.

quotation highest bid to buy and the lowest offer to sell a security in a given market at a given time; also called *quote*. If you ask your broker for a quotation on a stock, the answer may be, for example, "26.25 to 26.50." This means that $26.25 was the highest price any buyer wanted to pay (bid) at the time the quotation was given on the exchange and that $26.50 was the lowest price at which any holder of the stock offered to sell.

quoted price price at which the last purchase and sale of a specific security or commodity were made. *See also* QUOTATION.

R

r symbol used in *The Wall Street Journal* and similar publications indicating that there were no trades on that option today, so there is no last quote to report.

R-squared (R^2) percentage of a fund's movement that can be explained by changes in the S&P 500. In statistics, it is called the *coefficient of determination*, designated R^2 (read as R-squared). Simply put, R^2 tells us how good the overall relationship is between the dependent variable y and the explanatory variable x. An R^2 of 60.84% means that about 60.84% of the total variation in the XYZ Fund returns is explained by the market (represented by the S&P 500 Index). A relatively low R^2 indicates that there is little correlation between the XYZ Fund and the market. If the R^2 of a mutual fund is close to 100%, the fund is well diversified. The farther away a mutual fund is from 100%, the less the fund is diversified. Morningstar Inc. (800) 876-5005 offers R^2 values of major funds as does its web site at *www.morningstar.net*. The following presents R-squared values for some selected international funds:

R-SQUARED VALUES FOR SOME SELECTED INTERNATIONAL MUTUAL FUNDS

Company	Ticker Symbol	R-squared
GAM: International	GMMNX	0.09
Harbor International	HAINX	0.53
Strong International	STISX	0.24
Fidelity Overseas	FOSFX	0.63
Templeton International A	TEGEX	0.27
Vanguard International Growth	VWIGX	0.53

Source: MSN Money Central Investor (*http://moneycentral.msn.com/investor/contents.asp*), April 3, 2001.

Note: Generally, a higher R-squared will indicate a more useful BETA figure. If the R-squared is lower, then the beta is less relevant to the fund's performance.

See also ALPHA, BETA FOR A MUTUAL FUND; STANDARD DEVIATION.

rally brisk rise following a decline in the general price level of the market or of an individual stock.

random walk theory espoused by French mathematician Louis Bachelier in 1900 that states that past share prices are of no use in predicting future prices. A theory stating that all current information is reflected in current security prices and that future price movements are random (that is, take place without a pattern), because they are caused by unexpected news. According to the theory, share prices reflect reactions of the market to information being fed into the market completely randomly. Since the information is coming in randomly, the price movements they cause are not predictable. Random walk theory is diametrically opposed to TECHNICAL ANALYSIS. The theoretical underpinning of technical analysis is that markets react in a consistent way to share price movements. By looking at charts of past price movements, investors can identify patterns that have occurred before, and can anticipate future price movements because the market tends to react in the same way.

random walk theory   *see* RANDOM WALK.

range   lowest to highest market prices of a stock, bond, commodity, or overall market index (for example, Dow Jones Industrial Average) over a specified period. An example is the 52-week high and low price figures for stocks. It is significant when a stock price breaks out of its trading range, whether on the upside or downside. For example, a stock moving out of the upper boundary may go higher. It is an important development from a technical analysts' perspective.

rate of return   *see* YIELD.

rating   evaluation of investment grade and credit risk of a security as determined by rating services, such as Moody's, Fitch Investors Service, and Standard & Poor's. *See also* BOND RATINGS; PREFERRED STOCK RATINGS.

rating evaluation   rating assigned to an issue's investment quality. It is performed by a credit rating agency, such as Moody's or Standard & Poor's.

rating reliability   degree to which an analyst or investor can rely on the correctness of a quality ranking of a company or security by a financial rating agency such as Moody's. Rating agencies have been known to make mistakes on occasion.

reaction   term used to describe a short-term drop in prices.

real cost of hedging   extra cost of HEDGING as opposed to not hedging. A *negative* real cost would signify that hedging was more favorable than not hedging.

Real Estate Investment Trusts (REITs)   corporations that operate much like CLOSED-END MUTUAL FUNDS, investing shareholders' money in diversified real estate or mortgage portfolios instead of stocks or bonds. Their shares trade on the major stock exchanges or OVER-THE-COUNTER. By law, REITs must distribute 95% of their net earnings to shareholders, and in turn they are exempt from corporate taxes on income or gains. Since REIT earnings are not taxed before they are distributed, you get a larger percentage of the profits than with stocks. REIT yields are high, ranging between $5^1/_2$ to $10^1/_2$%. There are three types of REITs: equity REITs invest primarily in income-producing properties; mortgage REITs lend funds to developers or builders; and hybrid REITs do both.

real exchange rate   exchange rate adjusted by the inflation differential between two countries.

real gain or loss   real income or YIELD discounted for inflation. Real gain or loss represents real purchasing power. This is obtained by dividing the amount of money received by a cost-of-living index such as the CONSUMER PRICE INDEX.

real interest rate   rate of interest that is adjusted for inflation.

real return on investment   YIELD after subtracting the effects of inflation. It is the return on investment expressed in real PURCHASING POWER.

real time   describing stock, bond, option, or futures quote, which reports the most current price available when a security changes hands. A delayed quote shows a security's price 15 minutes and sometimes 20 minutes after a trade takes place.

realized gain (loss)   Excess (deficiency) in selling price relative to cost of a security. Realized gains or losses are included in net income in the year of sale as a separate item. Realized gains or losses (not unrealized gains or losses) are included on the tax return.

realized yield   yield realized on a bond before it matures. You need a measure of return to evaluate the investment appeal of any bonds you intend to buy and sell. Realized yield is used for this purpose. This measure is simply a variation of YIELD TO MATURITY, as only two variables are changed in the yield to maturity formula. The future price is used in place of PAR VALUE ($1000), and the length of the HOLDING PERIOD is substituted for the number of years to maturity.

EXAMPLE:
Assume that you anticipate holding the bond for only three years and that you have estimated interest rates will change in the future so that the price of the bond will move to about $925 from its present level of $877.70. You will therefore buy the bond today at a market price of $877.70 and sell the issue three years later at a price of $925. Then the realized yield is:

$$\text{Realized yield} = \frac{\$80 + (\$925 - \$877.70)/3}{(\$925 + \$877.70)/2} = \frac{\$80 + \$15.77}{\$901.35}$$

$$= \frac{\$95.77}{\$901.35} = 10.63\%$$

See also BOND YIELD; YIELD TO CALL.

recession   lower phase of a BUSINESS CYCLE, in which the economy's output (GDP), income, corporate profits, and employment are declining, coupled with a declining rate of business investment and consumer spending. Two to three successive quarterly declines in GNP are usually the sign of recession. Economists, however, have never made the distinction between recession and depression clear. It is the old rule of thumb that if your neighbor loses his or her job, it is a recession, and if you lose yours, it is a depression. *See also* RECOVERY.

record date   date on which a shareholder must officially own shares in order to be entitled to a DIVIDEND. After the date of record the stock is said to be EX-DIVIDEND.

recovery
  1. period of increasing prices after a drop in prices.
  2. expansion (prosperity) phase in the business or economic cycle. See below.

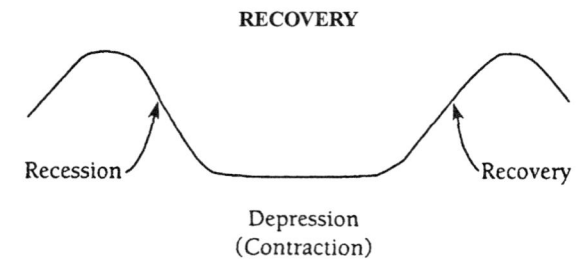

RECOVERY

Recession

Recovery

Depression
(Contraction)

red herring   slang term for a preliminary prospectus that outlines the important features of a new security issue. This does not contain selling price information or offering date. It is so named because it is stamped in red ink telling the reader that the document is not an official offer to sell the securities.

redemption (call) price   price at which a bond or PREFERRED STOCK can be called by the issuing company. In the case of a bond, it is repurchased before maturity. The call price typically exceeds the FACE VALUE of the bond, called *call premium*, recognizing that the holder will lose income and ownership from the forced BUYBACK.

redemption (exit) fees   fees that a mutual fund charges when an investor sells a share of a fund. These fees can range from a flat $5 to 2% of the amount withdrawn. The redemption fee may decline on a sliding basis depending on how long the funds were invested; for example, 3% after one year, 2% after two years, 1% after three years, and no fee thereafter. *See also* MUTUAL FUND.

redemption price
1. price at which a bond may be redeemed before maturity, at the option of the issuer. Redemption value also applies to the price the company must pay to call in certain types of PREFERRED STOCK.
2. price per share mutual fund shareholders receive when they cash in the shares. The value of the shares depends on the market value of the fund's portfolio of securities at the time.

regional funds mutual funds that invest in a particular region of the world, such as an Asian fund or a Latin American fund. Investors are advised to consider regional funds for only two reasons: (1) they should be an investor in that region for the long haul, at least five years; (2) the region has been beaten down recently and offers good value. Do not buy a regional fund because it produced stunning results last year. Further, consider more than one fund.

regional stock exchanges organized securities exchanges other than the New York Stock Exchange (NYSE) and the American Stock Exchange (AMEX) that deal primarily in securities having a local or regional flavor.

registered bond
1. bond recorded in the holder's name on either the issuing company's records or the issuer's registrar. If a registered owner wants to transfer the bond to another party, he or she must endorse it. In the case of a registered bond, principal of such a bond and interest, if registered as to interest, is paid to the owner of the bond listed on the record of the issuing company. It contrasts with BEARER (coupon) BONDS, where detachable coupons must be presented to the issuer for interest payment. Some registered bonds pay interest through electronic transfers.
2. public issue registered with the Securities and Exchange Commission.

registered representative *see* BROKER; FINANCIAL PLANNER.

registration process of filing the necessary documentation with the appropriate authorities for an offering of securities to the public, and having this registration declared effective. In Europe, filing is generally made with the stock market(s) on which the stock is to be traded, as well as with the competent authorities for such filings of the country of the stock market(s). In the United States, the registration statement (qv) is filed with the SEC, which also declares it effective.

Regulation Q Federal Reserve Board regulation that sets deposit interest rate ceilings and regulates advertising of interest on savings accounts. This regulation applies to all commercial banks. It is a rule, first instituted in the Banking Act of 1933.

Regulation T Federal Reserve Board regulation governing the amount of credit that may be advanced by brokers and dealers to customers for the purchase of securities. *See also* INITIAL MARGIN; MARGIN BUYING; MAINTENANCE MARGIN REQUIREMENT.

Regulation U Federal Reserve Board regulation governing the amount of credit that may be advanced by a bank to its customers for the purchase of securities.

reinvestment load fees subtracted from reinvested interest, dividends, and capital gains of a mutual fund. For example, if you receive a capital gains distribution of $400 and the reinvestment fee is 8%, the fund will keep $32 and reinvest $368.

relative strength measure of the market performance of a stock in comparison to its own industry and/or a market index for a stated time period. Stocks that have been strong relative to all other stocks should continue to be relatively stronger in the future, and securities that have been relatively weak tend to continue to be weaker. *See also* MOMENTUM; RELATIVE STRENGTH ANALYSIS.

relative strength analysis analysis of the price performance of a company's stock compared to the price performance of an overall market and/or industry index. In addition, the investor can compare how the performance of the stocks within an industry has done relative to the overall market. Market indexes that might be used are the Dow Jones Industrial Average, Standard & Poor's 500, and New York Stock Exchange Composite. Relative strength is an approach used in technical investment analysis by CHARTISTS. Relative strength for a company's stock may be computed using one or both of the following ratios:

$$\frac{\text{Monthly average stock price}}{\text{Monthly average market index}}$$

$$\frac{\text{Monthly average stock price}}{\text{Monthly average industry group index}}$$

An increase in these ratios means that the company's stock is performing better than the overall market or industry. This is a positive sign. A relative strength index (RSI) also may be computed for a security as follows:

$$RSI = 100 - \frac{100}{1 + RS}$$

where

$$RS = \frac{\text{14-day average of up closing prices}}{\text{14-day average of down closing prices}}$$

Relative strength for an industry also may be determined as follows:

$$\frac{\text{Specific industry group price index}}{\text{Total market index}}$$

An increasing ratio indicates that the industry is outperforming the market. Brokerage research reports, *Value Line Investment Survey*, and new stock reports from Morningstar Inc. may provide relative strength information on companies and industries. Investors also may compute the monthly average price of a company's stock and that of a market index by referring to price quotations in newspapers. Relative strength is an approach that helps the investor determine the quality of a price trend of an index or stock by comparing it with the trend in another index or stock. If there is an improvement in relative strength after a drastic decline, this is an indicator of strength. If there is a deterioration in relative strength after a prolonged increase in price, weakness exists.

Rembrandt bonds Dutch guilder-denominated bonds issued within the Netherlands by a foreign issuer (borrower).

resistance level price at which a particular security or the overall market tends to stop increasing. Technical analysts are encouraged when the market price of a stock rises above the resistance line since it may indicate that new highs will be reached. *See also* SUPPORT AND RESISTANCE LEVELS.

retention term that applies to the UNDERWRITING of securities referring to how many units are assigned to a participating investment banker less the units held back by the syndicate manager to facilitate sales to institutional investors, as well as to allocate to nonsyndicate members, which are part of the selling group.

retracement going back over again a past trend in price of a security.

return reward for investing. The investor must compare the expected return for a given investment with the risk involved. The return on an investment consists of the following sources of income: (1) periodic cash payments, called current income; (2) APPRECIATION (or DEPRECIATION) in market value, called CAPITAL GAINS (OR CAPITAL LOSSES). Current income, which is received on a periodic basis, may take the form of interest, dividends, rent, and the like. Capital gains or losses represent changes in market value. A capital gain is the amount by which the proceeds from the sale of an investment exceed its original purchase price. If the investment is sold for less than its purchase price, then the difference is a capital loss. *See also* BOND YIELD; HOLDING PERIOD RETURN (HPR); TOTAL RETURN.

return on equity measures the return, expressed as a percentage, earned on a company's common stock investment for a specific period. It is calculated by dividing common stock equity, or a company's net worth, into net income. The calculation is performed after preferred stock dividends and before common stock dividends. The

return relative return measured on a slightly different basis than TOTAL RETURN. This type of measure is necessary for calculating a COMPOUND (GEOMETRIC) AVERAGE RETURN, because negative returns cannot be used in the calculation. The return relative (RR) solves this problem by adding 1.0 to the total return. Although return relatives may be less than 1.0, they will be greater than zero, thereby eliminating negative numbers.

$$RR = \frac{C + (P_1 - P_0)}{P_0} + 1$$

where C = current dividend income, P_1 = price at year-end, P_0 = price at the beginning of the year, and $(P_1 - P_0)$ = change in price (gain or loss).

This can simply be reduced to the following formula (by using the price at the end of the HOLDING PERIOD in the numerator, rather than the *change* in price):

$$RR = \frac{C + P_1}{P_0}$$

EXAMPLE:
A total return of 0.10 for some holding period is equivalent to a return relative of 1.10 (0.10 + 1.0), and a total return of −0.15 is equivalent to a return relative of 0.85 (−0.15 + 1.0). *See also* ARITHMETIC AVERAGE RETURN; COMPOUND (GEOMETRIC) AVERAGE RETURN; HOLDING PERIOD RETURN; TOTAL RETURN.

reversal
1. change in direction, as when stock or commodity prices begin to fall after they have risen.
2. change in the direction in the price of a futures contract. See the chart below.

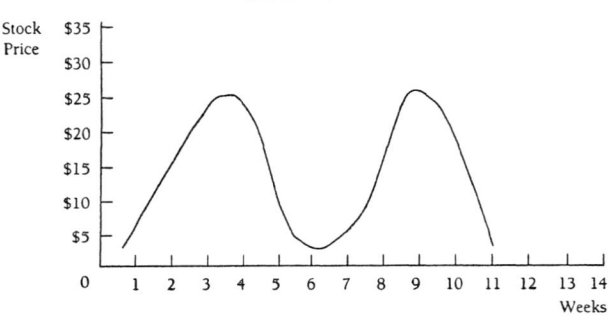

REVERSAL

reverse stock split issuing company's reduction in the amount of shares outstanding. With fewer shares outstanding but with the same total market value, each share will increase in price. For example, if a company with 500,000 shares outstanding selling at $40 per share (total market value of $20,000,000) has a reverse 1 for 5 split, we will now have 100,000 shares outstanding with a market price of $200 per share (total market value remains at $20,000,000). A company may opt for a reverse stock split if it desires to increase the market price per share because they believe the price per share currently is either too low to attract investors or the low market price may give the impression the company is of lower quality. *See also* STOCK SPLIT.

rights allowing a company's stockholders to buy the new shares ahead of other buyers in proportion to the number of shares each owns when the company issues additional stock. In general, the stockholders pay less than the public will be asked to pay.

rising bottoms term used by TECHNICAL ANALYSTS to depict an increasing trend in the low prices of a security or commodity. On a chart, the daily lows in prices move in an upward direction. In rising bottoms, there is evidence of high support levels. If this situation is combined with second tops, a BULLISH indication exists. See the chart below.

RISING BOTTOMS

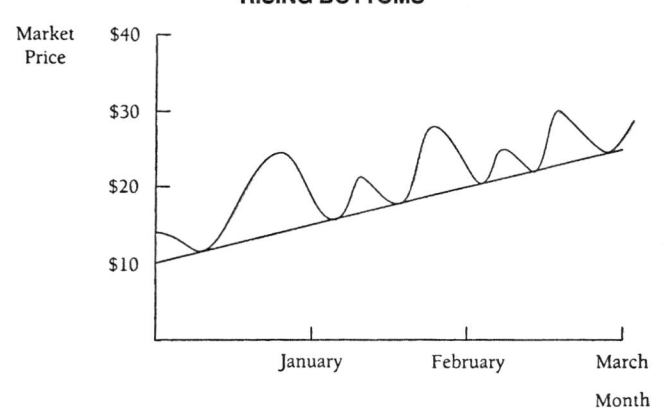

risk
 1. variability about income, returns, or other financial variable.
 2. possibility of losing value.
 3. peril insured against.

RISK

Among the commonly encountered types of risk are

- **business risk**: risk caused by fluctuations of earnings before interest and taxes (operating income). Business risk depends on variability in demand, sales price, input prices, and amount of operating leverage.
- **currency exchange risk**: risk arising from the fluctuation in foreign exchange rates.
- **default risk**: risk that a borrower will be unable to make interest payments or principal repayments on debt; for example, there is a great amount of default risk inherent in the bonds of a company experiencing financial difficulty.
- **economic risk**: negative impact of a company from economic slowdowns. For example, airlines have lower business volume in recession.
- **industry risk**: The uncertainty of the inherent nature of the industry such as high-technology, product liability, and accidents.
- **inflation (purchasing power) risk**: risk that relates to the possibility that an investor will receive a lesser amount of PURCHASING POWER than was originally invested. Bonds are most affected by this risk since the issuer will be paying back in cheaper dollars during an inflationary period.
- **interest rate risk**: term that refers to the fluctuations in the value of an asset as the interest rates and conditions of the money and capital markets change. Interest rate risk relates to fixed-income securities such as bonds; for example, if interest rates rise (fall), bond prices fall (rise).
- **international and political risks**: risks stemming from foreign operations in politically unstable foreign countries. An example is a U.S. company having a location and operations in a hostile country.
- **liquidity risk**: risk that represents the possibility that an asset may not be sold on short notice for its market value. If an investment must be sold at a high discount, then it is said to have a substantial amount of liquidity risk.
- **market risk**: changes in a stock's price that result from changes in the stock market as a whole, regardless of the fundamental change in a firm's earning power. Prices of all stocks are correlated to some degree with broad swings in the stock market.
- **social risk**: Problems facing the company due to ethnic boycott, discrimination cases, and environmental concerns.
- **systematic and unsystematic risk**: when investors hold more than one financial asset: The portion of a security's risk, called UNSYSTEMATIC RISK, can be controlled through diversification. This type of risk is unique to a given security. Business, liquidity, and default risks fall in this category. NONDIVERSIFIABLE RISK, more commonly referred to as SYSTEMATIC RISK, results from forces outside of the firm's control and are therefore not unique to the given security. Purchasing power, interest rate, and market risks fall

into this category. This type of risk is measured by the BETA COEFFICIENT.

risk averse opposed to RISK; a subjective attitude against risk taking. An investor not willing to take risk may place his or her funds into U.S. Treasury bills.

risk aversion term used to describe the fact that investors tend to be reluctant to take risk for the same level of expected return. To take more risk, they require compensation by a risk premium.

risk-free rate rate of return earned on a riskless security if no inflation were expected. A PROXY for a risk-free return is a rate of interest on short-term U.S. Treasury securities in an inflation-free world.

risk management analysis of and planning for potential risks and their subsequent losses. The objective of risk management is to try to minimize the financial consequence of random losses. *See also* INVESTMENT PLANNING.

risk measures quantitative measures of risk. They attempt to assess the degree of variation or uncertainty about earnings or return. There are several measures, including the STANDARD DEVIATION, coefficient of variation, and BETA. The standard deviation is a statistical measure of dispersion of the probability distribution of possible returns. The smaller the deviation, the tighter the distribution, and thus, the lower the riskiness of the investment. One must be careful in using the standard deviation to compare risk since it is only an absolute measure of dispersion (risk) and does not consider the dispersion of outcomes in relationship to an expected return. In comparisons of securities with differing expected returns, we commonly use the *coefficient of variation*. The coefficient of variation is computed simply by dividing the standard deviation for a security by its expected value. The higher the coefficient, the more risky the security. Beta measures a stock's or mutual fund's volatility relative to the general market.

risk neutral adjective describing an individual who neither fears nor enjoys risk but views it in an objective rational manner with a view toward its control when beneficial.

risk premium amount by which the required return on an asset or security exceeds the RISK-FREE RATE, such as the T-bill rate. The risk premium is the additional return required to compensate an investor for assuming a given level of risk. The higher this premium, the more risky the security and vice versa.

risk-return trade-off concept that the higher the return or yield, the larger the risk, or vice versa. All investment decisions involve some sort of balance between risk and return. You must compare the expected return from a given investment with the risk associated with it. Generally speaking, the higher the risk undertaken, the more

RISK-RETURN TRADE-OFF

ample the return, and conversely, the lower the risk, the more modest the return. In the case of investing in stock, you would demand higher return from a speculative stock to compensate for the higher level of risk. On the other hand, U.S. T-bills have minimal risk so a low return is appropriate. The proper assessment and balance of the various risk-return trade-offs is part of creating a sound investment plan. The first graph below depicts the risk-return trade-off, where the risk-free rate is the rate of return commonly required on a risk-free security such as a U.S. Treasury bill. *Note:* Generally speaking, the safer the investment, the lower the yield. In general, the risk-return characteristics of each of the major investment instruments can be displayed in a risk-return graph, as shown in the second graph. The third one illustrates risk-return trade-off of internationally diversified portfolios over the period 1976–1999.

RISK-RETURN TRADE-OFF

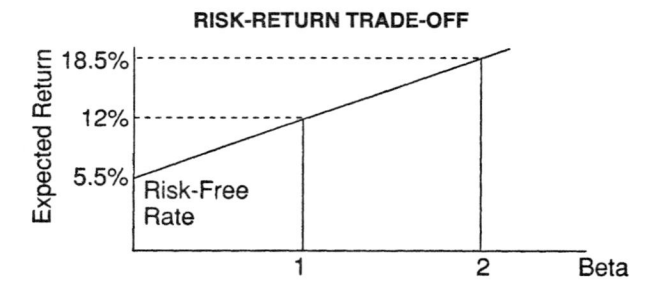

RISK-RETURN TRADE-OFFS FOR VARIOUS INVESTMENT VEHICLES

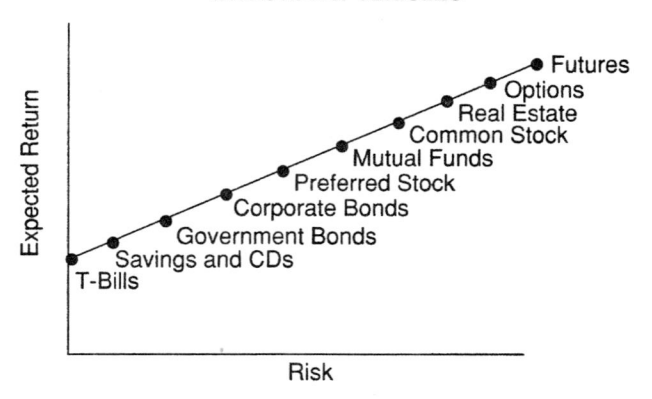

RISK-RETURN TRADE-OFF OF AN INTERNATIONALLY DIVERSIFIED PORTFOLIO OVER THE PERIOD 1976–1999

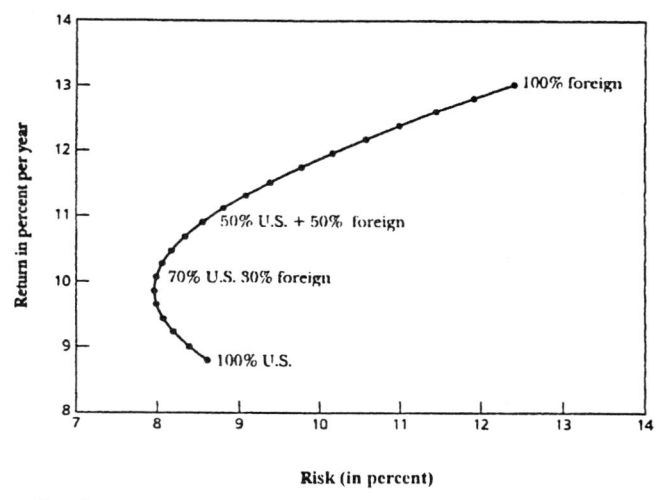

[Graph: Return in percent per year (y-axis, 8 to 14) vs. Risk (in percent) (x-axis, 7 to 14). Curve shows points labeled: 100% U.S. (~8.6, 8.7); 70% U.S. 30% foreign (~8, 10); 50% U.S. + 50% foreign (~8.3, 11); 100% foreign (~12.5, 13).]

See also INTERNATIONAL DIVERSIFICATION.

risk taker person who is not fearful of uncertainty and may even enjoy risky, speculative situations. He or she is a person who will take a chance or gamble in hopes of winning.

road show process during a PUBLIC OFFERING in which the management of an issuing company and the underwriters meet with groups of prospective investors to stimulate interest in an issue. Road shows are conducted during the "waiting period" shortly before the registration statement becomes effective. Road shows may take place in multiple cities and countries.

round lot unit of trading or a multiple thereof on a securities exchange. For example, a round lot on the New York Stock Exchange is 100 shares of stock or one $1000 face value bond (although brokers may have their own higher round lot requirements in the case of bonds). Inactive stocks have a 10 share round lot. By buying a round lot, the investor is not burdened with the differential associated with ODD LOT buys or sells. The round lot for institutional trading is taken by some to be 500 shares. The round lot for large certificates of deposit is $1 million.

round trip buying and selling a particular stock, bond, or commodity within a short time period. The commission for the round trip transaction is most apt to be for the buy-sell together. Round trip trading eats into profits because commissions tend to be significant. This strategy should be attempted only by sophisticated investors.

round turn   procedure by which a long or short position is offset by an opposite transaction or by accepting or making delivery of the actual financial instrument or physical commodity. This complete buy/sell or sell/buy is a *round turn*.

Rule of 69   very similar to the RULE OF 72; a rule stating that an amount of money invested at r percent per period will double in 69/r (in percent) + .35 periods.

EXAMPLE:
You bought a share of ADR yielding an annual return of 25%. The investment will double in a little over three years. 69/25 + .35 = 2.76 + .35 = 3.11 years.

Rule of 72   formula used to determine how many years it takes to double investment money at a given growth or interest rate. Under this method, dividing the number 72 by the fixed rate of return equals the number of years it takes for annual earnings from the investment to double, that is, 72/r (in percent).

EXAMPLE:
You bought a share of ADR yielding an annual return of 25%. The investment will double in less than three years. 72/25 = 2.88 years. The rule can also be reversed.

EXAMPLE:
If you know that your money doubled in four years, you can divide 72 by 4. You will see that you earned roughly 18% per year.

Note: The Rule of 72 does not work, however, when dealing with extreme numbers. For example, dividing 72 by a 72% return indicates that you expect to double your money in one year. It is not true. It would rather take a 100% return. Furthermore, it is more accurate when dealing with somewhat higher returns to use 76, not 72.

Rule 144A   rule for many companies that seek to raise capital in the U.S. markets privately by issuing restricted securities, which do not require SEC review. Rule 144A facilitates the trading of privately placed securities by sophisticated institutional investors (also known as Qualified Institutional Buyers, or QIBs; they must own or manage at least $100 million in securities). *See also* AMERICAN DEPOSITARY RECEIPT (ADR).

Russell 2000 Index   top barometer of performance for small company stock in the United States. It received growing attention in the late 1990s as large stock consistently outperformed smaller ones. The index is calculated by Frank Russell Co. of Seattle (*www.russell.com*). Russell first ranks all U.S. stocks from largest to smallest based on market capitalization each May 31. Russell excludes stocks trading below $1.00, generally limits only one class of a company's stock, and does not include CLOSED-END MUTUAL FUNDS,

LIMITED PARTNERSHIPS, royalty trusts, non-U.S. domiciled stocks, foreign stocks, and the like. Russell indexes can be used to detect the quality of the second tier market. Many studies have shown that over time small company stocks have performed better than large company shares. The Russell 2000 represents approximately 10% of the total market capitalization of all U.S. shares. As of May 31, 1998, the median market capitalization was approximately $500 million and the largest company in the index had an approximate market capitalization of $1.4 billion. An investor looking to catch the next upswing in small company stock might watch the relative performance of the Russell 2000 versus the Russell 1000, relative to the Dow Jones Industrial Average and the S&P 500. If the Russell 2000 is consistently underperforming, that could be a buy signal. The 3000 largest stocks become the RUSSELL 3000 INDEX, which tracks the broad U.S. market. The largest 1000 of those 3000 become the *Russell 1000 Index*, which tracks large U.S. stocks. The remaining 2000 is the roster of the Russell 2000.

Russell 3000 Index   index seen as a vane for the broad U.S. market. It also offers some interesting subindexes that track various industries:

- Russell 3000 Autos and Transportation Index—what are traditionally known as transportation companies plus auto companies.
- Russell 3000 Consumer Discretionary and Services Index—makers of products and providers of services directly to the customer.
- Russell 3000 Consumer Staples Index—companies that provide products directly to the consumer that are typically considered nondiscretionary items based on consumer purchasing habits.
- Russell 3000 Financial Services Index—financial-service firms.
- Russell 3000 Health Care Index—firms in medical services or health care.
- Russell 3000 Integrated Oils Index—oil companies in exploration, production, and refining processes.
- Russell 3000 Materials and Processing Index—companies that extract or process raw materials.
- Russell 3000 Other Energy Index—energy-related businesses other than integrated oils.
- Russell 3000 Producer Durables Index—companies that convert unfinished goods into finished durables used to manufacture other goods or provide services.
- Russell 3000 Technology Index—electronics and computer industries or makers of products based on the latest applied science.
- Russell 3000 Utilities Index—utilities companies in industries heavily regulated.

The following table compares key market indexes.

RUSSELL 3000 INDEX

RUSSELL INDEXES VERSUS OTHER KEY INDEXES

Index	Dow Jones Industrial Average	Standard & Poor's 500	NASDAQ Composite	Russell 3000	Russell 2000	Russell 1000
Tracks? Companies in index?	Large Cap 30	Broad market 500	NASDAQ 5500	Broad market 3000	Small Cap 2000	Large Cap 1000
How constructed/weighted?	By price	By market capitalization	By market capitalization	By market capitalization	By market capitalization	By market capitalization
Criteria for a stock's inclusion?	Selection committee; to be representative of U.S. industry	Selection committee; to include biggest U.S. stocks	All domestic shares traded on NASDAQ's National market and Small Cap exchange	Top 3000 NYSE, NASDAQ, and AMEX domestic stocks, ranked by market capitalization	Smallest 2000 stocks, by market cap, in Russell 3000	Largest 1000 stocks, by market cap, in Russell 3000
Median market cap of index stocks?	$4.9 billion	$5 billion	Not available	$790 million	$500 million	$3.7 billion
Percent of index on NYSE, by market cap?	100%	89.5%	0	83.9%	50.6%	87.2%
Percent of index on NASDAQ, by market cap?	0	10.2%	100%	15.5%	46.4%	12.4%
Percent of index on AMEX, by market cap?	0	0.3%	0	0.7%	3%	0.4%
Maximum time between changes in index members?	None	None	None	1 year	1 year	1 year

S

s symbol used in *The Wall Street Journal* and similar publications indicating that an option does not exist. The options exchange has not opened trading on that option.

SAI *see* STATEMENT OF ADDITIONAL INFORMATION.

sales (revenue) per share total sales revenue divided by the number of shares outstanding.

sales surprises levels of revenue that are either higher or lower than Wall Street's consensus forecasts. These surprises are now far more likely to trigger a share price reaction than EARNINGS SURPRISES. There are two reasons for this trend:
1. Analysts pay more attention to earnings (the BOTTOM LINE), and are more accurate in their predictions.
2. Companies have become extremely adept at "managing" earnings, so that expectations and actual results tally. By contrast, there is less leeway, or less effort made, to massage sales results. Fundamentally, companies have been finding things below the sale line (the top line) that they can use to manage earnings.

Salomon Smith Barney Broad Investment Grade Bond Index (BIG) considered by many to be the key BENCHMARK to gauge a money manager's performance in the bond market. It is a comprehensive index of bond prices for securities that have a minimum value of $25 million. BIG reflects the total return rate earned on corporate, mortgage, and Treasury securities with a maturity of one year or more. The index includes about 3750 mortgages and bonds predominantly comprised of corporate issues. The index is updated monthly for changes in its component issues and revised bond ratings.

Salomon Smith Barney World Government Bond Index index that tracks debt issues traded in 14 world government bond markets. Issues included in the Index have fixed-rate coupons and maturities of at least one year.

same store sales term used when analyzing the retail sector; compares sales in stores that have been open for a year or more. It allows you to compare what proportion of new sales has come from sales growth rather than resulting from the opening of new stores.

samurai bond yen-denominated bonds issued in Japan by a foreign borrower. This contrasts with SHOGUN BONDS. *See also* FOREIGN BONDS.

saucer technical chart pattern showing that the price of a stock or bond has bottomed out and is now rising. On the other hand, an inverse saucer shows that the price of the security has topped out and is declining. See the graph below.

SAUCER

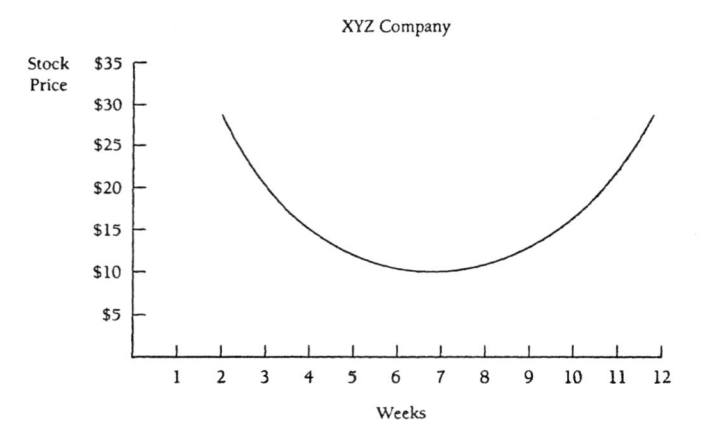

XYZ Company

[Graph showing stock price on y-axis ($5 to $35) and Weeks on x-axis (1 to 12), with a U-shaped curve bottoming around week 6-7 at $10 and rising to approximately $28 at both ends.]

SBF 250 (Société des Bourses Françaises (SBF) 250) market value-weighted barometer of the company issues of the 250 largest companies in the French market.

scale order order to buy or sell a security in given amounts at various prices.

scalper trader who buys and sells quickly to take advantage of small price fluctuations. Usually, a scalper is ready to buy at the bid and sell at the asked price, providing liquidity to the market. The term *scalper* is used because these traders attempt to scalp a small amount on a trade.

seasoned issue high-quality stocks of well-known and mature companies that enjoy strong following among investors. Such securities are actively traded and marketable in the SECONDARY MARKET.

SEC *see* SECURITIES AND EXCHANGE COMMISSION.

SEC Edgar the Securities and Exchange Commission uses electronic data gathering, analysis, and retrieval to transmit company documents to investors. Those documents, which are available via Smart Edgar service, include 10-Qs (quarterly reports), 8-Ks (significant developments such as the sale of a company unit), and 13-Ds (disclosures by parties who own 5% or more of a company's shares).

second section index market value-weighted barometer that reflects the performance of the smaller, less-established, and newly listed companies of the TOKYO STOCK EXCHANGE.

secondary distribution redistribution of a block of previously issued securities; also called *secondary offering*. The sale is generally handled through an underwriting company or SYNDICATE, and the shares are usually offered at a fixed price that is related to the current market price of the securities. The securities may be listed or unlisted. There are certain block dispositions requiring SEC sanction.

secondary market market in which previously issued securities are traded between investors. *See also* PRIMARY MARKET.

sector different segment of the economy. The sector can be an industry or a group of industries.

sector (mutual) fund mutual fund that operates several specialized industry sector portfolios under one umbrella. Transfers between the various portfolios can usually be executed by telephone at little or no cost. It invests in one or two fields or industries (sectors). These funds are risky in that they rise and fall depending on how the individual fields or industries do. An example is Prudential Bache Utility Fund.

securities analyst *see* ANALYST.

Securities and Exchange Commission (SEC) federal agency that regulates the U.S. financial markets. Established by Congress to help protect investors, the SEC administers the Securities Act of 1933, the Securities Exchange Act of 1934, the Trust Indenture Act, the Investment Company Act, the Investment Advisers Act, and the Public Utility Holding Company Act, and the amendments to some of these contained in the Securities Acts Amendments of 1964.

securities market indices indices that measure the value of a number of securities chosen as a sample to reflect the behavior of the general market of investments. *See also* MARKET INDICES AND AVERAGES.

securities markets markets in which financial assets such as stocks, bonds, and other financial instruments are traded. *See also* FINANCIAL INSTITUTIONS; FINANCIAL MARKETS.

securitization
1. development of financial markets for various new negotiable instruments so that borrowers and lenders are matched up.
2. process of converting nonmarketable financial assets such as loans or mortgages into negotiable securities issued in capital markets.
3. spreading risk by combining debt securities in a pool, and then selling new securities backed by the pool.

security paper proving ownership of stocks, bonds, and other investments. This table compares major types of securities.

COMPARISON OF SECURITIES

	Debt	Preferred Stock	Common Stock
Voting rights	No	No	Yes
Risk	Low	Medium	High
Appreciation in value of company	No	Yes	Yes
Fixed annual return	Yes	Yes	No
Partial tax exclusion for interest or dividends	No	Yes	Yes

security analysis various kinds, such as of the economy of the securities markets, of the industry of concern, and of the firm on which the security is issued, which help in the evaluation of the quality and general desirability of a security investment. *See also* FINANCIAL ANALYSIS; FUNDAMENTAL ANALYSIS; TECHNICAL ANALYSIS.

SEDOL code identification number assigned to all foreign stocks by the International Stock Exchange of London. SEDOL stands for Stock Exchange Daily Official List. Foreign stocks that do not have a CUSIP NUMBER and that do not trade actively in the United States can be identified by their SEDOL code.

sell-off very significant selling of securities after a sharp drop in market price. Investors sell their positions quickly before incurring additional losses.

sell on the news practice of selling a security when the actual earnings news came about after buying on the anticipated earnings expectations.

sell price price received when a security is sold.

selling climax condition in the securities markets in which a sudden selling surge develops, accompanied by high volume, resulting in investor panic. Prices drop precipitously, indicating the bottom of a market's selling pressure. This event implies that a rally is soon to develop. See the following graph.

SELLING CLIMAX

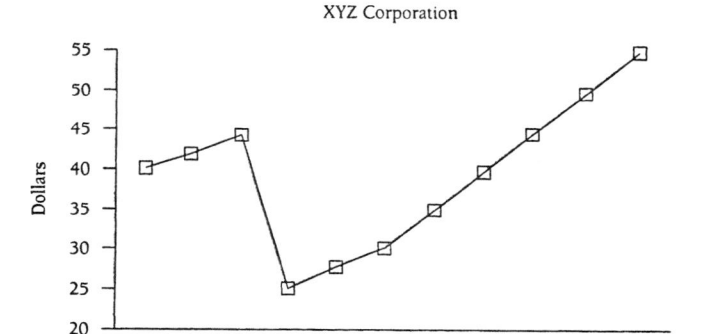

XYZ Corporation

selling short   *see* SHORT SALE.

sensitivity   percentage change in the price of a particular stock relative to the percentage change in the overall stock market. This is often measured by the BETA COEFFICIENT.

sentiment indicators   measure to appraise optimistic or pessimistic views of the market by investors. Many TECHNICAL ANALYSTS make recommendations that are opposite of what the sentiment indicators point to. This is one contrary opinion approach. For example, when most investors are BEARISH, the market might go up.

Series I savings bond   *see* U.S. SERIES I SAVINGS BOND.

settlement date
  1. time at which a security transaction must be paid by the buyer and the securities delivered by the seller. Stocks and bonds have a settlement date of three business days subsequent to the trade date. Listed options and government securities must be settled by the next business day.
  2. date a deed to real estate is transferred.

settlement price   official closing price of a futures contract set by the CLEARINGHOUSE at the end of the day and used for marking to market the margin.

settlement risk   form of CREDIT RISK; also called HERSATT RISK. It is the risk that a bank's counterpart is unable to deliver money in a foreign exchange deal.

SHADOW STOCKS

shadow stocks small stocks with low institutional interest that have had positive annual earnings for the two prior years. They are out of the spotlight and in the shadows of Wall Street.

shakeout
1. sudden, drastic decline in securities prices forcing speculative investors to sell their securities at significant loss.
2. change in the market environment forcing low-quality companies in the industry to go out of business. This situation can take place when oversupply exists for the major product of the industry or the product line is now technologically obsolete (as in typewriters, sewing machines).

Shanghai "B" Shares Index index that tracks Chinese shares that can be purchased by foreigners and that are traded on the Shanghai Exchange. "A" shares can be purchased only by Chinese citizens.

shareholder value indicator created by Valuation Technologies, a California-based research company, it measures the proportion of any change in market capitalization that is attributable to management. This indicator purports to filter out short-term fluctuations, while still providing a measure that investors can use to compare companies and sectors. It can be used as a tool in evaluation management and assessing executive pay and compensation. This metric was first introduced in *Shareholder Magazine* (*www.kennedyinfo.com*).

shares equity ownership or stake of an entity.

shares outstanding all the shares a corporation has issued less Treasury shares bought back. Some may be owned by insiders, while the rest are held by the public, including institutional and individual investors. *See also* FLOAT.

shares per ADR number of ordinary shares that each ADR or ADS represents for foreign companies trading AMERICAN DEPOSITARY RECEIPTS (ADRS) or American Depositary Shares (ADSs).

Sharpe ratio *see* SHARPE'S RISK-ADJUSTED RETURN.

Sharpe's risk-adjusted return risk-adjusted grades that compare five-year, risk-adjusted return, developed by Nobel Laureate William Sharpe. The fund manager is thus able to view his excess returns per unit of risk. This measure combines STANDARD DEVIATION and mean total return to show a risk-adjusted measure of the fund's performance. The higher this number is, the better. *Note:* As a rule of thumb, a Sharpe ratio of more than 1.00 is pretty good.

$$\text{Sharpe measure} = \frac{\text{Excess returns}}{\text{Fund standard deviation}}$$
$$= \frac{\text{Total fund return} - \text{Risk-free rate}}{\text{Fund standard deviation}}$$

EXAMPLE:

If a fund has a return of 10%, the risk-free rate is 6%, and the fund and standard deviation is 18%, the Sharpe measure is .22, as shown below.

$$\text{Sharpe measure} = \frac{10\% - 6\%}{18\%} = \frac{4\%}{18\%} = .22$$

Mutual fund analysis by Morningstar Inc. (*www.morningstar.net*) and others use it.

The following presents Sharpe ratios for some selected international funds:

BETAS FOR SOME SELECTED INTERNATIONAL MUTUAL FUNDS

Company	Ticker Symbol	Sharpe Ratio
GAM: International	GMMNX	−0.90
Harbor International	HAINX	−0.01
Strong International	STISX	−0.23
Fidelity Overseas	FOSFX	−0.07
Templeton International A	TEGEX	−0.05
Vanguard International Growth	VWIGX	−0.03

Source: MSN Money Central Investor (*http://moneycentral.msn.com/investor/contents.asp*), April 3, 2001.

shogun bonds
1. foreign currency-denominated bonds issued within Japan by Japanese companies.
2. bonds issued and distributed solely in Japan by a non-Japanese firm and denominated in a currency other than yen.

short term used to indicate that an investor does not own the stock. *See also* LONG.

short covering act of buying back borrowed securities sold SHORT in the market. This process is completed by a *short seller* either to lock in a profit, prevent a loss in a rising market, or to close out a HEDGE position.

short fund traditional type of HEDGED FUND taking short and long bets in COMMON STOCKS.

short hedge transaction that reduces or eliminates the risk of a drop in the price of a security or commodity without involving ownership; also called *cash hedge*. It generally involves selling futures contracts to cover a cash position. *See also* LONG HEDGE.

short interest total open interest in shares sold SHORT in a particular security market. The total number of shares sold short on the New York Stock Exchange is published monthly. The number of shares sold short gives an indication of investor sentiment. A large

SHORT-INTEREST RATIO is BULLISH in that these investors would have to cover their positions if the market began to rise. Conversely, a small short-interest ratio is BEARISH, as it indicates that investors are fully invested. *See also* SHORT-INTEREST THEORY; SHORT POSITION.

short-interest ratio (SIR) measure of the number of stocks sold SHORT in the market at any given time that have not yet been repurchased to close out short positions. The ratio is the latest reported short interest position for the month divided by the daily average trading volume. The SIR is more closely watched than the trading volume of shares sold short. A high ratio is BULLISH and a low ratio is BEARISH. In the past, the ratio for all stocks on the NYSE has hovered between 1.0 and 1.75. A ratio above 1.8 is considered bullish, while a ratio below 1.15 is deemed bearish. For example, a ratio of 2 represents 2.0 days of potential buying power. The SIR works best as a bullish indicator after a long-term decline in prices instead of after a long upturn.

short-interest theory theory predicting upward price movements of securities based on the SHORT-INTEREST RATIO. A rule-of-thumb measure states that the short-interest ratio is BULLISH if it exceeds $1\frac{1}{2}$ to 2 times the average daily volume of a security. However, with the advent of the covered call writing strategy, investors tend to borrow stock after being exercised by a stock purchaser, significantly distorting the effectiveness of classic short-interest theory. *See also* SHORT INTEREST; SHORT POSITION.

short position stock sold SHORT and not covered as of a particular date. On the New York Stock Exchange, a tabulation is issued a few days after the middle of the month listing all issues on the Exchange in which there was a short position of 5000 or more shares, and issues in which the short position had changed by 2000 or more shares in the preceding month. This tabulation is based on reports of positions on member firms' books. Short position also means the total amount of stock an individual has sold short and has not covered, as of a particular date. Initial margin requirements for a short position are the same as for a long position. *Note:* To find the number of shares sold short in any major stock, go to NASDAQ on the Web (*www.nasdaq.com*). Under the *Quotes* banner in the upper left corner, click *Fundamentals*, then click *Short Interest*. *See also* SHORT SALE.

short sale trading technique in which one sells security investors do not own (by borrowing from a broker) and later buying a like amount of the same security. This technique is used to make a profit from a fall in stock price. The rationale behind short selling goes as follows: It is well known that the simplest way to make money in the stock market is to buy a stock at a low price and sell it later at a higher one. In a short selling situation, investors are reversing the sequence; they are selling high, expecting to buy back the stock later at what they hope will be a lower price. If the stock price falls, they make money. If it rises and they have to buy back their stocks for more than they sold it, they lose money. The following example illustrates several scenarios that result in a profit or loss.

EXAMPLE:
You have a hunch that sales at XYZ Technology Inc. are going to weaken and that its stock is likely to plunge when the market finds out, so you decide to sell "short" 200 shares of XYZ. Here's how the transaction would work, and the possible outcomes:

The Sale: In your on-line trading account, you submit a regular "sell" order for 200 XYZ shares. Because you do not own XYZ stock, the brokerage recognizes it as a short sale. The firm sells the shares at XYZ's current price of $60, crediting the $12,000 in proceeds to your account. Behind the scenes, the brokerage has borrowed the shares from other customers or from other brokerages. Investors and firms that are long-term holders of stock frequently agree to allow their shares to be borrowed for short-sale purposes, because they are confident the shares will be there if they need them. Now you are $12,000 richer, but the proceeds from the short sale don't earn interest, unlike other funds you may have on deposit at the brokerage.

Scenario 1: You have guessed correctly, and XYZ's shares fall a week later to $50. You have $2000 in paper profit on the transaction. You decide to close out your bet and take the profit.

To close out the short sale, you would submit a buy order for 200 shares at $50, or a total of $10,000. Your brokerage would return the borrowed shares to the account that lent them, and you would keep the $2000 difference between the two transactions as profit (less brokerage commissions).

Scenario 2: XYZ has fallen to $50, but you decide it could decline much more sharply. You decide to wait. There is generally no time limit for returning borrowed shares in a short sale.

Scenario 3: Within a week, XYZ sinks to $30. You figure you've had enough: You close out the trade by buying 200 shares at $30, or a total of $6000. Now you have made a handsome profit of $6000 on the trade.

Scenario 4: Your bet has been dead wrong: Instead of falling, XYZ's shares have surged since you sold the stock short at $60. The price now is $70. You decide you can't take the risk that the stock will continue to rise. You close out your short sale by buying 200 XYZ shares at $70, or a total of $14,000. You have lost $2000 on the trade, before the deduction of brokerage commissions.

Scenario 5: Though XYZ rises to $70, you believe it will sink again. You decide to hold on, even though you have a paper loss. But within a week, XYZ stock has soared to $100. You can't take the pain anymore: You close out the trade by buying 200 shares at $100, or a total of $20,000. Now you have lost $8000 on the trade.

An investor who wants to sell short has to set up a MARGIN account with a stockbroker and comply with rules established by the federal government, the SEC, and the brokerage house. The reason for this requirement is that the government and the brokerage house want to ensure that the investor will be able to buy back the stock if the price suddenly rises; thus, the Federal Reserve requires that you have in your account cash or securities worth at least 50% of the market value of the stock you want to sell short. Another requirement is that a stock can be sold short only when the stock price has risen (UPTICK); thus you cannot sell short a listed stock that drops steadily from $50 to $30, for example. Stocks traded OVER-THE-COUNTER, on the other hand, may be sold short any time. The short seller normally pays no interest charge. You must, however, keep the proceeds from the sale in your brokerage account. The brokerage firm invests that money in short-term securities and keeps the interest. The firm also gets its normal commission.

Note: Since selling short can be extremely risky, you are advised to use some strategies. Here are two of the most common short-selling strategies.

1. Go short because you think the stock price is going to decline.
2. Go short to protect yourself if you own the stock but for some reason cannot sell. If, for example, you buy stock through a payroll purchase plan at the end of each quarter but do not get the certificates until several weeks later, it may make sense to sell your shares short to lock in the gain.

short selling *see* SHORT SALE.

short-term national financial markets markets, in different countries, for short-term instruments such as bank deposits and government bills in different nations; also called *national money markets*. Typically, local bank deposits and short-term investments in government securities give the firm an interest-earning opportunity for its locally available funds. This contrasts with LONG-TERM NATIONAL FINANCIAL MARKETS.

SIC (Standard Industrial Classification) Code four-digit code that indicates the company's line of business.

SIMEX Singapore International Monetary Exchange.

single-country funds mutual funds invested in securities of a single country. Single-country funds are the most focused and therefore by far the most aggressive foreign stock funds. Almost all single-country funds are CLOSED-END FUNDS (exceptions are the Japan Fund and French Fund). Because of their aggressive investment style, single-country closed-end funds have been recognized to sell at both large discounts and premiums to their NET ASSET VALUE.

sinking fund fund set aside for periodic payments, aimed at amortizing a financial obligation such as a bond. The funds can be invested in income-producing securities. The objective is to accumulate principal and investment income sufficient to retire the obligation at its maturity. *See* BALLOON BOND.

size effect observed tendency for smaller firms to have higher stock returns than larger firms, on a risk-adjusted basis. This size effect appears to have persisted for over 40 years.

slack market security or commodity market in which demand is slow.

sleeper
   1. investment, such as a stock, that suddenly is a favorite and substantially increases in price.
   2. security having strong future growth possibilities but at the present time shows little fluctuation in price.

small-company growth fund mutual fund investing in small companies having growth potential; however, this is a SPECULATIVE INVESTMENT approach.

smart money grade type or class of investment attractive to informed investors such as INSTITUTIONAL INVESTORS.

Society for Worldwide Interbank Financial Telecommunications (SWIFT) Belgian cooperative furnishing communication services to the international banking community such as payment mechanisms.

soft landing term used to describe, in Fed language, the economy slowing enough to eliminate the need for the Fed to further raise interest rates to lessen activity, but not enough to threaten a RECESSION, which is what results when the economy contracts instead of expands. HARD LANDING, on the other hand, could mean a recession.

soft market situation in which supply exceeds demand for securities and property. It may be characterized by one or more of the following: low trading volume, significant decline in price, and increasing spreads between bid-ask prices.

solvency ability of long-term assets to pay long-term debt. Excessive debt may make it difficult for the company to borrow funds at reasonable interest rates during tight money markets. Solvency also relates to corporate earning power.

sovereign risk risk that a government may default on its debt. *See also* POLITICAL RISK.

special distinct, unique, unusual, exceptional perceived investment opportunity. An example is an investor receiving from his or her brokerage firm a "hot" INITIAL PUBLIC OFFERING (IPO).

special drawing right (SDR) artificial official reserve asset held on the books of the International Monetary Fund (IMF).

specialist matchmaker of the stock exchange who undertakes to keep an orderly market in a specified stock by buying or selling on his or her own account when bids and offers by the public are not matched well enough to maintain an orderly market. If a broker cannot fill an order immediately, the order will be left with the specialist at the post. The specialist keeps lists of these unfilled orders and, as the market price moves up and down, looks for opportunities to fill each order. In this way, the specialist acts as the broker to the brokers, charging them commissions for every order successfully executed.

specialists/public (S/P) short ratio ratio used with the assumption that the speculative public makes an error at market turns and speculators who SHORT are among the least astute. What short selling is not done on the exchange by members is by definition done by the public, which may include a few institutions but they are not really active in short selling. This is one of many so-called smart money rules under which specialists might provide unusual insight into the future. It is derived by dividing the specialists shorts by the public shorts. It is found in the Market Laboratory section of *Barron's*. It is recommended to smooth the ratio over a four-week average. A ratio of around 3.5 (especially greater than 4.0) is interpreted as a BEARISH signal since it is a reflection of too much optimism. An S/P ratio below about 1.8 (especially near 1.0) indicates considerable pessimism and tends to be BULLISH.

specialized (mutual) fund mutual fund specializing in the securities of a particular industry or group of industries, special types of securities, or regional investments; also called SPECIALTY FUND.

specialty fund *see* SPECIALIZED (MUTUAL) FUND.

speculation employment of funds by a speculator. The safety of principal is a secondary factor.

speculative investment investment involving considerable risk of loss but has the chance of large gain.

speculative risk risk that exists when there is a marked chance of either a loss or a gain. Examples include starting a business, making an investment, or gambling at a casino.

speculative stock stock purchased by an investor who is willing to bear a greater amount of investment risk in the hope of receiving large capital appreciation. It is a stock considered to be risky and characterized by wide price fluctuations. PENNY STOCKS are considered speculative. It is a stock lacking a track record of high profitability and dividends. Regardless of uncertain earnings, speculative stocks have the potential for a very high return but there is a lot of risk. You can lose significant amounts or even your entire investment. Examples are oil and gas stocks and new biotechnology companies.

speed limits rate at which the economy can grow without triggering inflation.

spin-off situation in which a company can create an independent company from an existing part of the company by selling or distributing new shares.

split amendment of a firm's charter to increase (split up) or decrease (split down) the number of authorized shares. It requires stockholder approval. If a company with one million shares did a two-for-one split, the company would have two million shares. An investor, for example, with 100 shares before the split would hold 200 shares after the split. The investor's percentage of equity in the company remains the same. *Note*: For stock split announcements, go to *www.stocksplits.net/*

split-adjusted term used to describe that a stock price has been changed to reflect stock SPLITS that have transpired over time.

EXAMPLE:
Coca-Cola (stock symbol, K) went public in 1919 and has split its stock 10 times since then. Its year 2000 stock price is in the $60-per-share range. That does not mean that its shares have appreciated only roughly 50% since then. In late 1970 Coke's stock price was about $1.67, split-adjusted. The actual price then was about $80 per share, but in order to compare it with today's price, you need to adjust the price for splits that took place between then and now.

You will see that Coke's shares have not dropped from $80 to $60 in approximately 30 years, but instead have advanced considerably, from the equivalent of $1.67 to $60. For this reason, when you look up historical stock prices, you will see the term *split-adjusted*.

split commission
1. commission shared among the broker making a trade on behalf of an investor and the individual (for example, financial planner, investment adviser) who gave the business to that broker.
2. commission shared among brokers, as in the real estate industry.

split order large transaction in stocks, bonds, or commodities that is segregated into parts for execution over a specified time period so as not to cause a drastic price change in the market. Its purpose is to avoid a chaotic situation and make it orderly. For example, if a very large mutual fund decides to sell all of its position in a thinly traded security, it may decide to break the order down.

sponsored ADR *see* AMERICAN DEPOSITARY RECEIPT (ADR).

spot method of buying or selling foreign currency in which the VALUE DATE follows within two working days of the trade date. Products commonly "sold at spot" include foreign currency drafts and wires.

spot commodity commodity traded in cash and for immediate delivery; also called *cash commodity*. See also COMMODITIES FUTURES.

spot exchange rate exchange rate of one currency for another for immediate delivery; also called *current exchange* or *cash exchange rate*. Spot rate can be defined as the rate that exists in today's market. A typical listing of foreign exchange rates is found in the business section of daily newspapers, and *The Wall Street Journal*. For example, the British pound is quoted at 1.5685 per dollar. This rate is the spot rate. It means you can go to the bank today and exchange $1.5685 for £1.00. In reality, for example, if you need £10,000 for paying off an import transaction on a given day, you would ask your bank to purchase £10,000. The bank would not hand you the money, but instead it would instruct its English subsidiary to pay £10,000 to your English supplier and it would debit your account by (10,000 × 1.5685) $15,685. See also FORWARD EXCHANGE RATE.

spot market cash market for immediate delivery, as opposed to a futures market that provides the delivery at a future date.

spot (or cash) rate effective exchange rate for a foreign currency for delivery "on the spot."

spot price current market price of a security; also called *cash price*.

spot transaction transaction involving the purchase and sale of commodities, currency, and financial instruments for immediate delivery; also called *cash transaction*. This is settled (paid for) on the second following business day. A spot transaction contrasts with a *forward transaction*, which provides the delivery at a future date.

spread
  1. difference between the BID and ASKED PRICES of a security. *Note*: When PINK SHEET ADRs are traded, the spread can climb into the double digits. That means if you sell shares on the bid, having bought them on the asked, you could lose 12 or 15% immediately.
  2. difference between the purchase price paid by an investment banking firm and expected resale price of a new issue of securities.
  3. difference in YIELD between various grades of securities at comparable maturity dates.
  4. refers to a markup paid by a given borrower over the market interest rate paid by a top-quality borrower.

spread order type of order for the simultaneous purchase and sale of two options of the same type (calls or puts) on the same underlying stock. If placed with a LIMIT, the two options must be traded for a specified price difference or better.

stag speculator who gets in and out of stocks for a quick profit rather than holding for the long term.

stagflation incidence of rising prices during a slowdown in business activity. *See also* INFLATION; RECESSION.

Standard & Poor's Depositary Receipt (SPDR) shares of a security designed to track the value of the S&P 500; also called *Spiders*. Spiders trade on the American Stock Exchange under the symbol SPY. One SPDR unit is valued at approximately one-tenth of the value of the S&P 500. Dividends are distributed quarterly, and are based on the accumulated stock dividends held in trust, less any expenses of the trust.

Standard & Poor's 500 Stock Composite (S&P 500) 500 Stock Composite Index calculated by Standard & Poor's. It differs from the Dow Jones Industrial Average (DJIA) in that it is a value-weighted (rather than price-weighted) index. This means that the index considers not only the price of a stock but also the number of shares outstanding. That is to say, it is based on the aggregate market value of the stock, for example, price times number of shares. An advantage of the index over the DJIA is that STOCK SPLITS and STOCK DIVIDENDS do not affect the index value. A disadvantage is that large capitalization stocks—those with a large number of shares outstanding—heavily influence the index value. The S&P 500 actually consists of four separate indexes: the 400 industrials, the 40 utilities, the 20 transportation, and the 40 financial. *See also* MARKET INDICES AND AVERAGES.

Standard & Poor's Guide to International Ratings current assessment of the creditworthiness of a foreign borrower with respect to a specific obligation. Debt obligations of issuers *outside* the United States and its territories are rated on the same basis as domestic corporate and municipal issues. The ratings measure the creditworthiness of the obligor to repay in the currency of denomination of the issue. *Note*: The S&P does not assess the foreign exchange risk that the investor may bear. The S&P ratings are based, in varying degrees, on the following considerations: (1) likelihood of DEFAULT; (2) nature and provisions of the obligation; (3) protection afforded by, and relative position of, the obligation in the event of bankruptcy, reorganization, or other arrangements under the laws of bankruptcy and other laws affecting creditors' rights. *See also* BOND RATINGS.

standard deviation common measure of risk, often calculated using a time series of returns observed over the past, equal to the square root of the variance. The higher this number is, the more volatile the fund's returns have been. It indicates how much the fund has deviated from its mean total return over a specified time period.

EXAMPLE:
ABC Fund has returned on the average 10% over the last six quarters and the variability about its average return was 10.41%. The

high standard deviation (10.41%) relative to the average return of 10% indicates that the fund is very risky.

Morningstar Inc. (800) 876-5005 offers standard deviation values of major funds as does its web site at *www.morningstar.net*. The following presents standard deviation figures for some selected international funds:

STANDARD DEVIATION VALUES FOR SOME SELECTED INTERNATIONAL MUTUAL FUNDS

Company	Ticker Symbol	Standard Deviation
GAM: International	GMMNX	19.36
Harbor International	HAINX	17.44
Strong International	STISX	30.07
Fidelity Overseas	FOSFX	20.39
Templeton International A	TEGEX	16.02
Vanguard International Growth	VWIGX	17.26

Source: MSN Money Central Investor (*http://moneycentral.msn.com/investor/contents.asp*), April 3, 2001.

See also ALPHA; BETA FOR A MUTUAL FUND; R-SQUARED.

standardized (or SEC) yield   method of calculating a fund's yield that assumes that all portfolio securities are held until maturity. The Securities and Exchange Commission (SEC) requires all fixed-income funds to calculate this yield.

start-up   new business venture in its earliest stage of development. *See also* ANGEL.

state municipal bond funds—long-term   mutual funds that work just like NATIONAL MUNICIPAL BOND FUNDS except that their portfolios primarily contain the issues of one state. For residents of that state, the income from these securities is typically free from both federal and state taxes. For some taxpayers, a portion of income may be subject to the federal alternative minimum tax.

statement of additional information (SAI)   statement containing more detailed information about a mutual fund, which is not provided in the prospectus. This includes the compensation for officers of the fund, the fund's audited financial statement, and other pertinent information.

stochastics index   overbought/oversold MOMENTUM oscillator that is based on the principle that as prices advance, the closing price moves to the upper end of its range. In a downtrend, closing prices usually appear near the bottom of their recent range. Time periods of 9 and 14 days are usually employed in its construction.

stock commission   amount charged by the brokerage firm for buying or selling stock. Stock commissions are determined by the number of shares being transacted and the price of the stock. Brokerage houses offer competitive rates and the investor can do comparison shopping for the best rate.

stock company company fully owned by shareholders as evidenced by stock certificates. The stockholders have limited liability for the company's debts and share in profits and losses.

stock dividend pro rata distribution of additional shares of a corporation's own stock to its stockholders (or a SUBSIDIARY's shares being spun off) instead of cash. A stock dividend may be declared when the cash position of the firm is inadequate and/or when the company wishes to prompt more trading by reducing the market price of stock. A small stock dividend (less than 20%–25% of the shares outstanding at the date of declaration) decreases retained earnings and increases the capital accounts (capital stock and paid-in capital) for an amount equal to the fair value of the shares issued. A large stock dividend (in excess of 20%–25% of shares outstanding) decreases retained earnings and increases capital stock at the par or stated value only. If a company with 500,000 shares outstanding declares a 10% stock dividend, the total shares for the stock dividend will be 50,000. From a tax perspective, the stockholder is not taxed on the stock received until the time it is sold whereas a cash dividend is taxable income in the year received.

stock exchange marketplace in which buyers and sellers are brought together to trade securities, such as the NEW YORK STOCK EXCHANGE (NYSE).

Stock Exchange Automated Quotation Service (SEAQ) computerized system at the London Stock Exchange that continuously updates prices and trade reports for U.K. securities (shares, GILTS, and so on). SEAQ lists the market makers' bid and offer prices, together with the NORMAL MARKET SIZE at which those prices will be honored. Shares traded using SEAQ are said to be traded on the "quote book."

Stock Exchange Automated Trading System (SEATS) Plus trading system that handles the trading of all AIM and listed U.K. equities whose turnover is insufficient for the market making system or the STOCK EXCHANGE ELECTRONIC TRADING SERVICE (SETS).

Stock Exchange Trading Service (SETS) automated trading system introduced in 1997 for the largest companies quoted on the main list of the London Stock Exchange. Trades through SETS match buyers and sellers automatically, cutting out the need for a market maker, which theoretically means a more narrow bid-offer spread. Smaller companies continue to use the SEAQ "quote" book system, with market makers quoting prices to brokers and trades being done on a semiautomatic rather than fully automatic basis.

STOCK EXCHANGE INDICES

stock exchange indices　*see* MARKET INDICES AND AVERAGES.

stock index futures　futures contracts written on broad-based measures of stock market performance such as the S&P Stock Index.

stock index option　put or call option written on a specific market index such as the S&P Stock Index.

stock insurance company　insurance company owned by stockholders that receives the firm's profits in the form of stockholder dividends; however, policyholders' interests come before those of stockholders.

stock limit order　*see* LIMIT ORDER.

stock market　market in which securities are traded. Securities traded include common stock, convertibles, preferred stock, rights, and warrants. The principal stock markets in the United States are the New York Stock Exchange, the American Stock Exchange, and the NASDAQ (Over-the-Counter) Stock Market.

stock option　right to buy or sell a stock at a particular price within a given time period. A stock option enables one to speculate in stocks with a minimal investment. There is great potential for return; however, the entire investment may be lost if the stock does not move sufficiently in the right direction. Stock options can also be used to HEDGE one's position in other securities. *See also* CALL; PUT.

stock option plan　plan giving the holder the right to buy a certain number of shares of stock at a certain price by a specified date. Stock option plans are typically used to compensate corporate officers and other employees for their services. Typically, a stock option may not be exercised until the employee has worked a specified number of years (for instance, three years) after the date the option is granted. The value of the compensation of the stock option is measured by the quoted market price of the stock less the option price to the employee. Assume that an employee has the option to buy 2000 shares at an option price of $10 having a current market price of $15. The value of the compensation of the stock option is $10,000 (2000 shares × $5).

stock order　instruction given to a broker to buy or sell a stock. Most stock orders are verbal instructions. *See also* BUY ORDER.

stock purchase plan　employee benefit designed to facilitate the purchase of a company's stock often at a price lower than the market price or at a reduced commission cost. These plans often include an employer's payment toward the acquisition of the stock. The plans are continual over time and companies often offer to reinvest the dividends in more stock accumulation. An employee stock ownership plan (ESOP) is another form of a stock purchase plan in which the employees eventually have ownership control of the company.

stock ratings evaluations of stocks based on the company's financial health and management quality. Stocks are rated by such services as Fitch's Investor Service, Moody's, and Standard & Poor's. Stocks having higher ratings include many of the BLUE CHIP stocks and the *Fortune 500* companies.

stock right privilege giving a current stockholder the first right to buy shares in a new offering below the market price, thus maintaining the stockholder's proportionate ownership interest; also called PREEMPTIVE RIGHT. Assume an investor owns 1% of Company ABC. If the company issues 10,000 additional shares, the investor may receive a stock rights offering—an opportunity to buy 1%, or 100 shares, of the new issue. The right enables the investor to buy new common stock at a subscription price for a short time, typically no more than several weeks. The subscription price (exercise price) is typically lower than the public offering price of the stock. A single right is the privilege applicable to the holder of one old share of capital stock to purchase a certain number of shares of new capital stock.

stock split issuance of a substantial amount of additional shares, thus reducing the PAR VALUE of the stock on a proportionate basis. (A stock split also means that dividends per share will also fall proportionately.) No journal entry need be made, because the company's accounts do not change; however, there should be a memorandum entry describing the stock split. A stock split is often prompted by a desire to reduce the market price per share in order to stimulate investor buying. Assume XYZ Company has 1000 shares of $20 par value common stock. The total par value is thus $20,000. A two-for-one stock split is issued. There will now be 2000 shares at a $10 par value. The total par value remains at $20,000. Typically, the market price per share of the stock should also drop to one-half of what it was before the split. In the event that a stock split mandates an increase in authorized shares and/or a change in the par value per share, a modification to the corporate charter will be required that must be approved by the shareholders. *See also* REVERSE STOCK SPLIT; SPLIT; SPLIT-ADJUSTED.

stock split order *see* SPLIT ORDER.

stock swap use of shares you own to exercise your options. This could lower your tax bill.

stock symbol abbreviation assigned to a company's stock by the respective stock exchange where it trades; also called *trading symbol*. Stocks trading on the New York Stock Exchange have one to three letters, for example T for AT&T, and IBM for IBM. Stocks trading on the American Stock Exchange have three or four symbols, while stocks trading OVER THE COUNTER have four or five symbols. Mutual fund tickers end with the letter "X." Options tickers have their own help tables.

stock ticker lettered symbol assigned to securities and mutual funds that trade on U.S. financial exchanges.

stock transfer agent agent selected by a company to keep the records of its issued equity and debt securities. The agent lists the names of new owners of the securities, issues new certificates to buyers, cancels old certificates of sellers, and replaces lost certificates. A fee is assessed when replacement certificates are needed because of theft or loss. The agent prepares a list of all stockholders and the shares owned so dividends may be properly paid. The transfer agent makes sure that an overissuance of certificates does not occur. Although a transfer agent is typically an outside party, often a commercial bank, the issuing company may act as its own transfer agent.

stockholder of record stockholder whose name is registered on the books of the issuing corporation.

stop-limit order order triggered when the stock reaches a certain price rather than a market order. Other than that, this works the same as a STOP-LOSS ORDER. *See also* BUY ORDER.

stop-loss order *see* STOP ORDER.

stop order (or stop) investor order to his or her stockbroker to purchase or sell at the market price once the security or option has traded at a given price (STOP PRICE). A stop order to purchase is set at a stop price higher than the present market price. The reasons for this might be to protect a gain or to limit a loss on a short sale. A stop order to sell is set at a price below the present market price. The reasons might be to protect a gain or to limit a loss on a stock previously bought at a higher price. The speculative nature of stop orders is that they may be transacted at prices several points above or below the top price due to market orders preceding the stop order.

Note: It is recommended to set the order at about 20% below your initial cost or the highest price over the last 52 weeks.

EXAMPLE:
You own 2000 shares of ABC Company having a market price of $100 per share. You give a stop-loss order to sell the stock if it decreases to $90. Because you initially bought the stock at $55 a share, your stop-loss order locks in a gain of $35 per share ($90 − $55).

There are different kinds of stop orders including a DAY ORDER, time-limit order, and GOOD-TILL-CANCELLED ORDER.

stop price instruction from an investor to the broker to enter a market order after a security transaction takes place at the stipulated stop price.

STOXX indexes FOREIGN STOCK INDEXES created by Stoxx, Ltd., a joint venture between Dow Jones and some European investment banking firms, such as the Dow Jones Stoxx and the Dow

straddle option strategy that integrates a put and call on the same stock with the identical exercise (STRIKE) price and exercise date. It is employed to take advantage of significant variability in stock price. High BETA stocks might be most suited for this. A straddle may be bought either to maximize return or to minimize risk. This investment approach should be left to sophisticated investors. A straddle is not traded on listed exchanges but rather must be acquired through brokerage houses and members of the Put and Call Brokers and Dealers Association.

EXAMPLE:
An investor buys a call and put for $4 each on September 30 when the stock price is $42. The expiration period is four months. The investment is $8, or $800 in total. Assume the stock increases to $60 at expiration of the options. The difference between the selling price ($60) and cost ($42) is $18. The call earns a profit of $14 ($18 − $4) and the loss on the put is $4. The net gain is $10, or $1000 altogether.

straight bond
1. bond with a fixed interest rate.
2. bond with one maturity date as distinguished from a serial bond that matures in installments.
3. bond that is nonconvertible.

Straits Times Index the best-known of Singapore's stock market indexes. It is a narrow-based index of 30 companies listed on the Stock Exchange of Singapore. *See also* BUSINESS TIMES INDEX.

strap option contract comprised of one put and two calls of the same series. This contract can be purchased at a lower cost than the three options bought separately. The calls and put have similar features of underlying security, exercise price, and time period. *See also* STRIP.

strategic asset allocation investor's skillful planning of how to intelligently allocate funds among different investments based on the investor's predetermined criteria.

strategy
1. investor's planning of goals that can be achieved by a certain date. Examples of goals are desired net worth, retirement age, and career success. The investor plans how those goals are to be accomplished.
2. one of the various kinds of option investments, such as long call, covered write, bull spread, and so on.

street New York financial community concentrated in the Wall Street area. If one hears that the street recommends ABC stock, it means that investment analysts favor that company.

street broker broker dealing with OVER-THE-COUNTER securities rather than those listed on an exchange.

street name when securities are held in the name of a broker instead of the customer's name, they are said to be carried in street name. This occurs when the securities have been bought on margin or when the customer wishes the securities to be held by the broker. Corporate interest and dividend checks go directly to the broker instead of the investor. The transfer of securities upon sale is easier when the stock is registered in the broker's name than in the customer's. The client gives his or her authorization for transactions in that security. Monthly brokerage statements are received outlining activities for the month. The holding of securities in street name hastens the execution and transfer of securities transactions.

strike price price at which a call option or a put option can be exercised, normally at a price set close to the market price of the stock at the time the option is issued; also called STRIKING PRICE or *exercise price*. It is the exercise price for an option.

striking price *see* STRIKE PRICE.

strip
1. individual's purchase of an option contract combining two puts and one call on the same security. The puts and call have similar features, such as STRIKE PRICES and expiration dates. Compares with STRAP.
2. purchase of stock with the major aim of collecting dividends.
3. practice of a brokerage firm of distinguishing between the principal and coupon interest of a bond, which are then issued individually in the form of a zero-coupon security. The use of lowercase, *strip*, distinguishes broker strips from Treasury-issued Strips.

stripped bond bond divided into its principal and interest payments, which are then sold separately as a ZERO-COUPON BOND; also called STRIPS.

stripped treasuries ZERO-COUPON BONDS sold by the U.S. Treasury and created by stripping the coupons from a Treasury bond and selling them separately from the principal; also called STRIPS.

strong market market characterized by a prevalence of buyers over sellers and an increasing price trend. *See also* WEAK MARKET.

subscriber one who agrees to the terms of a SUBSCRIPTION at the SUBSCRIPTION PRICE.

subscription contractual understanding of an investor to purchase newly issued securities.

subscription price price that a current stockholder must pay to buy common shares in connection with a rights or warrant offering.

subscription privilege (right) right of current stockholders to purchase a new issue of stock before it goes public, typically below the PUBLIC OFFERING price. The right usually has a two-to-four-week life, and may be transferred. In most instances, one share of ownership gives the stockholder one right; however, the number of rights necessary to purchase a new share may vary. In exercising the right, the stockholder delivers the necessary number of rights plus the payment for the new shares.

subscription warranty security typically issued along with a bond or preferred stock allowing the holder to purchase a proportionate amount of common stock at a later date at a given price. A warrant is usually a SWEETENER for a fixed-income securities issuance. Warrants may be traded in the market.

subsidiary company owned by another, which controls more than 50% of its voting stock.

substitution
1. exchange of securities; for example, a SECURITIES ANALYST recommends replacing one stock in an industry by another in that same industry.
2. replacement of a different security of the same value for another security serving as collateral in a margin account.

sunrise industries industries at the beginning of their product or service life cycle.

sunset industries mature industries near the end of their product or service life cycle.

Super Bowl theory theory that stock prices will increase for the year if the Super Bowl winner is or was a member of the original National Football League.

support and resistance levels support level is the lower end of a trading range; a resistance level is the upper end. At the support level, there is support not to have a further decline in price, while at the resistance level there is resistance to a further price decline. These levels are considered in technical investment analysis. A chart may be prepared showing the price over time of an individual stock or overall market. The support and resistance prices based on the historical trend are depicted along with the breakout points. Support and resistance lines are actually trend lines drawn through high and low prices. See the following chart for the support level. *See also* RESISTANCE LEVEL.

SUPPORT LEVEL

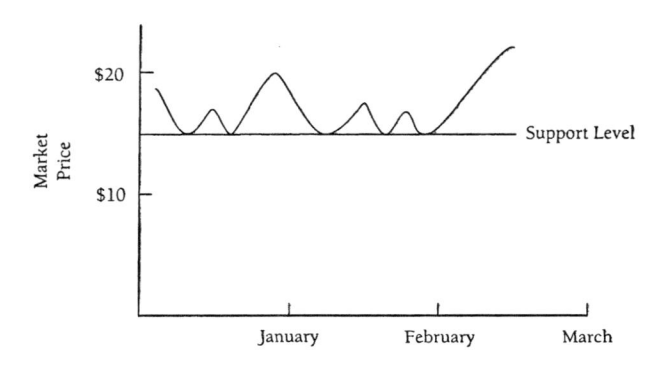

Figure: Market Price chart showing fluctuations above the Support Level line between $10 and $20, across January, February, and March.

sushi bonds EURODOLLARS, or other non-yen-denominated bonds issued by a Japanese firm for sale to Japanese investors.

swap to sell one security and buy another security for the purpose of improving overall yield with little or no market or credit risk. There are two primary types of swaps: (1) *extension swaps*, which try to determine whether extending the maturity of an instrument would improve overall return, based on yield curve analysis; and (2) YIELD SPREAD *swaps* or *quality swaps*, which rely on the differences in yield spreads between the various investments to enhance total yield. Typically, there is no exchange of the instruments themselves. Swaps may be tied to various underlying financial instruments, indices, or commodities. Examples are currency swaps and interest rate swaps. Swaps are not publicly traded on exchanges.

swap rate forward exchange rate quotation expressed in terms of the number of points by which the forward rate differs from the SPOT rate (for example, as a discount from, or a premium on, the spot rate). The interbank market quotes the forward rate this way.

swaptions options on SWAPS giving the holder the right to contract a swap at a particular future date at specified terms or to lengthen or terminate an existing swap.

sway to move toward one investment approach rather than another.

sweep account fund account set up to receive dividend and interest payments or sales proceeds from a discount brokerage or real estate fund.

sweetener attractive feature added to the issuance of a security to prompt readier purchase of it. An example is the CONVERSION feature added to a preferred stock or bond. *See also* WARRANT.

switching
   1. selling one security and buying another.
   2. transferring between different funds within a mutual fund.

switching privilege   *see* EXCHANGE PRIVILEGE.

symbol   *see* STOCK SYMBOL.

syndicates
   securities: group of INVESTMENT BANKERS brought together for the purpose of underwriting and distributing a new issue of securities or a large block of an outstanding issue.
   real estate: limited partnership that invests in various types of real estate and is professionally managed. It is registered with the SEC and includes a great number of limited partners.

systematic investment plan   plan in which the shareholder makes specified deposits each period to a savings or investment account, such as a mutual fund.

systematic risk   risk that cannot be diversified away; also called *nondiversifiable*, or *noncontrollable*, risk. This results from forces outside of a firm's control. Purchasing power, interest rate, and market risks fall in this category. This type of risk is assessed relative to the risk of a diversified portfolio of securities, or the market portfolio. It is measured by the BETA COEFFICIENT used in the CAPITAL ASSET PRICING MODEL (CAPM). The systematic risk is simply a measure of a security's volatility relative to that of an average security. For example, $b = 0.5$ means the security is only half as volatile, or risky, as the average security; $b = 1.0$ means the security is of average risk; and $b = 2.0$ means the security is twice as risky as the average risk. The higher the beta, the higher the return required.

T

T+3 (or trade date plus three) term used to define the date for settlement of trades as being within three business days of the date of the trade itself. Accordingly, shares are issued and money is received three business days after the effective date of a registration statement. T+3 is the goal that the G30 countries have agreed to aim for, and is applied in the United States by the SEC and in Europe by EASDAQ. The period varies from country to country.

takedown
1. investment banker's proportionate share of a new or secondary securities issue that is to be distributed to the public.
2. price that securities are allocated among underwriters.

takeup
1. investor who remits the balance due on a margin account, so as to obtain complete ownership.
2. an underwriter who directly sells stocks or bonds to the public.

taking a position
1. investor's purchase of a security, often with the intention of keeping it for a long time. If you buy 5% or more of a company's stock, you must file information with the Securities and Exchange Commission, respective stock exchange, and the company itself.
2. broker/dealer's retaining securities in inventory. The intent may be to hold them for the long term or short term.

taking delivery accepting receipt of products, securities certificates, or physical commodities following a purchase.

tangible assets tangible items of real and personal property that generally have a long life, such as housing and other real estate, automobiles, jewelry, cash, and other physical assets.

tap procedure by which a borrower can keep issuing additional amounts of an old bond at its current market value. This procedure is used for bond issues, notably by the British and French governments, as well as for some short-term debt instruments.

target *see* CLEARING HOUSE INTERBANK PAYMENTS SYSTEM (CHIPS).

tax equivalent yield yield on a tax-free municipal bond that needs to be looked at on an equivalent before-tax yield basis, because the interest received is not subject to federal income taxes. The formula used to equate interest on municipals to other investments is

$$\text{Tax equivalent yield} = \text{Tax-exempt yield}/(1 - \text{tax rate})$$

EXAMPLE:
If you have a marginal tax rate of 28% and are evaluating a municipal bond paying 10% interest, the equivalent before-tax bond yield on a taxable investment is calculated below.

$$10\%/(1-.28) = 13.9\%$$

Thus, you could choose between a taxable investment paying 13.9% and a tax-exempt bond paying 10% and be indifferent between the two. *See also* BOND YIELD.

tax-exempt bonds municipal bonds where interest income is not subject to federal tax, although the *Tax Reform Act (TRA) of 1986* imposed restrictions on the issuance of tax-exempt municipal bonds. Municipal bonds may carry a lower interest than taxable bonds of similar quality and safety; however, after-tax yield from these bonds is usually more than a bond with a higher rate of taxable interest. Municipal bonds are subject to two principal risks: interest rate and DEFAULT.

tax-exempt money market funds—national mutual funds seeking the highest level of federal tax-free income consistent with preserving investment principal. These funds invest in short-term municipal securities issued by states and municipalities to finance local projects. For some taxpayers, a portion of income may be subject to the federal alternative minimum tax.

tax-exempt money market funds—state mutual funds that work just like TAX-EXEMPT MONEY MARKET FUNDS—NATIONAL except that their portfolios invest primarily in issues from one state. A resident in that state typically receives income exempt from federal and state taxes. For some taxpayers, a portion of income may be subject to the federal alternative minimum tax.

technical analysis forecasting method for asset prices based solely on information about past prices. *See also* TECHNICAL INVESTMENT ANALYSIS.

technical forecasting use of historical exchange rates to predict future values. For example, the fact that a given currency has increased in value over four consecutive days may provide an indication of how the currency will move tomorrow. It is sometimes conducted in a judgmental manner, without statistical analysis.

technical investment analysis as the antithesis of FUNDAMENTAL ANALYSIS, investment analysis that concentrates on past price and volume movements, while totally disregarding economic fundamentals, to forecast a security price or currency rates. The two primary tools of technical analysts are CHARTING and key indicators. Charting means plotting the stock's price movement over time, as on the graph that follows. A security may have moved up and down in price, but remained within a band bounded by the lower limit (support level) and the higher limit (resistance level). Key indicators of market and security performance include trading volume, market breadth, mutual fund cash position, SHORT SELLING, ODD-LOT THEORY, and the INDEX OF BEARISH SENTIMENT. *See also* TECHNICAL FORECASTING.

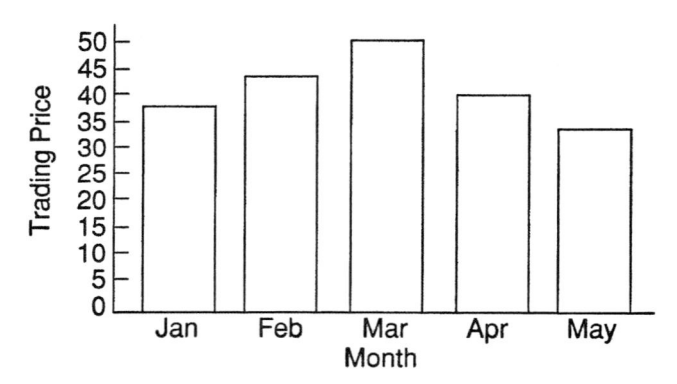

ted spread   yield spread between U.S. Treasury bills and EURODOLLARS.

telegraphic transfers   *see* WIRE TRANSFERS.

10-K   annual filing with the SECURITIES AND EXCHANGE COMMISSION (SEC) for publicly traded companies. Financial statements and supporting details are provided. Form 10-K typically contains more financial information than the ANNUAL REPORT to stockholders. Audited basic financial statements are included. Examples of disclosures are sales, operating income, segmental sales by major line of business for the last five years, and general business information.

10-Q   quarterly filing with the SECURITIES AND EXCHANGE COMMISSION (SEC) by publicly traded companies. It contains interim financial statements and related disclosures and may cover one particular quarter or be cumulative. It should present comparative figures for the same period of the prior year. The statements may or may not be audited. Form 10-Q is less comprehensive than form 10-K.

tenure   year the current manager took over the fund.

term structure of interest rates   *see* YIELD CURVE.

test   price of a stock or commodity, or the overall stock market, when it goes to a prior high or low. In effect, this tests the validity of a previous TREND LINE.

thinly traded   stocks with smaller FLOATS.

thin market   market in which there are comparatively few bids to buy or offers to sell, or both. The term applies to a single stock or to the entire stock market. In a thin market, buying or selling a few shares of stock can affect its price disproportionately in either direction. Price volatility is therefore generally greater than in markets with more liquidity.

third market   market in which all off-exchange transactions in securities listed on the organized exchanges take place. Today a few third-market brokers provide investors with the flexibility to trade when the NYSE is closed. They make a market in a stock by matching buyers and sellers (and collecting commissions).

tick   change in the price of a security. An UPTICK occurs when the last trade in a security takes place at a higher price than the prior trade. A DOWNTICK occurs when the last trade in a security takes place at a lower price than the prior trade. An indicator may be fashioned from the difference between the number of NYSE issues showing upticks on the last trade and the number of NYSE issues showing downticks on the last trade. This indicator is known as the *tick*, and is found on many quote screens. A tick of +236 means 236 more NYSE issues last traded on upticks than those trading on downticks.

ticker   instrument that prints prices and volume of security transactions in cities and towns throughout the United States within minutes after each trade on the floor. Today's ticker is a computer screen.

ticker symbols   letters used in a TICKER that identify a company for trading purposes. *See also* STOCK SYMBOL; STOCK TICKER.

ticker tape   *see* TICKER.

tight market   market in which the spreads between the BID and ASKED PRICE of a security are very small. This is a sign that the security is in abundant supply and being actively traded.

time horizon   minimum suggested length of time expected to keep your money in an investment. In mutual funds, aggressive funds, which are volatile, require a longer time horizon because the risk of losing money over the short term is great.

time order   order to sell at a particular price during a specified time or until withdrawn:

EXAMPLE:
You wish to sell 100 shares of Company XYZ at $50 per share, and you anticipate the price of the stock to increase to $50 in one month. You execute a time order with your broker to sell your shares at $50 within a month period. *See also* BUY ORDER.

time value
1. component of an option's value that is related to the length of time until expiration. It is essentially the amount that the premium of an option exceeds its intrinsic value. It reflects the statistical possibility that the option premium will increase in value rather than finishing at zero dollars. If an option is OUT-OF-THE-MONEY, then its entire premium consists of time value.
2. *see* TIME VALUE OF MONEY.

time value of money concept that states that money is worth different sums at different time periods. In other words, $1 today is worth more than $1 tomorrow. Time value of money is a critical consideration in financial and investment decisions. For example, compound interest (future value) calculations are needed to determine future earnings resulting from an investment in financial assets such as stocks and bonds. Discounting, or the calculation of present value, which is inversely related to compounding, is used to determine today's value of future cash flows associated with investments in stocks and bonds.

timing decisions decisions about when to buy and when to sell. A good time to buy may be when stock prices are depressed after a prolonged DOWNTURN. One theory is to BUY ON BAD NEWS. A good time to sell might be after a buying climax that is substantially run up in stock prices with very high volume. This scenario takes place at the culmination of an upward price trend. One theory is to sell on good news.

tipper individual who informs another person of material information that has not been made public relating to a public company. In the United States, under the Securities Exchange Act of 1934, the tipper is jointly liable with the tippee who trades on the basis of the inside information and is subject to civil penalties of up to the greater of three times the profit gained or loss avoided or $1,000,000, and to criminal penalties of up to 10 years in jail.

tips supposedly "inside" information on corporation affairs.

Tokyo Stock Exchange (TSE) largest stock exchange in Japan, with more than 80% of all transactions. Osaka is the second largest exchange, with about 15% of all transactions. By tradition, the TSE is an auction, order-driven market without market makers. Order clerks conclude trades by matching buyers and sellers without taking positions for their own accounts.

Tokyo Stock Exchange Index (TOPIX) index that covers all of approximately 1200 shares and is viewed as a major barometer of Japanese market conditions. Although the Nikkei 225 Index is quoted more often, Topix is in some ways a more representative index.

tombstone also called TUMBSTONE.

1. advertisement that states the borrower's name, gives the conditions of an issue, and lists the various banks taking part in the issue.
2. short printed announcement about a proposed or completed offering of registered securities, usually appearing in the financial section of newspapers or other publications.

top-down approach   process of building an investment portfolio in such a way as to first analyze economic trends, then select a suitable industry, and finally invest in an attractive company in that industry. For the international investor, top-down research is aimed at identifying the regions or countries of the world that have the macroeconomic environments suitable to the kinds of companies and stocks that fit together with your investment philosophy—GROWTH INVESTING or VALUE INVESTING. For the value investor, that means identifying countries where markets have fallen because the economy is weak, there are political problems, or something else is undermining investor confidence. Growth investors, on the other hand, are looking for countries or regions where economic growth is shifting into high gear. That's where they expect to find companies profiting from that growth by increasing market share or providing new products or services. Also, that is where the HOT MONEY will soon be headed and where the stock market performance is most likely to take off. *See also* BOTTOM-UP APPROACH.

TOPIX   *see* TOKYO STOCK EXCHANGE INDEX.

topping out   reference to a market or a security that is at the end of a period of increasing prices and whose price is now expected to remain fairly constant or decline.

Toronto Stock Exchange (TSE)   largest stock exchange in Canada, listing more than 1200 company stocks and 33 options. The TSE (*www.tse.com*) uses both OPEN OUTCRY and the Computer-Assisted Trading System (CATS). TSE is home to many natural resource companies in the mining, paper, timber, and other natural industries, but also trades manufacturing, biotechnology, and telecommunications issues. The *TSE Composite Index*, known as the TSE 300, is the most widely quoted index tracking this marketplace. The TORONTO 35-STOCK INDEX, made up of a cross section of major Canadian stocks, is the base for derivative products such as the *Toronto 35 Index option* (TXO) and futures (TXF). The TSE 100 INDEX is a performance benchmark for institutional investors, and is the base for the TSE 100 Index option and TSE 100 Index futures contracts.

Toronto Stock Exchange (TSE) 300 Index   market value-weighted barometer of 300 company issues traded in the Canadian market; also known as the *TSE Composite Index*.

Toronto 35-Stock Index   most widely quoted index tracking the Canadian stock market. The index, made up of a cross section of

TOTAL DOLLAR RETURN

major Canadian stocks, is the base for derivative products such as the Toronto 35 Index option (TXO) and futures (TXF).

total dollar return   *see* TOTAL RETURN.

total return   return received on an investment over a specified period of time. It is composed of two basic elements—the current yield such as dividend, interest, and rental income, and capital gains or losses. It is usually expressed as an annual percentage. Return is measured considering the relevant time period (holding period), called a HOLDING PERIOD RETURN.

$$\text{Holding Period Return (HPR)} = \frac{\text{Current income} + \text{Capital gain (or loss)}}{\text{Purchase price}}$$

Consider the investment in stocks A and B over one period of ownership:

STOCK

	A	B
Purchase price (beginning of year)	$100	$100
Cash dividend received (during the year)	$13	$18
Sales price (end of year)	$107	$97

The current income from the investment in stocks A and B over the one-year period are $13 and $18, respectively. For stock A, a capital gain of $7 ($107 sales price − $100 purchase price) is realized over the period. In the case of stock B, a $3 capital loss ($97 sales price − $100 purchase price) results.

Combining the capital gain return (or loss) with the current income, the total return on each investment is summarized below.

STOCK

Return	A	B
Cash dividend	$13	$18
Capital gain (loss)	7	(3)
Total return	$20	$15

Thus, the returns on investments A and B are

$$\text{HPR (stock A)} = \frac{\$13 + (\$107 - \$100)}{\$100} = \frac{\$13 + \$7}{\$100} = \frac{\$20}{\$100} = 20\%$$

$$\text{HPR (stock B)} = \frac{\$18 + (\$97 - \$100)}{\$100} = \frac{\$18 - \$3}{\$100} = \frac{\$15}{\$100} = 15\%$$

See also TOTAL RETURN FROM FOREIGN INVESTMENTS; YIELD.

total return decomposition   breakdown of an international portfolio's TOTAL RETURN, measured in base currency, into the three main sources of return: (1) capital gains (or loss), in local currency; (2) yield; and (3) currency. *See also* INTERNATIONAL RETURNS.

total return from foreign investments total dollar return on a foreign investment made up of three separate elements: (1) dividend/interest income; (2) capital gains (losses); and (3) currency gains (losses).

bonds: The one-period total dollar return on a foreign bond investment. Total dollar return can be calculated as follows:

Total dollar return (R) =

Foreign currency bond return × Currency gain (loss)

$$1+R = 1+\frac{B_1 - B_0 - I}{B_0}(1+\%C)$$

where B_1 = foreign currency bond price at year-end
B_0 = foreign currency bond price at the beginning of the period
I = foreign currency bond coupon income
$\%C$ = percent change in dollar value of the foreign currency

EXAMPLE:
Suppose the initial British bond price is £102, the coupon income is £9, the end-of-period bond price is £106, and the local currency appreciates by 8.64% against the dollar during the period. According to the formula, the total dollar return is 22.49%:

$$1+R = [1+(£106-£102+£9)/£102] \times (1+0.0864)$$
$$1+R = [1+(£13/£102)] \times 1.0864$$
$$1+R = 1.2249$$
$$R = 0.2249 = 22.49\%$$

Note: The currency gain applies to both the local currency principal and to the local currency return.

stocks: The one-period total dollar return on a foreign stock investment can be calculated as follows:

Total dollar return =

Foreign currency stock return × currency gain (loss)

$$1+R = 1+\frac{P_1 - P_0 - D}{P_0}(1+\%C)$$

where P_1 = foreign currency stock price at year-end
P_0 = foreign currency stock price at the beginning of the period
D = foreign currency dividend income
$\%C$ = percent change in dollar value of the foreign currency

TOTAL RISK

EXAMPLE:
Suppose that, during the year, Honda Motor Company moved from ¥11,000 to ¥9,000, while paying a dividend of ¥60. At the same time, the exchange rate moved from ¥105 to ¥110. The total dollar return from this stock investment is a loss, which is computed as follows:

$$1+R = [1 + (¥9,000 - ¥11,000 + ¥60)/¥11,000] \times (1 - 0.0455)$$
$$R = -0.2123 = -21.23\%$$

Note: The percent change in the yen rate is 0.00455 = (¥105 − ¥110)/¥110. In this example, the investor suffered both a capital loss on the foreign currency principal and a currency loss on the dollar value of the investment.

total risk sum of all the risks associated with a particular investment; for example, global investing will involve all types of domestic or local risks plus currency risk. *See also* RISK.

tracking error measure of relative risk. Investors want to see how closely their portfolios, or parts of their portfolios, track a BENCHMARK. Active portfolio managers take bets to beat a benchmark, but they also bear risks when they deviate from the benchmark. A tracking error is the STANDARD DEVIATION of EXCESS RETURNS from the benchmark.

tracking stock stock created by a company to follow, or "track" the performance of one of its divisions—typically one that is in a line of business that is fast growing and commands a higher industry PRICE/EARNINGS RATIO than the parent's main business. Some companies distribute tracking stock to their existing shareholders. Others sell tracking stock to the investing public, raising additional cash for themselves. Some companies do both. Tracking stock, however, does not typically provide voting rights. Issuing tracking stock is an increasingly popular corporate-financing technique.

trade balance balance of a country's exports and imports. Statistics on trade deficits are available on numerous web sites such as *www.economy.com*.

trade secret information, such as a formula, pattern, device, or process, that is not known to the public and that gives the person possessing the information a competitive advantage. It may include customer lead lists, marketing and/or business plans, and suppliers.

trade sizes amount of stock available for buyers and sellers. In a stock with a bid price of 18 and an ask price of $18^1/_2$, for example, a trade size of 10 × 5 indicates that investors have bids in to buy 10 blocks of 100 shares at the price of 18. Sellers, on the other hand, are willing to sell five blocks of 100 shares at $18^1/_2$.

trader one who buys and sells for his or her own account for short-term profit. It may also be a broker who buys and sells in the OVER-THE-COUNTER MARKET.

trading *see* CURRENCY TRADING; DAY TRADING.

trading halt suspension in trading of a stock, bond, option, or futures contract that can be made by an exchange while news is being broadcast about the security.

trading on equity use of borrowed funds to magnify return; also called FINANCIAL LEVERAGE. Trading profitably on the equity, also known as positive (favorable) financial leverage, means that the borrowed funds generate a higher rate of return than the interest rate paid for the use of the funds. The excess accrues to the benefit of the owner because it magnifies, or increases, his/her earnings. *See also* LEVERAGE.

trading post trading location at which stocks assigned to that location are bought and sold on the exchange floor.

trading range
1. region in which a stock or a market has traded during a particular period.
2. trading limit set by a commodities futures exchange on a given commodity.

trading rules rules that dictate trading for stock exchanges. Some rules are:
1. If two orders are equal, the first order receives priority.
2. If two orders are equal and simultaneous, the larger order gets priority.
3. If two orders are equal in all respects, they flip a coin.

trading volume number of shares traded on a stock exchange or for an individual security for a specified period of time, usually daily. A tabulation is made of the number of shares transacted for the day. Trading volume of the overall market and individual stocks can be found in the financial pages of newspapers (for example, *Barron's, Investor's Business Daily,* and *The Wall Street Journal*) and other financial publications. A "net volume" service for major listed stocks is published by Muller and Company. Program trading activity can be found in *The Wall Street Journal* based on information furnished by the NYSE. Trading volume trends indicate the health of the market. Price follows volume; for example, increased price can be expected on increased volume.

tranch CD *see* TRANCHES.

tranches
1. French for *slice*; a portion of a security issue that is designed for a specific category of investors.

2. subunits of a large ($10–$30 million) EURODOLLAR certificate of deposit that are marketed to smaller investors in $10,000 denominations. Tranches are represented by separate certificates and have the same interest rate, issue date, interest payment date, and maturity of the original instrument, which is called a TRANCH CD.
   3. in the United Kingdom, fixed-rate security issues often prearranged by governments, local authorities, or corporations, then brought out in successive rounds, called *tranches*. One therefore speaks of new tranches of existing securities. A variation of the term, TRANCHETTES, refers to small tranches of gilt-edged securities (government bonds) sold by the government to the Bank of England, which then sells them into the market at times it deems appropriate.
   4. risk maturity or other classes into which a multiclass security, such as a COLLATERALIZED MORTGAGE OBLIGATION (CMO) is split. For example, the typical CMO has A, B, C, and Z tranches, representing fast pay, medium pay, and slow pay bonds plus an issue (tranch) that bears no coupon but receives the cash flow from the collateral remaining after the other tranches are satisfied. More sophisticated CMO versions have multiple Z tranches and a Y tranch incorporating a SINKING FUND schedule.

tranchettes   *see* TRANCHES.

transaction risk   risk resulting from *transaction exposure* and losses from changing foreign currency rates. It involves a receivable or a payable denoted in a foreign currency.

transfer agent/registrar   agent of a company responsible for the issuing of stock certificates, for the registration of stockholders' names, and reregistration of new holders when transfering stock.

Treasuries   debt obligations issued and backed of the full credit and faith by the U.S. government. Depending on their denominations and maturities, they are classified into three types: TREASURY BILLS, TREASURY NOTES, and TREASURY BONDS. The income earned on Treasuries is exempt from state and local taxes. Treasuries, backed by the government, are considered riskless. *Note:* They carry the lowest markup, and can even be bought without commission directly from Federal Reserve branches (for information, go to *www.publicdebt.treas.gov*). Treasury yields are published daily in the larger newspapers and on numerous web sites. *See also* TREASURY DIRECT.

Treasury bill (T-bill)   short-term obligation of the U.S. government, which may be purchased for a minimum of $10,000, but at a discount, with maturities of three months, six months, or one year. T-bills are perhaps the safest investment, 100% guaranteed by the U.S. government. They are available through banks or other financial institutions for a small fee, or through Federal Reserve offices. Although T-bills cannot be cashed early, they are usually fairly easy to sell since there is an active SECONDARY MARKET. The interest is exempt from state and local taxes. T-bills are sold at a discount to face value.

EXAMPLE:
A one-year T-bill is bought at a stated interest rate of 8.5%. The amount of discount is $850 (8.5% × $10,000). The price the buyer will pay is $9150 ($10,000 − $850). The EFFECTIVE INTEREST RATE (EFFECTIVE ANNUAL YIELD) is 9.29% ($850/$9150).

Treasury bond
1. long-term debt instrument issued by the U.S. Treasury with maturity of 10 years, initially selling for face value, and paying a fixed rate of interest semiannually throughout its life. It is issued in minimum denominations of $1000.
2. BOND issued by a corporation and later repurchased. Such a bond is considered retired when repurchased.

Treasury direct mechanism through which an individual investor can purchase TREASURIES directly from Federal Reserve banks and branches, thus going around middlemen such as banks or broker-dealers and avoiding their fees. The minimum purchase is $10,000.

Treasury issues *see* TREASURIES.

Treasury note U.S. government security that can be bought in $1000 and $10,000 denominations, with a maturity of one to ten years, and a semiannual fixed interest rate slightly higher than a TREASURY BILL. Like Treasury bills, they are liquid, marketable, and virtually risk free.

Treasury stock issued shares that have been reacquired by the company. Treasury stock although issued is not outstanding. Treasury shares may be held indefinitely, resold, or cancelled. Dividends are not paid on Treasury shares nor are voting rights associated with them. Treasury stock may be bought for several reasons, such as: (1) having fewer shares outstanding making it more difficult for the company to be acquired by a suitor; (2) an increase in MARKET PRICE per share by having fewer shares outstanding; (3) an increase in earnings per share by having fewer shares outstanding; (4) generating shares for the exercise of stock options and warrants; and (5) providing shares in anticipation of the conversion of convertible securities.

trend general direction (upward, downward, sideways) in price or volume movement of a stock, bond, commodity, or the overall market. An accelerating trend is one having a slope, up or down, that is increasing sharply. A downtrend is a series of descending peaks and troughs, while an uptrend is a series of ascending peaks and troughs. Trendless describes a flat, sideways market. A trending market occurs when prices go in one direction, typically closing at an extreme for the day. An uptrend line is one drawn through two or more AS-

CENDING BOTTOMS; a downtrend line is drawn through DESCENDING TOPS. A violation of an up or down trend line often is a sign of a change in trend. A primary trend is the predominant movement of a market, whether it be for stocks, bonds, or commodities. A secondary trend is a market movement in security prices in the appropriate direction of the primary trend. A secondary trend is a temporary interruption in a BULL or BEAR market. *Note:* A trend may also apply to other financial measures, such as interest rates.

trend line   line drawn by technicians to chart the historical direction (movement) of a stock or commodity so as to aid in making future price predictions (see chart below). A trend line connects the lowest or highest prices a stock or commodity has reached within a specified period. A downtrend or uptrend is indicated by the angle of the trend line. A new direction is indicated when price rises above a downward sloping trend line or falls below a rising uptrend line.

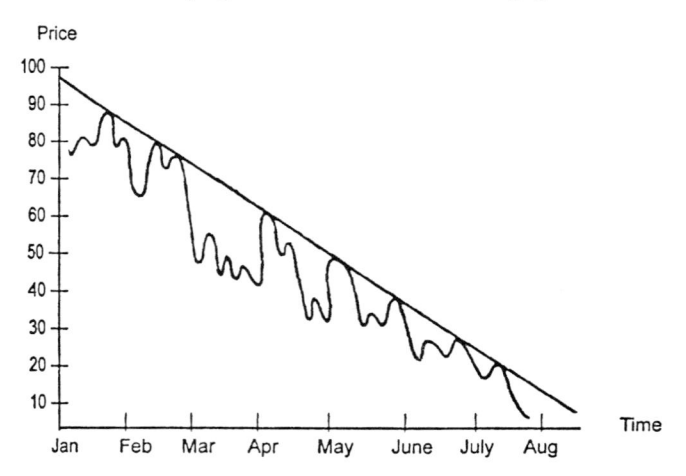

Treynor's performance measure   used to measure portfolio performance. It is concerned with systematic (BETA) risk.

$$T_p = \frac{\text{Risk premium}}{\text{Portfolio's beta coefficient}}$$

EXAMPLE:
An investor wants to rank two stock mutual funds he owns. The risk-free interest rate is 6%. Information for each fund follows:

Growth Fund	Return	Fund's Beta
A	14%	1.10
B	12	1.30

$$T_A = \frac{14\% - 6\%}{1.10} = 7.27 \text{ (First)}$$

$$T_B = \frac{12\% - 6\%}{1.30} = 4.62 \text{ (Second)}$$

Fund A is ranked first because it has a higher return relative to Fund B.

The index can be computed based on information obtained from financial newspapers such as *Barron's* and *The Wall Street Journal*. *See also* SHARPE'S RISK-ADJUSTED RETURN.

triple witching hour *see* PROGRAM TRADING.

TSE 100 Index performance BENCHMARK for institutional investors in the Canadian stock market.

TSE 200 Index small- to medium-cap index composed of 200 stocks in the TSE 300 that are not represented in the TSE 100.

tumbstone *see* TOMBSTONE.

turnaround
  1. positive reversal in an investor's portfolio, such as when securities prices increase after a downturn.
  2. company improves itself.

turning point reversal or change in direction in terms of price or volume of a security or an overall market.

turnover volume of business in a security or the entire market. For example, if turnover on the New York Stock Exchange is reported at 3,000,000 shares on a particular day, 3,000,000 shares changed hands. ODD-LOT turnover is tabulated separately and ordinarily is not included in reported volume. The same concept is applied to individual securities and the portfolio of individual or institutional investors.

turnover ratio measure of a mutual fund's trading history that is expressed as a percentage. A fund with a 100% turnover generally changes the composition of its entire portfolio each year. A 200% turnover means the fund's portfolio changes twice a year.

12b-1 fees fees of a mutual fund that cover advertising and marketing costs, but do nothing to improve the performance of the fund. Their main purpose is to bring new customers to the fund, and ultimately more money for the fund's management to invest.

U

uncovered *see* UNCOVERED OPTION.

uncovered option investment in which the written options are not matched with a long stock position or a long option position that expires no earlier than the written options. The loss potential with such a strategy is thereby unlimited. *See also* NAKED OPTION.

underlying term that refers to a security on which a derivative contract is written. It is a commodity price, interest rate, share price, foreign exchange rate, index of prices, or other variable applied to an amount specified in the contract so as to compute cash settlement or other exchange per the contract provision. While an underlying may be the price of an asset or liability, it is not itself an asset or liability.

underlying futures contract security specified in a futures contract that is transferred upon exercise of the futures contract.

underlying stock stock specified in an option contract that is transferred upon exercise of the option contract.

undervalued describing a stock worth more than its current price, because of better-than-average corporate earnings, favorable market trends, or low PRICE/EARNINGS RATIO. *See also* FULLY VALUED.

underwriting act of buying the securities from the issuing company, thus guaranteeing the company the capital it seeks, and in turn selling the securities, at a markup, to the investing public or institutions.

undigested securities recently issued stocks or bonds that continue to be undistributed due to inadequate public interest.

unissued stock shares that have been authorized but have not been issued. Assume authorized shares of 500,000 and issued shares of 200,000. The unissued shares are 300,000. There are no dividends or voting rights associated with unissued shares. *Note:* Shares required for but as yet not exercised attributable to employee stock options, warrants, rights, or convertible securities cannot be issued while such commitments are in effect. Unissued shares are disclosed in the stockholders' equity section of the BALANCE SHEET besides the issued and outstanding shares.

unit security consisting of two separate securities bundled together, for example a share of stock plus a WARRANT.

unit investment trust (UIT) closed-end investment company in which the proceeds from the sale of original shares are invested in a fixed portfolio of taxable or tax-exempt bonds and held until maturity. Like a mutual fund, a unit investment trust offers to small investors the advantages of a large, professionally selected and diversified portfolio. Unlike a mutual fund, however, its portfolio is fixed; once structured, it is not actively managed; therefore, fees are very low. Unit investment trusts are also available for money market securities, corporate bonds of different grades; mortgage-backed securities; preferred stocks; utility common stocks; and other investments. UITs are most suitable for people who need a fixed income and a guaranteed return of capital. They disband and pay off investors after the majority of their investments have been redeemed. *See also* INVESTMENT COMPANY; INVESTMENT TRUST.

unit trust   *see* UNIT INVESTMENT TRUST.

United States government securities   *see* TREASURIES.

unlisted   security not listed on a stock exchange.

unrealized gain (loss)   difference between market price and carrying value of an unsold security.

unsponsored ADR   *see* AMERICAN DEPOSITARY RECEIPT (ADR).

unsystematic risk   amount of RISK that can be removed by DIVERSIFICATION; also called DIVERSIFIABLE RISK, *company-specific risk*, or *controllable risk. See also* CAPITAL ASSET PRICING MODEL (CAPM); SYSTEMATIC RISK; BETA COEFFICIENT.

upside trend   comparatively long-lasting trend in upward price movement of an individual security or the broad market. Upside trends are never even, and they are often punctuated by downside reversals.

uptick   term used to designate a price higher than that on the preceding transaction in the stock; also called *plus tick*. A stock may be sold short only on an uptick, or on a ZERO-PLUS TICK. A zero-plus tick is a term used for a transaction at the same price as the preceding trade but higher than the preceding different price. Conversely, a DOWNTICK, or minus tick, is a term used to designate a transaction made at a price lower that the preceding trade. A ZERO-MINUS TICK is a transaction made at the same price as the preceding sale but lower than the preceding different price. A plus sign, or a minus sign, is displayed throughout the day next to the last price of each company's stock traded at each trading post on the floor of the New York Stock Exchange (NYSE).

uptrend   *see* UPSIDE TREND.

U.S. government income funds   mutual funds seeking income by investing in a variety of U.S. government securities, including Treasury bonds, federally guaranteed mortgage-backed securities, and other government-backed issues.

U.S. Series I savings bond   U.S. savings bond designed to protect the purchasing power of your principal and guarantee a real fixed rate of return above inflation for the life of the bond (10 to 30 years). The current Series I savings bond, called *I-bond* for short, guarantees 3% above inflation. You can purchase up to $30,000 worth of the bonds each year, you can never lose principal, earnings are free from state and local taxes, and federal taxes are deferred until you redeem the bond. Plus, there are no fees when you buy or sell these bonds. Although you can cash an I-bond six months after the issue date, there is a three-month earnings penalty if you redeem them in less than five years. I-bonds are sold in denominations of $50 to $10,000 at most banks and also on-line at *www.savingsbonds.gov*.

V

valuation process of determining the intrinsic value of an asset, such as a security, business, or a piece of real estate. The process of determining security valuation involves finding the present value of an asset's expected future cash flows using the investor's required rate of return. Thus, the basic security valuation model can be defined mathematically as follows:

$$V = \sum_{t=1}^{n} \frac{CF_t}{(1+r)^t}$$

where V = intrinsic value (or present value) of an asset
CF_t = expected future cash flows in period $t = 1, ..., n$
r = investor's required rate of return

See also COMMON STOCK VALUATION.

value current price of the security multiplied by the number of shares you own. If you own 1000 shares of Nokia, and the shares are selling for $25, the value is $25,000.

value averaging investment strategy to make the investor's stock holdings increase by some preset amount (such as $1000) each period. The investor would sell part of his or her investment if the value goes up too high. For example, if after four months, the investor's investment was worth $5000, he or she would sell $1000 worth of shares the fifth month to bring the account value down to $4000. In other words, value averaging forces the investor to sell high. The value averaging approach takes emotions out of the investment process; the investor can invest without worrying whether this is the right time to buy or sell. Value averaging works well for a fund that stays fully invested in stocks, such as one that tracks the Standard & Poor's 500 Index. In fact, it works best with NO-LOAD index funds that charge no commission to buy or sell. The drawbacks are more work and will probably result in more taxable transactions. Value averaging is a little more complex than DOLLAR COST AVERAGING but can usually generate higher returns at lower per share costs.

value date date on which GOOD FUNDS settlement is made for a transaction. Until the value date, funds are not available for use.

value investing strategy associated with buying out-of-favor stocks. Value issues often are perceived to have lower risks because their share prices already have been discounted compared to other shares in the market. Value-styled portfolios traditionally contain stocks that have lower-than-average price-to-book ratios and/or PRICE/EARNINGS RATIOS. Investors seeking value investments must obtain these or other ratios of value for the investment they are reviewing as well as key market BENCHMARK or peer securities. John Templeton, perhaps the best-known international value investor, uses many different tools: price/earnings ratios, price relative to cash flow, and even price relative to the breakup value of a company. Taking all that into account, he then measures one company against other similar companies to determine which one is cheapest. *Note:* Some international value investors prefer price-to-book value ratios to price/earnings ratios, not trusting the way in which earnings can be manipulated in many countries. *See also* GROWTH INVESTING.

Value Line Composite Average a broad-based measure of prices of NYSE, AMEX, and NASDAQ BLUE CHIP and second-tier stocks; it represents approximately 95% of the market value of all U.S. securities. It was developed and has been maintained, and published since 1961 by Arnold Bernhard and Co., which was renamed Value Line, Inc., upon its reorganization in October 1982. To be included, a stock must (1) have a reasonable market value, or capitalization; (2) have a strong trading volume, which is a measure of investor interest; and (3) have a high degree of investor interest, as represented by the number of requests for information on a specific stock by the subscribers of the VALUE LINE INVESTMENT SURVEY. Component stocks are rarely dropped from the index; if one is, it is because the company has either (1) gone bankrupt with little hope of revitalization and continued investor interest; (2) merged with another company; or (3) gone private.

Value Line Investment Survey investment advisory service, based in New York (P.O. Box 3988, New York, NY 10008-3988; *www.valueline.com*), which is renowned for its surveys. It ranks the quality of hundreds of companies. The service predicts which stocks will perform the best and worst over the next year. The service looks at stocks in terms of timeliness, safety, risk, and similar features. The ranking system goes from 1 (highest rank) to 5 (lowest rank). The organization is a publisher of *Value Line Average* and also runs a family of mutual funds.

value stock stock perceived by the marketplace to be undervalued based on criteria such as its PRICE/EARNINGS RATIO, price-to-book ratio, dividend yield, and so on.

variation margin
1. profits or losses on open positions in futures and option contracts that are paid or collected daily.
2. amount to be paid to satisfy MAINTENANCE MARGIN.

venture capital funds invested in companies that normally do not have access to conventional sources of capital, usually for a new, risky, start-up, business venture. Providers usually demand significant control of the equity ownership.

vertical spread strategy where an option is bought at one STRIKE PRICE while at the same time another option is sold on the same class at the next higher or lower strike price. The expiration dates of both options are the same.

virtual currency options options that do not require the payment or delivery of the underlying currency; also called *3-Ds* (dollar-denominated-delivery). Currently, 3-D options are available on the Deutsche mark and the Japanese yen. They are European-style options that mature any time from one week to nine months, and they settle weekly. *See also* CURRENCY OPTION.

volatility yardstick for risk of a security—a stock or an ADR—both up and down. It is a measure of the amount by which a security is expected to fluctuate in a given period of time. Volatility in stock prices may be due to many factors, such as instability in earnings, economic uncertainty, thinly traded security, and erratic economic or political conditions. Stocks with greater volatility exhibit wider price swings and their options are higher in price than less volatile stocks. This describes the fluctuations in the price of a stock or other type of security. If the price of a stock is capable of large swings, the stock has a high volatility. The pricing of options contracts depends in part on volatility. A stock with high volatility, for example, commands higher prices in the options market than one with low volatility. Volatility may be gauged by several measures, one of which involves calculating a security's STANDARD DEVIATION. Stock investors sometimes prefer to measure a stock's volatility versus that of an index, such as the Standard & Poor's 500 Index. This is known as a stock's BETA. A beta of 1.2 implies a stock that is 20% more volatile than the S&P 500. When the S&P rises 10%, the stock is expected to rise 12%.

volume daily number of shares of a security that changes hands between a buyer and a seller.

voting right stockholder's right to vote his or her stock in the affairs of the company. Most common shares have one vote each. Preferred stock usually has the right to vote when preferred dividends are in default. The right to vote may be delegated by the stockholder to another person.

W

W formation   pattern in which the price of a security or commodity reaches the SUPPORT LEVEL on two occasions and then moves up again.

***Wall Street Week* Technical Market Index**   index based on a survey of ten technical investment analysis methods. These technical indicators include financial conditions, market activity, investor behavior, insider purchases, calls and puts, and monetary policy. The index is used to substantiate an upward or downward trend in the stock market. Fundamental analysis is not taken into account. This measure is based on assigning +1 for a BULLISH characteristic, −1 for a BEARISH situation, and 0 for no effect for each of the ten technical indicators. The ratings are then added to obtain a total. The ten indicators in the index are

1. **Market Breadth:** a moving average for ten days for the net effect of advancing issues relative to declining issues.
2. **Put/Call Options Premium:** ratio of premium on PUT options to premium on CALL options.
3. **Arms Short-Term Trading Index:** advance/decline ratio of "Big Board" stocks shown by the rate, low of volume increasing to volume decreasing.
4. **Insider Buy/Sell Ratio:** ratio of insider buys to insider sells.
5. **Low-Price Activity Percentage:** volume of low-priced "risky" securities to the volume of high-quality stocks.
6. **Bearish Sentiment Index:** indicator of how investment newsletters perceive the future condition of the stock market.
7. **DJIA Momentum Ratio:** the difference between the closing DJIA and the average DJIA for 30 days.
8. **NYSE High-Low Index:** the number of stocks accomplishing new highs relative to those reaching new lows over the previous ten trading days applied on a daily basis.
9. **NYSE Securities at Market Prices Above 10-Week and 30-Week Moving Averages:** the percentage of stocks selling above their 10-week and 30-week highs.
10. **Ratio of Ending Prices on Fed Funds to the Discount Rate:** When the Federal Reserve Board tightens the money supply, the Fed funds rate increases relative to the discount rate, because the Fed charges a higher rate between individual member banks than it charges between member banks and the Fed.

The upper and lower limits for the Wall Street Week Technical Market Index is +10 to −10. A reading of +1 to −1 is neutral. A reading of +5 or more is a buy signal, while a reading of −5 is a sell signal. The index is found in *Futures and Investor's Analy-*

sis magazine (published by Robert Nurock). The index indicates from a technical standpoint whether the bottom or top is indicated. At market bottom there is a buy indicator, while at market top there is a sell indicator. For example, at the market bottom stock prices are expected to increase.

wallflower stocks stocks to which security analysts are giving little or no attention; as a result, investor interest in the stocks are nonexistent or minimal. The company is not being evaluated by professionals and its stock is either not being recommended or recommended infrequently. Wallflower stocks may be very small companies, very young companies, or companies that have previously disappointed investors. These stocks usually have low price/earnings multiples. Of course, an investor who buys a wallflower stock that turns itself around and becomes followed and recommended by security analysts can significantly profit.

warrant paper giving its holder the right to buy a security at a price, either within a specified period or perpetually. A warrant is generally offered with another security as an added inducement or SWEETENER to buy. Warrants are like call options, but with much longer time spans—sometimes years. *Note:* When you buy a warrant, you're paying a small price now for the right to buy a certain number of shares at a fixed price when the stock is finally issued. Consequently, you pay now and own later. You do this only if you think the price of the stock will rise.

EXAMPLE:
Suppose that you pay $1 a share for warrants that give you the right to buy shares at $6 when they're issued. If the shares are eventually issued at $11 a share, it will have cost you only $7 ($1 + $6) for an $11 stock.

wash sale
1. sale of a security for which no loss is recognized for tax purposes because within 30 days preceding or after the disposal date the investor bought a substantially identical security. Such sales are now forbidden by stock exchange rules.
2. manipulation of stock prices upward when two or more parties buy the stock from each other at higher prices. The objective is to give the false implication of market activity in a security so that unsuspecting investors become interested in it, further driving up the price. The manipulator then sells the security at the inflated price.

watch list
1. list of securities a brokerage firm or individual stockbroker may single out to observe, either because of unique investment characteristics, such as being possible takeover candidates, or for other investor interest.

2. closely monitored list, established by the government, of banks in danger of failing.

watered stock capital stock issued in exchange for assets having fair market values below the par or stated value. As a result, assets are recorded at overstated values. If the board of directors acted in bad faith, this practice is illegal. Watered stock got its name from the cattlemen's practice of encouraging their stock to drink large quantities of water, induced by salt, before taking them to market. Thus, the stock would appear larger and perhaps become more valuable.

weak market market characterized by a predominance of sellers over buyers and a declining price trend. *See also* STRONG MARKET.

weighted average cost of capital (WACC) *see* COST OF CAPITAL.

weighted-average exchange rate mean or average exchange rate used in translating income and expense accounts at the end of an accounting period. It takes into account the relative change of exchange rates during the period and adjusts the consolidated statement with this weighted average rate.

when distributed security trading in advance of the printing of the certificate.

when issued short form of "when, as, and if issued." The term indicates a conditional transaction in a security authorized for issuance but not as yet actually issued. All "when issued" transactions are on an "if" basis, to be settled if and when the actual security is issued and the National Association of Securities Dealers or an exchange rules the transactions are to be settled.

Wilshire 5000 Index broadest weighted index of all common stock issues on the NYSE, AMEX, and the most active issues on the OVER-THE-COUNTER MARKET. Approximately 85% of the securities are traded on the NYSE. The index's value is in billions of dollars. It includes about 6000 stocks (not 5000 as its name would suggest) so it is representative of the overall market. The stocks included in the index are weighted by market value. It covers total prices of all stocks with daily quotations. The Wilshire Index is published by Wilshire Associates (Santa Monica, California). The index is reported weekly in *Barron's* and in each issue of *Forbes*. It is reported daily in many newspapers such as *Investor's Business Daily, The New York Times*, and *The Wall Street Journal*. The investor should use the Wilshire 5000 Index as a barometer of the overall stock market condition. In a BULL MARKET the index will be increasing; in a BEAR MARKET the index will be decreasing. A stock may be bought if the index is on an upward move and the investor feels that prices will continue moving up. However, if stock conditions are deteriorating as evidenced by a declining index, the investor should sell the stock if he or she believes that conditions will worsen.

whipsawed condition in which an investor's security transaction is quickly followed by an opposite reaction. Sometimes referred to as "being whipped."

whisper number rumored earnings numbers about to be reported (sometimes leaked by an employee). Whisper numbers are especially useful when they differ from the consensus forecast. They are available on two well-known web sites: *www.earningswhispers.com/* and *www.whispernumbers.com/*

white knight slang term for an individual or company who saves a corporation from an unfriendly takeover by taking it over himself or herself. This way the targeted corporation is rescued from the unwanted bidder's control.

white sheets sheets published daily by the National Quotation Bureau providing information on OVER-THE-COUNTER securities, including data on prices (bid and asked prices and dealers in the stock. *See also* PINK SHEETS; YELLOW SHEETS.

wholesale market maker MARKET MAKER who caters to small-investor trades.

wide opening unusually large difference between the bid and asked prices of a security at the opening of a trade session.

widow and orphan stock secure stock with a record of high dividends. It typically is fairly stable in market price. In most cases, the company is very cyclical in nature. An example would be a large and mature utility.

wire *see* NEWS TICKER.

wire transfers electronic payment orders issued through bank channels; also called *telegraphic transfers*.

World Bank integrated group of international institutions that provides financial and technical assistance to developing countries. The World Bank (*http://www.worldbank.org*) includes the International Bank for Reconstruction and Development and the International Development Association. World Bank affiliates, legally and financially separate, include the International Center for Settlement of Investment Disputes, the International Finance Corporation, and the Multilateral Investment Guarantee Agency. World Bank headquarters are in Washington, D.C.

World Equity Benchmark Shares (WEBS) fund created by Morgan Stanley that tracks a predesignated index (one of Morgan Stanley's international capital indices) for each of 17 countries. These are closed-end funds, and trade on the AMEX.

wrap account special brokerage arrangement, in which investors place their funds and pay a comprehensive annual fee in return for investment management, including the making and implementing of decisions, as well as the administering of them.

write investor who sells an option contract not currently held (selling the option short) is said to *write* the option.

writer individual who sells covered options on underlying securities in an attempt to maximize an investment return; also called a *grantor*.

X

X or XD symbol used in the financial world to signify that a stock is trading without dividend (EX-DIVIDEND). The symbol X can also mean a bond selling without interest, usually at a deep discount from its face value.

xenocurrency currency that trades outside of its own borders.

XETRA (eXchange Electronic TRAding) *see* FRANKFURT STOCK EXCHANGE.

Y

Yankee bonds dollar-denominated bonds issued within the United States by a foreign corporation. These bonds would be sold in the United States when market conditions are more conducive to them relative to the EUROBOND market or in domestic markets overseas.

Yankee CD certificate of deposit (CD) issued in the U.S. market by a branch of a foreign bank.

Yankee stock offerings offerings of stock by non-U.S. companies in the U.S. markets.

year-end dividend corporate dividend paid to investors at period-end. It is based on the firm's profitability for the year, and is typically in the form of an *additional* dividend.

Yellow Book book of listing rules of the LONDON STOCK EXCHANGE (LSE). Separate listing rules exist for the LSE's junior market—the Alternative Investment Market.

yellow sheets daily issue of the National Quotation Bureau that lists the BID AND ASKED quotes and dealers in OVER-THE-COUNTER corporate bonds. *See also* PINK SHEETS; WHITE SHEETS.

yield to final maturity (YFM) equal to YIELD TO MATURITY (YTM) only for those bonds that are reimbursed on the final date.

yield to call yield of a bond, if it is held until the call date. This yield is valid only if the security is called prior to maturity. The calculation of yield to call is based on the coupon rate, length of time to the call date, and the market price. In general, bonds are callable over several years and normally are called at a small premium. If the bond may be called prior to maturity, the YIELD TO MATURITY (YTM) formula will have the call price in place of the PAR VALUE of $1000. For example, a 20-year bond was initially issued at a 13.5% coupon rate, and after two years, rates have dropped. The bond is currently selling for $1180, the yield to maturity on the bond is 11.15%, and the bond can be called in five years after issue at $1090. Thus, if an investor buys the bond two years after issue, his or her bond may be called back after three more years at $1090. Then the yield to call is:

$$\frac{\$135 + (\$1090 - \$1180)/3}{(\$1090 + \$1180)/2} = \frac{\$135 + (-\$90/3)}{\$1135} = \frac{\$105}{\$1135} = 9.25\%$$

Note that the yield to call figure of 9.25% is 190 basis points less than the yield to maturity of 11.15%. Clearly, the investor needs to be aware of the differential because a lower return is earned. *See also* BOND YIELD.

yield to maturity (YTM) the annual rate of return that a bondholder purchasing a bond today and holding it to maturity would receive on his or her investment. It is the EFFECTIVE RATE OF RETURN on a bond calculated from its market price, face value, coupon rate, and time remaining to maturity. The YTM incorporates the stated rate of interest on the bond as well as any discount or premium that may have been generated when bought.

The exact way of calculating this measure is the same as the one for the INTERNAL RATE OF RETURN. But the approximate method is

$$\text{Yield} = \frac{I + (M - V)/n}{(M + V)/2}$$

where V = the market value of the bond
I = dollars of interest paid per year
n = number of years to maturity

For example, the YTM of a 10-year, 8% coupon, $1000 par value bond at a price of $877.60 is:

$$\text{Yield} = \frac{\$80 + (\$1000 - \$877.60)/10}{(\$1000 + \$877.60)/2} = \frac{\$80 + \$12.24}{\$938.80}$$

$$= \frac{\$92.24}{\$938.80} = \$9.8\%$$

See also BOND YIELD.

yield (rate of return) also called *real return*, *real rate of return*, or EFFECTIVE RATE OF RETURN.

in general: The income earned on an investment, usually expressed as a percentage of the market price.

stocks: Percentage return earned on a common stock or preferred stock in dividends. It is figured by dividing the total of dividends paid in the preceding 12 months by the current market price. For example, a stock with a current market value of $40 a share, which has paid $2 in dividends in the preceding 12 months is said to return 5% ($2/$40). If an investor paid $20 for the stock five years earlier, the stock would be returning 10% on the original investment. *See also* DIVIDEND YIELD.

bonds: CURRENT YIELD or YIELD TO MATURITY (YTM). *See also* BOND YIELD; INTERNAL RATE OF RETURN; REALIZED YIELD; YIELD TO CALL.

Note: Yield is *not* the same thing as the coupon interest rate. Actually, yield may be higher or lower than the bond's interest rate. If, for instance, a bond costs $1000 and pays 8% interest, you'd receive $80 a year from this bond, so it would yield 8%. If, however, a year later, the bond loses value and it's sold for $800, the new buyers would still receive the $80 a year. However, because they paid only $800, the yield for them would be 10%. In contrast, should the bond be sold next year at a premium, say $1200, the $80 a year interest would be a yield of only 6.67% (see below).

HOW YIELD FLUCTUATES

Yield from a bond with an interest rate of 8%	Interest Payment	Yield
If you buy at par—$1000	$80.00	8%
If you buy at a discount price of $800	$80.00	10%
If you buy at a premium price of $1200	$80.00	6.67%

See also INTERNAL RATE OF RETURN.

yield curve curve showing the relationship between yield (interest rate) and maturity for a set of similar securities; also called the *term structure of interest rates*. For example, the yield curve can be drawn for U.S. Treasuries. Other factors such as default risk and tax treatment are held constant. An understanding of this relationship is important to investors who must decide whether to buy long- or short-term bonds. A yield curve may take any number of shapes. The graphs below show alternative yield curves; a flat (vertical) yield curve (A), a positive (ascending) yield curve (B), an inverted (descending) yield curve (C), and a humped (ascending and then descending) yield curve (D). *Note:* Different yield curves are drawn for ZERO-COUPON BONDS (zero-coupon yield curve) and for coupon bonds quoted at par (par yield curve).

ALTERNATIVE TERM-STRUCTURE PATTERNS

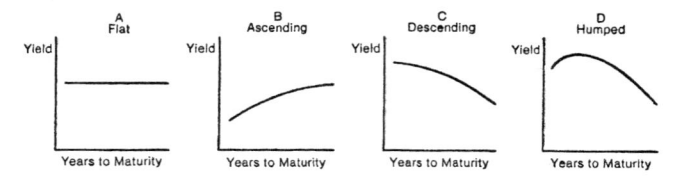

yield spread difference between the yields received on two different types of bonds with different ratings. In times of economic uncertainty, the yield spread increases because investors demand higher premiums on risky issues to compensate for the increased chance of default. *See also* BOND RATINGS.

yield to average life (YTAL) the ACTUARIAL YIELD that takes the mandatory SINKING FUND into account. The average life of a bond is usually defined as the average maturity of the whole issue. Average life takes into account the fact that some bonds are reimbursed early and others late, which makes it a weighted average of the maturities on each bond.

yo-yo stock stock that is volatile in price. Its ups and downs in price are fast and resemble the movement of a yo-yo.

Z

zero-cost collars package of options (buying some and selling others) so that the net investment is zero.

zero-coupon bond bond bought at a deep discount; also called simply *zeros*, or ORIGINAL ISSUE DISCOUNT (OID) bond. The interest, instead of being paid out directly, is added to the principal semiannually and both the principal and the accumulated interest are paid at maturity. Although a fixed rate is implicit in the discount and the specific maturity, these bonds are not fixed-income securities in the traditional sense because they provide for no periodic income. Although the interest on the bonds is paid at maturity, accrued interest is taxable yearly as ordinary income. Zero-coupon bonds have two basic advantages over regular coupon-bearing bonds: (1) a relatively small investment is required to buy these bonds and (2) a specific yield is assured throughout the term of the investment. Many investors are interested in an investment that accumulates and compounds interest automatically rather than paying interest regularly. This eliminates the need for reinvestment of periodic interest income, perhaps at lower rates than the initial investment. *See also* BEARER BOND; DEEP DISCOUNT BOND.

zero-coupon government bonds GOVERNMENT BONDS that are purchased at a deep discount and pay no cash income, unlike regular bonds.

zero-minus tick sale that is made at the same price as the prior transaction, but at a lower price than the last different price; also called a *zero downtick*. *See also* ZERO-PLUS TICK.

zero-plus tick sale that is made at the same price as the prior sale, but at a higher price than the last different price; also called a *zero uptick*. *Note:* Short sale must be executed only on plus ticks or zero-plus ticks. *See also* SHORT SALE.

zero-sum game investment situation in which the total wealth of all traders remains the same. Total gains of winners exactly equal the total losses of losers and thus the trading simply redistributes the wealth among the traders. An example is futures and options trading.

zombies companies that continue to trade despite having no product or substantive business activity; also called *brain dead*, *undead*, or *living dead*.

Appendix A
Present Value Tables

PRESENT VALUE OF $1 = T1

Periods	4%	6%	8%	10%	12%	14%	16%	18%	20%	22%	24%	26%	28%	30%	40%
1	.962	.943	.926	.909	.893	.877	.862	.847	.833	.820	.806	.794	.781	.769	.714
2	.925	.890	.857	.826	.797	.769	.743	.718	.694	.672	.650	.630	.610	.592	.510
3	.889	.840	.794	.751	.712	.675	.641	.609	.579	.551	.524	.500	.477	.455	.364
4	.855	.792	.735	.683	.636	.592	.552	.516	.482	.451	.423	.397	.373	.350	.260
5	.822	.747	.681	.621	.567	.519	.476	.437	.402	.370	.341	.315	.291	.269	.186
6	.790	.705	.630	.564	.507	.456	.410	.370	.335	.303	.275	.250	.227	.207	.133
7	.760	.665	.583	.513	.452	.400	.354	.314	.279	.249	.222	.198	.178	.159	.095
8	.731	.627	.540	.467	.404	.351	.305	.266	.233	.204	.179	.157	.139	.123	.068
9	.703	.592	.500	.424	.361	.308	.263	.225	.194	.167	.144	.125	.108	.094	.048
10	.676	.558	.463	.386	.322	.270	.227	.191	.162	.137	.116	.099	.085	.073	.035
11	.650	.527	.429	.350	.287	.237	.195	.162	.135	.112	.094	.079	.066	.056	.025
12	.625	.497	.397	.319	.257	.208	.168	.137	.112	.092	.076	.062	.052	.043	.018
13	.601	.469	.368	.290	.229	.182	.145	.116	.093	.075	.061	.050	.040	.033	.013
14	.577	.442	.340	.263	.205	.160	.125	.099	.078	.062	.049	.039	.032	.025	.009
15	.555	.417	.315	.239	.183	.140	.108	.084	.065	.051	.040	.031	.025	.020	.006

APPENDIX A PRESENT VALUE TABLES

PRESENT VALUE OF $1 = T1 (cont.)

Periods	4%	6%	8%	10%	12%	14%	16%	18%	20%	22%	24%	26%	28%	30%	40%
16	.534	.394	.292	.218	.163	.123	.093	.071	.054	.042	.032	.025	.019	.015	.005
17	.513	.371	.270	.198	.146	.108	.080	.060	.045	.034	.026	.020	.015	.012	.003
18	.494	.350	.250	.180	.130	.095	.069	.051	.038	.028	.021	.016	.012	.009	.002
19	.475	.331	.232	.164	.116	.083	.060	.043	.031	.023	.017	.012	.009	.007	.002
20	.456	.312	.215	.149	.104	.073	.051	.037	.026	.019	.014	.010	.007	.005	.001
21	.439	.294	.199	.135	.093	.064	.044	.031	.022	.015	.011	.008	.006	.004	.001
22	.422	.278	.184	.123	.083	.056	.038	.026	.018	.013	.009	.006	.004	.003	.001
23	.406	.262	.170	.112	.074	.049	.033	.022	.015	.010	.007	.005	.003	.002	
24	.390	.247	.158	.102	.066	.043	.028	.019	.013	.008	.006	.004	.003	.002	
25	.375	.233	.146	.092	.059	.038	.024	.016	.010	.007	.005	.003	.002	.001	
26	.361	.220	.135	.084	.053	.033	.021	.014	.009	.006	.004	.002	.002	.001	
27	.347	.207	.125	.076	.047	.029	.018	.011	.007	.005	.003	.002	.001	.001	
28	.333	.196	.116	.069	.042	.026	.016	.010	.006	.004	.002	.002	.001	.001	
29	.321	.185	.107	.063	.037	.022	.014	.008	.005	.003	.002	.001	.001	.001	
30	.308	.174	.099	.057	.033	.020	.012	.007	.004	.003	.002	.001	.001	.001	
40	.208	.097	.046	.022	.011	.005	.003	.001	.001						

APPENDIX A PRESENT VALUE TABLES

PRESENT VALUE OF AN ANNUITY OF $1 = T2

Periods	4%	6%	8%	10%	12%	14%	16%	18%
1	0.962	0.943	0.926	0.909	0.893	0.877	0.862	0.847
2	1.886	1.833	1.783	1.736	1.690	1.647	1.605	1.566
3	2.775	2.673	2.577	2.487	2.402	2.322	2.246	2.174
4	3.630	3.465	3.312	3.170	3.037	2.914	2.798	2.690
5	4.452	4.212	3.993	3.791	3.605	3.433	3.274	3.127
6	5.242	4.917	4.623	4.355	4.111	3.889	3.685	3.498
7	6.002	5.582	5.206	4.868	4.564	4.288	4.039	3.812
8	6.733	6.210	5.747	5.335	4.968	4.639	4.344	4.078
9	7.435	6.802	6.247	5.759	5.328	4.946	4.607	4.303
10	8.111	7.360	6.710	6.145	5.650	5.216	4.833	4.494
11	8.760	7.887	7.139	6.495	5.938	5.453	5.029	4.656
12	9.385	8.384	7.536	6.814	6.194	5.660	5.197	4.793
13	9.986	8.853	7.904	7.103	6.424	5.842	5.342	4.910
14	10.563	9.295	8.244	7.367	6.628	6.002	5.468	5.008
15	11.118	9.712	8.559	7.606	6.811	6.142	5.575	5.092
16	11.652	10.106	8.851	7.824	6.974	6.265	5.669	5.162
17	12.166	10.477	9.122	8.022	7.120	6.373	5.749	5.222
18	12.659	10.828	9.372	8.201	7.250	6.467	5.818	5.273
19	13.134	11.158	9.604	8.365	7.366	6.550	5.877	5.316
20	13.590	11.470	9.818	8.514	7.469	6.623	5.929	5.353
21	14.029	11.764	10.017	8.649	7.562	6.687	5.973	5.384
22	14.451	12.042	10.201	8.772	7.645	6.743	6.011	5.410
23	14.857	12.303	10.371	8.883	7.718	6.792	6.044	5.432
24	15.247	12.550	10.529	8.985	7.784	6.835	6.073	5.451
25	15.622	12.783	10.675	9.077	7.843	6.873	6.097	5.467
26	15.983	13.003	10.810	9.161	7.896	6.906	6.118	5.480
27	16.330	13.211	10.935	9.237	7.943	6.935	6.136	5.492
28	16.663	13.406	11.051	9.307	7.984	6.961	6.152	5.502
29	16.984	13.591	11.158	9.370	8.022	6.983	6.166	5.510
30	17.292	13.765	11.258	9.427	8.055	7.003	6.177	5.517
40	19.793	15.046	11.925	9.779	8.244	7.105	6.234	5.548

Payments (or receipts) at the *end* of each period.

Appendix B
Web Sites for Global Investing

WEB ADDRESS	PRIMARY FOCUS
www.global-investor.com/	The Internet Resource for International Investors
www.worldlyinvestor.com/	Global On-line Investing
www.investorguide.com/ International.htm	International Investing
www.knewmoney.com/ www.adr.com	Foreign Currency Investing ADR Quotations from J. P. Morgan
www.gefn.com	General Electric Financial Network, "How do exchange rates affect my foreign fund?"
www.cbs.marketwatch.com	General Financial Market Information. Includes Extensive List of Global Market, Sector and Bond Indexes
www.bankofny.com/adr	Educational Material on the Definition and Trading of ADRs, Along with a Listing of all ADRs in the U.S. Markets
www.bloomberg.com	General Financial Market Information. Includes Listing of World Indexes
www.cyberhost3.com/stockcit/adr/ index.html	Listing of ADRs
www.ft-se.co.uk	International Investment Information and Extensive Global Index Listings
www.healthwealthsolutions.com/ globaltrading	A Good Site on the Need for and Approach to Global Investing

(*cont.*)

APPENDIX B WEB SITES FOR GLOBAL INVESTING

WEB ADDRESS	PRIMARY FOCUS
www.ingbarings.com/pweb/ research/research_frame.htm	International Investment Site with Links and Index Listings
www.msci.com	Global Investment Information and Index Listings
www.spglobal.com	Listing of S&P Global Indexes
www.ratings.com/criteria/ sovereigns.index *www.moodys.com/repldata/ ratings/ratsov.html*	Bond Ratings
www.bradynet.com	Emerging Market Bonds
www.securitis.com	Financial Data for Emerging Markets
www.irasis.com	Financial Information for U.S. Treasuries
www.fidelity.com *www.mldirect.com* *www.etrade.com* *www.csfbdirect.com* *www.schwab.com*	Bond Trading on the Web
www.economy.com *www.dismal.com*	The Economy.com Network —a complete source for analysis, data, forecasts, and information on the U.S. and world economies
www.stats.bls.gov *www.census.gov/econ/*	Government Sites for Economic Data

Appendix C
World Stock Markets

Stock Exchange	Symbol	Country
American Stock Exchange	AMEX	USA
Amman Financial Market	AFM	Jordan
Amsterdam Exchanges	AEX	Netherlands
Arizona Stock Exchange	AZX	USA
Athens Stock Exchange	ASE	Greece
Australian Stock Exchange	ASX	Australia
Bahrain Stock Exchange	BSE	Bahrain
Baltic Exchange	BIFFEX	UK
Bangalore Stock Exchange Limited	BGSE	India
Beirut Stock Exchange	BSE	Lebanon
Belgrade Stock Exchange	BELEX	Yugoslavia
Bermuda Stock Exchange	BSX	Bermuda
Bolsa Boliviana de Valores	BBV	Bolivia
Bolsa de Barcelona		Spain
Bolsa de Bogotá		Colombia
Bolsa de Comercio de Buenos Aires	SBA	Argentina
Bolsa de Comercio de Santiago	BSAN	Chile
Bolsa de Madrid	BM	Spain
Bolsa de Valores de Caracas	CSE	Venezuela
Bolsa de Valores de Guayaquil—Ecuador	BVG	Ecuador
Bolsa de Valores de Lima—Peru	BVL	Peru
Bolsa de Valores de Nicaragua	BVN	Nicaragua
Bolsa de Valores de Panamá	BVP	Panama
Bolsa de Valores de Quito—Ecuador	BVQ	Ecuador
Bolsa de Valores de São Paulo—Brazil	BVSPA	Brazil
Bolsa de Valores de Rio de Janeiro	BVRJ	Brazil
Bolsa de Valores Nacional S.A. Guatemala	BVNSA	Guatemala
Bolsa Electronica de Chile	BEC	Chile
Bolsa Mexicana de Valores	BMV	Mexico
Bombay Stock Exchange	BSE	India
Boston Stock Exchange	BSE	USA
Botswana Stock Exchange		Botswana
Bourse de Paris		France
Brussels Exchange	BXS	Belgium
Bucharest Stock Exchange	BSE	Romania
Budapest Stock Exchange	FORNAX	Hungary
Bulgarian Stock Exchange	BSE	Bulgaria
Cairo & Alexandria Stock Exchange	CASE	Egypt
Canadian Venture Exchange	CDNX	Canada

(cont.)

APPENDIX C WORLD STOCK MARKETS

WORLD STOCK MARKETS

Stock Exchange	Symbol	Country
Cayman Islands Stock Exchange	CIE	Cayman Is.
Cincinnati Stock Exchange	CSE	USA
Colombo Stock Exchange		Sri Lanka
Copenhagen Stock Exchange	CSE	Denmark
Cyprus Stock Exchange	CSE	Cyprus
Dhaka Stock Exchange	DSE	Bangladesh
Ghana Stock Exchange	GSE	Ghana
Gruppe Deutsche Börse	FSE	Germany
Helsinki Stock Exchange	HEX	Finland
Hong Kong Stock Exchange	HKSE	Hong Kong
Stock Exchanges of India	ISE	India
Irish Stock Exchange	ISE	Ireland
Istanbul Stock Exchange	ISE	Turkey
Italian Stock Exchange		Italy
Jakarta Stock Exchange	JSX	Indonesia
Jamaica Stock Exchange	JSE	Jamaica
Johannesburg Stock Exchange	JSE	South Africa
Karachi Stock Exchange	KSE	Pakistan
Korea Stock Exchange	KSE	Korea
Kuala Lumpur Stock Exchange	KLSE	Malaysia
Lisbon Stock Exchange	BVL	Portugal
Ljubljana Stock Exchange	LJSE	Slovenia
London Stock Exchange		UK
Luxembourg Stock Exchange	LSE	Luxembourg
Macedonian Stock Exchange	MSE	Macedonia
Malaysian Exchange of Securities Dealing & Automated Quotation	MESDAQ	Malaysia
Montreal Exchange	ME	Canada
Nagoya Stock Exchange	NSE	Japan
Namibian Stock Exchange	NSE	Namibia
NASDAQ	NASDAQ	USA
National Stock Exchange of India	NSEI	India
National Stock Exchange of Lithuania	NSE	Lithuania
New York Stock Exchange	NYSE	USA
New Zealand Stock Exchange	NZSE	New Zealand
OM Stockholm Stock Exchange	OMX	Sweden
Oslo Stock Exchange	OSE	Norway
OTC Bulletin Board	OTCBB	USA
Pacific Exchange	PCX	USA
Palestine Securities Exchange	PSE	Israel
Philadelphia Stock Exchange	PHLX	USA
Philippine Stock Exchange	PSE	Philippines
Prague Stock Exchange	PSE	Czech Rep.
Riga Stock Exchange	RSE	Latvia

WORLD STOCK MARKETS

Stock Exchange	Symbol	Country
San Diego Stock Exchange	SDSE	USA
Singapore Stock Exchange	SES	Singapore
Stock Exchange of Newcastle	NSX	Austrailia
Stock Exchange of Thailand	SET	Thailand
Surabaya Stock Exchange	SSX	Indonesia
Swiss Stock Exchange	SWX	Switzerland
Taiwan Stock Exchange	TSE	Taiwan
Tallinn Stock Exchange	TALSE	Estonia
Tehran Stock Exchange	TSE	Iran
Tel Aviv Stock Exchange	TASE	Israel
Tokyo Stock Exchange	TSE	Japan
Toronto Stock Exchange	TSE	Canada
Tradepoint Stock Exchange		UK
Trinidad and Tobago Stock Exchange	TTSE	Trinidad & Tobago
Warsaw Stock Exchange	WSE	Poland
Wiener Börse AG	WBAG	Austria
Winnipeg Stock Exchange	WSE	Canada
Zagreb Stock Exchange	ZSE	Croatia
Zimbabwe Stock Exchange	ZSE	Zimbabwe

WORLD OPTIONS & FUTURES EXCHANGES

Options/Futures Exchange	Symbol	Location
Asian Capacity Exchange	ACE	Asia
Bolsa de Comercio de Santa Fe		Argentina
Bolsa de Mercadorias & Futuros	BM&F	Brazil
Chicago Board of Trade	CBOT	USA
Chicago Board Options Exchange	CBOE	USA
Chicago Mercantile Exchange	CME	USA
Commodity and Monetary Exchange of Malaysia	COMMEX	Malaysia
French Futures & Options Exchange	MATIF	France
Hong Kong Futures Exchange	HKFE	Hong Kong
International Petroleum Exchange	IPE	London
International Securities Exchange	ISE	USA
Kansas City Board of Trade	KCBT	USA
Kuala Lumpur Options and Financial Futures Exchange	KLCE	Malaysia
London International Financial Futures and Options Exchange	LIFFE	London
London Metal Exchange	LME	London
Meff Renta Fija	MEFF	Spain
Meff Renta Variable	MEFF	Spain

(cont.)

APPENDIX C WORLD STOCK MARKETS

WORLD OPTIONS & FUTURES EXCHANGES

Options/Futures Exchange	Symbol	Location
MidAmerica Commodity Exchange	MidAm	USA
Minneapolis Grain Exchange	MGE	USA
Marche des Options Negociables de Paris	MONEP	France
New York Mercantile Exchange	NYMEX	USA
Osaka Securities Exchange	OSA	Japan
Russian Exchange	RE	Russia
Shanghai Metal Exchange	SHME	China
Singapore International Monetary Exchange	SIMEX	Singapore
South African Futures Exchange	SAFEX	South Africa
Sydney Futures Exchange Ltd.	SFE	Australia
Tokyo Commodity Exchange	TOCOM	Japan
Tokyo Grain Exchange	TGE	Japan
Tokyo International Financial Futures Exchange	TIFFE	Japan
Twin Cities Board of Trade	TCBT	USA
Winnipeg Commodity Exchange	WCE	Canada

Appendix D
Foreign Ticker Symbols

CBS MARKETWATCH
(*www.cbs.marketwatch.com*)

Currency	Symbol
AMERICAN DEPOSITARY RECEIPT INDEXES	
AMEX INTERNATIONAL MARKET	
BONY ADR ASIA	XX:1821233
BONY ADR COMPOSITE	XX:1821211
BONY ADR EMERGING MKTS	XX:1821330
BONY ADR EUROPE	XX:1821222
BONY ADR LATIN AMERICA	XX:1821244
NASDAQ ADR	XX:1800414
FOREIGN CURRENCY	
CBOE Australian Dollar	CAD
CBOE British Pound	CBP
CBOE Canadian Dollar	CCD
CBOE Deutsche Mark	CDM
CBOE French Franc	CFF
CBOE Japanese Yen	CJY
Currency Exchange Rate US $ for 100 Argentina $	23199058
Currency Exchange Rate US $ for 100 Australian $	23199007
Currency Exchange Rate US $ for 100 Austria $	23199008
Currency Exchange Rate US $ for 100 Bahrain $	23199034
Currency Exchange Rate US $ for 100 Belg Co $	23199009
Currency Exchange Rate US $ for 100 Belg Fi $	23199010
Currency Exchange Rate US $ for 100 Brazil $	23199059
Currency Exchange Rate US $ for 100 Chile $	23199035
Currency Exchange Rate US $ for 100 China $	23199036
Currency Exchange Rate US $ for 100 Colombia $	23199037
Currency Exchange Rate US $ for 100 Czech $	23199038
Currency Exchange Rate US $ for 100 Denmark $	23199011
Currency Exchange Rate US $ for 100 Dutch $	23199012
Currency Exchange Rate US $ for 100 Ecuador $	23199039
Currency Exchange Rate US $ for 100 Finland $	23199013
Currency Exchange Rate US $ for 100 Greece $	23199014
Currency Exchange Rate US $ for 100 Hong Kong $	23199015
Currency Exchange Rate US $ for 100 Hungary $	23199041
Currency Exchange Rate US $ for 100 India $	23199042
Currency Exchange Rate US $ for 100 Indonesia $	23199030

(*cont.*)

APPENDIX D FOREIGN TICKER SYMBOLS

Currency	Symbol
Currency Exchange Rate US $ for 100 Ireland $	23199016
Currency Exchange Rate US $ for 100 Kuwait $	23199044
Currency Exchange Rate US $ for 100 Lebanon $	23199045
Currency Exchange Rate US $ for 100 Malaysia $	23199028
Currency Exchange Rate US $ for 100 Malta $	23199046
Currency Exchange Rate US $ for 100 Mexico $	23199020
Currency Exchange Rate US $ for 100 New Zealand $	23199029
Currency Exchange Rate US $ for 100 Norway $	23199021
Currency Exchange Rate US $ for 100 Pakistan $	23199047
Currency Exchange Rate US $ for 100 Peru New $	23199033
Currency Exchange Rate US $ for 100 Philippines $	23199048
Currency Exchange Rate US $ for 100 Poland $	23199049
Currency Exchange Rate US $ for 100 Portugal $	23199022
Currency Exchange Rate US $ for 100 Russia $	23199050
Currency Exchange Rate US $ for 100 S Arab $	23199051
Currency Exchange Rate US $ for 100 S Korea $	23199053
Currency Exchange Rate US $ for 100 Singapore $	23199023
Currency Exchange Rate US $ for 100 Slovak $	23199052
Currency Exchange Rate US $ for 100 South Africa $	23199024
Currency Exchange Rate US $ for 100 Spain $	23199025
Currency Exchange Rate US $ for 100 Sweden $	23199026
Currency Exchange Rate US $ for 100 Taiwan $	23199031
Currency Exchange Rate US $ for 100 Thai $	23199032
Currency Exchange Rate US $ for 100 Turkey $	23199054
Currency Exchange Rate US $ for 100 U Arab $	23199055
Currency Exchange Rate US $ for 100 Uruguay $	23199056
Currency Exchange Rate US $ for 100 Venezuela $	23199057
PHLX AUSTRALIAN DOLLAR	
PHLX BRITISH LB/DEUTS MARK-PMX	
PHLX BRITISH POUND	
PHLX CANADIAN DOLLAR	
PHLX DEUTSCHE MARK/JAPAN YEN-MYX	
PHLX DEUTSCHE MARK	
PHLX EUROPEAN CURRENCY UT-AMER	
PHLX EUROPEAN CURRENCY UT-EURO	
PHLX FRENCH FRANC	
PHLX ITALIAN LIRA	
PHLX JAPANESE YEN	
PHLX SWISS FRANC	
Utd Kingdom BANK OF ENGLAND ATS	XX:1885143
Utd Kingdom BANK OF ENGLAND AUD	XX:1885176
Utd Kingdom BANK OF ENGLAND BEF	XX:1885079
Utd Kingdom BANK OF ENGLAND CAD	XX:1885068
Utd Kingdom BANK OF ENGLAND CHF	XX:1884957
Utd Kingdom BANK OF ENGLAND DEM	XX:1884979
Utd Kingdom BANK OF ENGLAND DKK	XX:1885132

(*cont.*)

APPENDIX D FOREIGN TICKER SYMBOLS

Currency	Symbol
Utd Kingdom BANK OF ENGLAND ESP	XX:1885024
Utd Kingdom BANK OF ENGLAND FIM	XX:1885154
Utd Kingdom BANK OF ENGLAND FRF	XX:1885080
Utd Kingdom BANK OF ENGLAND GRD	XX:1885046
Utd Kingdom BANK OF ENGLAND IEP	XX:1884991
Utd Kingdom BANK OF ENGLAND ITL	XX:1884968
Utd Kingdom BANK OF ENGLAND JPY	XX:1884946
Utd Kingdom BANK OF ENGLAND NLG	XX:1885091
Utd Kingdom BANK OF ENGLAND NOK	XX:1884980
Utd Kingdom BANK OF ENGLAND NZD	XX:1885057
Utd Kingdom BANK OF ENGLAND PTE	XX:1885165
Utd Kingdom BANK OF ENGLAND SEK	XX:1885121
Utd Kingdom BANK OF ENGLAND STERLING	XX:1800298
Utd Kingdom BANK OF ENGLAND USD	XX:1885035

FOREIGN BOND INDEXES

Jp Morgan GBI AUSTRALIA(GDY)	XX:1817191
Jp Morgan GBI AUSTRALIA(LC)(TR)	XX:1803811
Jp Morgan GBI AUSTRALIA(USD)(TR)	XX:1803907
Jp Morgan GBI BELGIUM(GDY)	XX:1817179
Jp Morgan GBI BELGIUM(LC)(TR)	XX:1801707
Jp Morgan GBI BELGIUM(USD)(TR)	XX:1803918
Jp Morgan GBI CANADA(GDY)	XX:1817210
Jp Morgan GBI CANADA(LC)(TR)	XX:1803833
Jp Morgan GBI CANADA(USD)(TR)	XX:1803929
Jp Morgan GBI DENMARK(GDY)	XX:1817180
Jp Morgan GBI DENMARK(LC)(TR)	XX:1803800
Jp Morgan GBI DENMARK(USD)(TR)	XX:1803930
Jp Morgan GBI EUROPE(LC)(TR)	XX:1803822
Jp Morgan GBI EUROPE(USD)(TR)	XX:1803974
Jp Morgan GBI FRANCE(GDY)	XX:1817168
Jp Morgan GBI FRANCE(LC)(TR)	XX:1801699
Jp Morgan GBI FRANCE(USD)(TR)	XX:1803941
Jp Morgan GBI GERMANY(GDY)	XX:1817146
Jp Morgan GBI GERMANY(LC)(TR)	XX:1801075
Jp Morgan GBI GERMANY(USD)(TR)	XX:1803952
Jp Morgan GBI GLOBAL(GDY)	XX:1817135
Jp Morgan GBI GLOBAL(LC)(TR)	XX:1801064
Jp Morgan GBI GLOBAL(USD)(TR)	XX:1804041
Jp Morgan GBI GLOBAL(X-UK)(GDY)	XX:1815269
Jp Morgan GBI GLOBAL(X-UK)(USD) (TR)	XX:1800771
Jp Morgan GBI GLOBAL(X-US)(USD) (TR)	XX:1804052
Jp Morgan GBI IRELAND(LC)(TR)	XX:1815054
Jp Morgan GBI IRELAND(USD)(TR)	XX:1815065
Jp Morgan GBI ITALY(GDY)	XX:1817221
Jp Morgan GBI ITALY(LC)(TR)	XX:1803844

(*cont.*)

APPENDIX D FOREIGN TICKER SYMBOLS

Indexes	Symbol
Jp Morgan GBI ITALY(USD)(TR)	XX:1803963
Jp Morgan GBI JAPAN(GDY)	XX:1817232
Jp Morgan GBI JAPAN(LC)(TR)	XX:1803855
Jp Morgan GBI JAPAN(USD)(TR)	XX:1803985
Jp Morgan GBI NETHERLANDS(GDY)	XX:1817157
Jp Morgan GBI NETHERLANDS(LC) (TR)	XX:1801655
Jp Morgan GBI NETHERLANDS(USD) (TR)	XX:1803996
Jp Morgan GBI NEW ZEALAND(LC) (TR)	XX:1815076
Jp Morgan GBI NEW ZEALAND(USD) (TR)	XX:1815087
Jp Morgan GBI SPAIN(GDY)	XX:1817243
Jp Morgan GBI SPAIN(LC)(TR)	XX:1803866
Jp Morgan GBI SPAIN(USD)(TR)	XX:1804007
Jp Morgan GBI SWEDEN(GDY)	XX:1817254
Jp Morgan GBI SWEDEN(LC)(TR)	XX:1803877
Jp Morgan GBI SWEDEN(USD)(TR)	XX:1804018
Jp Morgan GBI UTD KINGDOM(GDY)	XX:1817265
Jp Morgan GBI UTD KINGDOM(LC) (TR)	XX:1803888
Jp Morgan GBI UTD KINGDOM(USD) (TR)	XX:1804029
Jp Morgan GBI UTD STATES(GDY)	XX:1817276
Jp Morgan GBI UTD STATES(LC)(TR)	XX:1803899
Jp Morgan GBI UTD STATES(USD)(TR)	XX:1804030
SALOMON BROS INDEX WGBI 10 YR (LC)	XX:1800920
SALOMON BROS INDEX WGBI 10 YR (USD)	XX:1800931
SALOMON BROS INDEX WGBI AUSTRALIA (LC)	XX:1884162
SALOMON BROS INDEX WGBI AUSTRALIA (USD)	XX:1884173
SALOMON BROS INDEX WGBI AUSTRIA(LC)	XX:1884281
SALOMON BROS INDEX WGBI AUSTRIA(USD)	XX:1884292
SALOMON BROS INDEX WGBI BELGIUM(LC)	XX:1884184
SALOMON BROS INDEX WGBI BELGIUM(USD)	XX:1884195
SALOMON BROS INDEX WGBI CANADA(LC)	XX:1884128
SALOMON BROS INDEX WGBI CANADA(USD)	XX:1884139
SALOMON BROS INDEX WGBI DENMARK(LC)	XX:1884203
SALOMON BROS INDEX WGBI DENMARK (USD)	XX:1884214
SALOMON BROS INDEX WGBI EUROPE(LC)	XX:1811256
SALOMON BROS INDEX WGBI EUROPE(USD)	XX:1811267
SALOMON BROS INDEX WGBI FRANCE(LC)	XX:1884087
SALOMON BROS INDEX WGBI FRANCE(USD)	XX:1884098
SALOMON BROS INDEX WGBI GERMANY(LC)	XX:1884065
SALOMON BROS INDEX WGBI GERMANY (USD)	XX:1884076
SALOMON BROS INDEX WGBI ITALY(LC)	XX:1884140
SALOMON BROS INDEX WGBI ITALY(USD)	XX:1884151
SALOMON BROS INDEX WGBI JAPAN(LC)	XX:1884043

(cont.)

APPENDIX D FOREIGN TICKER SYMBOLS

Indexes	Symbol
SALOMON BROS INDEX WGBI JAPAN(USD)	XX:1884054
SALOMON BROS INDEX WGBI NETHERLANDS (LC)	XX:1884225
SALOMON BROS INDEX WGBI NETHERLANDS (USD)	XX:1884236
SALOMON BROS INDEX WGBI NON-JPY(USD)	XX:1883590
SALOMON BROS INDEX WGBI NON-USD OVER 10 YR(LC)	XX:1811074
SALOMON BROS INDEX WGBI NON-USD OVER 10 YR(US)	XX:1811245
SALOMON BROS INDEX WGBI NON-USD(LC)	XX:1884010
SALOMON BROS INDEX WGBI NON-USD(USD)	XX:1884021
SALOMON BROS INDEX WGBI SPAIN(LC)	XX:1884247
SALOMON BROS INDEX WGBI SPAIN(USD)	XX:1884258
SALOMON BROS INDEX WGBI SWEDEN(LC)	XX:1884269
SALOMON BROS INDEX WGBI SWEDEN(USD)	XX:1884270
SALOMON BROS INDEX WGBI SWITZERLAND (LC)	XX:1816400
SALOMON BROS INDEX WGBI SWITZERLAND (USD)	XX:1816411
SALOMON BROS INDEX WGBI UTD KINGDOM (LC)	XX:1884106
SALOMON BROS INDEX WGBI UTD KINGDOM (USD)	XX:1884117
SALOMON BROS INDEX WGBI(LC)	XX:1810316
SALOMON BROS INDEX WGBI(USD)	XX:1810305
Ubs Benchmark Bond AUSTRALIA(USD)(TR)	XX:1800533
Ubs Benchmark Bond BELGIUM(EUR)(TR)	XX:1800845
Ubs Benchmark Bond BELGIUM(USD)(TR)	XX:1800481
Ubs Benchmark Bond CANADA(USD)(TR)	XX:1800492
Ubs Benchmark Bond DENMARK(EUR)(TR)	XX:1800889
Ubs Benchmark Bond DENMARK(USD)(TR)	XX:1800544
Ubs Benchmark Bond EURO(EUR)(TR)	XX:1800908
Ubs Benchmark Bond EURO(USD)(TR)	XX:1800265
Ubs Benchmark Bond EUROPE(EUR)(TR)	XX:1800038
Ubs Benchmark Bond FINLAND(EUR)(TR)	XX:1800953
Ubs Benchmark Bond FINLAND(USD)(TR)	XX:1800577
Ubs Benchmark Bond FRANCE(EUR)(TR)	XX:1800674
Ubs Benchmark Bond FRANCE(USD)(TR)	XX:1800113
Ubs Benchmark Bond GERMANY(EUR)(TR)	XX:1800652
Ubs Benchmark Bond GERMANY(USD)(TR)	XX:1800555
Ubs Benchmark Bond GLOBAL(USD)(TR)	XX:1876073
Ubs Benchmark Bond IRELAND(EUR)(TR)	XX:1800919
Ubs Benchmark Bond IRELAND(USD)(TR)	XX:1800522
Ubs Benchmark Bond ITALY(EUR)(TR)	XX:1800704
Ubs Benchmark Bond ITALY(USD)(TR)	XX:1800317

(cont.)

APPENDIX D FOREIGN TICKER SYMBOLS

Indexes	Symbol
Ubs Benchmark Bond JAPAN(USD)(TR)	XX:1800061
Ubs Benchmark Bond NETHERLANDS(EUR)(TR)	XX:1800726
Ubs Benchmark Bond NETHERLANDS(USD)(TR)	XX:1800340
Ubs Benchmark Bond NEW ZEALAND(USD)(TR)	XX:1800588
Ubs Benchmark Bond NORWAY(EUR)(TR)	XX:1800942
Ubs Benchmark Bond NORWAY(USD)(TR)	XX:1800566
Ubs Benchmark Bond SPAIN(EUR)(TR)	XX:1800715
Ubs Benchmark Bond SPAIN(USD)(TR)	XX:1800328
Ubs Benchmark Bond SWEDEN(EUR)(TR)	XX:1800878
Ubs Benchmark Bond SWEDEN(USD)(TR)	XX:1800500
Ubs Benchmark Bond SWITZERLAND(EUR)(TR)	XX:1800696
Ubs Benchmark Bond SWITZERLAND(USD)(TR)	XX:1800243
Ubs Benchmark Bond UTD KINGDOM(EUR)(TR)	XX:1800685
Ubs Benchmark Bond UTD KINGDOM(USD)(TR)	XX:1800254
Ubs Benchmark Bond UTD STATES(USD)(TR)	XX:1800049

FOREIGN STOCK INDEXES—GENERAL

AMEX EUROPE TOP 100	
AMEX HONG KONG 30	
AMEX INTL MARKET	XX:1807965
AMEX JAPAN	
AMEX MEXICO	
CBOE ASIA 100	XX:1819658
CBOE IPC (MEXICO)	XX:1819636
CBOE ISRAELI INDEX	
CBOE LATIN 15	XX:1819669
CBOE MEXICO	
CBOE NIKKEI 300 INDEX	
DOW JONES TAIWAN	
DOW JONES WORLD STOCK	XX:1819841
VALUE LINE EUROPEAN INDEX	

FOREIGN STOCK INDEXES—DETAILED

Australia ASX 100	XX:1800276
Australia ASX 100 INDUSTRIALS	XX:1881367
Australia ASX 100 INDUSTRIALS(ACC)	XX:1881378
Australia ASX 100 RESOURCES	XX:1881345
Australia ASX 100 RESOURCES(ACC)	XX:1881356
Australia ASX 100(ACC)	XX:1881118
Australia ASX 20 LEADERS	XX:1801428
Australia ASX 20 LEADERS(ACC)	XX:1801451
Australia ASX 50 LEADERS	XX:1805204
Australia ASX 50 LEADERS(ACC)	XX:1801291
Australia ASX ALCOHOL & TOBACCO	XX:1807738
Australia ASX ALCOHOL & TOBACCO(ACC)	XX:1807749

(*cont.*)

APPENDIX D FOREIGN TICKER SYMBOLS

Indexes	Symbol
Australia ASX ALL INDUSTRIALS	XX:1803361
Australia ASX ALL INDUSTRIALS(ACC)	XX:1801309
Australia ASX ALL MINING	XX:1803350
Australia ASX ALL MINING(ACC)	XX:1800210
Australia ASX ALL ORD(X-100)INDS	XX:1881141
Australia ASX ALL ORD(X-100)INDS(ACC)	XX:1881152
Australia ASX ALL ORDINARIES	XX:1803349
Australia ASX ALL ORDINARIES(ACC)	XX:1801365
Australia ASX ALL ORDS(X-100)	XX:1881389
Australia ASX ALL ORDS(X-100)(ACC)	XX:1881390
Australia ASX ALL ORDS(X-100)RES	XX:1881408
Australia ASX ALL ORDS(X-100)RES(ACC)	XX:1881419
Australia ASX ALL RESOURCES	XX:1803372
Australia ASX ALL RESOURCES(ACC)	XX:1801310
Australia ASX ASIAN	XX:1885819
Australia ASX ASIAN(ACC)	XX:1885820
Australia ASX BANCASSURANCE	XX:1819498
Australia ASX BANCASSURANCE(ACC)	XX:1819506
Australia ASX BANKS & FINANCE	XX:1801031
Australia ASX BANKS & FINANCE(ACC)	XX:1801321
Australia ASX BUILDING MATLS	XX:1800964
Australia ASX BUILDING MATLS(ACC)	XX:1801194
Australia ASX CHEMICALS	XX:1801097
Australia ASX CHEMICALS(ACC)	XX:1801224
Australia ASX DEV & CONTRACTORS	XX:1800599
Australia ASX DEV & CONTRACTORS(ACC)	XX:1801172
Australia ASX DIVD.INDUSTRIAL	XX:1801417
Australia ASX DIVD.INDUSTRIAL(ACC)	XX:1801462
Australia ASX DIVERS.RESOURCES	XX:1801138
Australia ASX DIVERS.RESOURCES(ACC)	XX:1801268
Australia ASX ENERGY	XX:1803383
Australia ASX ENERGY(ACC)	XX:1801161
Australia ASX ENGINEERING	XX:1801086
Australia ASX ENGINEERING(ACC)	XX:1801235
Australia ASX FOOD & H/HLD GOODS	XX:1800975
Australia ASX FOOD & H/HLD GOODS(ACC)	XX:1801202
Australia ASX GOLD	XX:1801149
Australia ASX GOLD(ACC)	XX:1801279
Australia ASX H/CARE & BIOTECH	XX:1857391
Australia ASX H/CARE & BIOTECH(ACC)	XX:1857432
Australia ASX INFRASTRUCT & UTIL	XX:1815894
Australia ASX INFRASTRUCT & UTIL(ACC)	XX:1857357
Australia ASX INSURANCE	XX:1801020
Australia ASX INSURANCE(ACC)	XX:1801332
Australia ASX INV & FINL SVCS	XX:1801376
Australia ASX INV & FINL SVCS(ACC)	XX:1801440

(cont.)

APPENDIX D FOREIGN TICKER SYMBOLS

Indexes	Symbol
Australia ASX MEDIA	XX:1801116
Australia ASX MEDIA(ACC)	XX:1801246
Australia ASX MIDCAP 50	XX:1881282
Australia ASX MIDCAP 50(ACC)	XX:1881293
Australia ASX MIDCAP INDUSTRIALS	XX:1881323
Australia ASX MIDCAP INDUSTRIALS(ACC)	XX:1881334
Australia ASX MIDCAP RESOURCES	XX:1881301
Australia ASX MIDCAP RESOURCES(ACC)	XX:1881312
Australia ASX MISC INDUSTRIALS	XX:1801406
Australia ASX MISC INDUSTRIALS(ACC)	XX:1801473
Australia ASX OTHER METALS	XX:1801398
Australia ASX OTHER METALS(ACC)	XX:1800209
Australia ASX PAPER & PACKAGING	XX:1801042
Australia ASX PAPER & PACKAGING(ACC)	XX:1801280
Australia ASX PROPERTY	XX:1801127
Australia ASX PROPERTY(ACC)	XX:1801257
Australia ASX RETAIL	XX:1800986
Australia ASX RETAIL(ACC)	XX:1801343
Australia ASX TELECOMMUNICATIONS	XX:1850000
Australia ASX TELECOMMUNICATIONS(ACC)	XX:1857379
Australia ASX TOURISM & LEISURE	XX:1881129
Australia ASX TOURISM & LEISURE(ACC)	XX:1881130
Australia ASX TRANS TASMAN 100	XX:1850044
Australia ASX TRANS TASMAN 100 (ACC)	XX:1819487
Australia ASX TRANSPORT	XX:1801105
Australia ASX TRANSPORT(ACC)	XX:1801354
Australia ASX/RUSSELL ALL GROWTH	XX:1816154
Australia ASX/RUSSELL ALL GROWTH(ACC)	XX:1816217
Australia ASX/RUSSELL ALL VALUE	XX:1816143
Australia ASX/RUSSELL ALL VALUE(ACC)	XX:1816206
Australia ASX/RUSSELL GROWTH 100	XX:1816176
Australia ASX/RUSSELL GROWTH 100 (ACC)	XX:1816239
Australia ASX/RUSSELL SMALL GRTH	XX:1816198
Australia ASX/RUSSELL SMALL GRTH(ACC)	XX:1816251
Australia ASX/RUSSELL SMALL VAL	XX:1816187
Australia ASX/RUSSELL SMALL VAL(ACC)	XX:1816240
Australia ASX/RUSSELL VALUE 100	XX:1816165
Australia ASX/RUSSELL VALUE 100(ACC)	XX:1816228
Austria ATX	XX:1889316
Austria ATX 50	XX:1816455
Austria ATX MIDCAP	XX:1816466
Austria CA-BV BOND	XX:1801570
Austria CA-BV SHARE	XX:1803413
Austria WBK REAL ESTATE	XX:1806434
Bahrain BSE BANKS	XX:1884474

(cont.)

APPENDIX D FOREIGN TICKER SYMBOLS

Indexes	Symbol
Bahrain BSE COMPOSITE	XX:1889112
Bahrain BSE HOTELS & TOURISM	XX:1884797
Bahrain BSE INDUSTRIAL	XX:1884786
Bahrain BSE INSURANCE	XX:1884764
Bahrain BSE INVESTMENT	XX:1884526
Bahrain BSE SERVICES	XX:1884775
Belgium ALLERLEI DIENSTEN	XX:1850215
Belgium ALLERLEI INDUSTRIEEN	XX:1850226
Belgium BANKS	XX:1850066
Belgium BEL-20	XX:1889286
Belgium BEL-20(INSTITUTIONAL)	XX:1810004
Belgium BEL-20(PRIVATE)	XX:1800663
Belgium B-GOLD	XX:1800157
Belgium B-GOLD(SETTLEMENT)	XX:1850055
Belgium B-GOLD(TR)	XX:1800168
Belgium BOUW	XX:1850077
Belgium BSE ALL SHARE	XX:1803424
Belgium BSE ALL SHARE(TR)	XX:1803435
Belgium BSE FORWARD(DOMESTIC)	XX:1801592
Belgium BSE FORWARD(FOREIGN)	XX:1805215
Belgium CHEMICALS	XX:1850088
Belgium DISTRIBUTIE	XX:1850099
Belgium ELECTRICITY & GAS	XX:1850107
Belgium HOLDINGS	XX:1850118
Belgium IN VEREFFENING/TIJDELIJKE	XX:1850129
Belgium METAAL-ELECTRONICA	XX:1850130
Belgium MID CAPS CASH	XX:1800403
Belgium NON-FERRO	XX:1850141
Belgium PETROLEUM	XX:1850152
Belgium SMALL CAPS CASH	XX:1800050
Belgium STAAL	XX:1850163
Belgium TROPISCHE	XX:1850174
Belgium VASTGOED	XX:1850185
Belgium VERZ. & FIN. DIENSTEN	XX:1850260
Belgium VERZEKERINGEN	XX:1850196
Belgium VLAM21	XX:1800306
Belgium VOEDING	XX:1850204
Brazil BOVESPA	XX:1802647
Brazil IBV	XX:1802807
Canada TSE 100	XX:1811472
Canada TSE 35	XX:1801666
Canada TSE COMMUNICATIONS & MEDIA	XX:1800005
Canada TSE COMPOSITE(300)	XX:1804524
Canada TSE CONSUMER PRODUCTS	XX:1807976
Canada TSE FINANCIAL SERVICES	XX:1800027

(cont.)

APPENDIX D FOREIGN TICKER SYMBOLS

Indexes	Symbol
Canada TSE GOLD	XX:1800094
Canada TSE INDUSTRIAL PRODUCTS	XX:1801600
Canada TSE MERCHANDISING	XX:1800124
Canada TSE METALS & MINERALS	XX:1800180
Canada TSE MGMT COMPANIES	XX:1800191
Canada TSE OIL & GAS	XX:1805828
Canada TSE PAPER & FOREST PRODUCTS	XX:1805839
Canada TSE PIPELINES	XX:1801611
Canada TSE REAL ESTATE	XX:1805840
Canada TSE TRANSPORT	XX:1801622
Canada TSE UTILITIES	XX:1801633
China SHANGHAI SE 30	XX:1838749
China SHANGHAI SE A SHARE	XX:1801730
China SHANGHAI SE ALL SHARE	XX:1801677
China SHANGHAI SE B SHARE	XX:1801815
China SHANGHAI SE COMMERCE	XX:1838750
China SHANGHAI SE COMPOSITE	XX:1838664
China SHANGHAI SE INDUSTRIAL	XX:1838772
China SHANGHAI SE PROPERTY	XX:1838738
China SHANGHAI SE UTILITY	XX:1838761
China SHENZHEN SE A SHARE	XX:1801718
China SHENZHEN SE A SHARE SUB	XX:1838642
China SHENZHEN SE B SHARE	XX:1801729
China SHENZHEN SE B SHARE SUB	XX:1838697
China SHENZHEN SE COMMERCIAL	XX:1838675
China SHENZHEN SE COMPOSITE	XX:1801688
China SHENZHEN SE COMPOSITE SUB	XX:1838727
China SHENZHEN SE CONGLOMERATE	XX:1838653
China SHENZHEN SE FINANCIAL	XX:1838631
China SHENZHEN SE INDUSTRIAL	XX:1838686
China SHENZHEN SE PROPERTY	XX:1838716
China SHENZHEN SE UTILITY	XX:1838705
Czech Republic PSE AGRICULTURE	XX:1815935
Czech Republic PSE BEVERAGE & TOBACCO	XX:1815957
Czech Republic PSE BUILDING	XX:1816002
Czech Republic PSE CHEMICAL PHARM & RUBBER	XX:1815991
Czech Republic PSE ELECTRICAL ENG ELECTRON	XX:1816035
Czech Republic PSE ENERGY	XX:1816046
Czech Republic PSE FINANCE & BANKING	XX:1816079
Czech Republic PSE FOOD PRODUCTION	XX:1815946
Czech Republic PSE INVESTMENT FUNDS	XX:1816109
Czech Republic PSE JEWELLERY GLASS&CERAM	XX:1816091

(cont.)

APPENDIX D FOREIGN TICKER SYMBOLS

Indexes	Symbol
Czech Republic PSE MECHANICAL ENGINEERING	XX:1816024
Czech Republic PSE METALLURGY	XX:1816013
Czech Republic PSE MINING	XX:1815968
Czech Republic PSE OTHERS	XX:1816110
Czech Republic PSE PX-50	XX:1884601
Czech Republic PSE PX-D	XX:1819562
Czech Republic PSE PX-GLOB	XX:1816132
Czech Republic PSE SERVICES	XX:1816080
Czech Republic PSE TEXTILES	XX:1815979
Czech Republic PSE TRADE	XX:1816068
Czech Republic PSE TRANSPORTATION	XX:1816057
Czech Republic PSE WOOD & PAPER	XX:1815980
Denmark CSE ALL SHARE	XX:1804535
Denmark CSE BANKS	XX:1801741
Denmark CSE INDUSTRY	XX:1801785
Denmark CSE INSURANCE	XX:1801752
Denmark CSE SHIPPING	XX:1801774
Denmark FUTOP BOND	XX:1862340
Denmark KFX	XX:1801804
Egypt CAIRO SE GENERAL	XX:1814181
Estonia EVK	XX:1815258
Estonia TALSE	XX:1887451
Euro Nm BELGIUM(PERF)	XX:1894967
Finland FOX	XX:1854198
Finland FOX	XX:1801837
Finland HEX 20	XX:1801848
Finland HEX 20(YLD)	XX:1877452
Finland HEX BANKS & FINANCE	XX:1801860
Finland HEX BANKS & FINANCE(YLD)	XX:1877474
Finland HEX CHEMICALS	XX:1887622
Finland HEX CHEMICALS(YLD)	XX:1887633
Finland HEX CONSTRUCTION	XX:1887514
Finland HEX CONSTRUCTION(YLD)	XX:1887525
Finland HEX ENERGY	XX:1887536
Finland HEX ENERGY(YLD)	XX:1887547
Finland HEX FOOD INDUSTRY	XX:1887495
Finland HEX FOOD INDUSTRY(YLD)	XX:1887503
Finland HEX FOREST INDUSTRY	XX:1801912
Finland HEX FOREST INDUSTRY(YLD)	XX:1877526
Finland HEX GENERAL	XX:1805538
Finland HEX GENERAL(YLD)	XX:1877441
Finland HEX INSURANCE	XX:1801871
Finland HEX INSURANCE(YLD)	XX:1877485
Finland HEX INVESTMENT	XX:1887569

(cont.)

APPENDIX D FOREIGN TICKER SYMBOLS

Indexes	Symbol
Finland HEX INVESTMENT(YLD)	XX:1887570
Finland HEX LIST	XX:1810446
Finland HEX LIST(YLD)	XX:1810190
Finland HEX MEDIA & PUBLISHING	XX:1887581
Finland HEX MEDIA & PUBLISHING(YLD)	XX:1887592
Finland HEX METAL & ENGINEERING	XX:1801901
Finland HEX METAL & ENGINEERING(YLD)	XX:1877515
Finland HEX MULTI-BUSINESS	XX:1809961
Finland HEX MULTI-BUSINESS	XX:1801923
Finland HEX MULTI-BUSINESS(YLD)	XX:1877537
Finland HEX NEW MARKET	XX:1810435
Finland HEX NEW MARKET(YLD)	XX:1810413
Finland HEX OTHER INDUSTRIES	XX:1801934
Finland HEX OTHER INDUSTRIES(YLD)	XX:1877548
Finland HEX OTHER SERVICES	XX:1887600
Finland HEX OTHER SERVICES	XX:1801882
Finland HEX OTHER SERVICES(YLD)	XX:1887611
Finland HEX OTHER SERVICES(YLD)	XX:1877496
Finland HEX PORTFOLIO	XX:1886760
Finland HEX PORTFOLIO(YLD)	XX:1886771
Finland HEX TELECOM & ELEC	XX:1887644
Finland HEX TELECOM & ELEC(YLD)	XX:1887655
Finland HEX TRADE	XX:1809905
Finland HEX TRADE(YLD)	XX:1809950
Finland HEX TRANSPORT	XX:1887666
Finland HEX TRANSPORT(YLD)	XX:1887677
France CAC 40	XX:1804546
France MID CAC	XX:1805806
France SBF 120	XX:1876415
France SBF 250	XX:1876404
France SBF 250 FINANCIALS	XX:1876716
France SBF 250 INDUSTRIALS	XX:1876738
France SBF 250 SERVICES	XX:1876493
France SBF 80	XX:1876545
France SBF AGRIFOOD	XX:1876482
France SBF AUTOMOTIVE	XX:1876460
France SBF CAPITAL GOODS	XX:1876459
France SBF CONSTRUCTION	XX:1876448
France SBF CONSUMER GOODS	XX:1876471
France SBF ENERGY	XX:1876426
France SBF FINANCIAL COS	XX:1876523
France SBF INTERMEDIATE GOODS	XX:1876437
France SBF INVESTMENT COS	XX:1876727
France SBF OTHER SERVICES	XX:1876512
France SBF REAL ESTATE	XX:1876705

(cont.)

APPENDIX D FOREIGN TICKER SYMBOLS

Indexes	Symbol
France SBF RETAILING	XX:1876501
France SBF SECOND MARKET	XX:1876749
Germany DAX	XX:1805969
Germany DAX	XX:1804579
Germany DAX 100	XX:1802142
Germany DAX 100 AUTO/TPT	XX:1815526
Germany DAX 100 AUTO/TPT BEST ASK	XX:1816541
Germany DAX 100 AUTO/TPT BEST BID	XX:1816530
Germany DAX 100 AUTO/TPT(PERF)	XX:1816552
Germany DAX 100 AUTO/TPT(PERF)	XX:1815270
Germany DAX 100 BANKS	XX:1815560
Germany DAX 100 BANKS BEST ASK	XX:1816820
Germany DAX 100 BANKS BEST BID	XX:1816819
Germany DAX 100 BANKS(PERF)	XX:1816585
Germany DAX 100 BANKS(PERF)	XX:1815463
Germany DAX 100 BEST ASK	XX:1816529
Germany DAX 100 BEST BID	XX:1816518
Germany DAX 100 CHEM/PHARM	XX:1815548
Germany DAX 100 CHEM/PHARM BEST ASK	XX:1816789
Germany DAX 100 CHEM/PHARM BEST BID	XX:1816778
Germany DAX 100 CHEM/PHARM(PERF)	XX:1816563
Germany DAX 100 CHEM/PHARM(PERF)	XX:1815292
Germany DAX 100 CONSTRUCTION(PERF)	XX:1816831
Germany DAX 100 CONSTRUCTION	XX:1815537
Germany DAX 100 CONSTRUCTION BEST ASK	XX:1816767
Germany DAX 100 CONSTRUCTION BEST BID	XX:1816756
Germany DAX 100 CONSTRUCTION(PERF)	XX:1815281
Germany DAX 100 ELECTRICAL(PERF)	XX:1815452
Germany DAX 100 INSURANCE	XX:1815601
Germany DAX 100 INSURANCE BEST ASK	XX:1816660
Germany DAX 100 INSURANCE BEST BID	XX:1816659
Germany DAX 100 INSURANCE(PERF)	XX:1816626
Germany DAX 100 INSURANCE(PERF)	XX:1815504
Germany DAX 100 MACHINERY	XX:1815571
Germany DAX 100 MACHINERY BEST ASK	XX:1816701
Germany DAX 100 MACHINERY BEST BID	XX:1816693
Germany DAX 100 MACHINERY(PERF)	XX:1816596
Germany DAX 100 MACHINERY(PERF)	XX:1815474
Germany DAX 100 RETAIL	XX:1815612
Germany DAX 100 RETAIL(PERF)	XX:1816637
Germany DAX 100 RETAIL(PERF)	XX:1815515
Germany DAX 100 SOFT/TECH	XX:1815559
Germany DAX 100 SOFT/TECH BEST ASK	XX:1816808
Germany DAX 100 SOFT/TECH BEST BID	XX:1816790

(cont.)

APPENDIX D FOREIGN TICKER SYMBOLS

Indexes	Symbol
Germany DAX 100 SOFT/TECH(PERF)	XX:1816574
Germany DAX 100 STEEL	XX:1815593
Germany DAX 100 STEEL BEST ASK	XX:1816745
Germany DAX 100 STEEL BEST BID	XX:1816734
Germany DAX 100 STEEL(PERF)	XX:1816615
Germany DAX 100 STEEL(PERF)	XX:1815496
Germany DAX 100 TRD & RTL BEST ASK	XX:1816682
Germany DAX 100 TRD & RTL BEST BID	XX:1816671
Germany DAX 100 UTILITIES	XX:1815582
Germany DAX 100 UTILITIES BEST ASK	XX:1816723
Germany DAX 100 UTILITIES BEST BID	XX:1816712
Germany DAX 100 UTILITIES(PERF)	XX:1816604
Germany DAX 100 UTILITIES(PERF)	XX:1815485
Germany DAX 100(PERF)	XX:1816648
Germany DAX BEST ASK	XX:1816477
Germany DAX BEST BID	XX:1816488
Germany DAX(200 DAY MVG AVE)	XX:1802175
Germany DAX(40 DAY MVG AVE)	XX:1802164
Germany DAX(PERF)	XX:1876534
Hong Kong HANG SENG	XX:1804580
Hong Kong HANG SENG 100	XX:1896208
Hong Kong HANG SENG ASIA	XX:1815924
Hong Kong HANG SENG CHINA AFFILIATED	XX:1887332
Hong Kong HANG SENG CHINA ENTERPRISES	XX:1876653
Hong Kong HANG SENG COMM & INDY	XX:1802238
Hong Kong HANG SENG COMM & IND SUBINDEX	XX:1813218
Hong Kong HANG SENG FINANCE	XX:1802250
Hong Kong HANG SENG FINANCE SUBINDEX	XX:1813207
Hong Kong HANG SENG LONDON REFERENCE	XX:1800362
Hong Kong HANG SENG MIDCAP 50	XX:1808924
Hong Kong HANG SENG PROPERTIES	XX:1802272
Hong Kong HANG SENG PROPERTY SUBINDEX	XX:1813229
Hong Kong HANG SENG UTILITIES	XX:1802261
Hong Kong HANG SENG UTILITY SUBINDEX	XX:1813230
Hong Kong HKSE 30	XX:1802324
Hong Kong HKSE ALL ORDINARIES	XX:1805282
Hong Kong HKSE CONSD ENTERPRISES	XX:1802283
Hong Kong HKSE FINANCIALS	XX:1802294
Hong Kong HKSE HOTELS	XX:1802302
Hong Kong HKSE INDUSTRIALS	XX:1802313
Hong Kong HKSE MISCELLANEOUS	XX:1865372
Hong Kong HKSE PROPERTIES	XX:1802335
Hong Kong HKSE UTILITIES	XX:1802346
Hungary BUX	XX:1802755

(cont.)

APPENDIX D FOREIGN TICKER SYMBOLS

Indexes	Symbol
Iceland ICEX 15	XX:1841941
Iceland ICEX ALL SHARES	XX:1887268
Iceland ICEX CONSTRUCTION	XX:1841985
Iceland ICEX EQUITY FUNDS & INV COS	XX:1887279
Iceland ICEX FINANCE & INSURANCE	XX:1842007
Iceland ICEX FISHERIES	XX:1887280
Iceland ICEX GROWTH LIST	XX:1841963
Iceland ICEX INDUSTRY & MANUFACT	XX:1887309
Iceland ICEX INFORMATION TECHNOLOGY	XX:1841974
Iceland ICEX MAIN LIST	XX:1841952
Iceland ICEX OIL DISTRIBUTION	XX:1887321
Iceland ICEX PHARMACEUTICAL	XX:1841996
Iceland ICEX SERVICES & COMMERCE	XX:1887291
Iceland ICEX TRANSPORT	XX:1887310
India BSE 100	XX:1803543
India BSE 200	XX:1801514
India BSE DOLLEX	XX:1801525
India BSE SENSEX (BSE30)	XX:1803532
Indonesia JSX AGRICULTURE	XX:1887343
Indonesia JSX BASIC INDUSTRY	XX:1887365
Indonesia JSX COMPOSITE	XX:1803554
Indonesia JSX CONS GOOD IND	XX:1887387
Indonesia JSX FINANCE	XX:1887417
Indonesia JSX INFRASTRUCTURE	XX:1887406
Indonesia JSX LQ45	XX:1887440
Indonesia JSX MANUFACTURE	XX:1887439
Indonesia JSX MINING	XX:1887354
Indonesia JSX MISC INDUSTRY	XX:1887376
Indonesia JSX PROPERTY	XX:1887398
Indonesia JSX TRADE	XX:1887428
Ireland DAVY	XX:1803673
Ireland ISE FINANCIAL	XX:1803725
Ireland ISE FINANCIAL(TR)	XX:1818406
Ireland ISE GENERAL	XX:1803736
Ireland ISE GENERAL(TR)	XX:1818417
Ireland ISE OVERALL	XX:1803714
Ireland ISE OVERALL(TR)	XX:1818398
Ireland RIADA GILT TOT CML(ALL)	XX:1815913
Ireland RIADA GILT TOT CML(OV 15 YR)	XX:1815902
Ireland RIADA GILT TOT CML(OV 5 YR)	XX:1818332
Ireland RIADA GILT XD(ALL STKS)	XX:1803770
Ireland RIADA GILT XD(OVER 15 YR)	XX:1803769
Ireland RIADA GILT XD(OVER 5 YR)	XX:1818321
Ireland RIADA GILT(5–15 YR)	XX:1800618
Ireland RIADA GILT(ALL STKS)	XX:1803758

(cont.)

APPENDIX D FOREIGN TICKER SYMBOLS

Indexes	Symbol
Ireland RIADA GILT(OVER 10 YR)	XX:1800436
Ireland RIADA GILT(OVER 15 YR)	XX:1803747
Ireland RIADA GILT(OVER 5 YR)	XX:1800425
Ireland RIADA GILT(UNDER 5 YR)	XX:1800458
Israel TA-100	XX:1884407
Israel TA-25	XX:1884418
Israel TACT	XX:1892938
Italy BCI COMIT-30	XX:1806014
Italy BCI GENERAL	XX:1804591
Italy MIB 30	XX:1800016
Italy MIB 30 R	XX:1885529
Italy MIB BANKS(CUR)	XX:1885477
Italy MIB BANKS(HIST)	XX:1885745
Italy MIB BUILDING(CUR)	XX:1885392
Italy MIB BUILDING(HIST)	XX:1885660
Italy MIB CHEMICALS(CUR)	XX:1885325
Italy MIB CHEMICALS(HIST)	XX:1885659
Italy MIB ELECTRONICS & ENG(CUR)	XX:1885400
Italy MIB ELECTRONICS & ENG(HIST)	XX:1885671
Italy MIB FINANCIAL COS(CUR)	XX:1885455
Italy MIB FINANCIAL COS(HIST)	XX:1885723
Italy MIB FINANCIAL SVS(CUR)	XX:1885518
Italy MIB FINANCIAL SVS(HIST)	XX:1885789
Italy MIB FOOD MFG(CUR)	XX:1885295
Italy MIB FOOD MFG(HIST)	XX:1885604
Italy MIB GENERAL(CUR)	XX:1806003
Italy MIB GENERAL(HIST)	XX:1892110
Italy MIB HOLDING COS(CUR)	XX:1885488
Italy MIB HOLDING COS(HIST)	XX:1885756
Italy MIB INDUSTRIALS(CUR)	XX:1885284
Italy MIB INDUSTRIALS(HIST)	XX:1885596
Italy MIB INSURANCE COS(CUR)	XX:1885466
Italy MIB INSURANCE COS(HIST)	XX:1885734
Italy MIB MEDIA(CUR)	XX:1885251
Italy MIB MEDIA(HIST)	XX:1885563
Italy MIB METALS MIN & OIL(CUR)	XX:1885433
Italy MIB METALS MIN & OIL(HIST)	XX:1885701
Italy MIB MISC FINL SVS(CUR)	XX:1885499
Italy MIB MISC FINL SVS(HIST)	XX:1885767
Italy MIB MISC INDUSTRIALS(CUR)	XX:1885422
Italy MIB MISC INDUSTRIALS(HIST)	XX:1885693
Italy MIB MOTORCARS(CUR)	XX:1885303
Italy MIB MOTORCARS(HIST)	XX:1885615
Italy MIB PAPER(CUR)	XX:1885314
Italy MIB PAPER(HIST)	XX:1885626

(cont.)

APPENDIX D FOREIGN TICKER SYMBOLS

Indexes	Symbol
Italy MIB PLANT & MACH(CUR)	XX:1885411
Italy MIB PLANT & MACH(HIST)	XX:1885682
Italy MIB PUBLIC SVS(CUR)	XX:1885262
Italy MIB PUBLIC UTILITIES(HIST)	XX:1885574
Italy MIB REAL ESTATE(CUR)	XX:1885507
Italy MIB REAL ESTATE(HIST)	XX:1885778
Italy MIB RETAIL(CUR)	XX:1885240
Italy MIB RETAIL(HIST)	XX:1885552
Italy MIB RNC(HIST)	XX:1885530
Italy MIB SERVICES(CUR)	XX:1885239
Italy MIB SERVICES(HIST)	XX:1885541
Italy MIB TEXT CLOTH & ACC(CUR)	XX:1885444
Italy MIB TEXT CLOTH & ACC(HIST)	XX:1885712
Italy MIB TRANSP/TOURISM(CUR)	XX:1885273
Italy MIB TRANSP/TOURISM(HIST)	XX:1885585
Italy MIBTEL	XX:1884753
Italy MIDEX	XX:1897955
Japan JASDAQ	XX:1810480
Japan JASDAQ CB	XX:1803402
Japan JASDAQ(ARITHMETIC)	XX:1810383
Japan JASDAQ(WEIGHTED)	XX:1810338
Japan NIKKEI AIR TRANSPORTATION	XX:1802959
Japan NIKKEI AUTO	XX:1802960
Japan NIKKEI AVERAGE(225)	XX:1804610
Japan NIKKEI AVERAGE(300)	XX:1885002
Japan NIKKEI AVERAGE(500)	XX:1802948
Japan NIKKEI BANKS	XX:1802971
Japan NIKKEI CHEMICALS	XX:1802982
Japan NIKKEI COMMUNICATIONS	XX:1802993
Japan NIKKEI CONSTRUCTION	XX:1804803
Japan NIKKEI DRUGS	XX:1804814
Japan NIKKEI ELECTRIC APPL.	XX:1804825
Japan NIKKEI ELECTRICITY	XX:1804836
Japan NIKKEI FISHERY	XX:1804847
Japan NIKKEI FOODS	XX:1804858
Japan NIKKEI GAS	XX:1804869
Japan NIKKEI GLASS & CERAMICS	XX:1804870
Japan NIKKEI INSURANCE	XX:1804881
Japan NIKKEI LAND TRANSPORTATION	XX:1804892
Japan NIKKEI MACHINERY	XX:1804900
Japan NIKKEI MINING	XX:1804911
Japan NIKKEI NON-FER.METALS	XX:1804922
Japan NIKKEI OIL	XX:1804933
Japan NIKKEI OTC	XX:1818428
Japan NIKKEI OTHER FINANCIALS	XX:1804944

(cont.)

APPENDIX D FOREIGN TICKER SYMBOLS

Indexes	Symbol
Japan NIKKEI OTHER MAKERS	XX:1804955
Japan NIKKEI PAPER & PULP	XX:1804966
Japan NIKKEI PREC.INSTRUM.	XX:1804977
Japan NIKKEI RAILWAYS	XX:1804988
Japan NIKKEI REAL ESTATE COS	XX:1804999
Japan NIKKEI RETAILERS	XX:1805000
Japan NIKKEI RUBBER GOODS	XX:1805011
Japan NIKKEI SEA TRANSPORTATION	XX:1805022
Japan NIKKEI SECURITIES	XX:1805033
Japan NIKKEI SERVICES	XX:1805044
Japan NIKKEI SHIPBUILDING	XX:1805055
Japan NIKKEI STEELS	XX:1805066
Japan NIKKEI TEXTILES	XX:1805077
Japan NIKKEI TRADING COS	XX:1805088
Japan NIKKEI TRANSP.EQUIP.	XX:1805099
Japan NIKKEI WAREHOUSING	XX:1805107
Japan TOPIX 100	XX:1822979
Japan TOPIX 500	XX:1823013
Japan TOPIX AIR TRANSPORT(SPI)	XX:1825053
Japan TOPIX AIR TRANSPORTATION	XX:1883880
Japan TOPIX BANKS	XX:1883976
Japan TOPIX BANKS(SPI)	XX:1826001
Japan TOPIX CHEMICALS	XX:1883932
Japan TOPIX CHEMICALS(SPI)	XX:1823091
Japan TOPIX COMMUNICATION	XX:1883909
Japan TOPIX COMMUNICATION(SPI)	XX:1825075
Japan TOPIX CONSTRUCTION	XX:1883675
Japan TOPIX CONSTRUCTION(SPI)	XX:1823057
Japan TOPIX CORE 30	XX:1822957
Japan TOPIX ELECTRONIC APPLIANCES	XX:1883794
Japan TOPIX ELECTRONIC APPS(SPI)	XX:1824083
Japan TOPIX FIN BUSINESS(SPI)	XX:1826034
Japan TOPIX FINANCING BUSINESS	XX:1884009
Japan TOPIX FISH AGRIC & FOR(SPI)	XX:1823035
Japan TOPIX FISHERY AGRI & FOREST	XX:1883653
Japan TOPIX FOODS	XX:1883686
Japan TOPIX FOODS(SPI)	XX:1823068
Japan TOPIX GAS	XX:1883910
Japan TOPIX GAS(SPI)	XX:1825020
Japan TOPIX GLASS & CERAMICS PROD	XX:1883749
Japan TOPIX GLASS & CERAMICS(SPI)	XX:1824038
Japan TOPIX INSURANCE	XX:1883998
Japan TOPIX INSURANCE(SPI)	XX:1826023
Japan TOPIX IRON & STEEL	XX:1883750
Japan TOPIX IRON & STEEL(SPI)	XX:1824049

(cont.)

APPENDIX D FOREIGN TICKER SYMBOLS

Indexes	Symbol
Japan TOPIX LAND TRANSPORT(SPI)	XX:1825031
Japan TOPIX LAND TRANSPORTATION	XX:1883868
Japan TOPIX LARGE 70	XX:1822968
Japan TOPIX MACHINERY	XX:1883783
Japan TOPIX MACHINERY(SPI)	XX:1824072
Japan TOPIX MARINE TRANSPORT(SPI)	XX:1825042
Japan TOPIX MARINE TRANSPORTATION	XX:1883879
Japan TOPIX METAL PRODUCTS	XX:1883772
Japan TOPIX METAL PRODUCTS(SPI)	XX:1824061
Japan TOPIX MID 400	XX:1823002
Japan TOPIX MINING	XX:1883664
Japan TOPIX MINING(SPI)	XX:1823046
Japan TOPIX NONFERROUS METALS	XX:1883761
Japan TOPIX NONFERROUS METALS(SPI)	XX:1824050
Japan TOPIX OIL & COAL PRODS(SPI)	XX:1824016
Japan TOPIX OIL & COAL PRODUCTS	XX:1883727
Japan TOPIX OTHER PRODUCTS	XX:1883824
Japan TOPIX OTHER PRODUCTS(SPI)	XX:1825019
Japan TOPIX PHARMACEUTICAL	XX:1883943
Japan TOPIX PHARMACEUTICAL(SPI)	XX:1824005
Japan TOPIX PRECISION EQUIPMENT	XX:1883813
Japan TOPIX PRECISION INSTS(SPI)	XX:1825008
Japan TOPIX PULP & PAPER	XX:1883705
Japan TOPIX PULP & PAPER(SPI)	XX:1823080
Japan TOPIX REAL ESTATE	XX:1883857
Japan TOPIX REAL ESTATE(SPI)	XX:1826045
Japan TOPIX RETAILS TRADE	XX:1883965
Japan TOPIX RETAILS TRADE(SPI)	XX:1825097
Japan TOPIX RUBBER PRODUCTS	XX:1883738
Japan TOPIX RUBBER PRODUCTS(SPI)	XX:1824027
Japan TOPIX SECURITIES	XX:1883987
Japan TOPIX SECURITIES(SPI)	XX:1826012
Japan TOPIX SERVICES	XX:1883921
Japan TOPIX SERVICES(SPI)	XX:1826056
Japan TOPIX SMALL	XX:1823024
Japan TOPIX TEXTILES & APPARELS	XX:1883697
Japan TOPIX TEXTILES & APPS(SPI)	XX:1823079
Japan TOPIX TRANSPORT EQUIP	XX:1883802
Japan TOPIX TRANSPORTATION(SPI)	XX:1824094
Japan TOPIX WAREHOUSING	XX:1883891
Japan TOPIX WAREHOUSING(SPI)	XX:1825064
Japan TOPIX WHOLESALE TRADE	XX:1883954
Japan TOPIX WHOLESALE TRADE(SPI)	XX:1825086
Japan TSE 2ND SECTION	XX:1805118
Japan TSE 2ND SECTION(SPI)	XX:1807006

(cont.)

APPENDIX D FOREIGN TICKER SYMBOLS

Indexes	Symbol
Japan TSE 2ND SECTION(WA)	XX:1807062
Japan TSE STK PRICE(L)	XX:1807103
Japan TSE STK PRICE(L)(SPI)	XX:1807028
Japan TSE STK PRICE(L)(WA)	XX:1807073
Japan TSE STK PRICE(M)	XX:1807114
Japan TSE STK PRICE(M)(SPI)	XX:1807039
Japan TSE STK PRICE(M)(WA)	XX:1807084
Japan TSE STK PRICE(S)	XX:1807125
Japan TSE STK PRICE(S)(SPI)	XX:1807040
Japan TSE STK PRICE(S)(WA)	XX:1807095
Japan TSE STK PRICE(SPA)	XX:1807017
Japan TSE STK PRICE(TOPIX)	XX:1804609
Japan TSE STK PRICE(WA)	XX:1807051
Korea KOSPI 200	XX:1815634
Korea KOSPI 200 CIRCULATIVE	XX:1890824
Korea KOSPI 200 CONSTRUCTION	XX:1890835
Korea KOSPI 200 ELEC & COMMUN	XX:1890846
Korea KOSPI 200 FINANCIAL	XX:1890857
Korea KOSPI 200 MANUFACTURING	XX:1890868
Korea KOSPI COMPOSITE	XX:1807211
Korea KSE BANKING (MIN)	XX:1897836
Korea KSE BASIC METALS INDS (MAJ)	XX:1890880
Korea KSE BEVERAGE (MIN)	XX:1897847
Korea KSE CHEMICAL COMP (MAJ)	XX:1890891
Korea KSE CHEMICALS (MIN)	XX:1807158
Korea KSE CONSTRUCTION (MAJ)	XX:1807169
Korea KSE DRUG & MEDICAL (MIN)	XX:1897858
Korea KSE ELECTRICAL (MIN)	XX:1807170
Korea KSE FABRICATED METAL (MAJ)	XX:1891139
Korea KSE FABRICATED METAL (MIN)	XX:1897869
Korea KSE FINANCE (MAJ)	XX:1807181
Korea KSE FIRST SECTION (MIN)	XX:1897870
Korea KSE FISHING (MAJ)	XX:1891322
Korea KSE FOOD & BEVERAGE (MAJ)	XX:1891764
Korea KSE FOOD (MIN)	XX:1897881
Korea KSE INSURANCE (MAJ)	XX:1893102
Korea KSE INVESTMENT (MIN)	XX:1897892
Korea KSE IRON & STEEL (MIN)	XX:1890879
Korea KSE LAND TRANS (MIN)	XX:1897900
Korea KSE LARGE SIZE	XX:1897911
Korea KSE MACHINERY (MIN)	XX:1888153
Korea KSE MEDIUM SIZE	XX:1888164
Korea KSE MINING (MAJ)	XX:1893113
Korea KSE NON FERROUS (MIN)	XX:1888175
Korea KSE NON METALLIC (MIN)	XX:1888186
Korea KSE OTHER MANUFACTURE (MAJ)	XX:1893124

(*cont.*)

APPENDIX D FOREIGN TICKER SYMBOLS

Indexes	Symbol
Korea KSE PAPER PRODUCTS (MAJ)	XX:1893135
Korea KSE PRODUCTION (MIN)	XX:1888197
Korea KSE RUBBER (MIN)	XX:1888205
Korea KSE SECOND SECTION (MIN)	XX:1888216
Korea KSE SECURITIES (MIN)	XX:1888227
Korea KSE SMALL SIZE	XX:1888238
Korea KSE TEXTILE & WEAR (MAJ)	XX:1893146
Korea KSE TEXTILE (MIN)	XX:1889383
Korea KSE TRANS & STORAGE (MAJ)	XX:1893180
Korea KSE TRANSP & EQUIP (MIN)	XX:1807192
Korea KSE WATER TRANS (MIN)	XX:1889394
Korea KSE WEARING (MIN)	XX:1890813
Korea KSE WHOLESALE & TRADE (MAJ)	XX:1893210
Korea KSE WHOLESALE & TRADE (MIN)	XX:1807200
Korea KSE WOOD PRODUCTS (MAJ)	XX:1893771
Lithuania LITIN	XX:1818291
Lithuania LITIN 10	XX:1818514
Lithuania LITIN A	XX:1818309
Lithuania LITIN G	XX:1818310
Lithuania LITIN VVP	XX:1818503
Malaysia KLSE 2ND BOARD	XX:1807299
Malaysia KLSE COMPOSITE	XX:1807307
Malaysia KLSE CONSTRUCTION	XX:1808894
Malaysia KLSE CONSUMER PRODUCT	XX:1808883
Malaysia KLSE EMAS	XX:1882229
Malaysia KLSE FINANCE	XX:1807255
Malaysia KLSE INDUSTRIAL PROD	XX:1808902
Malaysia KLSE INDUSTRIALS	XX:1807244
Malaysia KLSE MINING	XX:1807288
Malaysia KLSE PLANTATIONS	XX:1807277
Malaysia KLSE PROPERTIES	XX:1807266
Malaysia KLSE TRADING SERVICES	XX:1808913
Netherlands AEX ALL SHARE	XX:1814200
Netherlands AEX ALL SHARE AEX	XX:1814211
Netherlands AEX ALL SHARE AEX & AMX	XX:1814233
Netherlands AEX ALL SHARE AEX & AMX (TR)	XX:1825514
Netherlands AEX ALL SHARE AEX(TR)	XX:1818978
Netherlands AEX ALL SHARE AMX	XX:1814222
Netherlands AEX ALL SHARE AMX(TR)	XX:1818990
Netherlands AEX ALL SHARE NMAX	XX:1814255
Netherlands AEX ALL SHARE NMAX(TR)	XX:1825536
Netherlands AEX ALL SHARE(TR)	XX:1825503
Netherlands AEX AUTOMOBILES	XX:1817209
Netherlands AEX AUTOMOBILES(TR)	XX:1825688
Netherlands AEX BANKS	XX:1818860

(*cont.*)

APPENDIX D FOREIGN TICKER SYMBOLS

Indexes	Symbol
Netherlands AEX BANKS(TR)	XX:1825945
Netherlands AEX BASIC INDS	XX:1815753
Netherlands AEX BASIC INDS(TR)	XX:1825570
Netherlands AEX BEVERAGES	XX:1818473
Netherlands AEX BEVERAGES(TR)	XX:1825718
Netherlands AEX CHEMICALS	XX:1815764
Netherlands AEX CHEMICALS(TR)	XX:1825581
Netherlands AEX CONST & BLDG MATLS	XX:1815872
Netherlands AEX CONST & BLDG MATLS(TR)	XX:1825592
Netherlands AEX CYC CONSUMER GOODS	XX:1817113
Netherlands AEX CYC CONSUMER GOODS(TR)	XX:1825677
Netherlands AEX CYCLICAL SERVICES	XX:1818707
Netherlands AEX CYCLICAL SERVICES(TR)	XX:1825785
Netherlands AEX DISTRIBUTORS	XX:1818718
Netherlands AEX DISTRIBUTORS(TR)	XX:1825796
Netherlands AEX DIVERSIFIED INDLS	XX:1817083
Netherlands AEX DIVERSIFIED INDLS(TR)	XX:1825644
Netherlands AEX ELECTRON & ELEC EQUIP	XX:1817094
Netherlands AEX ELECTRON & ELEC EQUIP(TR)	XX:1825655
Netherlands AEX ENGINEERING & MACH	XX:1817102
Netherlands AEX ENGINEERING & MACH(TR)	XX:1825666
Netherlands AEX FINANCIALS	XX:1818859
Netherlands AEX FINANCIALS (AFSX)	XX:1819755
Netherlands AEX FINANCIALS(TR)	XX:1825934
Netherlands AEX FOOD & DRUG RETAIL	XX:1818796
Netherlands AEX FOOD & DRUG RETAIL(TR)	XX:1825882
Netherlands AEX FOOD PROD & PROC	XX:1818484
Netherlands AEX FOOD PROD & PROC(TR)	XX:1825729
Netherlands AEX FORESTRY & PAPER	XX:1815883
Netherlands AEX FORESTRY & PAPER(TR)	XX:1825600
Netherlands AEX GENERAL INDUSTRIES	XX:1816381
Netherlands AEX GENERAL INDUSTRIES(TR)	XX:1825622
Netherlands AEX GENERAL RETAILERS	XX:1818729
Netherlands AEX GENERAL RETAILERS(TR)	XX:1825804
Netherlands AEX HEALTH	XX:1818495
Netherlands AEX HEALTH(TR)	XX:1825730
Netherlands AEX HOUSEHOLD GDS & TXT	XX:1818008
Netherlands AEX HOUSEHOLD GDS & TXT(TR)	XX:1825699
Netherlands AEX INFO TECH	XX:1818923
Netherlands AEX INFO TECH (AISX)	XX:1819766
Netherlands AEX INFO TECH HARDWARE	XX:1818934
Netherlands AEX INFO TECH HARDWARE(TR)	XX:1838619
Netherlands AEX INFO TECH(TR)	XX:1838608
Netherlands AEX INSURANCE	XX:1818871
Netherlands AEX INSURANCE(TR)	XX:1825956
Netherlands AEX INVESTMENT COS	XX:1818893

(cont.)

APPENDIX D FOREIGN TICKER SYMBOLS

Indexes	Symbol
Netherlands AEX INVESTMENT COS(TR)	XX:1825978
Netherlands AEX LEISURE ENT & HOT	XX:1818730
Netherlands AEX LEISURE ENT & HOT(TR)	XX:1825815
Netherlands AEX LIFE ASSURANCE	XX:1818882
Netherlands AEX LIFE ASSURANCE(TR)	XX:1825967
Netherlands AEX MEDIA & PHOTOGRAPHY	XX:1818741
Netherlands AEX MEDIA & PHOTOGRAPHY(TR)	XX:1825826
Netherlands AEX MID-KAP (AMX)	XX:1811580
Netherlands AEX MID-KAP(TR)	XX:1818989
Netherlands AEX MINING	XX:1814277
Netherlands AEX MINING(TR)	XX:1825558
Netherlands AEX NON-CYC CONS GOODS	XX:1818462
Netherlands AEX NON-CYC CONS GOODS(TR)	XX:1825707
Netherlands AEX NON-CYC SERVICES	XX:1818785
Netherlands AEX NON-CYC SERVICES(TR)	XX:1825860
Netherlands AEX OIL & GAS	XX:1814288
Netherlands AEX OIL & GAS(TR)	XX:1825569
Netherlands AEX PACKAGING	XX:1818666
Netherlands AEX PACKAGING(TR)	XX:1825741
Netherlands AEX PERS CARE & H/H PRODS	XX:1818677
Netherlands AEX PERS CARE & H/H PRODS(TR)	XX:1825752
Netherlands AEX PHARMACEUTICALS	XX:1818688
Netherlands AEX PHARMACEUTICALS(TR)	XX:1825763
Netherlands AEX REAL ESTATE	XX:1818901
Netherlands AEX REAL ESTATE(TR)	XX:1825989
Netherlands AEX RESOURCES	XX:1814266
Netherlands AEX RESOURCES(TR)	XX:1825547
Netherlands AEX SMALLER COS (ASCX)	XX:1814244
Netherlands AEX SMALLER COS(TR)	XX:1825525
Netherlands AEX SOFTWARE & COMP	XX:1818945
Netherlands AEX SOFTWARE & COMP(TR)	XX:1838620
Netherlands AEX SPECIAL & OTH FIN	XX:1818912
Netherlands AEX SPECIAL & OTH FIN(TR)	XX:1825990
Netherlands AEX STEEL & OTHER METALS	XX:1816370
Netherlands AEX STEEL&OTHER METALS(TR)	XX:1825611
Netherlands AEX STOCK (AEX)	XX:1810101
Netherlands AEX STOCK(TR)	XX:1818967
Netherlands AEX SUPPORT SERVICES	XX:1818763
Netherlands AEX SUPPORT SERVICES(TR)	XX:1825848
Netherlands AEX TELECOM SERVICES	XX:1818804
Netherlands AEX TELECOM SERVICES(TR)	XX:1825871
Netherlands AEX TOP 5	XX:1810112
Netherlands AEX TRANSPORT	XX:1818774
Netherlands AEX TRANSPORT(TR)	XX:1825859
Norway BRIX	XX:1885648
Norway GOVT BONDS—0.25 YEAR	XX:1811557

(*cont.*)

APPENDIX D FOREIGN TICKER SYMBOLS

Indexes	Symbol
Norway GOVT BONDS—0.5 YEAR	XX:1811568
Norway GOVT BONDS—1 YEAR	XX:1811535
Norway GOVT BONDS—3 YEAR	XX:1811579
Norway GOVT BONDS—5 YEAR	XX:1811546
Norway OSE ALL-SHARE	XX:1810208
Norway OSE BUILDING & CONSTRUCT	XX:1810640
Norway OSE FINANCE	XX:1810178
Norway OSE GFB	XX:1810651
Norway OSE INDUSTRY	XX:1804687
Norway OSE INFORMATION TECHNOLOGY	XX:1810598
Norway OSE OBX	XX:1885637
Norway OSE SHIPPING	XX:1810189
Norway OSE SMB	XX:1857335
Pakistan KSE 100	XX:1810220
Philippines MANILA S.E.COMML-INDL.	XX:1810242
Philippines MANILA S.E.COMPOSITE	XX:1810275
Philippines MANILA S.E.MINING	XX:1810253
Philippines MANILA S.E.OIL	XX:1810264
Philippines MANILA S.E.PROPERTY	XX:1813241
Philippines PSE ALL SHARES	XX:1817298
Philippines PSE BANKING & FINL SERVICES	XX:1817306
Poland MIDWIG	XX:1854132
Poland NIF	XX:1854143
Poland WIG	XX:1810286
Poland WIG 20	XX:1884719
Poland WIRR	XX:1810673
Portugal BTA LISBON	XX:1810297
Portugal BVL 30	XX:1888249
Portugal BVL GENERAL	XX:1800607
Portugal PSI 20	XX:1885808
Russia AK&M BANK	XX:1884838
Russia AK&M COMPOSITE	XX:1884849
Russia AK&M ENERGY	XX:1884894
Russia AK&M FERROUS METALS	XX:1884883
Russia AK&M INDUSTRIAL	XX:1884827
Russia AK&M MACHINERY	XX:1884913
Russia AK&M NON-FERROUS METALS	XX:1884872
Russia AK&M OIL & GAS EXTRACTION	XX:1884850
Russia AK&M PETROCHEMISTRY	XX:1884861
Russia AK&M TELECOMMUNICATION	XX:1884924
Russia AK&M TIMBER INDUSTRY	XX:1884902
Russia AK&M TRANSPORT	XX:1884935
Russia ASP 12(RUB)	XX:1801826
Russia ASP 12(USD)	XX:1807868
Russia ASP BANKING(RUB)	XX:1807910
Russia ASP BANKING(USD)	XX:1807921

(cont.)

APPENDIX D FOREIGN TICKER SYMBOLS

Indexes	Symbol
Russia ASP ENGINEERING(RUB)	XX:1808690
Russia ASP ENGINEERING(USD)	XX:1808742
Russia ASP PACIFIC(USD)	XX:1817038
Russia ASP PAPER & FOREST PRODS(RUB)	XX:1817049
Russia ASP PAPER & FOREST PRODS(USD)	XX:1817050
Russia ASP TRADING(RUB)	XX:1808656
Russia ASP TRADING(USD)	XX:1808667
Russia MOSCOW TIMES(RUB)	XX:1807891
Russia MOSCOW TIMES(USD)	XX:1807909
Russia ROS(CSFB)	XX:1817124
Russia SKATE 100(RUB)	XX:1807879
Russia SKATE 100(USD)	XX:1807880
Russia SKATE ENGINEERING(RUB)	XX:1818235
Russia SKATE ENGINEERING(USD)	XX:1818246
Russia SKATE FERROUS METALS(RUB)	XX:1817061
Russia SKATE FERROUS METALS(USD)	XX:1817072
Russia SKATE INDUSTRIALS(RUB)	XX:1807932
Russia SKATE INDUSTRIALS(USD)	XX:1808270
Russia SKATE NON-FERR METALS(RUB)	XX:1808678
Russia SKATE NON-FERR METALS(USD)	XX:1808689
Russia SKATE OIL & GAS(RUB)	XX:1808601
Russia SKATE OIL & GAS(USD)	XX:1808612
Russia SKATE POWER INDUSTRY(RUB)	XX:1808775
Russia SKATE POWER INDUSTRY(USD)	XX:1808786
Russia SKATE RETAILING(RUB)	XX:1818213
Russia SKATE RETAILING(USD)	XX:1818224
Russia SKATE TELECOM(RUB)	XX:1808753
Russia SKATE TELECOM(USD)	XX:1808764
Russia SKATE TRANSPORTATION(RUB)	XX:1808797
Russia SKATE TRANSPORTATION(USD)	XX:1808805
Singapore BT COMPOSITE	XX:1800737
Singapore DBS 50	XX:1810510
Singapore DBS(C.P.F.STOCKS)	XX:1810361
Singapore SES ALL COMMERCE	XX:1802744
Singapore SES ALL CONSTRUCTION	XX:1802915
Singapore SES ALL FINANCE	XX:1810327
Singapore SES ALL HOTEL	XX:1810349
Singapore SES ALL INDL. & COMML.	XX:1810394
Singapore SES ALL MANUFACTURING	XX:1802733
Singapore SES ALL MULTI INDUSTRIAL	XX:1802722
Singapore SES ALL PROPERTY	XX:1810402
Singapore SES ALL SHARE	XX:1810372
Singapore SES ALL TRANS/STORAGE/COMMS	XX:1802904
Singapore SES ELECTRONICS	XX:1815678
Singapore SES FOREIGN	XX:1815667
Singapore SES MAIN BOARD	XX:1815656

(*cont.*)

APPENDIX D FOREIGN TICKER SYMBOLS

Indexes	Symbol
Singapore SES REGIONAL	XX:1802711
Singapore UOB BLUE CHIP	XX:1810491
Singapore UOB BLUE CHIP(30)	XX:1810521
Singapore UOB BLUE CHIP(90)	XX:1810532
Singapore UOB OTC	XX:1810509
Singapore UOB OTC(90)	XX:1810576
Singapore UOB SESDAQ	XX:1810350
Singapore UOB SESDAQ(90)	XX:1810554
Slovakia SAX	XX:1803037
Slovenia BIO	XX:1805981
Slovenia PIX	XX:1854154
Slovenia SBI	XX:1808634
South Africa JSE ALL GOLD	XX:1805259
South Africa JSE BANKS	XX:1806508
South Africa JSE BANKS & FINANCIAL SVCS	XX:1888863
South Africa JSE BEVERAGES	XX:1806519
South Africa JSE BLDG CONST & ENGINEER	XX:1806520
South Africa JSE CHEMICALS OILS&PLASTICS	XX:1806531
South Africa JSE CLOTHING & TEXTILES	XX:1806542
South Africa JSE COAL	XX:1806553
South Africa JSE CURTAILED OPERATIONS	XX:1806575
South Africa JSE DEVELOPMENT CAPITAL	XX:1806597
South Africa JSE DEVELOPMENT STAGE	XX:1815173
South Africa JSE DIAMONDS	XX:1806605
South Africa JSE DIVERSIFIED INDL	XX:1806672
South Africa JSE EDUCATION & STAFFING	XX:1895700
South Africa JSE ELECTRONIC & ELECTRICAL	XX:1806616
South Africa JSE ENGINEERING	XX:1806627
South Africa JSE FIN 15 TOP COS	XX:1838266
South Africa JSE FINANCIAL	XX:1804085
South Africa JSE FINANCIAL & INDUSTRIAL	XX:1806649
South Africa JSE FINANCIAL SERVICES	XX:1895670
South Africa JSE FOOD	XX:1806650
South Africa JSE FURNITURE & APPLIANCES	XX:1806661
South Africa JSE GOLD	XX:1806702
South Africa JSE GOLD MNG-RAND & OTHERS	XX:1806984
South Africa JSE GOLD O.F.S	XX:1806810
South Africa JSE GOLD-WEST WITWATERSRAND	XX:1806973
South Africa JSE HEALTHCARE	XX:1806735
South Africa JSE HOTELS & LEISURE	XX:1895711
South Africa JSE I.T.	XX:1895722
South Africa JSE INDL CONSUMER	XX:1895755
South Africa JSE INDUSTRIAL	XX:1805260
South Africa JSE INSURANCE	XX:1895681
South Africa JSE INVESTMENT TRUSTS	XX:1806694
South Africa JSE LIFE ASSURANCE	XX:1806683

(cont.)

APPENDIX D FOREIGN TICKER SYMBOLS

Indexes	Symbol
South Africa JSE MEDIA	XX:1838943
South Africa JSE METALS & MINERALS	XX:1806780
South Africa JSE METALS & MINERALS	XX:1806779
South Africa JSE METALS & MINLS-MANGANESE	XX:1806724
South Africa JSE METALS & MINERALS-COPPER	XX:1806564
South Africa JSE MID CAP	XX:1886748
South Africa JSE MIN PRO 15 TOP COS	XX:1838255
South Africa JSE MINING EXPLORATION	XX:1806746
South Africa JSE MINING FINANCIAL	XX:1806757
South Africa JSE MINING HLDGS & HOUSES	XX:1806768
South Africa JSE MINING HOLDING	XX:1804074
South Africa JSE MINING RESOURCES	XX:1893953
South Africa JSE MOTOR	XX:1806791
South Africa JSE NON-MINING RESOURCES	XX:1895636
South Africa JSE OVERALL	XX:1804063
South Africa JSE PACKAGING & PRINTING	XX:1888874
South Africa JSE PAPER	XX:1895647
South Africa JSE PLATINUM	XX:1806854
South Africa JSE PRIVATE EQUITY FUNDS	XX:1895658
South Africa JSE PROPERTY	XX:1806906
South Africa JSE PROPERTY LOAN STOCK	XX:1806887
South Africa JSE PROPERTY UNIT TRUST	XX:1806917
South Africa JSE REAL ESTATE	XX:1895766
South Africa JSE REDEVELOPMENT	XX:1888885
South Africa JSE RESOURCES	XX:1806809
South Africa JSE RESOURCES 20	XX:1895885
South Africa JSE RETAIL	XX:1806939
South Africa JSE SERVICE	XX:1895733
South Africa JSE SHORT TERM INSURANCE	XX:1895692
South Africa JSE SMALL MID CAP	XX:1886759
South Africa JSE STEEL & ALLIED	XX:1806928
South Africa JSE TELECOMMUNICATIONS	XX:1895744
South Africa JSE TRANSPORT	XX:1806940
South Africa JSE VENTURE CAPITAL	XX:1806962
South Africa JSE/ACT ALL GOLD 10	XX:1815214
South Africa JSE/ACT ALL SHARE 40	XX:1815195
South Africa JSE/ACT FIN & IND 30	XX:1815203
South Africa JSE/ACT INDUSTRIAL 25	XX:1815225
Spain BARCELONA SE BANKS	XX:1810145
Spain BARCELONA SE CEMENT & CONST	XX:1811427
Spain BARCELONA SE CHEMICALS	XX:1812903
Spain BARCELONA SE COMMERCE & FIN	XX:1811438
Spain BARCELONA SE ELECTRICITY	XX:1811449
Spain BARCELONA SE GENERAL	XX:1812787

(cont.)

APPENDIX D FOREIGN TICKER SYMBOLS

Indexes	Symbol
Spain BARCELONA SE METALLURGICAL	XX:1812884
Spain BARCELONA SE MID 50	XX:1824351
Spain BARCELONA SE MISC SERVICES	XX:1812958
Spain BARCELONA SE TEXTILE & PAPER	XX:1812970
Spain BILBAO SE BANKS	XX:1810156
Spain BILBAO SE CHEMICALS	XX:1812914
Spain BILBAO SE ELECTRICITY	XX:1811450
Spain BILBAO SE FINANCIAL STOCKS	XX:1813003
Spain BILBAO SE FOOD	XX:1810123
Spain BILBAO SE FOOD AGRIC & FOREST	XX:1810134
Spain BILBAO SE GENERAL	XX:1812798
Spain BILBAO SE INDUSTRIAL STOCKS	XX:1813014
Spain BILBAO SE INVESTMENT & INS	XX:1812851
Spain BILBAO SE IRON & STEEL	XX:1812969
Spain BILBAO SE MISC SERVICES	XX:1812947
Spain BILBAO SE REAL EST. & CONST	XX:1812839
Spain BILBAO SE TRANSPORT & COM	XX:1812992
Spain IBEX 35	XX:1808247
Spain IBEX COMPLEMENTARY	XX:1830046
Spain IBEX FINANCIALS	XX:1836549
Spain IBEX INDUSTRIALS	XX:1836561
Spain IBEX UTILITIES	XX:1836550
Spain MADRID SE BANKS/FINANCE	XX:1808708
Spain MADRID SE COMMUNICATION	XX:1803327
Spain MADRID SE CONSTRUCTION	XX:1808719
Spain MADRID SE FIX INT 3 YR YLD	XX:1812925
Spain MADRID SE FIX INT PRICES	XX:1812936
Spain MADRID SE FOOD	XX:1811524
Spain MADRID SE GENERAL	XX:1804706
Spain MADRID SE INVESTMENT	XX:1812806
Spain MADRID SE METAL WORKING	XX:1812817
Spain MADRID SE MISC INDS & SVCS	XX:1803316
Spain MADRID SE OIL & CHEMICAL	XX:1800782
Spain MADRID SE UTILITIES	XX:1808720
Spain VALENCIA SE BANKS	XX:1811494
Spain VALENCIA SE COMMERCE	XX:1811502
Spain VALENCIA SE CONSTRUCTION	XX:1811513
Spain VALENCIA SE ELECTRICITY/GAS	XX:1811461
Spain VALENCIA SE ENERGY/WATER	XX:1811483
Spain VALENCIA SE GENERAL	XX:1812828
Spain VALENCIA SE MANUFACTURING	XX:1812862
Spain VALENCIA SE METAL/MECHANICS	XX:1812873
Spain VALENCIA SE MINERAL & CHEM	XX:1812895
Spain VALENCIA SE REAL ESTATE	XX:1812840
Spain VALENCIA SE TRANSPORT & COM	XX:1812981
Sri Lanka COLOMBO S.E.	XX:1803305

(cont.)

APPENDIX D FOREIGN TICKER SYMBOLS

Indexes	Symbol
Sweden AFFARSVARLDEN GENERAL	XX:1804717
Sweden ALFRED BERG NORDIC	XX:1878842
Sweden OMX	XX:1889231
Sweden SX 3–5 YRS MATURITY	XX:1810479
Sweden SX 70 LEAST TRADED STOCKS	XX:1816369
Sweden SX BANKS	XX:1804320
Sweden SX ENGINEERING	XX:1804289
Sweden SX FOREST PRODUCTS	XX:1804278
Sweden SX GENERAL	XX:1804115
Sweden SX INVESTMENT COS	XX:1804331
Sweden SX LESS THAN 3 YRS MATURITY	XX:1810457
Sweden SX MISCELLANEOUS	XX:1804342
Sweden SX MORE THAN 5 YRS MATURITY	XX:1810565
Sweden SX O	XX:1810468
Sweden SX O LIST	XX:1804397
Sweden SX OTC	XX:1804386
Sweden SX PHARMACEUTICAL	XX:1804375
Sweden SX PUBLISHING	XX:1810543
Sweden SX REAL ESTATE	XX:1804353
Sweden SX SERVICE	XX:1800179
Sweden SX TOP 16	XX:1804126
Sweden SX TRADING	XX:1804319
Sweden VECKANS AFFARER TOP 16	XX:1804267
Sweden VECKANS AFFARER TOTAL	XX:1804256
Switzerland LOMBARD IND MILO	XX:1813285
Switzerland LOMBARD IND SILO	XX:1813296
Switzerland NEW BANKS	XX:1814846
Switzerland NEW BANKS(TR)	XX:1814835
Switzerland NEW BANKS(YLD)	XX:1814857
Switzerland NEW CONFED	XX:1814783
Switzerland NEW CONFED(TR)	XX:1814772
Switzerland NEW CONFED(YLD)	XX:1814794
Switzerland NEW DOMESTIC	XX:1814965
Switzerland NEW DOMESTIC(TR)	XX:1814954
Switzerland NEW DOMESTIC(YLD)	XX:1814976
Switzerland NEW ENERGY	XX:1814813
Switzerland NEW ENERGY(TR)	XX:1814802
Switzerland NEW ENERGY(YLD)	XX:1814824
Switzerland NEW FOREIGN	XX:1814998
Switzerland NEW FOREIGN(TR)	XX:1814987
Switzerland NEW FOREIGN(YLD)	XX:1815009
Switzerland NEW GENERAL	XX:1815032
Switzerland NEW GENERAL	XX:1815021
Switzerland NEW GENERAL(TR)	XX:1815010
Switzerland NEW INDUSTRY	XX:1814879
Switzerland NEW INDUSTRY(TR)	XX:1814868

(*cont.*)

APPENDIX D FOREIGN TICKER SYMBOLS

Indexes	Symbol
Switzerland NEW INDUSTRY(YLD)	XX:1814880
Switzerland NEW OTHER	XX:1814932
Switzerland NEW OTHER(TR)	XX:1814921
Switzerland NEW OTHER(YLD)	XX:1814943
Switzerland NEW STATES	XX:1814909
Switzerland NEW STATES(TR)	XX:1814891
Switzerland NEW STATES(YLD)	XX:1814910
Switzerland NON-LARGE UMWELT INDEX	XX:1813627
Switzerland OLD BANKS 87	XX:1814578
Switzerland OLD BANKS 87(TR)	XX:1814567
Switzerland OLD BANKS 87(YLD)	XX:1814589
Switzerland OLD CONFED 87	XX:1814512
Switzerland OLD CONFED 87(TR)	XX:1814501
Switzerland OLD CONFED 87(YLD)	XX:1814523
Switzerland OLD DOMESTIC 87	XX:1814697
Switzerland OLD DOMESTIC 87(TR)	XX:1814686
Switzerland OLD DOMESTIC 87(YLD)	XX:1814705
Switzerland OLD ENERGY 87	XX:1814545
Switzerland OLD ENERGY 87(TR)	XX:1814534
Switzerland OLD ENERGY 87(YLD)	XX:1814556
Switzerland OLD FOREIGN 87	XX:1814727
Switzerland OLD FOREIGN 87(TR)	XX:1814716
Switzerland OLD FOREIGN 87(YLD)	XX:1814738
Switzerland OLD GENERAL 87	XX:1814750
Switzerland OLD GENERAL 87(TR)	XX:1814749
Switzerland OLD GENERAL 87(YLD)	XX:1814761
Switzerland OLD INDUSTRY 87	XX:1814608
Switzerland OLD INDUSTRY 87(TR)	XX:1814590
Switzerland SBI DOMESTIC 1–3 YR	XX:1824964
Switzerland SBI DOMESTIC GOVT	XX:1814318
Switzerland SBI DOMESTIC GOVT (DURAT)	XX:1854013
Switzerland SBI DOMESTIC GOVT(TR)	XX:1814307
Switzerland SBI DOMESTIC GOVT(YLD)	XX:1854024
Switzerland SBI DOMESTIC NON-GOVT	XX:1824908
Switzerland SBI DOMESTIC NON-GOVT(TR)	XX:1824878
Switzerland SBI FOREIGN 1–3 YR	XX:1825161
Switzerland SBI FOREIGN CORP(DURAT)	XX:1854057
Switzerland SBI FOREIGN CORP(TR)	XX:1814460
Switzerland SBI FOREIGN CORP(YLD)	XX:1854068
Switzerland SBI FOREIGN GOVT	XX:1814437
Switzerland SBI FOREIGN GOVT(DURAT)	XX:1854079
Switzerland SBI FOREIGN GOVT(TR)	XX:1814426
Switzerland SBI FOREIGN GOVT(YLD)	XX:1854080
Switzerland SBI FOREIGN(DURAT)	XX:1854035
Switzerland SBI SUPRANATIONAL(DURAT)	XX:1854091

(cont.)

APPENDIX D FOREIGN TICKER SYMBOLS

Indexes	Symbol
Switzerland SNB GOVT.BOND YIELD	XX:1807846
Switzerland SPI INVESTMENT COS	XX:1830121
Switzerland SPI LARGE COS	XX:1813337
Switzerland SPI MEDIUM COS	XX:1813326
Switzerland SPI OTHER INDUSTRIES	XX:1807727
Switzerland SPI PTG CERTS	XX:1807589
Switzerland SPI SMALL & MEDIUM COS	XX:1813348
Switzerland SPI SMALL COS	XX:1813315
Switzerland SPI(X-INVESTMENT COS)	XX:1830132
Switzerland SPIX INVESTMENT COS	XX:1830109
Switzerland SPIX LARGE COS	XX:1813382
Switzerland SPIX MEDIUM COS	XX:1813371
Switzerland SPIX OTHER INDUSTRIES	XX:1813597
Switzerland SPIX PTG CERTS	XX:1813445
Switzerland SPIX SMALL & MEDIUM COS	XX:1813393
Switzerland SPIX SMALL COS	XX:1813360
Switzerland SPIX(X-INVESTMENT COS)	XX:1830143
Switzerland UBS INDEX FUND(ACC)	XX:1814147
Taiwan AUTOMOBILES	XX:1808731
Taiwan BANKING & INSURANCE	XX:1876589
Taiwan CEMENT	XX:1808571
Taiwan CEMENT	XX:1876556
Taiwan CHEMICAL	XX:1808560
Taiwan COMPOSITE AVERAGE	XX:1806445
Taiwan CONSTRUCTION	XX:1876567
Taiwan ELECTRICAL	XX:1809273
Taiwan ELECTRICALS	XX:1876578
Taiwan ELECTRONICS	XX:1809024
Taiwan FOOD	XX:1876590
Taiwan GLASS & CERAMICS	XX:1809035
Taiwan HOTEL	XX:1809080
Taiwan INDUSTRIAL AVERAGE	XX:1806456
Taiwan IRON & STEEL	XX:1809262
Taiwan MACHINERY	XX:1809091
Taiwan NON-FINANCIALS	XX:1876608
Taiwan OTHERS	XX:1805903
Taiwan PLASTICS	XX:1809143
Taiwan PULP & PAPER	XX:1876619
Thailand SET	XX:1805323
Thailand SET 50	XX:1815645
Thailand SET AGRIBUSINESS	XX:1808214
Thailand SET BANKING	XX:1807998
Thailand SET BUILDING & FURNISHING	XX:1808225
Thailand SET CHEMICALS & PLASTICS	XX:1813025
Thailand SET COMMERCE	XX:1808010

(cont.)

APPENDIX D FOREIGN TICKER SYMBOLS

Indexes	Symbol
Thailand SET COMMUNICATIONS	XX:1813036
Thailand SET ELEC PRODS & COMPUTER	XX:1808236
Thailand SET ELECTRONIC COMPONENTS	XX:1813069
Thailand SET ENERGY	XX:1813047
Thailand SET ENTERTAIN & RECREATION	XX:1813058
Thailand SET FINANCIALS	XX:1808009
Thailand SET FOOD & BEVERAGES	XX:1808162
Thailand SET HEALTH CARE SERVICES	XX:1813081
Thailand SET HOTEL & TRAVEL	XX:1808173
Thailand SET HOUSEHOLD GOODS	XX:1813070
Thailand SET INSURANCE	XX:1808184
Thailand SET JEWELLERY & ORNAMENTS	XX:1813092
Thailand SET MACHINERY & EQUIPMENT	XX:1813100
Thailand SET MINING	XX:1813111
Thailand SET OTHERS	XX:1813122
Thailand SET PACKAGING	XX:1813144
Thailand SET PHARMACEUTICALS	XX:1813133
Thailand SET PRINTING & PUBLISHING	XX:1808195
Thailand SET PROFESSIONAL SERVICES	XX:1813155
Thailand SET PROPERTY & DEVELOPMENT	XX:1808203
Thailand SET PULP & PAPER	XX:1813166
Thailand SET TEXTILES	XX:1808032
Thailand SET TRANSPORTATION	XX:1813188
Thailand SET VEHICLE & PARTS	XX:1813199
Thailand SET WAREHOUSE & SILO	XX:1813177
Turkey ISE NATIONAL 100	XX:1864443
Turkey ISE NATIONAL FINANCIALS	XX:1864454
Turkey ISE NATIONAL INDUSTRIALS	XX:1864465
United Kingdom FT 30	XX:1808269
United Kingdom FT GOLD MINES	XX:1808281
United Kingdom FT GOLD MINES—AFRICA	XX:1800351
United Kingdom FT GOLD MINES—AUSTRALASIA	XX:1800373
United Kingdom FT GOLD MINES—NORTH AMERICA	XX:1800384
United Kingdom FT GOVERNMENT SECURITIES	XX:1800287
United Kingdom FTSE 100(GBP)	XX:1805550
United Kingdom FTSE 100(TR)	XX:1812475
United Kingdom FTSE 250(GBP)	XX:1868003
United Kingdom FTSE 250(TR)	XX:1812486
United Kingdom FTSE 250(X-IT)(GBP)	XX:1868371
United Kingdom FTSE 250(X-IT)(TR)	XX:1812497
United Kingdom FTSE 350 LOWER YIELD(TR)	XX:1812527
United Kingdom FTSE 350(GBP)	XX:1868014
United Kingdom FTSE 350(TR)	XX:1812505
United Kingdom FTSE 350(X-IT)(GBP)	XX:1883545

(*cont.*)

APPENDIX D FOREIGN TICKER SYMBOLS

Indexes	Symbol
United Kingdom FTSE AIM(GBP)	XX:1815106
United Kingdom FTSE ALL-SHARE(GBP)	XX:1805549
United Kingdom FTSE ALL-SHARE(TR)	XX:1812550
United Kingdom FTSE ALL-SMALL(GBP)	XX:1838589
United Kingdom FTSE ALL-SMALL(TR)	XX:1838590
United Kingdom FTSE APCIMS BALANCED	XX:1880267
United Kingdom FTSE APCIMS BALANCED(TR)	XX:1857584
United Kingdom FTSE APCIMS GROWTH	XX:1880256
United Kingdom FTSE APCIMS GROWTH(TR)	XX:1857573
United Kingdom FTSE APCIMS INCOME	XX:1880278
United Kingdom FTSE APCIMS INCOME(TR)	XX:1857595
United Kingdom FTSE CHEMICALS(350)	XX:1875616
United Kingdom FTSE CHEMICALS(GBP)	XX:1869987
United Kingdom FTSE CHEMICALS(TR)	XX:1812099
United Kingdom FTSE DISTRIBUTORS(350)	XX:1875780
United Kingdom FTSE DISTRIBUTORS(GBP)	XX:1870569
United Kingdom FTSE DISTRIBUTORS(TR)	XX:1812259
United Kingdom FTSE DIVERSIFIED INDLS(TR)	XX:1812107
United Kingdom FTSE ELEC & ELEC(350)	XX:1875638
United Kingdom FTSE ELEC & ELEC(GBP)	XX:1870428
United Kingdom FTSE ELEC & ELEC(TR)	XX:1812118
United Kingdom FTSE ELECTRICITY(350)	XX:1875876
United Kingdom FTSE ELECTRICITY(GBP)	XX:1870752
United Kingdom FTSE ELECTRICITY(TR)	XX:1812345
United Kingdom FTSE FINANCIALS(GBP)	XX:1874851
United Kingdom FTSE FINANCIALS(TR)	XX:1812390
United Kingdom FTSE FLEDGLING(GBP)	XX:1811364
United Kingdom FTSE FLEDGLING(TR)	XX:1812561
United Kingdom FTSE FLEDGLING(X-IT)(TR)	XX:1812572
United Kingdom FTSE GAS DISTRIBUTION(350)	XX:1875887
United Kingdom FTSE GAS DISTRIBUTION(GBP)	XX:1873182
United Kingdom FTSE GAS DISTRIBUTION(TR)	XX:1812356
United Kingdom FTSE GENERAL INDLS(GBP)	XX:1868791
United Kingdom FTSE GENERAL INDLS(TR)	XX:1812066
United Kingdom FTSE GENERAL RETAILERS(TR)	XX:1812293
United Kingdom FTSE GILT-EDGED ACTIVITY	XX:1808979
United Kingdom FTSE INFO TECH(GBP)	XX:1830110
United Kingdom FTSE INSURANCE(350)	XX:1875940
United Kingdom FTSE INSURANCE(GBP)	XX:1874873
United Kingdom FTSE INSURANCE(TR)	XX:1812419
United Kingdom FTSE LIFE ASSURANCE(350)	XX:1875951
United Kingdom FTSE LIFE ASSURANCE(GBP)	XX:1874884
United Kingdom FTSE LIFE ASSURANCE(TR)	XX:1812420
United Kingdom FTSE NON FINANCIALS(GBP)	XX:1874840
United Kingdom FTSE NON FINANCIALS(TR)	XX:1812389
United Kingdom FTSE PHARMACEUTICALS(350)	XX:1875757

(cont.)

APPENDIX D FOREIGN TICKER SYMBOLS

Indexes	Symbol
United Kingdom FTSE PHARMACEUTICALS (GBP)	XX:1870536
United Kingdom FTSE PHARMACEUTICALS(TR)	XX:1812226
United Kingdom FTSE RESOURCES(GBP)	XX:1868434
United Kingdom FTSE RESOURCES(TR)	XX:1812022
United Kingdom FTSE SMALL CAP(GBP)	XX:1868382
United Kingdom FTSE SMALL CAP(TR)	XX:1812538
United Kingdom FTSE SUPPORT SERVICES(350)	XX:1875832
United Kingdom FTSE SUPPORT SERVICES(GBP)	XX:1870611
United Kingdom FTSE SUPPORT SERVICES(TR)	XX:1812301
United Kingdom FTSE TELECOM SERVICES(350)	XX:1875898
United Kingdom FTSE TELECOM SERVICES (GBP)	XX:1874044
United Kingdom FTSE TELECOM SERVICES(TR)	XX:1812367
United Kingdom FTSE TOBACCO(350)	XX:1875768
United Kingdom FTSE TOBACCO(GBP)	XX:1870547
United Kingdom FTSE TOBACCO(TR)	XX:1812237
United Kingdom FTSE TRANSPORT(350)	XX:1875843
United Kingdom FTSE TRANSPORT(GBP)	XX:1870622
United Kingdom FTSE TRANSPORT(TR)	XX:1812312
United Kingdom FTSE UTILITIES(GBP)	XX:1870644
United Kingdom FTSE UTILITIES(TR)	XX:1812334
United Kingdom FTSE WATER(350)	XX:1875906
United Kingdom FTSE WATER(GBP)	XX:1874390
United Kingdom FTSE WATER(TR)	XX:1812378
United Kingdom FTSE-A GOVT 10–15 YR	XX:1839894
United Kingdom FTSE-A GOVT 10–15 YR(TR)	XX:1839902
United Kingdom FTSE-A GOVT 5–10 YR	XX:1839872
United Kingdom FTSE-A GOVT 5–10 YR(TR)	XX:1839883
United Kingdom FTSE-A GOVT 5–15 YR	XX:1805572
United Kingdom FTSE-A GOVT 5–15 YR(TR)	XX:1839838
United Kingdom FTSE-A GOVT ALL	XX:1805602
United Kingdom FTSE-A GOVT ALL(TR)	XX:1839861
United Kingdom FTSE-A GOVT IRRED	XX:1805594
United Kingdom FTSE-A GOVT IRRED(TR)	XX:1839850
United Kingdom FTSE-A GOVT OVER 15 YR	XX:1805583
United Kingdom FTSE-A GOVT OVER 15 YR(TR)	XX:1839849
United Kingdom FTSE-A GOVT UP TO 15 YR	XX:1839913
United Kingdom FTSE-A GOVT UP TO 15 YR(TR)	XX:1839924
United Kingdom FTSE-A GOVT UP TO 20 YR	XX:1839935
United Kingdom FTSE-A GOVT UP TO 20 YR(TR)	XX:1839946
United Kingdom FTSE-A GOVT UP TO 5 YR	XX:1805561
United Kingdom FTSE-A GOVT UP TO 5 YR(TR)	XX:1839827
United Kingdom FTSE-A GOVT YLD(10)	XX:1840034
United Kingdom FTSE-A GOVT YLD(15)	XX:1840045
United Kingdom FTSE-A GOVT YLD(20)	XX:1840056

(*cont.*)

APPENDIX D FOREIGN TICKER SYMBOLS

Indexes	Symbol
United Kingdom FTSE-A GOVT YLD(25)	XX:1840067
United Kingdom FTSE-A GOVT YLD(30)	XX:1840078
United Kingdom FTSE-A GOVT YLD(35)	XX:1840089
United Kingdom FTSE-A GOVT YLD(40)	XX:1840090
United Kingdom FTSE-A GOVT YLD(45)	XX:1840108
United Kingdom FTSE-A GOVT YLD(5)	XX:1840023
United Kingdom FTSE-A GOVT YLD(50)	XX:1840119
United Kingdom FTSE-A GOVT YLD(IRRED)	XX:1805743
United Kingdom FTSE-A I/L 5–15 YR	XX:1839980
United Kingdom FTSE-A I/L ALL	XX:1805635
United Kingdom FTSE-A I/L ALL(TR)	XX:1839957
United Kingdom FTSE-A I/L OVER 15 YR	XX:1840001
United Kingdom FTSE-A I/L OVER 5 YR	XX:1805624
United Kingdom FTSE-A I/L OVER 5 YR(TR)	XX:1839979
United Kingdom FTSE-A I/L UP TO 5 YR	XX:1805613
United Kingdom FTSE-A I/L UP TO 5 YR(TR)	XX:1839968
United Kingdom FTSE-A I/L YLD (0% 5–15)	XX:1840153
United Kingdom FTSE-A I/L YLD (0% ALL)	XX:1840142
United Kingdom FTSE-A I/L YLD (0% OVER 15)	XX:1840164
United Kingdom FTSE-A I/L YLD (0% OVER 5)	XX:1805765
United Kingdom FTSE-A I/L YLD (0% UP TO 5)	XX:1805754
United Kingdom FTSE-A I/L YLD (15% 5–15)	XX:1840238
United Kingdom FTSE-A I/L YLD (15% ALL)	XX:1840205
United Kingdom FTSE-A I/L YLD (15% OVER 15)	XX:1840249
United Kingdom FTSE-A I/L YLD (15% OVER 5)	XX:1840227
United Kingdom FTSE-A I/L YLD (15% UP TO 5)	XX:1840216
United Kingdom FTSE-A I/L YLD (5% 5–15)	XX:1840186
United Kingdom FTSE-A I/L YLD (5% ALL)	XX:1840175
United Kingdom FTSE-A I/L YLD (5% OVER 15)	XX:1840197
United Kingdom FTSE-A I/L YLD (5% OVER 5)	XX:1805787
United Kingdom FTSE-A I/L YLD (5% UP TO 5)	XX:1805776
Venezuela CSE BANKING	XX:1801547
Venezuela CSE GENERAL	XX:1808151
Venezuela MERINVEST COMPOSITE	XX:1801503
Venezuela MERINVEST FINANCIAL	XX:1811386
Venezuela MERINVEST NON-FINANCIAL	XX:1811397

FOREIGN INDEXES—SUBSCRIPTION SERVICES

BARING EMERGING MARKETS INDEX EXT-ARGENTINA	06799W62
BARING EMERGING MARKETS INDEX EXT-ASIA INDEX	06799W69
BARING EMERGING MARKETS INDEX EXT-BRAZIL	06799W63
BARING EMERGING MARKETS INDEX EXT-CHILE	06799W65

(cont.)

APPENDIX D FOREIGN TICKER SYMBOLS

Indexes	Symbol
BARING EMERGING MARKETS INDEX EXT-CHINA	06799W64
BARING EMERGING MARKETS INDEX EXT-COLOMBIA	06799W66
BARING EMERGING MARKETS INDEX EXT-CZECHOSLOV	06799W90
BARING EMERGING MARKETS INDEX EXT-EGYPT	06799W98
BARING EMERGING MARKETS INDEX EXT-EUROPE IDX	06799W68
BARING EMERGING MARKETS INDEX EXT-GREECE IDX	06799W70
BARING EMERGING MARKETS INDEX EXT-HUNGARY	06799W31
BARING EMERGING MARKETS INDEX EXT-INDIA INDX	06799W72
BARING EMERGING MARKETS INDEX EXT-INDONESIA	06799W71
BARING EMERGING MARKETS INDEX EXT-JORDAN IDX	06799W73
BARING EMERGING MARKETS INDEX EXT-KOREA INDX	06799W74
BARING EMERGING MARKETS INDEX EXT-LATIN AMER	06799W75
BARING EMERGING MARKETS INDEX EXT-MALAYSIA	06799W77
BARING EMERGING MARKETS INDEX EXT-MEXICO IDX	06799W76
BARING EMERGING MARKETS INDEX EXT-MOROCCO	06799W96
BARING EMERGING MARKETS INDEX EXT-PAKISTAN	06799W78
BARING EMERGING MARKETS INDEX EXT-PERU INDEX	06799W79
BARING EMERGING MARKETS INDEX EXT-PHILIPPINES	06799W80
BARING EMERGING MARKETS INDEX EXT-POLAND IDX	06799W81
BARING EMERGING MARKETS INDEX EXT-PORTUGAL	06799W82
BARING EMERGING MARKETS INDEX EXT-RUSSIA	06799W97
BARING EMERGING MARKETS INDEX EXT-S. AFRICA	06799W83
BARING EMERGING MARKETS INDEX EXT-TAIWAN IDX	06799W86

(cont.)

APPENDIX D FOREIGN TICKER SYMBOLS

Indexes	Symbol
BARING EMERGING MARKETS INDEX EXT-THAILAND	06799W84
BARING EMERGING MARKETS INDEX EXT-TURKEY IDX	06799W85
BARING EMERGING MARKETS INDEX EXT-VENEZUELA	06799W28
BARING EMERGING MARKETS INDEX EXT-WORLD INDX	06799W67
BARING EMERGING MARKETS INDEX LON-ASIA INDEX	06799W02
BARING EMERGING MARKETS INDEX LON-CHINA INDX	06799W14
BARING EMERGING MARKETS INDEX LON-COLOMBIA	06799W23
BARING EMERGING MARKETS INDEX LON-CZECHOSLVK	06799W89
BARING EMERGING MARKETS INDEX LON-EGYPT	06799W91
BARING EMERGING MARKETS INDEX LON-EUROPE IDX	06799W03
BARING EMERGING MARKETS INDEX LON-GREECE IDX	06799W11
BARING EMERGING MARKETS INDEX LON-HUNGARY	06799W29
BARING EMERGING MARKETS INDEX LON-INDIA INDX	06799W15
BARING EMERGING MARKETS INDEX LON-INDONESIA	06799W05
BARING EMERGING MARKETS INDEX LON-JORDAN IDX	06799W25
BARING EMERGING MARKETS INDEX LON-KOREA INDX	06799W06
BARING EMERGING MARKETS INDEX LON-MALAYSIA	06799W07
BARING EMERGING MARKETS INDEX LON-MOROCCO	06799W93
BARING EMERGING MARKETS INDEX LON-PAKISTAN	06799W20
BARING EMERGING MARKETS INDEX LON-PHILIPPINES	06799W08
BARING EMERGING MARKETS INDEX LON-POLAND IDX	06799W24
BARING EMERGING MARKETS INDEX LON-PORTUGAL	06799W12
BARING EMERGING MARKETS INDEX LON-RUSSIA	06799W92

(*cont.*)

APPENDIX D FOREIGN TICKER SYMBOLS

Indexes	Symbol
BARING EMERGING MARKETS INDEX LON-SO AFRICA	06799W21
BARING EMERGING MARKETS INDEX LON-TAIWAN IDX	06799W09
BARING EMERGING MARKETS INDEX LON-THAILAND	06799W10
BARING EMERGING MARKETS INDEX LON-TURKEY IDX	06799W13
BARING EMERGING MARKETS INDEX LON-VENEZUELA	06799W26
BARING EMERGING MARKETS INDEX LON-WORLD INDX	06799W01
BARING EMERGING MARKETS INDEX NY-ARGENTINA	06799W53
BARING EMERGING MARKETS INDEX NY-ASIA INDEX	06799W41
BARING EMERGING MARKETS INDEX NY-BRAZIL INDX	06799W54
BARING EMERGING MARKETS INDEX NY-CHILE INDEX	06799W55
BARING EMERGING MARKETS INDEX NY-CHINA	06799W60
BARING EMERGING MARKETS INDEX NY-COLOMBIA	06799W61
BARING EMERGING MARKETS INDEX NY-CZECHOSLOVK	06799W88
BARING EMERGING MARKETS INDEX NY-EGYPT	06799W95
BARING EMERGING MARKETS INDEX NY-EUROPE INDX	06799W42
BARING EMERGING MARKETS INDEX NY-GREECE INDX	06799W49
BARING EMERGING MARKETS INDEX NY-HUNGARY	06799W30
BARING EMERGING MARKETS INDEX NY-INDONESIA	06799W52
BARING EMERGING MARKETS INDEX NY-KOREA INDEX	06799W44
BARING EMERGING MARKETS INDEX NY-LATIN AMER	06799W43
BARING EMERGING MARKETS INDEX NY-MALAYSIA	06799W45
BARING EMERGING MARKETS INDEX NY-MEXICO INDX	06799W56
BARING EMERGING MARKETS INDEX NY-PAKISTAN	06799W57

(*cont.*)

APPENDIX D FOREIGN TICKER SYMBOLS

Indexes	Symbol
BARING EMERGING MARKETS INDEX NY-PERU INDEX	06799W58
BARING EMERGING MARKETS INDEX NY-PHILIPPINES	06799W46
BARING EMERGING MARKETS INDEX NY-POLAND INDX	06799W87
BARING EMERGING MARKETS INDEX NY-PORTUGAL	06799W50
BARING EMERGING MARKETS INDEX NY-RUSSIA	06799W94
BARING EMERGING MARKETS INDEX NY-S AFRICA	06799W59
BARING EMERGING MARKETS INDEX NY-TAIWAN INDX	06799W47
BARING EMERGING MARKETS INDEX NY-THAILAND	06799W48
BARING EMERGING MARKETS INDEX NY-TURKEY INDX	06799W51
BARING EMERGING MARKETS INDEX NY-VENEZUELA	06799W27
BARING EMERGING MARKETS INDEX NY-WORLD INDEX	06799W40
Ft/S&P Awi AMERICAS(GBP)	XX:1804223
Ft/S&P Awi AMERICAS(LC)	XX:1804234
Ft/S&P Awi AMERICAS(USD)	XX:1804212
Ft/S&P Awi AMERICAS(YLD)	XX:1804245
Ft/S&P Awi AUSTRALIA(GBP)	XX:1808474
Ft/S&P Awi AUSTRALIA(LC)	XX:1808485
Ft/S&P Awi AUSTRALIA(USD)	XX:1808463
Ft/S&P Awi AUSTRALIA(YLD)	XX:1808496
Ft/S&P Awi AUSTRIA(GBP)	XX:1808537
Ft/S&P Awi AUSTRIA(LC)	XX:1808548
Ft/S&P Awi AUSTRIA(USD)	XX:1808526
Ft/S&P Awi AUSTRIA(YLD)	XX:1808559
Ft/S&P Awi BELGIUM(GBP)	XX:1808593
Ft/S&P Awi BELGIUM(LC)	XX:1809002
Ft/S&P Awi BELGIUM(USD)	XX:1808582
Ft/S&P Awi BELGIUM(YLD)	XX:1809013
Ft/S&P Awi BRAZIL(GBP)	XX:1804148
Ft/S&P Awi BRAZIL(LC)	XX:1804159
Ft/S&P Awi BRAZIL(USD)	XX:1804137
Ft/S&P Awi BRAZIL(YLD)	XX:1804160
Ft/S&P Awi CANADA(GBP)	XX:1809057
Ft/S&P Awi CANADA(LC)	XX:1809068
Ft/S&P Awi CANADA(USD)	XX:1809046
Ft/S&P Awi CANADA(YLD)	XX:1809079

(*cont.*)

APPENDIX D FOREIGN TICKER SYMBOLS

Indexes	Symbol
Ft/S&P Awi DENMARK(GBP)	XX:1809110
Ft/S&P Awi DENMARK(LC)	XX:1809121
Ft/S&P Awi DENMARK(USD)	XX:1809109
Ft/S&P Awi DENMARK(YLD)	XX:1809132
Ft/S&P Awi EUROPE(GBP)	XX:1804450
Ft/S&P Awi EUROPE(LC)	XX:1810855
Ft/S&P Awi EUROPE(USD)	XX:1805334
Ft/S&P Awi EUROPE(X-UK)(GBP)	XX:1805408
Ft/S&P Awi EUROPE(X-UK)(LC)	XX:1809637
Ft/S&P Awi EUROPE(X-UK)(USD)	XX:1805389
Ft/S&P Awi EUROPE(X-UK)(YLD)	XX:1809648
Ft/S&P Awi EUROPE(YLD)	XX:1810866
Ft/S&P Awi EUROPE/PACIFIC(GBP)	XX:1804483
Ft/S&P Awi EUROPE/PACIFIC(LC)	XX:1810930
Ft/S&P Awi EUROPE/PACIFIC(USD)	XX:1805367
Ft/S&P Awi EUROPE/PACIFIC(YLD)	XX:1810941
Ft/S&P Awi FINLAND(GBP)	XX:1807783
Ft/S&P Awi FINLAND(LC)	XX:1807794
Ft/S&P Awi FINLAND(USD)	XX:1807772
Ft/S&P Awi FINLAND(YLD)	XX:1807802
Ft/S&P Awi FRANCE(GBP)	XX:1809176
Ft/S&P Awi FRANCE(LC)	XX:1809187
Ft/S&P Awi FRANCE(USD)	XX:1809165
Ft/S&P Awi FRANCE(YLD)	XX:1809198
Ft/S&P Awi GERMANY(GBP)	XX:1809239
Ft/S&P Awi GERMANY(LC)	XX:1809240
Ft/S&P Awi GERMANY(USD)	XX:1809228
Ft/S&P Awi GERMANY(YLD)	XX:1809251
Ft/S&P Awi HONG KONG(GBP)	XX:1809295
Ft/S&P Awi HONG KONG(LC)	XX:1809303
Ft/S&P Awi HONG KONG(USD)	XX:1809284
Ft/S&P Awi HONG KONG(YLD)	XX:1809314
Ft/S&P Awi IRELAND(GBP)	XX:1809358
Ft/S&P Awi IRELAND(LC)	XX:1809369
Ft/S&P Awi IRELAND(USD)	XX:1809347
Ft/S&P Awi IRELAND(YLD)	XX:1809370
Ft/S&P Awi ITALY(GBP)	XX:1809411
Ft/S&P Awi ITALY(LC)	XX:1809422
Ft/S&P Awi ITALY(USD)	XX:1809400
Ft/S&P Awi ITALY(YLD)	XX:1809433
Ft/S&P Awi JAPAN(GBP)	XX:1809477
Ft/S&P Awi JAPAN(LC)	XX:1809488
Ft/S&P Awi JAPAN(USD)	XX:1809466
Ft/S&P Awi JAPAN(YLD)	XX:1809499
Ft/S&P Awi MALAYSIA(GBP)	XX:1809530
Ft/S&P Awi MALAYSIA(LC)	XX:1809541

(cont.)

APPENDIX D FOREIGN TICKER SYMBOLS

Indexes	Symbol
Ft/S&P Awi MALAYSIA(USD)	XX:1809529
Ft/S&P Awi MALAYSIA(YLD)	XX:1809552
Ft/S&P Awi MEXICO(GBP)	XX:1809585
Ft/S&P Awi MEXICO(LC)	XX:1809596
Ft/S&P Awi MEXICO(USD)	XX:1809574
Ft/S&P Awi MEXICO(YLD)	XX:1809604
Ft/S&P Awi NETHERLANDS(GBP)	XX:1809682
Ft/S&P Awi NETHERLANDS(LC)	XX:1809693
Ft/S&P Awi NETHERLANDS(USD)	XX:1809671
Ft/S&P Awi NETHERLANDS(YLD)	XX:1809701
Ft/S&P Awi NORDIC(GBP)	XX:1804461
Ft/S&P Awi NORDIC(LC)	XX:1808429
Ft/S&P Awi NORDIC(USD)	XX:1805345
Ft/S&P Awi NORDIC(YLD)	XX:1808430
Ft/S&P Awi NORWAY(GBP)	XX:1809808
Ft/S&P Awi NORWAY(LC)	XX:1809819
Ft/S&P Awi NORWAY(USD)	XX:1809790
Ft/S&P Awi NORWAY(YLD)	XX:1809820
Ft/S&P Awi NORTH AMERICA(GBP)	XX:1804494
Ft/S&P Awi NORTH AMERICA(LC)	XX:1810974
Ft/S&P Awi NORTH AMERICA(USD)	XX:1805378
Ft/S&P Awi NORTH AMERICA(YLD)	XX:1810996
Ft/S&P Awi SINGAPORE(GBP)	XX:1809864
Ft/S&P Awi SINGAPORE(LC)	XX:1809875
Ft/S&P Awi SINGAPORE(USD)	XX:1809853
Ft/S&P Awi SINGAPORE(YLD)	XX:1809886
Ft/S&P Awi SPAIN(GBP)	XX:1809983
Ft/S&P Awi SPAIN(LC)	XX:1809994
Ft/S&P Awi SPAIN(USD)	XX:1809972
Ft/S&P Awi SPAIN(YLD)	XX:1810587
Ft/S&P Awi SOUTH AFRICA(GBP)	XX:1809927
Ft/S&P Awi SOUTH AFRICA(LC)	XX:1809938
Ft/S&P Awi SOUTH AFRICA(USD)	XX:1809916
Ft/S&P Awi SOUTH AFRICA(YLD)	XX:1809949
Ft/S&P Awi SWEDEN(GBP)	XX:1810617
Ft/S&P Awi SWEDEN(LC)	XX:1810628
Ft/S&P Awi SWEDEN(USD)	XX:1810606
Ft/S&P Awi SWEDEN(YLD)	XX:1810639
Ft/S&P Awi SWITZERLAND(GBP)	XX:1810684
Ft/S&P Awi SWITZERLAND(LC)	XX:1810695
Ft/S&P Awi SWITZERLAND(USD)	XX:1810662
Ft/S&P Awi SWITZERLAND(YLD)	XX:1810703
Ft/S&P Awi THAILAND(GBP)	XX:1804182
Ft/S&P Awi THAILAND(LC)	XX:1804193
Ft/S&P Awi THAILAND(USD)	XX:1804171
Ft/S&P Awi THAILAND(YLD)	XX:1804201

(cont.)

APPENDIX D FOREIGN TICKER SYMBOLS

Indexes	Symbol
Ft/S&P Awi UTD KINGDOM(GBP)	XX:1810747
Ft/S&P Awi UTD KINGDOM(LC)	XX:1810758
Ft/S&P Awi UTD KINGDOM(USD)	XX:1810736
Ft/S&P Awi UTD KINGDOM(YLD)	XX:1810769
Ft/S&P Awi UTD STATES(GBP)	XX:1810800
Ft/S&P Awi UTD STATES(LC)	XX:1810811
Ft/S&P Awi UTD STATES(USD)	XX:1810792
Ft/S&P Awi UTD STATES(YTD)	XX:1810822
Ft/S&P Awi WORLD(GBP)	XX:1805464
Ft/S&P Awi WORLD(USD)	XX:1804449
Ft/S&P Awi WORLD(X-JPN)(GBP)	XX:1805453
Ft/S&P Awi WORLD(X-JPN)(LC)	XX:1811159
Ft/S&P Awi WORLD(X-JPN)(USD)	XX:1804438
Ft/S&P Awi WORLD(X-JPN)(YLD)	XX:1811160
Ft/S&P Awi WORLD(X-UK)(GBP)	XX:1805431
Ft/S&P Awi WORLD(X-UK)(LC)	XX:1811104
Ft/S&P Awi WORLD(X-UK)(USD)	XX:1804416
Ft/S&P Awi WORLD(X-UK)(YLD)	XX:1811115
Ft/S&P Awi WORLD(X-USA)(GBP)	XX:1805420
Ft/S&P Awi WORLD(X-USA)(LC)	XX:1811052
Ft/S&P Awi WORLD(X-USA)(USD)	XX:1804405
Ft/S&P Awi WORLD(X-USA)(YLD)	XX:1811063
Hsbc Jc ARGENTINA	XX:1806218
Hsbc Jc BRAZIL	XX:1806229
Hsbc Jc CGMT(GBP)	XX:1897386
Hsbc Jc CGMT(USD)	XX:1897375
Hsbc Jc CHILE	XX:1806230
Hsbc Jc COLOMBIA	XX:1806241
Hsbc Jc CROATIA(GBP)	XX:1897405
Hsbc Jc CROATIA(USD)	XX:1897397
Hsbc Jc CYPRUS(GBP)	XX:1897427
Hsbc Jc CYPRUS(USD)	XX:1897416
Hsbc Jc DRAGON 300	XX:1860043
Hsbc Jc DRAGON INDONESIA	XX:1860076
Hsbc Jc DRAGON KOREA	XX:1860087
Hsbc Jc DRAGON MALAYSIA	XX:1860098
Hsbc Jc DRAGON PHILIPPINES	XX:1860106
Hsbc Jc DRAGON SINGAPORE	XX:1860117
Hsbc Jc DRAGON TAIWAN	XX:1860128
Hsbc Jc DRAGON THAILAND	XX:1860139
Hsbc Jc ESTONIA(GBP)	XX:1897483
Hsbc Jc ESTONIA(USD)	XX:1897472
Hsbc Jc G&T(GBP)	XX:1897524
Hsbc Jc G&T(USD)	XX:1897513
Hsbc Jc GLOBAL COAL MINING	XX:1881431
Hsbc Jc GLOBAL DIVERSIFIED	XX:1806188

(*cont.*)

Indexes	Symbol
Hsbc Jc GLOBAL GOLD	XX:1806144
Hsbc Jc GLOBAL MINING	XX:1806133
Hsbc Jc GLOBAL MINING SM.COS	XX:1806199
Hsbc Jc GREECE(GBP)	XX:1897502
Hsbc Jc GREECE(USD)	XX:1897494
Hsbc Jc HONG KONG	XX:1806036
Hsbc Jc HUNGARY(GBP)	XX:1897546
Hsbc Jc HUNGARY(USD)	XX:1897535
Hsbc Jc INDIA	XX:1813263
Hsbc Jc KOREA	XX:1806047
Hsbc Jc LATIN AM MINING NEW	XX:1805873
Hsbc Jc LATIN AMERICA	XX:1806263
Hsbc Jc LATVIA(GBP)	XX:1897568
Hsbc Jc LATVIA(USD)	XX:1897557
Hsbc Jc LITHUANIA(GBP)	XX:1897580
Hsbc Jc LITHUANIA(USD)	XX:1897579
Hsbc Jc MALAYSIA	XX:1806058
Hsbc Jc MALTA(GBP)	XX:1897609
Hsbc Jc MALTA(USD)	XX:1897591
Hsbc Jc MEEM EX R(GBP)	XX:1897643
Hsbc Jc MEEM EX R(USD)	XX:1897632
Hsbc Jc MEEM EX R(USD)	XX:1830206
Hsbc Jc MEEM(GBP)	XX:1897621
Hsbc Jc MEEM(USD)	XX:1830198
Hsbc Jc MEXICO	XX:1806274
Hsbc Jc MM EX R(GBP)	XX:1897687
Hsbc Jc MM EX R(USD)	XX:1830187
Hsbc Jc MM(GBP)	XX:1897665
Hsbc Jc MM(USD)	XX:1897654
Hsbc Jc MM(USD)	XX:1830176
Hsbc Jc NTH AMERICAN BASE METALS	XX:1881420
Hsbc Jc NTH AMERICAN GOLD	XX:1806155
Hsbc Jc PAKISTAN	XX:1813274
Hsbc Jc PERU	XX:1806285
Hsbc Jc PHILIPPINES	XX:1806069
Hsbc Jc POLAND(GBP)	XX:1897706
Hsbc Jc POLAND(USD)	XX:1897698
Hsbc Jc ROMANIA(GBP)	XX:1897728
Hsbc Jc ROMANIA(USD)	XX:1897717
Hsbc Jc RUSSIA(GBP)	XX:1897740
Hsbc Jc RUSSIA(USD)	XX:1897739
Hsbc Jc SCEEM(GBP)	XX:1897762
Hsbc Jc SCEEM(USD)	XX:1897751
Hsbc Jc SINGAPORE	XX:1806070
Hsbc Jc SLOVAKIA(GBP)	XX:1897803
Hsbc Jc SLOVAKIA(USD)	XX:1897795

(cont.)

APPENDIX D FOREIGN TICKER SYMBOLS

Indexes	Symbol
Hsbc Jc SLOVENIA(GBP)	XX:1897784
Hsbc Jc SLOVENIA(USD)	XX:1897773
Hsbc Jc SMALLER AUSTRIAN	XX:1881464
Hsbc Jc SMALLER BELGIAN	XX:1881475
Hsbc Jc SMALLER DANISH	XX:1881486
Hsbc Jc SMALLER DUTCH	XX:1881497
Hsbc Jc SMALLER EURO(I-UK)(GBP)	XX:1805862
Hsbc Jc SMALLER EURO(X-UK)(GBP)	XX:1805851
Hsbc Jc SMALLER EUROLAND(EUR)	XX:1889156
Hsbc Jc SMALLER EUROLAND(GBP)	XX:1889145
Hsbc Jc SMALLER EUROLAND(USD)	XX:1889134
Hsbc Jc SMALLER EUROPEAN(I-UK)	XX:1803662
Hsbc Jc SMALLER EUROPEAN(X-UK)	XX:1889101
Hsbc Jc SMALLER FINNISH	XX:1881505
Hsbc Jc SMALLER FRENCH	XX:1881516
Hsbc Jc SMALLER GERMAN	XX:1881527
Hsbc Jc SMALLER GREEK	XX:1881538
Hsbc Jc SMALLER HONG KONG	XX:1816273
Hsbc Jc SMALLER INDONESIAN	XX:1816284
Hsbc Jc SMALLER IRISH	XX:1881549
Hsbc Jc SMALLER ITALIAN	XX:1881550
Hsbc Jc SMALLER JAPANESE(GBP)	XX:1805798
Hsbc Jc SMALLER JAPANESE(JPY)	XX:1805646
Hsbc Jc SMALLER KOREAN	XX:1816295
Hsbc Jc SMALLER LUXEMBOURG	XX:1881561
Hsbc Jc SMALLER MALAYSIAN	XX:1816303
Hsbc Jc SMALLER NORWEGIAN	XX:1881572
Hsbc Jc SMALLER PHILIPPINES	XX:1816314
Hsbc Jc SMALLER PORTUGUESE	XX:1881583
Hsbc Jc SMALLER SINGAPORE	XX:1816325
Hsbc Jc SMALLER SOUTH EAST ASIAN	XX:1816262
Hsbc Jc SMALLER SPANISH	XX:1881594
Hsbc Jc SMALLER SWEDISH	XX:1888948
Hsbc Jc SMALLER SWISS	XX:1889082
Hsbc Jc SMALLER TAIWAN	XX:1816336
Hsbc Jc SMALLER THAILAND	XX:1816347
Hsbc Jc SMALLER TURKISH	XX:1889093
Hsbc Jc SOUTH EAST ASIA	XX:1806025
Hsbc Jc SRI LANKA	XX:1881163
Hsbc Jc TAIWAN	XX:1806081
Hsbc Jc THAILAND	XX:1806092
Hsbc Jc TII EUROPEAN SMALL CAP	XX:1830154
Hsbc Jc TURKEY(GBP)	XX:1897825
Hsbc Jc TURKEY(USD)	XX:1897814
Hsbc Jc UK GREEN	XX:1806100
Hsbc Jc UK GREEN WASTE	XX:1806122

(cont.)

APPENDIX D FOREIGN TICKER SYMBOLS

Indexes	Symbol
Hsbc Jc UK SMALL GREEN	XX:1806111
Hsbc Jc VENEZUELA	XX:1806296
Hsbc Jc WLD(I-SMALLER US)(GBP)	XX:1850248
Hsbc Jc WLD(I-SMALLER US)(USD)	XX:1850237
Hsbc Jc WLD(X-SMALLER US)(GBP)	XX:1850033
Hsbc Jc WLD(X-SMALLER US)(USD)	XX:1850022
Morgan St Cap Intl AUSTRALIA(LC)	XX:1802829
Morgan St Cap Intl AUSTRIA(LC)	XX:1802830
Morgan St Cap Intl BELGIUM(LC)	XX:1802841
Morgan St Cap Intl BRAZIL(USD)	XX:1884582
Morgan St Cap Intl CANADA(LC)	XX:1803112
Morgan St Cap Intl CANADA(USD)	XX:1874947
Morgan St Cap Intl DENMARK(LC)	XX:1802863
Morgan St Cap Intl EAFE(FREE)(LC)	XX:1884441
Morgan St Cap Intl EAFE(LC)	XX:1800339
Morgan St Cap Intl EAFE(USD)	XX:1802818
Morgan St Cap Intl EAFE(X-UK)(LC)	XX:1884463
Morgan St Cap Intl EMF ASIA(USD)	XX:1884720
Morgan St Cap Intl EMF LATIN AMERICA(USD)	XX:1884731
Morgan St Cap Intl EMF(USD)	XX:1884593
Morgan St Cap Intl EMG(USD)	XX:1884634
Morgan St Cap Intl EUROPE(LC)	XX:1800221
Morgan St Cap Intl EUROPE(USD)	XX:1802788
Morgan St Cap Intl EUROPE(X-UK)(LC)	XX:1884485
Morgan St Cap Intl EUROPE(X-UK)(USD)	XX:1874936
Morgan St Cap Intl FAR EAST(LC)	XX:1884496
Morgan St Cap Intl FAR EAST(X-JPN)(LC)	XX:1850011
Morgan St Cap Intl FAR EAST(X-JPN)(USD)	XX:1874981
Morgan St Cap Intl FINLAND(LC)	XX:1803156
Morgan St Cap Intl FRANCE(LC)	XX:1802896
Morgan St Cap Intl GERMANY(LC)	XX:1803004
Morgan St Cap Intl HONG KONG(LC)	XX:1803123
Morgan St Cap Intl IRELAND(LC)	XX:1803167
Morgan St Cap Intl ISRAEL(USD)	XX:1884571
Morgan St Cap Intl ITALY(LC)	XX:1803015
Morgan St Cap Intl JAPAN(LC)	XX:1803048
Morgan St Cap Intl JAPAN(USD)	XX:1874958
Morgan St Cap Intl MALAYSIA(LC)	XX:1803178
Morgan St Cap Intl NETHERLANDS(LC)	XX:1803059
Morgan St Cap Intl NEW ZEALAND(LC)	XX:1803190
Morgan St Cap Intl NORDIC(LC)	XX:1884515
Morgan St Cap Intl NORDIC(USD)	XX:1883578
Morgan St Cap Intl NORWAY(LC)	XX:1803060
Morgan St Cap Intl NTH.AMERICA(LC)	XX:1884504
Morgan St Cap Intl PACIFIC(LC)	XX:1884537
Morgan St Cap Intl SINGAPORE FREE(LC)	XX:1807330

(*cont.*)

APPENDIX D FOREIGN TICKER SYMBOLS

Indexes	Symbol
Morgan St Cap Intl SINGAPORE(LC)	XX:1803134
Morgan St Cap Intl SPAIN(LC)	XX:1803071
Morgan St Cap Intl SWEDEN(LC)	XX:1803082
Morgan St Cap Intl SWITZERLAND(LC)	XX:1803093
Morgan St Cap Intl UTD KINGDOM(LC)	XX:1803101
Morgan St Cap Intl UTD KINGDOM(USD)	XX:1874969
Morgan St Cap Intl UTD STATES(LC)	XX:1803145
Morgan St Cap Intl UTD STATES(USD)	XX:1874970
Morgan St Cap Intl WORLD(LC)	XX:1800072
Morgan St Cap Intl WORLD(USD)	XX:1802777
Morgan St Cap Intl WORLD(X-JPN)(USD)	XX:1884548
Morgan St Cap Intl WORLD(X-UK)(LC)	XX:1884559
Morgan St Cap Intl WORLD(X-USA)(LC)	XX:1884560
RUSSELL/AUSTRALIA ASX—ALL GROWTH	XX:1816154
RUSSELL/AUSTRALIA ASX—ALL GROWTH (ACC)	XX:1816217
RUSSELL/AUSTRALIA ASX—ALL VALUE	XX:1816143
RUSSELL/AUSTRALIA ASX—ALL VALUE (ACC)	XX:1816206
RUSSELL/AUSTRALIA ASX—GROWTH 100	XX:1816176
RUSSELL/AUSTRALIA ASX—GROWTH 100 (ACC)	XX:1816239
RUSSELL/AUSTRALIA ASX—SMALL GRTH	XX:1816198
RUSSELL/AUSTRALIA ASX—SMALL GRTH (ACC)	XX:1816251
RUSSELL/AUSTRALIA ASX—SMALL VAL	XX:1816187
RUSSELL/AUSTRALIA ASX—SMALL VAL (ACC)	XX:1816240
RUSSELL/AUSTRALIA ASX—VALUE 100	XX:1816165
RUSSELL/AUSTRALIA ASX—VALUE 100(ACC)	XX:1816228
STOXX LIMITED DJES AUTO MANUF(EUR)	XX:1898118
STOXX LIMITED DJES AUTO MANUF(EUR)(TR)	XX:1898130
STOXX LIMITED DJES AUTO MANUF(USD)	XX:1898129
STOXX LIMITED DJES AUTO MANUF(USD)(TR)	XX:1898141
STOXX LIMITED DJES AUTO PARTS(EUR)	XX:1898152
STOXX LIMITED DJES AUTO PARTS(EUR)(TR)	XX:1898174
STOXX LIMITED DJES AUTO PARTS(USD)	XX:1898163
STOXX LIMITED DJES AUTO PARTS(USD)(TR)	XX:1898185
STOXX LIMITED DJES AUTO(EUR)	XX:1836657
STOXX LIMITED DJES AUTO(EUR)(TR)	XX:1837070
STOXX LIMITED DJES AUTO(USD)	XX:1837490
STOXX LIMITED DJES AUTO(USD)(TR)	XX:1837917
STOXX LIMITED DJES BANK(EUR)	XX:1836710
STOXX LIMITED DJES BANK(EUR)(TR)	XX:1837133
STOXX LIMITED DJES BANK(USD)	XX:1837553

(*cont.*)

APPENDIX D FOREIGN TICKER SYMBOLS

Indexes	Symbol
STOXX LIMITED DJES BANK(USD)(TR)	XX:1837973
STOXX LIMITED DJES BASIC MATLS(EUR)	XX:1895056
STOXX LIMITED DJES BASIC MATLS(EUR)(TR)	XX:1895089
STOXX LIMITED DJES BASIC MATLS(USD)	XX:1895067
STOXX LIMITED DJES BASIC MATLS(USD)(TR)	XX:1895078
STOXX LIMITED DJES BASIC RES(EUR)	XX:1836624
STOXX LIMITED DJES BASIC RES(EUR)(TR)	XX:1837047
STOXX LIMITED DJES BASIC RES(USD)	XX:1837467
STOXX LIMITED DJES BASIC RES(USD)(TR)	XX:1837887
STOXX LIMITED DJES BEVERAGES(EUR)	XX:1898215
STOXX LIMITED DJES BEVERAGES(EUR)(TR)	XX:1898259
STOXX LIMITED DJES BEVERAGES(USD)	XX:1898237
STOXX LIMITED DJES BEVERAGES(USD)(TR)	XX:1898260
STOXX LIMITED DJES BLDG MATLS(EUR)	XX:1898271
STOXX LIMITED DJES BLDG MATLS(EUR)(TR)	XX:1898293
STOXX LIMITED DJES BLDG MATLS(USD)	XX:1898282
STOXX LIMITED DJES BLDG MATLS(USD)(TR)	XX:1898301
STOXX LIMITED DJES CHEMICAL(EUR)	XX:1836613
STOXX LIMITED DJES CHEMICAL(EUR)(TR)	XX:1837036
STOXX LIMITED DJES CHEMICAL(USD)	XX:1837456
STOXX LIMITED DJES CHEMICAL(USD)(TR)	XX:1837876
STOXX LIMITED DJES COMM TECH(EUR)	XX:1898419
STOXX LIMITED DJES COMM TECH(EUR)(TR)	XX:1898453
STOXX LIMITED DJES COMM TECH(USD)	XX:1898442
STOXX LIMITED DJES COMM TECH(USD)(TR)	XX:1898464
STOXX LIMITED DJS AIRLINES(EUR)	XX:1899241
STOXX LIMITED DJS AIRLINES(EUR)(TR)	XX:1899285
STOXX LIMITED DJS AIRLINES(USD)	XX:1899274
STOXX LIMITED DJS AIRLINES(USD)(TR)	XX:1899296
STOXX LIMITED DJS AUTO MANUF(EUR)	XX:1899467
STOXX LIMITED DJS AUTO MANUF(EUR)(TR)	XX:1899519
STOXX LIMITED DJS AUTO MANUF(USD)	XX:1899478
STOXX LIMITED DJS AUTO MANUF(USD)(TR)	XX:1899531
STOXX LIMITED DJS AUTO PARTS(EUR)	XX:1899553
STOXX LIMITED DJS AUTO PARTS(EUR)(TR)	XX:1899605
STOXX LIMITED DJS AUTO PARTS(USD)	XX:1899586
STOXX LIMITED DJS AUTO PARTS(USD)(TR)	XX:1899616
STOXX LIMITED DJS AUTO(EUR)	XX:1836840
STOXX LIMITED DJS AUTO(EUR)(TR)	XX:1837263
STOXX LIMITED DJS AUTO(USD)	XX:1837683
STOXX LIMITED DJS AUTO(USD)(TR)	XX:1838103
STOXX LIMITED DJS AUTO(X-UK)(EUR)	XX:1842728
STOXX LIMITED DJS AUTO(X-UK)(EUR)(TR)	XX:1842739
STOXX LIMITED DJS AUTO(X-UK)(USD)	XX:1842717
STOXX LIMITED DJS AUTO(X-UK)(USD)(TR)	XX:1842740
STOXX LIMITED DJS BANK(EUR)	XX:1836903

(*cont.*)

APPENDIX D FOREIGN TICKER SYMBOLS

Indexes	Symbol
STOXX LIMITED DJS BANK(EUR)(TR)	XX:1837326
STOXX LIMITED DJS BANK(USD)	XX:1837746
STOXX LIMITED DJS BANK(USD)(TR)	XX:1838169
STOXX LIMITED DJS BANK(X-UK)(EUR)	XX:1842751
STOXX LIMITED DJS BANK(X-UK)(EUR)(TR)	XX:1842773
STOXX LIMITED DJS BANK(X-UK)(USD)	XX:1842762
STOXX LIMITED DJS BANK(X-UK)(USD)(TR)	XX:1842784
STOXX LIMITED DJS BASIC MATLS(EUR)	XX:1895410
STOXX LIMITED DJS BASIC MATLS(EUR)(TR)	XX:1895432
STOXX LIMITED DJS BASIC MATLS(USD)	XX:1895421
STOXX LIMITED DJS BASIC MATLS(USD)(TR)	XX:1895443
STOXX LIMITED DJS BASIC RES(EUR)	XX:1836817
STOXX LIMITED DJS BASIC RES(EUR)(TR)	XX:1837230
STOXX LIMITED DJS BASIC RES(USD)	XX:1837650
STOXX LIMITED DJS BASIC RES(USD)(TR)	XX:1838073
STOXX LIMITED DJS BASIC RES(X-UK)(EUR)	XX:1842795
STOXX LIMITED DJS BASIC RES(X-UK)(USD)	XX:1842803
STOXX LIMITED DJS BEVERAGES(EUR)	XX:1899144
STOXX LIMITED DJS BEVERAGES(EUR)(TR)	XX:1899166
STOXX LIMITED DJS BEVERAGES(USD)	XX:1899155
STOXX LIMITED DJS BEVERAGES(USD)(TR)	XX:1899177
STOXX LIMITED DJS BLDG MATLS(EUR)	XX:1899188
STOXX LIMITED DJS BLDG MATLS(EUR)(TR)	XX:1899207
STOXX LIMITED DJS BLDG MATLS(USD)	XX:1899199
STOXX LIMITED DJS BLDG MATLS(USD)(TR)	XX:1899218
STOXX LIMITED DJS CHEMICAL(EUR)	XX:1836806
STOXX LIMITED DJS CHEMICAL(EUR)(TR)	XX:1837229
STOXX LIMITED DJS CHEMICAL(USD)	XX:1837649
STOXX LIMITED DJS COMM TECH(EUR)	XX:1899348
STOXX LIMITED DJS COMM TECH(EUR)(TR)	XX:1899360
STOXX LIMITED DJS COMM TECH(USD)	XX:1899359
STOXX LIMITED DJS COMM TECH(USD)(TR)	XX:1899371
STOXX LIMITED DJS CYC GOODS(X-UK)(EUR)	XX:1842955
STOXX LIMITED DJS CYC GOODS(X-UK)(USD)	XX:1842977
STOXX LIMITED DJS N-CYC GDS(X-UK)(EUR)	XX:1842999
STOXX LIMITED DJS N-CYC GDS(X-UK)(USD)	XX:1843000
STOXX LTD DJES L&M AUTO(EUR)	XX:1854808
STOXX LTD DJES L&M AUTO(EUR)(TR)	XX:1854820
STOXX LTD DJES L&M AUTO(USD)	XX:1854819
STOXX LTD DJES L&M AUTO(USD)(TR)	XX:1854831
STOXX LTD DJES L&M BANK(EUR)	XX:1854886
STOXX LTD DJES L&M BANK(EUR)(TR)	XX:1855005
STOXX LTD DJES L&M BANK(USD)	XX:1854897
STOXX LTD DJES L&M BANK(USD)(TR)	XX:1855016
STOXX LTD DJES L&M BASIC RES(EUR)	XX:1855061
STOXX LTD DJES L&M BASIC RES(USD)	XX:1855072

(*cont.*)

APPENDIX D FOREIGN TICKER SYMBOLS

Indexes	Symbol
STOXX LTD DJES L&M CYC GOOD(EUR)	XX:1855384
STOXX LTD DJES L&M CYC GOOD(USD)	XX:1855395
STOXX LTD DJES LARGE(EUR)	XX:1854358
STOXX LTD DJES LARGE(EUR)(TR)	XX:1854370
STOXX LTD DJES LARGE(USD)	XX:1854369
STOXX LTD DJES LARGE(USD)(TR)	XX:1854381
STOXX LTD DJS L&M AUTO(EUR)	XX:1854842
STOXX LTD DJS L&M AUTO(EUR)(TR)	XX:1854864
STOXX LTD DJS L&M AUTO(USD)	XX:1854853
STOXX LTD DJS L&M AUTO(USD)(TR)	XX:1854875
STOXX LTD DJS L&M BANK(EUR)	XX:1855027
STOXX LTD DJS L&M BANK(EUR)(TR)	XX:1855049
STOXX LTD DJS L&M BANK(USD)	XX:1855038
STOXX LTD DJS L&M BANK(USD)(TR)	XX:1855050
STOXX LTD DJS L&M BASIC RES(EUR)	XX:1855102
STOXX LTD DJS L&M BASIC RES(USD)	XX:1855113
STOXX LTD DJS L&M CYC GOOD(EUR)	XX:1855425
STOXX LTD DJS L&M CYC GOOD(EUR)(TR)	XX:1855447
STOXX LTD DJS L&M CYC GOOD(USD)(TR)	XX:1855458
STOXX LTD DJS L&M N-CYC GDS(EUR)	XX:1855986
STOXX LTD DJS L&M N-CYC GDS(EUR)(TR)	XX:1856008
STOXX LTD DJS L&M N-CYC GDS(USD)	XX:1855997
STOXX LTD DJS L&M N-CYC GDS(USD)(TR)	XX:1856019
STOXX LTD DJS LARGE(EUR)	XX:1854392
STOXX LTD DJS LARGE(EUR)(TR)	XX:1854411
STOXX LTD DJS LARGE(USD)	XX:1854400
STOXX LTD DJS LARGE(USD)(TR)	XX:1854422
STOXX LTD DJS NORDIC LARGE(EUR)	XX:1854596
STOXX LTD DJS NORDIC LARGE(EUR)(TR)	XX:1854615
STOXX LTD DJS NORDIC LARGE(USD)	XX:1854604
STOXX LTD DJS NORDIC LARGE(USD)(TR)	XX:1854626

Appendix E
World Currencies and Symbols

Country	Currency / Symbol	Abbrev.	Subdivision
Afghanistan	Afghani / Af	AFA	100 puls
Albania	Lek / L	ALL	100 qindarka (or quintars)
Algeria	Dinar / DA	DZD	100 centimes
Australia	Dollar / A$	AUD	100 cents
Austria	Schilling / ATS	ATS	100 groschen
Bangladesh	Taka / Tk	BDT	100 paisa (or poisha)
Barbados	Dollar / Bds$	BBD	100 cents
Belgium	Franc / BF	BEF	100 centimes
Brunei	Ringgit / B$ (or Bruneian $)	BND	100 sen (or cents)
Bulgaria	Leva / Lv	BGL	100 stotinki
Cambodia	New Riel / CR	KHR	100 sen
Canada	Dollar / Can$	CAD	100 cents
China	Yuan Renminbi / RMB	CNY	10 jiao = 100 fen
Christmas Island	see Australia	—	—
Colombia	Peso / Col$	COP	100 centavos
Congo	Franc / CFAF	XAF	100 centimes
Cook Islands	see New Zealand	—	—
Croatia	Kuna / HRK	HRK	100 lipas
Czech Republic	Koruna / Kč (or Crown)	CZK	100 haléř (hellers)
Denmark	Krone (plural: kroner) / Dkr	DKK	100 øre
Egypt	Pound / £E	EGP	100 piasters or 1000 milliemes
Estonia	Kroon (plural: Krooni) / KR	EEK	100 senti
Ethiopia	Birr / Br	ETB	100 cents
European Union	Euro / €	EUR	100 euro-cents
Fiji	Dollar / F$	FJD	100 cents
Finland	Markka (plural: Markkaa) / Mk	FIM	100 pennia or 100 p
France	Franc / FR	FRF	100 centimes
French Polynesia	Franc / CFPF	XPF	100 centimes

APPENDIX E WORLD CURRENCIES AND SYMBOLS

Country	Currency / Symbol	Abbrev.	Subdivision
Gambia	Dalasi / D	GMD	100 butut
Germany	Deutsche mark / DM	DEM	100 pfennig
Greece	Drachma / Dr	GRD	100 lepta (singular: lepton)
Greenland	see Denmark	—	—
Guadeloupe	see France	—	—
Guam	see United States	—	—
Guatemala	Quetzal / Q	GTQ	100 centavos
Hong Kong	Dollar / HK$	HKD	100 cents
Hungary	Forint / Ft	HUF	—
Iceland	Króna / IKr	ISK	100 aurar (singular: aur)
India	Rupee / Rs	INR	100 paise
Indonesia	Rupiah / Rp	IDR	100 sen (no longer in use)
Iran	Rial / Rls	IRR	10 rials = 1 toman
Iraq	Dinar / ID	IQD	1000 fils
Ireland	Punt or £ / IR£	IEP	100 pingin or pence
Isle of Man	see United Kingdom	—	—
Israel	New shekel / NIS	ILS	100 new agorot
Italy	Lira (plural: Lire) / Lit	ITL	—
Jamaica	Dollar / J$	JMD	100 cents
Japan	Yen / ¥	JPY	100 sen (no longer in use)
Jordan	Dinar / JD	JOD	1000 fils
Kazakhstan	Tenge / Te	KZT	100 tiyn
Kenya	Shilling / K Sh	KES	100 cents
Korea, North	Won / Wn	KPW	100 chon
Korea, South	Won / W	KRW	100 chon
Kuwait	Dinar / KD	KWD	1000 fils
Kyrgyzstan	Som / S	KGS	100 tyyn
Laos	New kip / KN	LAK	100 at
Latvia	Lat / Ls	LVL	100 santims
Lebanon	Pound (Livre) / £L	LBP	100 piastres
Liberia	Dollar / $	LRD	100 cents
Libya	Dinar / LD	LYD	1000 dirhams
Lithuania	Litas (plural: Litai)	LTL	100 centu
Luxembourg	Franc / LuxF	LUF	100 centimes
Macao	Pataca / P	MOP	100 avos
Macedonia	Denar / MKD	MKD	100 deni
Madagascar	Ariayry = 5 Malagasy Francs /FMG	MGF	1 francs = 100 centimes

(cont.)

APPENDIX E WORLD CURRENCIES AND SYMBOLS

Country	Currency / Symbol	Abbrev.	Subdivision
Malawi	Kwacha / MK	MWK	100 tambala
Malaysia	Ringgit / RM	MYR	100 sen
Maldives	Rufiyaa / Rf	MVR	100 lari
Mali	Franc / CFAF	MLF	100 centimes
Malta	Lira (plural: Liri) / Lm	MTL	100 cents
Martinique	see France	—	—
Mauritius	Rupee / Mau Rs	MUR	100 cents
Mexico	Peso / Mex$	MXN	100 centavos
Monaco	see France	—	—
Mongolia	Tugrik (Tögroög, a.k.a. Tughrik) / T	MNT	100 mongos
Morocco	Dirham / DH	MAD	100 centimes
Mozambique	Metical / Mt	MZM	100 centavos
Myanmar	Kyat / K	MMK	100 pyas
Namibia	Dollar / N$	NAD	100 cents
Nepal	Rupee / NRs	NPR	100 paise
Netherlands	Guilder (or Florin, Gulden) / f.	NLG	100 cents
New Caledonia	Franc / CFPF	XPF	100 centimes
New Zealand	Dollar / NZ$	NZD	100 cents
Niger	Franc / CFAF	XOF	100 centimes
Nigeria	Naira / N	NGN	100 kobo
Norway	Krone (plural: kroner) / NKr	NOK	100 øre
Oman	Rial / RO	OMR	1000 baizas
Pakistan	Rupee / Rs	PKR	100 paisa
Papua New Guinea	Kina / K	PGK	100 toeas
Paraguay	Guarani / G	PYG	100 centimos
Peru	New sol / S	PEN	100 centimos
Philippines	Peso / P	PHP	100 centavos
Poland	Zloty / zl	PLZ	100 groszy
Portugal	Escudo / Esc	PTE	100 centavos
Puerto Rico	see United States	—	—
Qatar	Riyal / QR	QAR	100 dirhams
Romania	Leu (plural: Lei) / L	ROL	100 bani
Russia	Ruble / R	RUB	100 kopecks
Rwanda	Franc / RF	RWF	100 centimes
Saudi Arabia	Riyal / SRIs	SAR	100 halala
Serbia	see Yugoslavia	—	—
Seychelles	Rupee / SR	SCR	100 cents
Singapore	Dollars / SGD	SGD	100 cents

APPENDIX E WORLD CURRENCIES AND SYMBOLS

Country	Currency / Symbol	Abbrev.	Subdivision
Slovakia	Koruna / Sk	SKK	100 haliers (or haleru)
Slovenia	Tolar / SIT	SIT	100 stotinov (or stotins)
Solomon Islands	Dollar / SI$	SBD	100 cents
Somalia	Somali Shilling / Sh	SOS	100 centesimi
South Africa	Rand / R	ZAR	100 cents
Spain	Peseta / Ptas	ESP	100 centimos
Sri Lanka	Rupee / SLRs	LKR	100 cents
Sudan	Sudanese Dinar	SDP	100 piastres
Sweden	Krona (plural: Kroner) / Sk	SEK	100 öre
Switzerland	Franc / SFr	CHF	100 centimes
Taiwan	New dollar / NTD	TWD	100 cents
Thailand	Baht / Bht	THB	100 stang
Turkey	Lira / TL	TRL	100 kurus
Uganda	Shilling / USh	UGX	100 cents
United Kingdom	Pound sterling/ £	GBP	100 pence
United States of America	Dollar / USD	USD	100 cents
Yugoslavia	Dinar / Din	YUM	100 paras
Zimbabwe	Dollar / ZD	ZWD	100 cents

BARRON'S
Business Success Guides

For career-minded men and women, here are the facts, the tips, the wisdom, and the commonsense advice that will pave the way to success. A total to date of 32 short, pocket-size, entertaining and easy-to-read volumes advise on succeeding at all levels of management, marketing, and other important areas within the business and corporate world. They're written by the people who have been there, who currently hold top positions, who know the ropes—and know the facts *you* need to know!

Each book: Paperback, approximately 96 pages, priced individually

0-8120-9893-5: Conducting Better Job Interviews, 2nd Ed.—$6.95, Canada $8.95
0-7641-0403-9: Creative Problem Solving, 2nd Ed.—$6.95, Canada $8.95
0-7641-1410-7: Entrepreneurship 101—$7.95, Canada $11.50
0-7641-1113-2: Intercultural Business—$6.95, Canada $9.50
0-7641-0684-8: Interview Strategies That Lead to Job Offers—$6.95, Canada $9.50
0-8120-9892-7: Make Presentations with Confidence, 2nd Ed.—$6.95, Canada $8.95
0-7641-1950-8: Managing Your Boss—$7.95, Canada $11.50
0-7641-0400-4: Maximizing Your Memory Power, 2nd Ed.—$6.95, Canada $8.95
0-8120-9898-6: Motivating People—$7.95, Canada $11.50
0-7641-1645-2: 100+ Tactics for Office Politics—$7.95, Canada $11.50
0-7641-1644-4: 100+ Winning Answers to the Toughest Interview Questions—$7.95, Canada $11.50
0-7641-0883-2: Performance Management—$6.95, Canada $9.50
0-8120-9823-4: Running a Meeting That Works, 2nd Ed.—$6.95, Canada $8.95
0-7641-0401-2: Speed Reading, 2nd Ed.—$7.95, Canada $11.50
0-7641-0071-8: Successful Assertiveness—$6.95, Canada $8.95
0-7641-0074-2: Successful Direct Mail—$6.95, Canada $8.95
0-7641-0072-6: Successful Leadership—$7.95, Canada $11.50
0-7641-0073-4: Successful Team Building—$7.95, Canada $11.50
0-7641-0060-2: Successfully Managing Change—$6.95, Canada $8.95
0-7641-0402-0: Time Management, 2nd Ed.—$6.95, Canada $8.95
0-7641-1951-6: Understanding Body Language—$7.95, Canada $11.50
0-8120-9894-3: Winning with Difficult People, 2nd Ed.—$6.95, Canada $8.95
0-8120-9824-2: Writing Effective Letters and Memos, 2nd Ed.—$6.95, Canada $8.95

**Barron's Educational Series, Inc. • 250 Wireless Blvd., Hauppauge, NY 11788
Order toll-free: 1-800-645-3476 • Order by fax: 1-631-434-3217
Canadian orders: 1-800-247-7160 • Fax in Canada: 1-800-887-1594**

Visit us at www.barronseduc.com

Books and packages may be purchased at your local bookstore or by mail directly from Barron's. Enclose check or money order for total amount, plus sales tax where applicable and 18% for postage and handling (minimum $5.95). All books advertised here are paperback editions.
Prices subject to change without notice.

(#73) 9/01

More selected BARRON'S titles:

Dictionary of Accounting Terms, 3rd Ed.
0-7641-1259-7 $12.95, Can $17.95
Dictionary of Banking Terms, 3rd Ed.
0-7641-1260-0 $13.95, Can $19.50
Dictionary of Business Terms, 3rd Ed.
0-7641-1200-7 $14.95, Can $21.00
Dictionary of Computer and Internet Terms, 7th Ed.
0-7641-1265-1 $10.95, Can $15.50
Dictionary of Finance & Investment Terms, 5th Ed.
0-7641-0790-9 $13.95, Can $18.95
Dictionary of Insurance Terms, 4th Ed.
0-7641-1262-7 $13.95, Can $19.50

Dictionary of International Business Terms, 2nd Ed.
0-7641-1263-5 $13.95, Can $19.50
Dictionary of International Investment Terms
0-7641-1864-1 $11.95, Can $16.95
Dictionary of Marketing Terms, 3rd Ed.
0-7641-1214-7 $12.95, Can $17.95
Dictionary of Real Estate Terms, 5th Ed.
0-7641-1264-3 $13.95, Can $19.50

BARRON'S FOREIGN LANGUAGE BUSINESS DICTIONARIES
Seven bilingual dictionaries translate about 3000 business terms not found in most foreign phrasebooks.

French for the Business Traveler
0-8120-1768-4 $9.95, Can $12.95

Italian for the Business Traveler
0-8120-1771-4 $9.95, Can $12.95
Japanese for the Business Traveler
0-8120-1770-6 $11.95, Can $15.95
Russian for the Business Traveler
0-8120-1784-6 $11.95, Can $15.95
Spanish for the Business Traveler
0-8120-1773-0 $11.95, Can $15.95

All prices are in U.S. and Canadian dollars and subject to change without notice. Books may be purchased at your bookseller, or order direct, adding 18% for postage and handling (minimum charge $5.95) N.Y. state residents add sales tax. All books are paperback editions.

Barron's Educational Series, Inc.
250 Wireless Boulevard, Hauppauge, NY 11788
In Canada: Georgetown Book Warehouse
34 Armstrong Ave., Georgetown, Ontario L7G 4R9

Visit our website at: www.barronseduc.com

(#12) R 9/01

BARRON'S BUSINESS KEYS

Each "key" explains approximately 50 concepts and provides a glossary and index. Each book: Paperback, approx. 160 pp., 4 3/16" x 7", $4.95, $5.95, & $7.95 Can. $6.50, $7.95, $8.50, & $11.50.

Keys to Avoiding Probate and Reducing Estate Taxes (4668-4)
Keys to Buying Foreclosed and Bargain Homes, 2nd Edition *(1294-5)
Keys to Buying and Owning a Home, 3rd Edition *(1299-6)
Keys to Incorporating, 3rd Edition (1300-3)
Keys to Investing in Common Stocks, 3rd Edition *(1301-1)
Keys to Investing in Municipal Bonds (9515-4)
Keys to Investing in Mutual Funds, 3rd Edition (9644-4)
Keys to Investing in Options and Futures, 3rd Edition *(1303-8)
Keys to Investing in Real Estate, 3rd Edition *(1295-3)
Keys to Investing in Your 401(K), 2nd Edition *(1298-8)
Keys to Mortgage Financing and Refinancing, 3rd Edition (1296-1)
Keys to Personal Financial Planning, 2nd Edition (1919-9)
Keys to Purchasing a Condo or a Co-op, 2nd Edition *(1305-4)
Keys to Reading an Annual Report, 3rd Edition (1306-2)
Keys to Risks and Rewards of Penny Stocks (4300-6)
Keys to Starting a Small Business (4487-8)
Keys to Understanding the Financial News, 3rd Edition *(1308-9)
Keys to Understanding Securities, 2nd Edition *(1309-7)

Available at bookstores, or by mail from Barron's. Enclose check or money order for full amount plus sales tax where applicable and 18% for postage & handling (minimum charge $5.95). Prices subject to change without notice. $= U.S. dollars • Can. $= Canadian dollars • Barron's ISBN Prefix, 0-8120, *indicates 0-7641

Barron's Educational Series, Inc.
250 Wireless Boulevard • Hauppauge, NY 11788
In Canada: Georgetown Book Warehouse
34 Armstrong Avenue, Georgetown, Ont. L7G 4R9
www.barronseduc.com

(#10) R 9/01